Food Festival, U.S.A.

Klare

Food Festival, U.S.A.

Red, White, & Blue Ribbon Recipes from All 50 States

Becky Mercuri

Illustrated by Tom Klare

LAUREL GLEN

San Diego, California

Laurel Glen Publishing
An imprint of the Advantage Publishers Group
5880 Oberlin Drive, San Diego, CA 92121-4794
www.advantagebooksonline.com

ISBN 1-57145-775-5
Library of Congress Cataloging-in-Publication Data available upon request.

Publisher: Allen Orso
Associate Publisher: Rachel Petrella
Project Editors: Elizabeth McNulty, JoAnn Padgett
Production Editor: Mana Monzavi
Design: Duotribe, Inc.
Illustrator: Tom Klare

Printed in the United States by Von Hoffmann.
1 2 3 4 5   06 05 04 03 02

Dedication

This book is dedicated to my mother, Margaret Shaw Mayerat, who has made all things possible, and to the memory of my grandparents, Charles and Olive Shaw, who instilled in me a love and respect for fine food and cooking.

A portion of the proceeds from the sale of this book is being donated by the author to support the rescue of abused and abandoned pets and to assist in the care of wounded and orphaned wildlife.

Contents

Acknowledgments

A book of this type takes patience, determination, and fortitude coupled with encouragement and moral support from people who believe in the ultimate value of the finished product. I would thus like to express my heartfelt thanks to the individuals who made it all possible. My agent, Meredith Bernstein, who immediately believed in this book and who bravely and competently promoted a new author. My editors, JoAnn Padgett and Elizabeth McNulty, who calmly and capably guided me through the publishing process while answering my endless questions. Production editor Mana Monzavi, who provided cheerful assistance. John T. Edge who generously offered to write the foreword for this book despite his own demanding schedule. My friend Sue Erwin, publisher of *Cookbook Collectors Exchange*, who is always there for me. My mentor and friend, Dr. Mary Ellen Shaughnessy of SUNY Buffalo, who gave me a great deal of encouragement along with a mighty shove forward. My friend Josephine Bacon of American Pie and Pholiota Translations in London, who can always be counted on to provide inspiration and support. My husband Richard and friends and neighbors who devoured endless dishes as I tested recipes, and who provided nonstop encouragement: Randy, Mary Ann, Nicole, Jeremy and Sarah Vink; Fred and MariAnn Stiles; Bob, Becky, Dylan and Daniel Coates; Cindy Reese; and Tony, Fran, and Bill Green. Thanks to Tom Kiernan and Jeff Pallone who allowed me maximum flexibility in scheduling vacation time during this project. My friend Peter Tauber, an expert writer who provided just the right amount of advice interspersed with great good humor. And last, but by no means least, all the festival people, cooks, and chefs who so graciously provided information and shared their wonderful recipes.

Foreword

I dote on food festivals. I've been to the Shrimp and Petroleum Festival in Morgan City, Louisiana and the Okra Strut in Irmo, South Carolina, to name just a couple. Reading through Becky Mercuri's Food Festival U.S.A. compelled me to ink those festivals on my calendar for a return engagement. What is more, I added a host of new prospects to my list including the intriguing-sounding Prairie Dog Chili Cook Off and World Championship Pickled Quail Egg Eating, staged in Grand Prairie, Texas; and the Abalone Festival of Mendocino, California.

Mercuri's accounting of our nation's public culinary celebrations also stirred a bout of reminiscence–a recollection of a recent visit to Belzoni, Mississippi, the self-styled Catfish Capitol of the World, and host, on the first Saturday in April, to the World Catfish Festival.

My first taste of catfish came at a quarter 'til nine in the morning: a pinwheel of spinach and catfish, spiced with chili powder, bound by cream cheese, and tucked into a flour tortilla. By ten, I had downed a demi-baguette larded with catfish mousse and a few bagel chips slathered with a chunky artichoke and catfish tapenade. By eleven-thirty, I had polished off a couple of fried catfish filets and a few French fries. And I was just getting started.

To work up a sufficient appetite, I ambled about the courthouse square. Over the course of a lazy couple of hours, I caught a theatrical performance sponsored by the Belzoni Garden Club; dodged an errant unicyclist snacking on a corn dog as he lurched through the crowd; and watched as the outgoing Queen Catfish relinquished her sash and crown in a pomp and circumstance ceremony staged on a flag-draped dais. When my feet grew weary, I snagged a seat on a park bench and leafed through a copy of the Captain Catfish coloring books being handed out at the welcome center.

I kept my shopping to a minimum. Though I was tempted, I didn't purchase a clothes hamper constructed of kudzu vines. Ditto the sow-shaped concrete planters that were a bargain at twelve dollars a pair. If I did too much shopping, or dallied too long in front of the bandstand, I might miss the chance to taste something extraordinary. My concern was warranted, for this past year, in addition to showcasing the renowned fry cooks of the Delta, festival organizers had brought in some imported talent, chefs with James Beard pedigrees and Food Network followings, ready to wow rapt audiences of catfish consumers with feats of culinary derring-do with a cook-off. I planted myself front and center and strapped on the feedbag. Looking back, this seems to be the point at which everything caromed hopelessly out of control.

By one in the afternoon, I was tucking into a filet of sautéed catfish, crusted with quinoa, and drizzled with key lime mustard. This dish proved the perfect follow-up to a broiled teriyaki catfish with wasabi cucumber salad. Was I full? Yes. Did I stop? No. Next up was a filet of catfish, smothered in a sauce of morel mushrooms and spring onions, gilded with a shock of chervil. Last came roasted catfish Basquaise, wrapped in a blanket of bacon and napped with extra virgin olive oil, which proved my favorite of the day—and my eventual undoing.

Don't ask me who won the contest. As best as I can determine, I lost culinary consciousness somewhere between my second and third bites of catfish Basquaise. Reports have trickled in over the course of the past few months. So and So saw me at a barbecue stand, buying a sandwich of smoked catfish. Such and Such spied me at the at Baptist church-run booth, begging for a taste of catfish jambalaya. What I've been able to piece together is this: I stayed mobile for a good thirty minutes after the catfish Basquaise incident. In the end, I didn't so much faint as swoon. What I choose to call a nap followed. Sometime around three that afternoon, I felt a hand on my shoulder, heard a voice in my ear. Someone—obviously someone who knew me well—kept insisting that I be awakened in time to make the catfish-eating contest.

I finally came to under an oak tree, a plate of fried catfish and hushpuppies by my side. To this day, I don't know how I got there. Or how I got my hands on that plate of fish. The hushpuppies were still nice and warm though. I took a bite. And then another. They had a nice crunch to them. And the chopped jalapeno peppers added a nice kick.

In *Food Festival U.S.A*, Becky Mercuri sings a paean to the diversity of America's food heritage. Along the way, she manages to convey a few lessons in culinary history. So dive in. By the time you hit page 320, you'll be out the door, stomach rumbling, car keys in hand, hell-bent for the Prairie Dog Chili Cook Off and World Championship Pickled Quail Egg Eating. Look for me. I'll be there, too. I'll be the guy surrounded by spent chili bowls, napping under the bough of an oak.

John T. Edge

John T. Edge is the author of *Southern Belly: The Ultimate Food Lover's Companion to the South*. He lives in Oxford, Mississippi.

Introduction

Street food, carnival food, festival food—by whatever name, this is food that draws Americans together. Thousands of food festivals are held annually throughout the United Sates, attracting millions of visitors. Some are small, local events run by all-volunteer organizations with profits benefiting charitable causes. Others are giant productions, staged by professional organizers. Often, the celebration of a particular ethnic heritage is at the heart of a festival, while others are held as harvest festivals or promotional events for a regional crop or food product. Many of the events (and some entire festivals) are tongue-in-cheek, but are nonetheless irresistible, since they represent a truly American fondness for having fun.

In writing this book, I had the opportunity to speak with hundreds of Americans who work hard to produce the food festivals and ethnic celebrations that make up such a rich part of our collective culture. I shall be forever grateful to each and every one of these folks who went out of their way to locate special recipes, to provide historical information on festivals and foodways, or to introduce me to someone often described as "the best cook in these parts."

Throughout my research, I was continually reminded of the words of music and food writer Ronni Lundy, whom I interviewed several years ago. Author of *Butter Beans to Blackberries: Recipes from the Southern Garden,* an extraordinary book on Southern food and cooking, Ronni told me, "Music and cooking are my passions. They provide windows to look at culture." Indeed. Nearly every festival in this book boasts of that same basic combination of music and food and gives us a peek into the very essence of life in a particular region or ethnic group.

A treasure trove of recipes can be found in festival cookbooks and archives. Many of the recipes herein are the unique creations of those who have entered festival cooking contests. Others are ethnic favorites, generously shared by people who have safeguarded the formulas as family heirlooms and who hope to see them preserved for generations yet to come. Still other recipes are from locally prominent chefs who have devised dishes that incorporate and showcase foods in new, innovative, and always delicious ways. Collectively, these recipes illustrate the fact that we reach out to honor and preserve our historic foodways while embracing the new. Certainly, there is no better souvenir of a food festival than the recipe for a special treat we have discovered and enjoyed.

In a world characterized by constant social and economic change, by the disappearance of the traditional family nucleus, and by the shift to commercially processed and prepared food products, we seek meaning in the celebration of food and food-related rituals. And increasingly, we seek out food that is different, that has a history of its own, and that gives us a sense of comfort and well-being. No wonder, then, that Americans have a renewed interest in food and that so many of us are driven to forge communal bonds around the common denominator that it provides. Such activity delivers a sense of history and identity, and we are compelled to resurrect and preserve recipes and traditions surrounding the preparation and consumption of food.

This book seeks to document a portion of our regional and ethnic foodways, to preserve them lest the great "Melting Pot of America" erases the diverse cultures and traditions upon which our country was founded and has grown and prospered. It represents my own small effort to preserve heritage recipes, to show how food has influenced our lives, how American ingenuity has created new dishes in response to diverse products, and how we have used food as a means of bringing about social interaction and bonding. The main activity of the food festival is the communal sharing of food, and, in a sense, food festivals have replaced the church socials of years ago. As such, they are a slice of pure Americana and should be revered and celebrated.

Now let's eat!

Chapter 1

The Northeast

Connecticut | Maine | Massachusetts | New Hampshire | New Jersey
New York | Pennsylvania | Rhode Island | Vermont

Connecticut

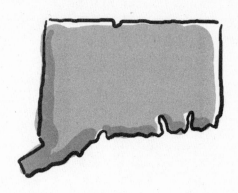

The southernmost of the New England states, Connecticut shares in the region's rich seafaring history, characterized by fishing, shipbuilding, and shipping. Connecticut now holds a predominant position in manufacturing and insurance, but the state retains a firm foothold in its maritime heritage. With a 250-mile-long southern coast bordered by Long Island Sound, Connecticut is a major destination for sport-fishing enthusiasts drawn to saltwater fishing for trophy striped bass and the hard-fighting bluefish. The latter is so esteemed that even Bridgeport's minor league baseball team carries the moniker of the Bluefish.

Bluefish Festival, Clinton, CT

Those with a penchant for bluefish gravitate to the Riverside Drive town dock in Clinton, Connecticut, where a festival has been held in honor of their favorite prey every August for over twenty-five years. Clinton lays claim to the title "Bluefish Capital of the World." In the early days, the festival included a bluefish fishing tournament with contenders battling to reel in the biggest "bulldog of the ocean." Today, 15,000 visitors to the festival feast on over 250 pounds of bluefish caught locally.

Rich Onofrio of the Clinton Rotary Club chairs the bluefish dinners, an integral part of the festival, which are held Friday night, Saturday, and Sunday. Rich took over from Willie Charles who passed along this never-fail recipe for preparing bluefish. Because it tends to be strongly flavored and oily, the dark bluefish needs to be dressed quickly and served promptly after it's caught. The Rotary Club also serves up lobster and chicken, with generous helpings of boiled red potatoes, corn on the cob, coleslaw, and beer.

Willie Charles' Famous Grilled Bluefish

Courtesy of Rich Onofrio, Clinton Rotary Club.

2 medium bluefish fillets
Butter
Lemon
Seasoned salt

Place each fillet on a piece of heavy-duty foil. Season with butter, lemon, and Lawry's Seasoned Salt, adjusting amounts according to the size of the fillet. Tightly close the foil so fish won't dry out and grill over a hot grill for 4½ minutes per side. Place foil-wrapped fish on serving plates accompanied by boiled red potatoes, corn on the cob, and coleslaw. Serves: 2.

Third Weekend in August

Maine

Folks in Maine think of their state as rural, but as Maine's economy evolves, its traditional industries of fishing and farming also change. Food processing has become big business in Maine and is closely aligned with the state's blueberry and potato crops, egg and poultry markets, and seafood harvest. Potatoes are the number one agricultural commodity of Maine, while eggs and milk are the leading livestock products. Maine is known as the "land of wild blueberries" because the low bush wild blueberry has grown in the region for thousands of years. Today ninety-five percent of U.S. production comes from the state's annual crop. The rapidly growing Maine salmon industry supplies almost twenty percent of U.S. domestic consumption, and Maine lobstermen still toil from dawn to dusk, bringing in their world-famous catch while taking care to conserve and manage the resource they depend upon. As the Maine Lobster Industry is working to preserve the oral history of generations of Maine lobstermen, Maine's Acadians seek to preserve and celebrate their unique culture and heritage.

Acadian Festival, Madawaska, ME

Last Week in June

In the late seventeenth century, a small group of French farmers settled in present-day Nova Scotia and northern Maine, a region known as "Acadia." The British took over the region in 1713, and in 1755, forcibly expelled the Acadians after they refused to swear loyalty. This is the diaspora that led to the Louisiana colony of Acadians, known as "'Cadians" or "Cajuns." Some original settlers remained along the St. John River, however, forming the town of Madawaska, and in 1978, Maine designated June 28 as Acadian Day.

The Acadian Festival was launched that same year, and today it is the largest cultural festival in Maine. Festival events vary from year to year, but usually include a parade and arts and crafts fair. A cultural display features local artisans demonstrating their skills, and organizers stage a reenactment of the first Acadian canoe landing. Held at the original site, it is followed by a traditional Acadian bean supper with beans cooked in holes dug in the ground.

Visitors can sample plenty of other Acadian cuisine that differs substantially from the fiery cooking of Louisiana Cajuns. Due to the huge difference in climate, Acadian food in Maine is often described as hearty and heavy, and not spicy. Only a sausage called *boudin* is held in common.

Acadian breakfast features *ployes*—buckwheat pancakes cooked thin and served folded, much like tortillas—eggs, and *grillades,* or fried pork rinds. Then there is the traditional Acadian supper that includes *pot-en-pot*, a rich stew layered with pork, beef, chicken, and vegetables; *fugère*, fiddlehead fern heads; *patates fricassé*, potatoes fried with salt pork and onion; *grillades en sauce blanche,* pork rinds in white sauce; and ployes in molasses for dessert.

Each year, an Acadian family celebrates its reunion as part of the festival. Some years, more than 4,000 family members have attended, swelling average attendance to over 15,000. The recipes have been documented in *Reunion Families' Favorite Recipes* by Geraldine Pelletier Chassé. The book is sold to raise funds for the Acadian Cultural Exchange.

Ployes Buckwheat Pancakes

A heritage recipe from Geraldine Pelletier Chassé of the Acadian Cultural Exchange.

1 cup buckwheat flour
1 cup all-purpose flour
2 teaspoons baking powder
1 teaspoon salt
1½ cups cold water
½–¾ cup hot (not boiling) water

Mix all dry ingredients in a large bowl with cold water until the mixture obtains the consistency of cake batter. Add hot water and mix well to thin. Spoon enough batter onto a very hot griddle to make a 4–8 inch pancake. Airholes will form in the ploye as it cooks. Cook on one side only. When the top of the pancake is dry, it is ready to eat.

Serve rolled or folded as a substitute for bread. At breakfast, serve ployes with *cretons*, a spicy pork spread (recipe follows). For lunch, ployes are served with butter, and at dinner, they are served with molasses or maple syrup as a dessert.

Cretons Pork Spread

Another heritage recipe from *Reunion Families' Favorite Recipes* by Geraldine Pelletier Chassé.

5–6 pounds pork
2–3 onions
Salt and pepper
Water
Additional onions to taste
Seasoning to taste: allspice, cloves, cinnamon, and nutmeg
Flour

Place pork in a large pot with onions, salt, and pepper, and cover with water. Boil until pork is tender. Remove pork and skim off excess fat from broth. Debone the pork and pass it through a meat grinder or food processor. Mince more onions to taste and add pork and onions to broth. Heat, then add the spices along with a little flour to thicken. Stir until all ingredients are well mixed. Store in the refrigerator until ready to serve as a spread for ployes.

Central Maine Egg Festival, Pittsfield, ME

Maine is a major producer of eggs, most of them brown as a result of the favored breed of chicken there. The Central Maine Egg Festival celebrates the state's major export with exhibits and demonstrations. Visitors to the cook tent who take part in the early bird breakfast can view one of the world's largest frying pans. Made by Alcoa and Tefloned by Dupont, it is ten feet one inch across and filled with that traditional American breakfast, ham and eggs. Because this is New England, diners are served a side of baked beans.

Breakfast aside, cheesecake is the preferred vehicle for eggs, and the annual cheesecake contest dictates that every entry must be made from scratch and include at least four brown eggs. Judging is followed by the cheesecake dessert luncheon and a chicken barbecue that runs throughout the afternoon.

Fourth Saturday in July

Double Chocolate Raspberry Marble Cheesecake

Dianne Berry, Corinna, ME, grand prize winner of the
Central Maine Egg Festival Cheesecake Contest.

½ cup butter, melted
1 package (10¼ ounces) fudge brownie mix
4 (8-ounce) packages cream cheese
4 large eggs
1½ cups sugar
1 cup heavy cream
1 teaspoon vanilla
½ cup raspberries
2 tablespoons sugar
½ ounce unsweetened chocolate, melted
Fresh raspberries and chocolate to garnish

Crust: Mix together butter and brownie mix and press into a 9-inch springform pan.

Filling: Beat cream cheese until smooth. Add eggs, one at a time, beating until smooth after each addition. Add sugar, cream, and vanilla, and beat until very smooth. Pour all but one cup of the filling into prepared crust.

Purée: Combine raspberries and sugar in a food processor. Mix in ½ cup of reserved filling mixture.

Topping: Mix remaining ½ cup of reserved filling mixture with the melted chocolate.

Assembly: Spoon purée on top of filling, followed by the topping. Draw a knife carefully through the mixture to create a marbling effect.

Bake cheesecake in a preheated 300° oven for one hour. If the cheesecake has not set, turn oven up to 350° and bake an additional 20–30 minutes, or just until center has set. Turn off oven, open door, and cool the cheesecake in oven. Chill in refrigerator for at least 8 hours. Garnish with additional fresh raspberries and shaved semisweet chocolate.

Eastport Salmon Festival, Eastport, ME

Eastport, Maine, is located on Moose Island, about as far east as you can get before land meets the Atlantic Ocean. The village is in the heart of Maine's salmon farming industry.

Since 1988, the locals have closed their historic downtown district to traffic in order to celebrate salmon on the first Sunday after Labor Day. Fine arts and crafts, live music, educational booths, and farmers' (and seafarmers') markets attract increasing numbers of attendees who flock to enjoy good food, shopping, and entertainment at the Salmon Festival.

The canopied lawns of the Peavey Memorial Library provide the perfect bucolic setting for barbecued salmon dinners featuring fresh salmon served with those equally famous baked Maine potatoes. Celebrity chefs and students from the nearby technical college lend a hand in the preparations, and diners are welcome to climb aboard one of two charter boats for a tour of salmon farm sites.

Mrs. Jett Peterson, proprietor of the Weston House Bed and Breakfast, is an expert on preparing Eastport's salmon and is the driving force behind a future Salmon Festival cookbook designed around the local specialty. Her recipe provides an excellent showcase for salmon.

Baked Salmon Passion with a Salsa of Nectarines, Blueberries, and Mint

Guests at Jett Peterson's Weston House Bed & Breakfast in Eastport, ME, have voted this recipe a real winner!

Fish:
2-pound side of salmon, boned and skinned
Olive oil
Sea salt or kosher salt
Jump Up and Kiss Me Hot Sauce with Passion
Additional fresh mint for garnish

Salsa:
2–3 nectarines, chopped into small cubes
1 cup fresh Maine blueberries
¼ cup chopped fresh mint leaves

Combine and mix salsa ingredients. Cover and chill for at least 30 minutes.

Preheat oven to 450°. Line a baking tray with foil and spray with nonstick spray. Place salmon on baking tray and cover top with a light coating of olive oil and salt. Spread with a coating of hot sauce. Bake salmon for 10 minutes per inch of thickness at the meatiest point. If you prefer salmon well done, bake approximately 10 minutes longer but do not overcook. When salmon is done, allow it to rest for 5–10 minutes. Place on a serving platter, garnish with salsa and additional mint sprigs, and serve immediately.
Serves: 2–4.

The First Sunday after Labor Day

Houlton Potato Feast Days, Houlton, ME

Houlton, Maine, is the "Shiretown" or county seat of Aroostook County. It's also smack dab in the middle of Maine's potato farm country. So it was only natural that Potato Feast Days was established in 1960 to pay homage to their crop.

This family-friendly festival is characterized by a parade of dolls, concerts, a road race, a quilt show, and contests like potato barrel rolling and various potato games for children. On Friday night, there is a big outdoor lobster "feed" to get things off on the right foot.

For spud lovers, the Potato Feast is the place to be. A baked potato sale with a huge assortment of toppings plays second fiddle only to the Potato Feast supper on Saturday evening, which includes an enormous variety of potato dishes along with roast beef and pork, fresh vegetables, homemade rolls, and desserts. For many years the festival included a potato cooking contest, and one of the favorite winners is just one such potato dessert.

Potato Custard Pie

Lona Putnam's Winning Recipe from *Favorite Potato Recipes*.

1 medium potato, about 6 ounces
2 tablespoons butter
¾ cup sugar
2 egg yolks, beaten
½ cup milk
1 tablespoon fresh lemon juice
1 teaspoon grated lemon rind
2 egg whites, stiffly beaten
1 (9-inch) deep-dish pie shell

Peel, cook, and mash potato. Add butter and sugar. Stir until creamy. Cool. Add egg yolks, milk, lemon rind, and juice. Fold in stiffly beaten egg whites. Pour into a 9-inch pastry shell and bake at 400° for 25–35 minutes or until top is golden. Cool on rack, then chill in refrigerator.

Last Full Weekend in August before Labor Day Weekend

Maine Lobster Festival, Rockland, ME

Lobster is king in the state of Maine where they bill their favorite crustacean as "the ultimate white meat." The first Maine Lobster Festival was held in 1948 and continues today in celebration of midcoast Maine's maritime heritage. Over 60,000 people converge upon Rockland's Harbor Park, the city's picturesque waterfront overlooking beautiful Penobscot Bay, for this annual summer event.

King Neptune and his court rule over the pageantry of the festival, which includes marine exhibits, boat rides, a carnival, and Maine crafts and products. Delicious Maine lobster is steamed in the world's largest lobster cooker.

One of the most prestigious events is the "Great Taste of Maine Lobster" culinary competition hosted at Blaine House, the governor's residence. Maine chefs compete for medals as part of an all-out effort to demonstrate the versatility of the lobster.

First Weekend of August

Lobster Risotto with Fresh Tomato and Basil

Chef Joseph Pirkola of Raspberri's at The Gorges Grant Hotel, Ogunquit, ME, won
a gold medal at the Great Taste of Maine Lobster competition with this recipe.
Reprinted with permission from the Maine Lobster Promotion Council.

Lobster Stock:
6 lobster bodies and shells from picked lobsters
2 onions, roughly diced
2 carrots, roughly diced
4 celery stalks, roughly diced
3 tomatoes, roughly diced
2 bay leaves
Basil stems
Parsley stems
Black peppercorns to taste
Pinch of salt

Rinse shells and lobster bodies and roast in a 300° oven for 20–30 minutes. Allow shells to cool and combine with remaining ingredients in a large pot. Fill pot with cold water to about 6 inches above shells and vegetables. Bring to a boil and reduce to a simmer. Skim off impurities that rise to the surface and simmer for no longer than 30 minutes. Strain through a fine strainer and cheesecloth and return to stove to reduce to concentrate flavor before use.

Lobster Risotto:
6 cups lobster stock
4 tablespoons butter
1 cup diced onion
2 tablespoons finely chopped garlic
1½ cups Arborio rice
¼ cup freshly grated Parmesan cheese

Salt and pepper to taste
6 (1¼-pound) lobsters, steamed and meat removed from shells
1 cup yellow and red Roma tomatoes, peeled, seeded, and julienned
2 tablespoons fresh basil

In a saucepan, bring stock to a simmer and maintain the simmer during preparation. In a large saucepan, melt 2 tablespoons of the butter and sauté the onion and garlic until translucent. Add rice and stir for 1–2 minutes until well coated with butter and slightly translucent. Add ½ cup of the stock and stir continuously until the stock is absorbed by the rice. Continue adding ½ cup of stock at a time, stirring until almost all of the stock is absorbed before adding more stock. Keep stirring until rice is tender but slightly crunchy in the center, about 20–25 minutes. Add Parmesan cheese and season with salt and pepper to taste.

In a separate pan, add remaining hot lobster stock and stir in reserved lobster meat, the remaining 2 tablespoons butter, the tomatoes, and basil. Serve risotto in a warm pasta bowl while rice is still fluid and creamy, arranging lobster meat over rice and surrounded by additional broth with tomato and basil between the rim of the bowl and the risotto. Serves: 6.

Wild Blueberry Festival, Machias, ME

In Machias, Maine, townsfolk gather every August to celebrate the harvest of the wild blueberry—a delicious sweet-sour North American berry that is smaller than its cultivated Midwestern cousin. The festival started small back in 1976, but today, word has spread, and upward of 10,000 visitors are likely to show up. And no wonder—this is Maine food at its down-home best.

A Friday night fish fry kicks the event off to a good start. On Saturday morning, participants enjoy wild blueberry pancakes before the five-mile Blueberry Run. All that running works up an appetite for the New England-style lunch to follow: lobster, corn, steamed clams, and fish chowder.

But what about the blueberries? Besides the blueberry pancake breakfast, there's a wild blueberry dessert bar in the Centre Street Congregational Church, where visitors can also view a display of blueberry quilts. Each year, the festival organizers stage a "home-grown" musical on a silly blueberry theme, such as "It's a Wonderful Blueberry." There's a pie-eating contest and a wild blueberry baking contest. Naturally, blue ribbons are awarded—one for the overall winner, in addition to the best blueberry pie champion.

Blueberry Strudel

By Tyler Robertson from *Prize-Winning Recipes from the Machias Blueberry Festival.*

6 tablespoons fresh bread crumbs
2–3 cups fresh blueberries
¼ cup golden raisins (optional)
½ tablespoon lemon juice
½ cup sugar
¼ teaspoon cinnamon
5 sheets of phyllo pastry
½ cup unsalted butter, melted
⅓ cup finely chopped macadamia nuts
Powdered sugar

Toast bread crumbs in a 325° oven for 10 minutes. Mix together blueberries, raisins, lemon juice, sugar, and cinnamon. Preheat oven to 425°. Place phyllo dough on a sheet of waxed paper and keep covered with a clean, damp dishtowel, removing one sheet at a time, so it does not dry out. Layer sheets of phyllo dough, brush each sheet with melted butter, and add a sprinkling of toasted bread crumbs and macadamia nuts. Place filling 2 inches away from the long side of one edge, fold the near edge over filling, tuck in ends, and roll up. Brush roll with remaining melted butter. Bake on a lightly buttered cookie sheet for 25 minutes. Cool and dust with powdered sugar.

Friday and Saturday of the Third Weekend in August

Massachusetts

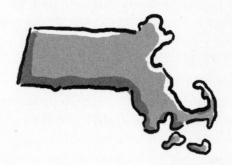

Since 1620, when the Pilgrims first landed on her shores, Massachusetts has been recognized as a haven for those seeking freedom from religious persecution. In 1790, the Shakers, who had first settled near Albany, New York, also established a colony in Massachusetts. Most early settlers were farmers, but with the opening of the Erie Canal in 1825, products began arriving more cheaply from the West and many farmers went to work in factories. For a small state, Massachusetts today ranks a huge sixth in manufacturing, but the state's farmers still produce livestock, milk, eggs, vegetables, and thirty percent of the nation's cranberries. Massachusetts has paid official homage to its food heritage by designating the cranberry as the state's official berry, and cranberry juice as the official state beverage. But they didn't stop there... the official state game bird is the wild turkey and the official state fish is the cod. The basis of Boston baked beans, the humble navy bean is recognized as the official state bean, and the corn muffin, a staple of New England cooking, is the state muffin. The state dessert, created in the nineteenth century, is Boston cream pie, and the state cookie is the chocolate chip, first developed by Ruth Wakefield at her famous Toll House Inn in Whitman, Massachusetts.

An Evening at Hancock Shaker Village, Pittsfield, MA

Hancock Shaker Village, home to Shakers from 1790 to 1960, is today an outdoor history museum that preserves and interprets the Shaker society and religion. In 1989, the folks at Hancock decided to develop a special program that would give visitors the opportunity to experience an authentic Shaker meal. The result was An Evening at Hancock Shaker Village, held on selected Saturday evenings in the restored 1830 Believers' Dining Room.

Shaker "sisters" were well known for their fine cooking, and they took pains to document their recipes—recipes which incorporate the high-quality produce, dairy products, and meats resulting from their communal labor. Today these dishes are prepared by local caterers using these historical recipes.

While the menus vary each week due to the use of fresh, seasonal ingredients, meals include soup, an entrée, a sidedish, and dessert. In September, guests might enjoy green salad, tomato soup, beef pot roast, roasted potatoes, Shaker squash, ginger beets, Believers' bread, and apple pie. The program includes a guided tour of the main buildings at the village, known as the "City of Peace," followed by a taste of specialty hard ciders in an 1830 kitchen. The meal itself is served family style at long tables. In typical Shaker tradition, no one goes away hungry.

Chocolate Pound Cake

A prized heritage recipe from *The Best of Shaker Cooking* by Amy Bess Miller and Persis Fuller. Reprinted with permission from Hancock Shaker Village.

1 cup butter
½ cup lard or vegetable shortening
3 cups sugar
5 eggs
3 cups sifted flour
½ cup cocoa
½ teaspoon baking powder
¼ teaspoon salt
1¼ cups milk
2 tablespoons grated chocolate
1 teaspoon vanilla

This is a round ring cake and should be baked in a 9-inch tube pan. Preheat oven to 325°. Cream the butter, shortening, and sugar together until light and fluffy. Add eggs, one at a time, beating well after each addition. Sift together the flour, cocoa, baking powder, and salt; add alternately with milk to egg mixture, stirring after each addition until well blended. Add chocolate. Stir in vanilla. Turn batter into greased and floured pan. Bake for 1½ hours or until cake tests done. Turn onto wire rack to cool. Center can be filled with whipped cream and shaved chocolate, if desired.

Saturdays Mid-July to Mid-August and Mid-September to Mid-October

Topsfield Fair, Topsfield, MA

Topsfield Fair is the oldest county fair in the United States, dating back to 1818. Despite its large size today, accommodating some half million people over its ten-day run, Topsfield remains, in essence, a country fair and, as such, abounds with traditional foods and cooking methods of New England.

The food committee makes and sells three or four kinds of bread daily. Several organizations hold luncheons and dinners during the fair, including the Congregational Church of Topsfield that produces home-cooked turkey dinners every day.

Topsfield offers all the trappings of an old-fashioned fair. Barn tours, milking demonstrations, a petting farm, and a chick-hatching exhibit all serve to acquaint the city slicker with life on the farm. A fall flower show, spinning and other arts and crafts demonstrations, and a farmers' market attract homemakers, while guys especially enjoy the antique car and tractor displays, decoy carving, and model building.

The All New England Giant Pumpkin Weigh-Off is a favorite of all, especially for competitors who spend the summer nervously feeding their pumpkin patch with secret concoctions in the hope of producing the most massive

pumpkin of the season. Competition is fierce, with entries ranging between 800 and 1,000 pounds. Pumpkins are judged on weight, but must also be free of splits, holes, and soft spots.

Topsfield Fair also features cooking contests aplenty. The general cooking competition covers everything from candy, cookies, cakes, and pies, to soups, breads, and, because this is New England, baked beans. The Topsfield apple pie contest has attracted national media attention thanks to Rosie O'Donnell, who has a penchant for this all-American dessert. The parent-and-child cookie celebration presents a great opportunity for a family partnership to take home both winning ribbons and cash. In an interesting twist, contestants in the King Arthur Flour baking competition must all prepare the same recipe, selected each year by the sponsor. Due to the different brands of ingredients used, taste and texture vary widely.

For many, there's no better combination than a hot bowl of chili and a cold beer. Topsfield capitalizes on this approach to good eating with its chili contest and its home-brew competition. Fire departments, ambulance crews, and other groups all vie for top prizes in hot and mild chili cooking divisions. And you know something's brewing when contestants enter their homemade beers. Past entries have ranged from Scandinavian Pilsner to British Bitter, with competition spirited, to say the least.

Topsfield joins over forty fairs around the country in participating in the Land O' Lakes quick bread contest. The winner goes on to compete in the company's national contest.

Walnut Tea Ring

Louise Bevilacqua of Haverhill, MA, won first place for this creation in the Land O' Lakes Quick Bread Contest.

½ cup butter, softened
½ cup canola oil
2 cups sugar
5 eggs, separated
1 tablespoon vanilla
1¾ cups ground walnuts
1 cup light sour cream
2 cups flour
1 teaspoon baking soda
⅓ cup finely minced candied pineapple
2 tablespoons grated orange peel
1 tablespoon poppy seeds

Icing:
3½ cups powdered sugar
6 ounces cream cheese, softened
6 ounces butter, softened
1 tablespoon grated orange peel
3 tablespoons orange juice
⅓ cup finely ground walnuts

Preheat oven to 350°. Grease two six-cup ring pans. Cream the butter and oil with the sugar. Add egg yolks and beat well. Add the vanilla, walnuts, sour cream, flour, baking soda, pineapple, orange peel, and poppy seeds. Stir until blended. Beat egg whites until fluffy. Fold into batter. Pour batter into prepared pans and bake for 40 minutes or until a toothpick comes out clean. Cool on a rack.

Combine all icing ingredients except the walnuts and beat until creamy. Stir in the walnuts. Spread the icing on cooled cake rings. Yield: 2 tea rings.

New Hampshire

New Hampshire is a remarkably beautiful land of rivers, lakes, and ponds, and home to the sparkling granite White Mountains (thus the Granite State), which form a majestic backdrop to its rolling hills and pastures. Since 1885, the state has been a haven for summer tourists escaping the heat of the great Eastern cities. In the late nineteenth century, over two hundred White Mountain hotels, inns, and boarding houses accommodated over 12,000 guests at a time. In the tradition of that Victorian era, these great hotels offered high tea service in tearooms. Meeting for tea and conversation in the late afternoon became a hallmark of elegance throughout society, and eventually, the custom spawned independent teahouses as well. Today, New Hampshire continues to cater to the tourist trade, and with America's renewed interest in tea as part of a healthier lifestyle, the inns, hotels, and bed-and-breakfast establishments of New Hampshire have revived the old tradition of afternoon tea.

Traditional Tea and Summer Fun
Lawn Party, Tamworth, NH

Usually the Third Saturday in July

Early New England village life is re-created at the Remick Country Doctor Museum and Farm in Tamworth, a lovely area nestled between the White Mountains and New Hampshire's lake region. In 1894, Dr. Edwin Remick established his medical practice in Tamworth, and his son, Dr. Edwin Crafts Remick, also a physician, served the community until his death in 1993. Through his generosity, the museum was established, giving visitors the opportunity to learn about life on a family farm and the activities of a country doctor.

Tamworth has hosted New Hampshire's summer tourists for over a century. Nineteenth-century Tamworth boasted multiple teahouses on the banks of the Chocorua River, and most accompanied the tea with English-style tea foods: finger sandwiches of cucumber and butter or walnuts and cream cheese, cookies, and lemon curd with scones and muffins. Family diaries kept by Tamworth women frequently mention taking tea on a regular basis throughout the year.

The tea tradition of Tamworth has today been revived at the Remick Country Doctor Museum and Farm with its annual Tea and Summer Fun Lawn Party. Women in Victorian dress serve tea, along with cookies and cakes made from historic recipes, to adults who luxuriate at tables in the flower garden set with fine linens from the Remick family's possessions, while the museum's director explains the history of tea. Children enjoy their own special tea party with lemonade, iced tea, and cookies, and are taught the basics of tea etiquette.

Melt-in-Your-Mouth-Delicious Blueberry Cake

This is the carefully guarded tea cake recipe of nurse Gertrude Henry Seiders, assistant to both Dr. Edwin Remick and Dr. Edwin Crafts Remick. The recipe is provided courtesy of Mrs. Seiders' niece, Earline Stevens Wright, and The Remick Country Doctor Museum and Farm.

2 eggs, separated
1 cup sugar
½ cup shortening
⅛ teaspoon salt
1 teaspoon vanilla
1½ cups sifted all-purpose flour
1 teaspoon baking powder
⅓ cup milk
1½ cups fresh blueberries tossed with
   1 tablespoon flour
Additional sugar for topping

Preheat oven to 350°. Beat the egg whites until stiff, adding about ¼ cup of the sugar to the egg whites to keep them stiff. Cream the shortening; add the salt and vanilla, add remainder of the sugar, and then add the egg yolks, beating until light and creamy. Sift the flour together with baking powder and add to creamed mixture alternately with milk. Fold in egg whites, then fold in blueberries. Spread mixture in a well-buttered 8 x 8-inch baking pan and sprinkle top lightly with sugar. Bake for 50 minutes or until done. Cool on a wire rack.

New Jersey

New Jersey's official nickname is the "Garden State," and today almost twenty percent of the state is composed of farmland. Over $800 million in annual revenue is generated by agriculture; the nursery, greenhouse, and sod industries are top producers, closely followed by vegetable and fruit crops, the dairy industry, and poultry and egg production. New Jersey also boasts an abundance from the sea. The commercial harvest includes oysters, scallops, several varieties of fish, and clams—in fact, the state's vast clam beds, extending from Barnegat Bay to Cape May, make New Jersey the U.S. leader in value of clams caught.

In the nineteenth century, improved transportation fueled industrial development in New Jersey, and thousands of Europeans arrived to work in factories. Beginning in the 1890s, earlier immigrants from Ireland and Germany were joined by Jews, Hungarians, and Italians, making for a mix of cultures and cuisines reflected in the incredible ethnic edibles throughout this agriculturally rich state.

Hungarian Festival, New Brunswick, NJ

For over twenty years, between 5,000 and 10,000 people of Hungarian descent and lovers of wonderful food have converged upon New Brunswick's Hungarian Festival each June. Against a backdrop of traditional music and folk dancing, visitors enjoy authentic crafts like color woodcuts, embroidery, porcelain, and laces. Then there's the food—an eight-block stretch of enticing Hungarian treats. For a casual lunch, there are *Kolbasz* sausage and *pecsenye* (pork cutlet sandwiches). Many cannot resist digging into a full-course meal that includes stuffed cabbage, beef goulash, *szekely gulyás* (pork stew with sauerkraut), and chicken *paprikas*. And for dessert, there's *langos* (fried dough similar to funnel cakes), *palacsintas* (crepes filled with cottage cheese or jelly), *fank* (jelly-filled doughnuts), *kalacs* (nut or poppy seed rolls), *kifli* (small pastries filled with nuts, prunes, or apricots), and strudel by the slice. Unable to eat their fill in a single day, many attendees purchase an array of pastries to take home.

First Saturday in June

Gulyásleves
Hungarian Gulyás Soup

A real winner from the *Hungarian Festival Cookbook*.

2 pounds beef, cut into 1-inch cubes
1 tablespoon salt
2 tablespoons vegetable oil
2 large onions, chopped
1 tablespoon Hungarian sweet paprika
4 cups beef broth
4 medium potatoes, diced
1 large green bell pepper, diced
¼ teaspoon black pepper
Pinch of caraway seeds

Mix the beef cubes with 1½ teaspoons of salt; set aside. Heat vegetable oil and sauté onions until golden. Add paprika, stir, then add beef. Let the beef simmer in its own juice over low heat for 1½ hours or until tender. Add the broth, potatoes, bell pepper, remaining salt, and black pepper. Simmer until potatoes are done. Add caraway seeds. Serves: 6–8.

Laci Pecsenye
Pork Fry Sandwich

The folks at the Hungarian Festival provided this recipe for their famous pork sandwiches.

1 (14-ounce) can sauerkraut
Beef broth
2 pounds lean pork butt, sliced thin or substitute thinly sliced, boneless pork chops
1 teaspoon salt
½ teaspoon pepper
½ teaspoon Hungarian sweet paprika
2 cloves garlic, crushed
Vegetable oil for deep-frying
Sliced fresh rye bread

Drain sauerkraut, place in a baking dish, add beef broth to barely cover, and bake, covered, at 350° for 1 to 2 hours. Leave in the oven. Sprinkle both sides of the pork slices with salt, pepper, paprika, and garlic. Let stand for about 10 minutes. Heat oil in skillet and fry pork. Serve the pork on slices of rye bread with hot sauerkraut. Serves: 4.

Long Beach Island Chowderfest, Beach Haven, NJ

Cooler temperatures and the end of the summer season on New Jersey's Long Beach Island mean it's time for the annual Chowderfest. Local merchants participate in an end-of-year tent sale, while more than twenty restaurants compete in the chowder cook-off, producing over a hundred gallons of chowder in an effort to win recognition for either the "best red" or "best white." Most folks think that festival patrons are the real winners since they get to enjoy unlimited chowder tastings in order to vote for the winners. Because Barnegat Bay is famous for its local shellfish and seafood, vendors sell other shore favorites like delicious fresh clams on the half shell and clams casino.

Morrison's Restaurant in Beach Haven is a family business and one of the last of the old fish houses in New Jersey. Peg and Pete Morrison opened a clam bar on the bay in 1946. Today, patrons in the know flock to the restaurant in order to enjoy Peg's clam chowder, the happy result of her efforts in gathering advice and recipes from old-timers in Beach Haven. This recipe, in addition to nearly one hundred other recipes from the chefs of thirty-seven local restaurants, appears in *Favorite Recipes from Long Beach Island Restaurants*.

Peg's Clam Chowder

Now you can duplicate the chowder that has folks lined up at Morrison's Restaurant in Beach Haven, New Jersey. Reprinted from *Favorite Recipes from Long Beach Island Restaurants* with permission of the publisher.

One Weekend before Columbus Day Weekend

½ pound bacon
2 quarts water
2 stalks celery, diced
3 cups diced onion
¼ cup chopped carrots
2 dozen chowder clams, minced (save juice)
Bottled clam juice (optional)
1 tablespoon oregano
1 quart whole, skinless tomatoes, chopped or 1 (28-ounce) can whole, skinless tomatoes in thick purée, undrained, and tomatoes chopped
1 cup tomato or vegetable juice
½ cup chicken broth
4 cups diced potatoes
Salt and pepper to taste

Fry, cool, and crumble bacon. Set aside. Start with 2 quarts water. Add the celery, onion, and carrots, and bring to a boil. Add the reserved clam juice (plus bottled clam juice if desired for flavor) and bring back to a boil. Add the oregano. Combine the tomatoes, tomato juice, and chicken broth and add to the broth. Bring back to a boil, then add the bacon and clams. Bring to a boil again. Add potatoes and simmer until they are tender. When potatoes are done, the chowder is done. Serves: 12.

National Lima Bean Festival, W. Cape May, NJ

For years, West Cape May, New Jersey, has been known along the East Coast for its cultivation of lima beans. So when local residents got to talking about having a celebration to promote their area, the "lowly lima" was a natural focal point. The large seeded lima bean dates back to between 5000 and 6000 B.C. when it was cultivated along the western coast of South America. Today, there are almost one hundred lima bean farms throughout New Jersey, making the state the unofficial lima bean capital of the world.

Although the company that purchased all those lima beans for processing decided to cancel their contract in the early 1990s in favor of more fashionable vegetables, the denizens of West Cape May decided that the event was too much fun to let it fall by the wayside and the festivities continued.

Today the only festival of this type in the world attracts thousands of visitors who participate in the lima bean pitching contest and watch the crowning of the Miss Lima Bean Queen. Local restaurants compete to produce innovative dishes using limas, with winners picked by the visitors who line up to check out the bean cuisine, including several varieties of lima bean soup. Pork sandwiches and fish platters are also served to round out the meal.

Saturday of Columbus Day Weekend

Key Lima Pie

From the *National Lima Bean Festival Cookbook* comes a winning recipe from the R.D. 2 Gang, Victoria Palchak, Susan Kornacki, and Margie Rosso.

1 (10-inch) deep-dish piecrust, unbaked
¼ pound Colby cheese, grated
8 ounces lump crabmeat
10 ounces cooked baby lima beans
4 eggs
2 cups heavy cream
¾ teaspoon salt
Pinch of nutmeg
Pinch of sugar
Pinch of cayenne pepper
1 red bell pepper

Preheat oven to 425°. Sprinkle pie shell with grated cheese. Sprinkle the crabmeat on top of cheese. Sieve cooked beans through a sieve mill. Whip eggs, cream, and spices together. Add beans and whip. Pour over the cheese and crabmeat. Cut 3 or 4 pepper rings and place on top. Bake for 15 minutes at 425°. Reduce oven temperature to 300° and bake 40 minutes longer or until knife inserted in center comes out clean. Let stand 5 minutes before slicing.

New York

Once an agricultural powerhouse, New York state today allots just about one-quarter of its land to farms. However, the dairy and livestock industries still thrive, and traditional crops like apples and grapes—New York boasts one of America's oldest commercial wine regions, dating back to the 1860s—are joined by exciting new gourmet tastes, like exotic mushrooms and hardy strains of garlic. This combination of old and new makes for one of the most diverse and delicious food festival circuits.

In the nineteenth century, New York's thriving economy was fueled by wave after wave of immigration. The populations of cities like New York and Buffalo reflect this history. In its glory days, Buffalo supplied textiles and steel to the rest of America, and Greeks, Germans, Irish, Italians, Poles, and other Eastern Europeans flocked to Buffalo in search of employment. Today, this "City of Good Neighbors" continues to celebrate the rich diversity of its ethnic heritage with a variety of food festivals.

Burgerfest, Hamburg, NY

Controversy surrounds the invention of the hamburger. Some believe that it originated in Hamburg, Germany. Then there is the hamburger listed on the 1834 menu of New York City's Delmonico's restaurant. But when it comes to enthusiasm, the claim of Hamburg, New York, wins hands-down. Reportedly, Charles and Frank Menches were selling sandwiches in their stand at the 1885 Erie County Fair, then called the "Hamburg Fair." When they ran short of pork, they began serving grilled beef patties on rolls. Being savvy entrepreneurs, they called the new sandwiches "hamburgers" in honor of the locals.

When Burgerfest was established in 1985, descendants of the Menches journeyed from their hometown of Akron, Ohio, to sell their original burgers. Today, there are plenty of burgermeisters who come to sell their own version of America's favorite sandwich—and to participate in the burger competition. The typical entry is based on a meat patty with various toppings, but there are a variety of whimsical entries too, like a halved doughnut containing chocolate filling with dollops of red and yellow frosting to simulate ketchup and mustard. The 15,000 attendees also feast on corn on the cob from nearby Eden, home of the Eden Corn Festival each August.

LETTUCE introduce you to the "Birthplace of the Hamburger"—Hamburg, NY. In 1885, the Menches brothers RELISHED life in Hamburg, where the people always cut the MUSTARD. While selling their sandwiches in PRIME time, they invented the first-known ground beef pattie in America and named it the hamburger. If ever GRILLED about the origin of America's favorite sandwich, the HAMBURGER, don't get in a PICKLE, just remember Hamburg, NY.

Reprinted with permission from the Hamburg, NY Chamber of Commerce.

Turkey Burger

Marie Cook and Nicole Trzepacz of Cook's Cozy Corner, Hamburg, NY, won the 1997 Burger Competition with this innovative entry.

Burgers:
1 pound ground turkey
½ cup finely chopped celery
½–¾ cup Italian-style bread crumbs
Salt and pepper to taste

Dijonnaise:
½ cup mayonnaise
1½ tablespoons Dijon mustard

4 miniature sub rolls, split and toasted
Alfalfa sprouts or chopped lettuce

Mix together all the burger ingredients. Form into four oblong patties and grill on barbecue until done. Make Dijonnaise by combining mayonnaise and mustard, mixing to taste. Spread both sides of roll with Dijonnaise, add burger, and top with alfalfa sprouts or chopped lettuce. Turkey burgers may also be panfried in 3 tablespoons butter until browned, crispy, and completely cooked in center. Serves: 4.

Fox Run Vineyards Garlic Festival, Penn Yan, NY

The Finger Lakes Region of New York State has long been known for its fine wines, but with ideal soil and cool climate, the area is also the homeland of garlic, especially the coveted hard-necked varieties. The latter have gained a reputation as the healthiest, priciest, and most intense of the various garlic strains.

The Garlic Festival celebrates the diversity of garlic varieties grown in the Finger Lakes area. Representatives of the Garlic Seed Foundation, an organization of regional growers, conduct tastings of the freshly harvested bulbs, and approximately 3,000 visitors take the opportunity to stock up.

Local chefs are on hand to demonstrate cooking techniques and signature dishes that incorporate the many varieties of Finger Lakes garlic as well as other specialties of the region, including the hand-crafted chevre, feta, and blue cheeses produced by Lively Run Goat Dairy.

The centerpiece of the festival is the Glorious Garlic Dinner, a ticketed event held on Saturday evening that showcases a lavish array of garlic-infused dishes created by award-winning chefs and paired with Fox Run wines. Served alfresco at the top of Fox Run Vineyards at dusk, overlooking shimmering Seneca Lake, the dinner combines a dramatic setting with elaborate cuisine.

Whole Roasted Garlic with New York State Goat Cheese

Mark Cupolo, chef/proprietor, Victor Grilling Company, Victor, NY, is the locally renowned and award-winning creator of this great appetizer.

6 heads fresh garlic
½ cup extra virgin olive oil
6 sprigs fresh thyme
Salt and pepper
6 ounces fresh goat cheese
Crostini or crackers
French green olives

Preheat oven to 350°. Cut each head of garlic in half horizontally. Brush each cut surface with olive oil and sprinkle with salt, pepper, and thyme leaves. Put the garlic heads back together and wrap in aluminum foil. Bake until the garlic is completely soft, about 1 hour. Serve the garlic with the goat cheese, crostini, French green olives, and the remaining olive oil.

The First Weekend in August

Greater Buffalo Italian Heritage Festival, Buffalo, NY

Wed.–Sun. Second Week of July

Buffalo was the destination for thousands of Italian immigrants in the early 1900s. The descendants of those first arrivals celebrate the old traditions and foods every year at the Italian Heritage Festival, begun in 1988.

Visitors can sample Italian foods at more than one hundred booths, many sponsored by local Italian restaurants. Favorites like Italian sausage, pizza, and calzones are just the beginning. The many regional specialty items include: *la cutina* (stuffed, rolled pigskin), *cardunes* (omelettes with burdock, a relative of the artichoke), *babaluci* (snails), *bistella di stipare* (stuffed hot peppers), and *caponatina* (eggplant with capers, onions, and tomatoes). And everyone saves room for dessert. Who could resist classics like *cannoli*, *gelato*, and *spumoni*? Then there are the local special pastries: *sfinge* (cream puffs), *pastaciotti* (cookies filled with ricotta and chocolate chips), and *gugilini* (sesame cookies). And espresso and cappuccino fortify the crowd as they dance to a variety of musical acts.

Veal GarAngelo

A winning recipe from Gary Tenebra, chef/proprietor, Cafe GarAngelo in Buffalo.

Eggplant:
1 cup peeled, cubed eggplant
1 clove garlic, chopped
2 tablespoons chopped onion
Olive oil

Veal:
2 (4-ounce) slices milk-fed veal or chicken breast, pounded thin and lightly floured
Olive oil
1 plum tomato, chopped
2 tablespoons chopped onion
1 teaspoon chopped garlic
Fresh chopped basil to taste (2–3 large leaves)
½ cup dry white wine
2 very thin slices prosciutto (Italian ham)
2 thin slices provolone cheese
2 ounces spaghetti, cooked al dente

Garnish:
1 lemon slice
Additional fresh basil (2–3 large leaves)
1 fresh plum tomato, chopped

Preheat oven to 400°. Combine eggplant with garlic and onion and add salt and pepper to taste. Sprinkle with oil and roast until browned, about 30 minutes. Set aside.

Sauté floured veal slices in hot olive oil; remove and place the slices side-by-side in a lightly oiled baking pan. To frying pan, add the tomato, onion, garlic, and basil. Add wine, a bit at a time, and salt and pepper to taste. Cook through and stir in the eggplant mixture. Meanwhile, place a piece of prosciutto on top of each veal slice, bunching it up so it doesn't hang over. Top with the provolone cheese. Place in a preheated 400° oven until cheese is melted. If thicker slices of chicken are used, this should take about 20 minutes. Transfer to a plate. Add cooked spaghetti to sauce in pan, and toss. Place the spaghetti next to veal, reserving a spoonful of sauce to top the veal. Garnish with a slice of lemon and additional chopped basil and plum tomato. Serves: 1.

Hellenic Festival, Buffalo, NY

Tsourekia (Sweet Bread)

Expert baker Marion Halstead shares her recipe used at the festival bake sale.

2 tablespoons active dry yeast
¾ cup plus 1 teaspoon sugar
¾ cup milk, warmed
1 tablespoon flour
10 tablespoons butter
3½–4 cups unsifted all-purpose flour
2 tablespoons ground mahlepi*
2 eggs, lightly beaten

*Mahlepi (aka mahleb) is the seed of the wild Persian cherry. It is available from several online or mail-order spice houses.

Dissolve yeast and 1 teaspoon sugar in ¼ cup warmed milk. Mix in 1 tablespoon flour, cover, and set in a warm place for 15 minutes or until mixture is bubbly. When yeast mixture is ready, combine ¾ cup sugar and ½ cup milk in a saucepan and warm mixture just enough to dissolve sugar. In another pan, melt the butter.

In a large bowl, combine 3½ cups of the flour with the mahlepi. Add yeast mixture and the warm milk and sugar mixture and stir. Add beaten eggs and stir. Add melted butter and mix until dough forms a ball. Add more flour, ¼ cup at a time, as needed to form a pliable dough. Knead dough on a floured board until smooth and satiny. Place dough in a large, greased bowl, cover, and set in a warm place to rise, about 1 hour or until doubled in bulk.

Punch dough down and divide into six pieces. Pinch and stretch each piece into a 19-inch rope. Braid three ropes together to form two braids 13 inches long. Place on a greased baking sheet. Cover braids and let rise in a warm place until doubled in size.

Preheat oven to 350°. Brush loaves with egg wash, sprinkle with sesame seeds, and bake for 20 to 25 minutes until golden. Remove loaves from baking sheets and cool on wire racks. Yield: 2 loaves.

Since 1977, the Hellenic Orthodox Church of the Annunciation has celebrated Buffalo's Greek life at the annual Hellenic Festival.

A boutique offers Greek clothing, jewelry, and souvenirs, while the *bakaliko* (market) provides a variety of Greek foods ranging from cheeses and olives to *loukoumi*, a candy known as "Greek delight." Imported Greek wines are also available, as well as ouzo, an anise liqueur. You'll find traditional music and dance at the "Good Time" tent, where *saganaki* is served. After lunch, head for the *zaharoplastion* (sweet shop) for some pastries (baklava, *diples*) and orange and butter cookies (*finikia* and *koulourakia*). There's also plenty of *tsourekia*, a braided Easter sweet bread that's delicious year-round.

Saganaki (Flaming Cheese Appetizer)

From *The Midas Touch II—Golden Greek Goodies*, the church cookbook.

1 pound Kasseri cheese, cut in wedges
2 tablespoons melted butter
2 tablespoons brandy
Juice of ½ lemon

Place cheese on a buttered broiler pan. Pour on melted butter. Broil 4–6 inches from heat until cheese is bubbly and golden. Warm brandy. Place cheese and butter in an ovenproof dish to flame at the table. Pour warmed brandy over hot cheese and ignite immediately. Squeeze lemon over cheese as flame begins to die. Serves: 6.

Hudson Valley Garlic Festival, Saugerties, NY

In 1989, Pat Reppert was looking for a way to promote the modest herb farm that she and her family run in Saugerties, New York (fifty miles north of New York City). She decided to hold a little garlic festival and set up a stall in her front yard. She cooked a few of her favorite garlic-based dishes and set out garlic and herbs for sale. With enough food to serve sixty people, Pat was overwhelmed when double that number showed up. The next year, 500 people came, and Pat's gardens were trampled beyond repair.

Today, the Hudson Valley Garlic Festival is no longer in Pat's yard. Sponsored by the Kiwanis Club of Saugerties, the festival hosts up to 40,000 visitors and a wide variety of down-home musical entertainment, from Appalachian to zydeco. Festival-goers can attend garlic-related lectures on such topics as making garlic braids and other gifts, the growing of garlic, and the health benefits of the herb, which, in New York State, consists of cold-hardy strains.

Last Full Weekend in September

Fresh garlic and garlic crafts are for sale, and vendors offer an enormous array of garlic-based foods. Main courses include barbecued pork with hot garlic sauce, garlic pizza, garlic brats and sausage, and steak sandwiches with garlic sauce. Garlic-eriffic variations on food festival favorites include garlic blooming onions, garlic fries, garlic fried dough, even garlic Cajun fries. And for the truly adventurous, there are desserts, such as garlic ice cream and garlic cotton candy. Those who want to know more about cooking with garlic, and perhaps invent new garlic sensations of their own, take in "Taste of the Gods," a series of cooking demonstrations by acclaimed area chefs who share some of their most successful recipes, all highlighting the joys of the local hard-neck garlic.

Vichyssoise with Roasted Hard-Neck Garlic

Richard Erickson, chef/owner of Blue Mountain Bistro, Woodstock, NY, shares the formula for his patrons' favorite dish.

4 medium leeks
2 pounds russet potatoes
3 tablespoons butter
6 cups chicken broth
Salt and freshly ground pepper
2 cups milk
½ cup heavy cream
2 or more heads roasted garlic (see below)
Fresh chives or garlic flower stems for garnish

Trim leeks, split, and rinse well. Cut the whites and light green portions into fine slices. Drop into a basin of cold water and let stand. This will clear them of grit and sand. Drain well in colander and then on paper towels. Peel potatoes, cut into thin slices, and hold them in cold water. Melt butter in a large saucepan and add the leeks. Cook for about 5–10 minutes over low heat, stirring often. Do not allow to brown. Add potatoes, chicken broth, salt, and pepper. Cook for about 30–40 minutes, adding milk and cream at the end. Check the seasoning, remembering that when served cold, it will need slightly more seasoning than usual. Purée the soup in a food mill or blender, adding the roasted garlic cloves to taste. Chill and serve, garnishing with fresh chives or garlic flower stems. Note: This soup is also delicious served hot. Serves: 6–8.

To roast garlic: Preheat oven to 350°. Cut each head of garlic in half horizontally. Brush each cut surface with olive oil. Put the halves of each head back together and wrap in aluminum foil. Bake until the garlic is completely soft, 1–1½ hours. Remove from oven, cool, then squeeze softened garlic from each clove.

Phelps Sauerkraut Festival, Phelps, NY

Sauerkraut (or "sour cabbage") is the German name for a dish that is actually quite ancient. A type of pickled cabbage was first invented by the Chinese to feed workers building the Great Wall. In the United States, long-lasting sauerkraut was the main source of vitamin C before citrus fruits were mass-shipped throughout the country, and by the 1930s, a huge six-building complex in Phelps, New York made most of the sauerkraut eaten in the world—at the height of production, an average of twenty tons of sauerkraut per day. Today, cabbage is still a major crop here, and to celebrate this history, Phelps hosts an annual Sauerkraut Festival.

The Sauerkraut Festival attracts some 10,000 people with a midway, parades, arts and crafts booths, and numerous bands to provide plenty of entertainment.

Sauerkraut is paired with barbecued pork, chicken, and spareribs, but many folks opt for good old-fashioned "kraut dogs" (hot dogs with sauerkraut). Perhaps the biggest festival treat of all is the traditional Sauerkraut Cake—a deep, rich chocolate cake baked by Phelps volunteer Cheryl Wysong that doesn't taste at all like sauerkraut. The cake weighs in at over one hundred pounds, and is served to the appreciative crowd by the Sauerkraut Prince and Princess.

Four Days during the First Weekend in August

Most sauerkraut today is consumed as a garnish for hot dogs and Reubens. The creation of this latter sandwich of corned beef, Swiss cheese, and sauerkraut on rye is contested. The dictionary credits Arnold Reuben, owner of the Manhattan deli Reuben's. Another story holds that the sandwich was invented by Reuben Kulakofsky, an Omaha grocer, for some late-night poker players. In 1956, an Omaha hotel waitress submitted the sandwich in a national contest and won.

Chocolate Sauerkraut Cake

The Comstock Michigan Fruit Company divulges the secret ingredient in this favorite festival recipe.

1 package (18¼-ounce) devil's food cake mix
⅔ cup water
3 eggs
½ cup vegetable oil
1 cup sauerkraut, rinsed, drained, and finely chopped
Powdered sugar or whipped cream for garnish

Preheat oven to 350°. Combine the cake mix, water, eggs, and oil in a large bowl. Blend at low speed until moistened. Beat 2 minutes at high speed. Stir in sauerkraut until well mixed. Pour into well-greased and floured tube pan, or two 9-inch round cake pans, or a 13 x 9-inch pan. Bake until wooden pick inserted in center comes out clean and cake springs back when touched lightly in center: about 35–40 minutes for tube pan, 25–35 minutes for round pans, or 30–40 minutes for 13 x 9-inch pan. Cool 15–25 minutes; remove from pan, and cool on rack. Serve sprinkled with powdered sugar or topped with whipped cream.

SerbFest, Lackawanna, NY

SerbFest, held annually at St. Stephen Serbian Orthodox Church and Cultural Center, is an absolute must for anyone who has never experienced the delights of Serbian food and culture. Lackawanna is a Buffalo suburb, and the church serves as a hub of religious and social activities for Serbians of the Western New York area.

Visitors can enjoy the sounds of Serbian orchestras and string instruments, watch folk dancers in authentic costumes, and browse through a *selo* (village) with a *pijaca* (store) featuring imported items.

A warm welcome is guaranteed to all who come, for these folks love to share their traditions and their food. And what food there is! The *kuhinja* (kitchen) delivers a spectacular Serbian-style barbecued lamb prepared by Stanley Kovacevic since the festival first began as a building fund way back in 1970. The *sarma*, a Balkan dish of seasoned meat wrapped in cabbage leaves, is truly delicious. The indoor grill features *cevapcici*, a seasoned miniature sausage made of three meats and served on a roll with chopped onion; tender, juicy *pecenica*, seasoned and thinly sliced pork on a roll; and *gra i kupus*, a thick savory soup of beans and sauerkraut. To satisfy your sweet tooth, the *pekarna* (bakery) offers a seemingly endless array of home-made Serbian desserts—tortes, nut rolls, and a layered Serbian sweet called *gibanica*.

Pineapple Cream Cheese Kifle

A hands-down winner from
The Best of Two Worlds Cookery.

1 (20-ounce) can crushed pineapple, undrained
1 cup sugar
3 tablespoons cornstarch
1 (8-ounce) package cream cheese, softened
1 cup butter, softened
2 cups unsifted flour

Combine pineapple, sugar, and cornstarch and cook over medium-low heat until clear. Watch closely, as the syrup has a tendency to stick and burn.

Preheat oven to 350°. Cream together the cream cheese and butter. Gradually add flour and beat until smooth. Roll out on a floured board to a thickness of between $\frac{1}{16}$–$\frac{1}{8}$ inch. Keep turning dough over when first rolling so it doesn't stick to the board. Dough should be rolled in three batches. Cut into 2-inch squares. Place about ½ teaspoon pineapple on each square, lap two corners over and press lightly to keep them from opening up. Bake on ungreased cookie sheets for about 12 minutes; check midway through baking, as you may have to press the cookies closed again. Remove from oven when cookies just begin to brown. Cool on wire racks. Yield: about 135 small cookies.

Second to the Last Weekend in July

Pennsylvania

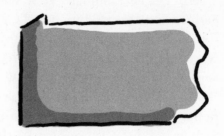

Pennsylvania boasts of some 55,000 farms and one of the largest rural populations in the United States—over three million people. The state's agricultural industry is noted for its dairy products as well as mushrooms, apples, and lots of other produce, including plentiful spring rhubarb. Southeastern Pennsylvania is the heart of the mushroom growing region that has put the state on the map as the number one producer of mushrooms in the country. With all that produce on hand, food processing is a major industry, attracting large companies, such as Smucker's, known for preserves and jellies, and since 1965, for its peanut butter, too.

Site of the Constitutional Congress, Pennsylvania has played a vital role in American history. Residents pay tribute to that history with many events throughout the year, including the Bean Soup in McClure, which commemorates Civil War veterans. Pennsylvania was founded as a refuge from religious persecution, and the Mennonites and Amish, who settled in eastern Pennsylvania in and around Lancaster County, are collectively known as the "Pennsylvania Dutch" (from "Deutsche" for their German ancestry). All adhere to a simple way of life, and their crafts and cooking annually attract large numbers of tourists curious to learn more about the "plain people" whose picturesque farms dot the countryside.

Annual Rhubarb Fest, Intercourse, PA

When the tender shoots of spring rhubarb have turned a rosy pink, it's time for the tiny village of Intercourse, Pennsylvania, to have their first festival of the season. The Annual Rhubarb Fest is held at Kitchen Kettle Village which started as a home-based jam and relish shop in 1954, but today is a major draw for visitors to Pennsylvania Dutch Country.

Rhubarb, sometimes called "pie plant" because of its use in pies and desserts, is sold in dozens of different dishes in stands and shops throughout the village. Rhubarb pie, strawberry rhubarb cookies, almond rhubarb pastry, and rhubarb pecan muffins number among visitors' favorites. At Kitchen Kettle Village, there's rhubarb and strawberry-rhubarb jams as well as a specialty, "bluebarb" (blueberry-rhubarb) jam, that's only made at festival time. Early arrivals enjoy strawberry rhubarb French toast, while those seeking lunch or dinner are in for treats like spiced rhubarb ham and rhubarb-glazed chicken kabobs.

The rhubarb arcade of games features the world's only rhubarb race-car derby with mini dragsters made of rhubarb stalks. Other games include a rhubarb regatta, rhubarb pick-up sticks, and the rhubarb bull's-eye toss. Many take advantage of the opportunity to have their picture taken with festival mascot Rupert Rhubarb.

Fresh rhubarb and rhubarb plants are sold along with *The Little Book of Rhubarb Recipes*. Adults can take part in the quilting bee and a rhubarb pie throwing contest, and bakers can enter the "Best Rhubarb Pie in Lancaster County" baking contest. With divisions designated for single crust, double crust, and chiffon/cream, entries are both diverse and delicious. Once judging is complete, and ribbons are awarded, the pies are sold by the slice with proceeds donated to charity.

Always the Third Saturday in May

Rhubarb Maple Muffins

A crowd pleaser from Kitchen Kettle Village's *Little Book of Rhubarb Recipes*.

1½ cups peeled, diced rhubarb
⅓ cup sugar
2½ cups flour
1 teaspoon salt
1 tablespoon baking powder
½ teaspoon allspice
½ teaspoon cinnamon
6 tablespoons butter
½ cup maple syrup
1 egg
½ cup milk

Combine rhubarb and sugar and let stand 1 hour. Preheat oven to 400°. Combine flour, salt, baking powder, allspice, and cinnamon. Cream together the butter, syrup, and egg. Blend in milk. Mix in rhubarb and dry ingredients, mixing just until combined. Spoon into muffin pans lined with muffin papers. Bake in the oven for 20–30 minutes. Yield: 12 muffins.

Kutztown Pennsylvania-German Festival, Kutztown, PA

Every year, more than 100,000 people attend this festival that celebrates the lifestyle of the Pennsylvania Dutch people in Berks County, Pennsylvania. Festival organizers are committed to documenting the heritage of the "plain people" in their staging of pageants showing Pennsylvania Dutch events like weddings and country auctions. There are also demonstrations of traditional crafts—quilting, blacksmithing, weaving, woodcarving, and chair caning.

The quilt barn displays over a thousand locally handmade wall hangings and quilts that are offered for sale during the festival. Many serious collectors make the annual pilgrimage to the famous opening-day quilt auction in order to bid on the top thirty prize-winning quilts.

Local churches, farm granges, the Rotary and Lions clubs, and a variety of women's organizations serve up food cooked from heritage recipes throughout the day. Family-style suppers offer a range of choices like country chicken and ham, ox roast, chicken potpie, *Schnitz und Knepp* (dried apples and dumplings), and corn pie—all of which include an array of side dishes such as cottage cheese with apple butter and pepper cabbage. Traditional treats like sweet homemade dumplings and local fruit pies follow for dessert.

The Week of 4th of July

For those visitors who prefer lighter meals or snacks, there is a wide range of items available: homemade soups, hot and cold sandwiches, Dutch fries (thickly sliced, deep-fried potatoes), soft pretzels, apple fritters, hex waffles, funnel cakes, and ice cream. The beverage of choice is Kutztown's old-fashioned birch beer.

The smell of freshly baked bread entices many a shopper to purchase a loaf or two to take home. The bread is baked in a standing stove oven, much like those from the nineteenth century, still found on area Pennsylvania-German farms.

The farmers' market is a haven for those who appreciate good food and who want to take area specialties home with them. Many shoppers carry bags bulging with jams and jellies, sweet rolls, fruit and shoofly pies, cookies, cakes, candies, pretzels, and an assortment of relishes both sweet and sour. Locally made cheeses are prized souvenirs. And then there are the delicious Pennsylvania Dutch meats, including summer sausages, sweet bolognas, fresh and smoked sausages, and deliciously cured hams.

Shoofly Pie

The recipe for this famous pie has been provided by the gracious folks at the Kutztown Pennsylvania-German Festival.

Pastry:
2 cups flour
Pinch of salt
¼ cup shortening
6 tablespoons water

Liquid:
1 cup molasses
2 cups brown sugar
1 egg
2 cups hot water
1 tablespoon baking soda

Crumbs:
3 cups flour
1 cup brown sugar
½ cup butter

Shoofly pie is so-named because the ooey-gooey molasses attracts flies. The pie lacks a top crust, so the flies must be shooed away by the vigilant baker.

Pastry: Mix flour and salt and cut in shortening. Stir in water and gather dough to form two balls. Roll out and line two 9-inch pie pans. Preheat oven to 350°.

Liquid: Combine the molasses, brown sugar, and egg. Stir until smooth. Mix together baking soda and hot water and gradually add to molasses mixture.

Crumbs: Combine the flour and brown sugar. Cut in butter until mixture is like coarse crumbs.

Assembly: Divide liquid mixture between two 9-inch pastry-lined pie pans. Cover each with half the crumb mixture. Bake pies for 40 minutes. Remove and cool on a rack. Yield: 2 pies.

McClure Bean Soup, McClure, PA

Christian town-dwellers say that McClure, Pennsylvania, has three holidays: Christmas, Easter, and the Bean Soup. No, it's not a festival or party, just the "Bean Soup."

This unique event traces its origins back to the Civil War when the Pennsylvania Volunteer Infantry marched and fought on a basic diet of salt pork or beef and hardtack (crackers). Since even these provisions were scarce, and most of the men had to cook for themselves, bean soup, easily cooked in large kettles over open fires, quickly became a favorite staple. It was flavored with the meat and served with the hardtack and coffee. Once the war ended, many veterans hungered not only for the companionship of old war buddies but for the taste of that soup. Annual reunions led to the first official McClure Bean Soup, held in October 1891, when veterans opened their gathering to the public.

Today, McClure Bean Soup organizers dish up almost 3,000 gallons of bean soup to some 70,000 customers. The soup is cooked in thirty-five-gallon iron kettles over open wood fires. The original recipe was simple: "twenty pounds of beef, a large bucketful of beans, and water. Cook and stir until tender." Today's festival recipe is not much different, but the home cook might want to throw in some spices to taste (if strict authenticity is not the first priority).

McClure Bean Soup

This is the soup that has folks lined up for second helpings at the festival. Courtesy of McClure Bean Soup chairman S. Kirby Bubb.

Into each 35-gallon cast-iron kettle, put 15 pounds of ground beef, 6 pounds of suet, and 25 pounds of dry navy beans. Use clear spring water. Cook over a wood fire for 2 hours or longer till beans are soft and disintegrated. As the soup simmers, stir constantly with a 10-pound wooden paddle with big wooden fingers to cream the soup by bruising the beans. Season with a handful of salt.

For the home cook:
1 pound dried navy beans
½–1 pound ground beef
3 ounces suet
Water
Salt and pepper

Second Tuesday in September through Saturday

Pick over beans and rinse clean. Place in a large bowl, cover with water, and let beans soak overnight to soften.

Drain beans and place in a large, heavy pot or Dutch oven. Brown the ground beef and add to the pot along with the suet. Add cold water to cover beans by about 2 inches, partially cover pot, and simmer for 1½–2 hours. Add more water during the cooking process if necessary. Stir frequently during the final half hour of cooking in order to bruise the beans and give the soup a creamy texture. Season with salt and pepper to taste, and serve piping hot. Serves: 8.

Note: Beef broth or stock can be substituted for the water, producing a richer (but less authentic) bean soup.

Mushroom Festival, Kennett Square, PA

Kennett Square is the birthplace of the American mushroom industry, and produces one quarter of all our culinary fungi. No wonder then that its nickname is "Mushroom Capital of the World."

Italian immigrants originally came to the area to work the quarries. When the quarries closed down, many switched to growing mushrooms. The Kennett Square festival was begun in 1986 and now attracts 30,000 visitors to sample the delights of their favorite fungi and enjoy the added fun of an arts and crafts show and parade. Visitors can also tour mushroom farms and learn about the complicated process of mushroom cultivation. Throughout the street festival area, educational exhibits familiarize the viewer with other fascinating aspects of the world of mushrooms.

A mushroom judging contest is followed by a public sale, allowing festivalgoers to take home prize-winning mushrooms, including shiitake, cremini, portobello, and button mushrooms. Local produce, flowers, and baked goods are available at the farmers' market, and visitors can sample a large variety of local microbrews.

Food vendors feature bountiful festival fare, with most menu items paying homage to the humble mushroom. Popular items include mushroom soup and fried mushrooms. Local chefs deliver cooking demonstrations using mushrooms in numerous quick and easy recipes. The National Mushroom Cook-Off attracts both amateur and professional chefs who prepare their creations in front of visitors. Once judging is complete, both the hungry and the curious can savor past winning recipes at a special tasting buffet.

Second Saturday and Sunday in September

Stuffed Chicken Breasts with Portobellos and Basil Over Sherry Caramel Sauce

Raymond Maxwell of Chadds Ford Inn, Chadds Ford, PA, easily walked away with First Place in the Professional Division when he entered this specialty in the Cook-Off. Reprinted with permission from the 1995 *National Mushroom Festival Tenth Anniversary Cookbook*.

2 (4-ounce) half breasts of chicken, boned and skinned for stuffing
½ cup Portobello mushrooms, diced
¼ cup basil, julienned
1 tablespoon butter
1 tablespoon fresh shallot, minced
½ teaspoon fresh garlic, minced
4 ounces additional chicken meat (for filling)
3–4 strips bacon
1 egg
Salt to taste
½ teaspoon pepper
1 teaspoon Worcestershire sauce
Flour
Butter

Sauce:
1 cup sugar
¼ cup sherry vinegar or Spanish wine vinegar
½ cup chicken stock
2 tablespoons cornstarch mixed with
  1 tablespoon cold water

With a small, sharp knife, slice the side of the chicken breast, creating a pocket for the stuffing—be careful not to cut all the way through. Lightly sauté mushrooms and basil with the butter, shallot, and garlic until tender. Meanwhile, in a food processor, purée the additional chicken meat with bacon, egg, salt, pepper, and Worcestershire sauce. Gently fold the mushrooms and basil into the mixture. Stuff the pockets of breasts until full. Refrigerate while making the sauce. Once sauce is prepared (see below), gently roll breasts in flour and sauté until lightly browned. Place in a well-buttered baking dish and finish in a preheated 400° oven for 10–15 minutes. Any leftover stuffing should be baked in a small buttered dish alongside the chicken. Serves: 2.

Sauce: Cook sugar on low heat until light brown in color. Deglaze with sherry vinegar and reduce by half. Add chicken stock and thicken with the cornstarch mixture. Keep warm while preparing chicken. Serve on warm plates with breasts sliced and fanned over the sauce. The sauce is very rich and should be served sparingly.

National Apple Harvest Festival, Biglerville, PA

The rolling hills of Adams County, Pennsylvania, are characterized by the well-drained soil and ideal weather conditions for growing apples. The area produces over half the state's annual eight million bushels of apples, earning the title "Apple Capital U.S.A."

Since 1964, the Upper Adams Jaycees have staged the National Apple Harvest Festival that now attracts over 100,000 visitors annually. Visitors enjoy delicious foods and exciting activities, all related to apples. One of the most interesting facets of the event is the use of antique equipment in the preparation of all sorts of apple products, providing a glimpse into the life of yesteryear. Fresh cider is pressed in an old-fashioned cider mill, and apple butter is cooked up in an authentic "boil," sending delicious aromas through the crowd.

All kinds of apple products—applesauce, apple pancake syrup, apple jellies, apple butter, apple salsa, you name it—are cooked and bottled on-site. Samples are freely available and the bottled products are sold to take home. The Old Tyme Butcher Shop features country ham and bacon along with scrapple, a popular Pennsylvania Dutch specialty made by simmering boneless pork scraps with cornmeal and spices, and served in fried slices.

The apple pancake and sausage breakfast fortifies everyone for a full day of nonstop entertainment. Then there's the apple-pie-eating contest, designed to test the mettle of even the most dedicated pie fan. A highlight of the festival is pit beef sandwiches made from beef roasted over mesquite charcoal and sliced from the pit right before the eyes of hungry customers. The apple-pie baking contest calls for two-crust pies, which are judged by a panel of experts and then auctioned off to benefit the St. Jude Children's Hospital.

Apple Harvest Festival Pancakes

Adams County's Apple Cookbook features this authentic Pennsylvania breakfast favorite.

2 cups Bisquick
1 teaspoon sugar
¼ cup dry milk
1¼ cups apple cider
1 egg
2 tablespoons melted butter
¾–1 cup peeled, cored, and finely chopped fresh apples (such as Granny Smith)

Mix together the Bisquick, sugar, and dry milk. Add the cider, egg, and butter and whisk until combined. Stir in the chopped apple. Pour slightly less than ¼ cup of batter for each pancake onto a hot, lightly greased griddle. Cook over medium heat until bubbles form on the top of each pancake. Turn and cook on second side until pancakes are golden brown. As pancakes are made, keep them warm on a cookie sheet in a 250° oven, separating layers with waxed paper. Serve topped with butter and maple syrup. Yield: 24 (4-inch) pancakes.

Peanut Butter Festival, New Bethlehem, PA

Folks in New Bethlehem, Pennsylvania, are pretty proud of the fact that their town is home to the only peanut-butter plant owned by the J. M. Smucker Company, known primarily for its fruit jams and jellies. In summer 1996, the town suffered a devastating flood. By fall, the town had rebounded and decided to celebrate with a joyful weekend tribute to peanut butter.

The Peanut Butter Festival, now an annual event, features a carnival, a mountain bike race, a 5K fitness run, an "anything that floats" race, and that old-fashioned favorite—a bed race. All that racing creates big appetites for the annual pig roast, and after dinner, folks make their way over to the Smucker's booth for delicious peanut-butter ice cream, or they sample the entries in the peanut-butter baking contest.

Peanut Butter Sandwich Cookies

Pam Crissman of New Bethlehem, PA, was an award winner with this original recipe. Reprinted from *Vittles of the Valley* with permission from the publisher.

1 cup butter-flavored shortening
1 cup creamy peanut butter
1 cup sugar
1 cup packed brown sugar
1 teaspoon vanilla
3 eggs
3 cups unbleached, unsifted flour
2 teaspoons baking soda
¼ teaspoon salt

Filling:
½ cup creamy peanut butter
3 cups sifted powdered sugar
1 teaspoon vanilla
6–8 tablespoons milk

Optional topping:
Semisweet chocolate chips, melted

Preheat oven to 375°. In a mixing bowl, cream shortening, one cup peanut butter, and sugars. Add vanilla. Add eggs, one at a time, beating well after each addition. Combine flour, baking soda, and salt; add to creamed mixture. Shape into 1-inch balls and place 2 inches apart on ungreased cookie sheets. Flatten to ⅜-inch thickness by pressing with a fork to make a crosshatch pattern. Bake for 7–8 minutes or until golden brown. Cool and remove from cookie sheets.

In a mixing bowl, beat filling ingredients until smooth. Spread on half the cookies and top with a second cookie. Lightly drizzle tops of cookies with melted chocolate if desired. Yield: 4 dozen filled cookies.

Friday through Sunday of the Third Weekend in September

Rhode Island

Rhode Island may be our smallest state, but it's in the big time when it comes to tourism. Boasting over four hundred miles of coastline and twenty percent of America's National Historic Landmarks, the state is geographically irresistible. And then there's the food…

After greenhouse and nursery products, milk is the second most valuable agricultural crop in Rhode Island, but it's rarely drunk straight. True Rhodies enjoy "coffee milk" made with Autocrat coffee syrup so much that they made it the official state drink. Since apples are the most valuable fruit crop, you can bet Rhode Islanders find plenty of excuses to use them in pies and other desserts. The state's fishing industry delivers a variety of fish, mollusks, and shellfish. Rhode Island even claims a unique state clam: the quahog. Everything—from "real" Rhode Island clam chowder (a broth) to beer fritters to "stuffies" (a type of stuffed, baked clam)—is made with these delicious large clams. Another local treat is the ubiquitous jonnycake. Since colonial days, Rhode Islanders have made these pancakes from the native white flint cornmeal. The same specialty cornmeal is also combined with milk and molasses to deliver Indian pudding, a dessert often laced with cinnamon and ice cream.

Conversion to Rhode Island tastes doesn't take long, and most visitors take home a stockpile of local ingredients, or at least the mail-order information, in order to satisfy their new cravings.

International Quahog Festival, Wickford, RI

Since 1983, folks have flocked to the International Quahog Festival that pays homage to Rhode Island's state shellfish. The quahog is an extra-large, hard-shell clam native to the waters around Rhode Island. The word "quahog" (or "quahaug" or "quohog") comes from the Narraganset word *poquaûhock*. Native Americans used the purple inner surface of the shells to make beads and ornaments used as currency.

Over the two-day festival, clam fans debate such topics as "when a clam is not a clam" and wonder at the marvels that a simple bivalve can deliver. Bakemaster Brian Casey pulls out all the stops with his traditional Rhode Island style clambake, and attendees can also try quahog chili, clam cakes, lobster, and chowder. Those who wish to show off their culinary skills compete in the "World's Best Stuffie" contest. For the uninitiated, a "stuffie" is a type of stuffed, baked clam: quahogs are chopped, mixed with a tangy seasoned stuffing, and then baked on the half shell.

Main Street Fish Market Stuffies

Chef Laura Harrington of Dan Montmarquet's Main Street Fish Market & Restaurant in historic Wakefield, RI, won first place in 2001.

2 dozen large quahogs in the shell
1 box Ritz crackers (4 sleeves)
1 loaf day-old bread
½ cup butter, melted
1 tablespoon Worcestershire sauce
1 tablespoon lemon juice
1 large onion
2 stalks celery
2 green peppers
½ pound chaurice (or chorizo) sausage
2 cups minced sea clams
1 tablespoon granulated onion
1 tablespoon salt
1 teaspoon white pepper
1 teaspoon granulated garlic
1 quart (4 cups) clam juice
Paprika

Fourth Weekend in August

Shuck quahogs, reserving the juice and shells. Run the quahog meat through a meat grinder. Strain the juice through a fine mesh strainer to remove any shell particles. In a large bowl, crush Ritz crackers and break bread into one-inch pieces. Add Worcestershire and lemon juice to melted butter. In a food processor, chop together the onion, celery, green peppers, and chaurice. Add all ingredients to the bread mixture and mix with your hands. Stuffing should be moist, yet stiff enough to hold the shape of a scoop. Add more clam juice or crackers as needed.

Preheat oven to 375°. Rinse the quahog shells and drain. Using a 4-ounce ice-cream scoop, fill the shells. Sprinkle with paprika and bake for 30 minutes. The stuffies can be baked, frozen, and then reheated. Yield: 48 stuffies (about 8 servings).

Rhode Island May Breakfasts

Throughout the Ocean State during the month of May, the May Breakfast has become a customary rite of spring. Every year, an estimated 25,000 residents and visitors enjoy breakfast in one of about two dozen celebrations.

First held as a fundraiser in 1867 at the Oak Lawn Baptist Church in Cranston, Rhode Island, the May Breakfast has since been adopted by groups statewide. Oak Lawn still serves up its original menu each year, and visitors are attended by hostesses in period dress.

May Breakfast menus include eggs, ham, bacon, baked beans, muffins, juice, coffee, tea, milk or coffee milk, and of course, that Rhode Island tradition, the jonnycake. Using a variety of hard corn grown only in the region, early settlers prepared this Native American recipe to make food for traveling called "journeycakes." Over the years, these hard little cakes lightened up considerably, were served with maple syrup or butter, and became known as "jonnycakes."

May is "Heritage Month" in Rhode Island since it was in this month, exactly two months before the rest of the colonies, that Rhode Island declared independence from Britain. May Breakfasts are scheduled throughout the month with each organization keeping its favorite day. Oak Lawn's traditional date is May 1, while many others favor May 4, Rhode Island's Independence Day.

South County Jonnycakes

Diane Smith and her husband Bob own and operate the historic Carpenter's Grist Mill on Moonstone Beach Road in Perryville, RI. Lucky visitors can often find Diane at the mill making these perfect jonnycakes on griddles heated over a gas grill. The recipe is from Diane's cookbook, *Good Tastes of Rhode Island's South County*, which features wonderful heritage recipes of the area.

1 cup jonnycake meal
1 tablespoon sugar
½ teaspoon salt
1 cup boiling water
3–4 tablespoons milk
Bacon grease or corn oil

Combine sugar and salt with meal in a large mixing bowl. Scald with boiling water and stir well. Thin immediately with milk to a mixture that will drop easily from a spoon (additional milk may be necessary—mixture should be the consistency of thin mashed potatoes). Drop by spoonfuls onto a medium-hot griddle greased with 1–2 tablespoons of bacon grease or corn oil. (Do not let griddle get dry.) Cook 5–6 minutes on each side until a brown, crunchy crust is formed and inside is soft. Add butter and serve hot. Yield: A dozen 3-inch cakes.

South County Museum Annual Harvest Festival and Apple Pie Contest, Narraganset, RI

Rhode Islanders are so serious about their clams that they are included as part of the standard bill of fare at the Annual Harvest Festival and Apple Pie Contest, which has been celebrated for more than twenty-five years. Held as a fundraiser to benefit the South County Museum, the event features famous Rhode Island jonny-cakes along with clam cakes, clam fritters, cider, and homemade root beer. Once judged, contest apple pies are sold by the slice.

But it's the clam chowder that takes center stage. South County clam chowder is a clear-broth clam chowder made from quahogs dug from local ponds. Both the juices and the broth created from steaming the clams are used for the liquid in this authentic recipe from Washington County, known as "South County" by the local populace.

Most visitors to the festival make a side trip to Carpenter's Grist Mill, located in the Perryville section of South Kensington. The mill was built in 1703 by Samuel E. Perry and has been in continuous operation ever since. Current owners Bob and Diane Smith use only Rhode Island corn to make their meal. Grown in the salubrious climate of Rhode Island's south shore, the corn's unique flavor is influenced by the area's soil and damp salt air, imparting a delicious flavor to the meal ground by water-powered granite stones.

Held on a Sunday in October

South County Quahog Chowder

Good Tastes of Rhode Island's South County by Diane Smith provides the definitive formula for authentic Rhode Island chowder. Reprinted with permission from Diane Smith, Carpenter's Grist Mill, Moonstone Beach Rd., Perryville, RI 02879.

6 pounds quahogs
6 cups water
¼ cup salt pork, cut into tiny cubes
1 cup chopped onion
4 cups cubed potatoes
¼ teaspoon salt
⅛ teaspoon black pepper

Scrub the quahogs clean. Place the shells in large kettle with water and cover. Place over medium heat until the shells open, about 5 minutes. Remove the meat and grind into small pieces. Discard the shells. Reserve all liquid. Fry salt pork to light brown color in a large pot. Add the onions and fry lightly. Add reserved liquid plus enough water to make 8 cups, potatoes, salt, and pepper. Simmer until potatoes are tender, about 5 minutes. Add chopped quahogs and bring to a light boil for 2 or 3 minutes. (For nonpurists, a small amount of milk or half-and-half may be added.) Chowder is better made a day ahead and reheated. Serves: 6.

Vermont

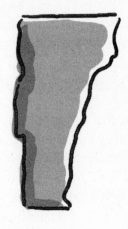

Vermont's countryside is dotted with picturesque dairy farms that are the backbone of its well-known cheese industry. Dairy and tourism are big business here, as are hunting and fishing. The heavily forested Green Mountains run north to south through the state, and the region is noted for its fresh streams, lakes, and ponds, making it an ideal habitat for fish and wildlife. Hunters are attracted by big game like the black bear, moose, and deer, but there's an abundance of smaller quarry as well: foxes, rabbits, beavers, raccoons, turkeys, pheasant, ruffled grouse, and partridge. Locals are generally comfortable out on their own in the wilds of the state, but for visitors, guided hunts are recommended. For armchair experts eschewing the thrill of the hunt, there are game dinners offering a taste of the wild.

Annual Wild Game Supper, Bradford, VT

The first Wild Game Supper to benefit The Congregational Church of the United Church of Christ was put on by Cliff and Helen McLam in 1957. They made $83.14, enough to pay for a new sidewalk along one side of the church. With such encouraging results, the Wild Game Supper has continued year after year. As many as 1,300 guests have been fed and 1,500 turned away in a single year. Today reservations are a must and attendance is limited to 1,000, a number that parishioners feel they can properly handle without sacrificing quality in food or service.

While the meat is prepared in the church kitchen, the pies, rolls, and gingerbread are baked at home by volunteers. Vegetables are cooked at the local high school and transported in steaming containers by pickup trucks two miles to the church.

Logistics aside, this is a bounteous buffet indeed, with a menu featuring roast venison, beaver, rabbit, bear, buffalo, and wild boar, all prepared in a variety of delicious ways. Entrées are subject to availability each year, but frequent favorites include venison chili, rabbit pie and pâté, moose burgers, and wild game sausage. There's also an annual surprise meat dish such as the Red Deer Sauerbraten served in 1994 or the Antelope Marsala that was a big hit in 1995. Accompaniments include mashed potatoes, rice, dressing, gravy, squash, cabbage salad, and homemade rolls. Be sure to save room for dessert—homemade gingerbread topped with real whipped cream.

Always the Saturday before Thanksgiving

Venison Meat Loaf

Armed with this recipe from the *Annual Wild Game Supper Cook Book—From Beaver to Buffalo*, any cook will win wild reviews.

Meat loaf:
¾ cup bread crumbs
½ cup milk
1½ pounds ground venison
½ pound ground pork
2 beaten eggs
½ cup chopped onion
¼ cup chopped green bell pepper
1½ teaspoons salt
¾ teaspoon sage
¼ teaspoon pepper

Topping for meatloaf:
½ cup prepared mustard
½ cup ketchup
2 tablespoons brown sugar

Preheat oven to 350°. Soak the crumbs in milk, add remaining ingredients, and mix well. Pack into a large loaf pan, score top, and bake for 1 hour. Meanwhile, combine topping ingredients. Spread topping on top of the meatloaf the last 15 minutes of baking. Remove the meatloaf from the oven and let stand 5–10 minutes before lifting it out of the pan.

Chapter 2

The South

Alabama | Arkansas | Delaware | Florida
Georgia | Kentucky | Louisiana | Maryland | Mississippi
North Carolina | South Carolina | Tennessee | Virginia
Washington, D.C. | West Virginia

Alabama

The state of Alabama is known as the "Heart of Dixie" primarily because of its central role in the Civil War. Not only was the constitution of the Confederacy drawn up in Montgomery, but the state capital also served as the first capital of the confederacy. Today, Alabama is known as the cradle of the Civil Rights Movement and has transitioned from an economy ruled by "King Cotton" to one with a strong industrial base and livestock industries. Cotton is still grown in the state, too, as are Alabama's famous peanuts, sweet potatoes, and pecans. George Washington Carver left a powerful legacy from his years at the Tuskegee Institute where he promoted over four hundred different products derived from these last three crops. Freshwater and saltwater fishing also contribute to the state's economy. Shrimp are the most valuable saltwater fishing product. Catfish are caught commercially in freshwater streams, and farm-raised, grain-fed catfish are an increasingly important new food crop.

Alabama Chitlin Jamboree, Clio, AL

When the folks in Clio, Alabama, began looking for a way to support the local hog raising industry, the result was the Alabama Chitlin Jamboree, an event that attracts more than 10,000 visitors to this small town of only 1,200 people.

In addition to music, clogging, arts and crafts, and a quilt show, the Chitlin Jamboree brings on the competition. For men, there's the tobacco spitting contest where the record is an awesome fourteen feet. The pork cook-off, headed by Lena Bell Smith, is popular among local ladies who compete for cash prizes.

The focus of this festival is not just chitlins, but the whole hog. It's served up in barbecued pork sandwiches with typical southern sides like black-eyed peas, turnip greens, coleslaw, and sweet potatoes. Over two tons of chitlins—aka hogs' intestines—are consumed. Chitlin plates are served two ways: deep-fried or boiled in broth.

Brunswick Stew, an old southern dish (the original sometimes included squirrel), has been revised by the folks of Clio to feature pork. Alex Brock, who has been chairman of the Chitlin Jamboree for some fifteen years, generously shared his mother's Brunswick Stew recipe which he says he has enjoyed all his life.

Always the Last Saturday in October

Granny Brock's Brunswick Stew

Alex Brock of Clio, AL, is greeted with
shouts of joy when he shows up at
the festival with this stew.

4 pounds of pork such as Boston Butt or pork
   shoulder blade butt roast
4 pounds of chicken (hens or fryers)
1 (15-ounce) can butter beans with juice
1 (14-ounce) can diced tomatoes with juice
1 (15-ounce) can cream-style corn
1½ pounds onions, chopped and sautéed in
   vegetable oil
3 cups ketchup
½ cup Louisiana hot sauce
Salt and pepper to taste
1 (48-ounce) can chicken broth
1 tablespoon dried parsley (optional)
1 tablespoon dried basil (optional)
Sour cream for serving (optional)

Separately roast the pork and chicken.
Remove skin from chicken, debone both pork
and chicken, and chop into small pieces. Mix
all ingredients together in a very large pot.
Season the stew to taste with salt and
pepper. The original recipe did not include
parsley and basil but it makes a lovely addition
to this dish. Bring stew to a boil, then simmer
over low heat for 30 minutes. If necessary,
thin the stew with additional chicken broth to
desired consistency. While this is certainly
committing heresy to a true Brunswick stew,
this dish is great served with a large dollop of
sour cream on top! Yield: 12–15 generous
servings.

Sausage Roll

Jeanette B. Hill of Clio, AL, won first place
in the Pork Cook-Off with this recipe.

1 loaf (1 pound) frozen bread dough
½ bell pepper
½ medium onion
2 sticks celery
2 carrot sticks
1 (16-ounce) package pork sausage (or sweet
   or hot Italian sausage)
Grated Parmesan cheese

Let dough thaw and rise according to
package directions. When dough is ready to
bake, put the pepper, onion, celery, and carrot
in a food processor and grind until fine. Place
mixture in a skillet and cook until tender. Add
sausage and cook until done. Drain off any
fat.

Preheat oven to 350°. Roll dough out on a
floured surface. Cover with sausage mixture
one-quarter inch from all edges. Sprinkle
generously with cheese and roll up, tucking in
and sealing edges. Bake for about 40
minutes. Yield: 10–12 slices.

Carver Sweet Potato Arts & Craft Festival, Tuskegee, AL

Every year, some 2,000 locals and visitors gather in downtown Tuskegee, Alabama, to honor sweet potatoes, an important local crop, and the man who did so much to promote them, Dr. George Washington Carver. Famed professor at Tuskegee University from 1896 to 1943, Carver spent considerable time investigating techniques for growing and developing several varieties of sweet potatoes.

Sponsored by the Sweet Potato Growers Arts and Craft Association of Macon County, the festival features sweet potato judging and a juried arts and crafts show in addition to gospel singing and a variety of children's activities.

Those with hearty appetites can participate in the sweet potato pie eating contest. Others bring their homemade creations for judging in the sweet potato pie baking contest. Visitors who come simply to enjoy the food do not leave disappointed. Everyone chooses from a vast array of specialties including sweet potato fries, pies, and pancakes, as well as ash-baked sweet potatoes. For dessert, there's sweet potato pecan ice cream, a traditional favorite at the festival.

Sweet Potato Pecan Ice Cream

George Washington Carver Sweet Potato Arts and Craft Association of Macon County, AL, shares their secret recipe for ice cream served at the festival.

3–4 pounds sweet potatoes (Carver or TU-1892s are recommended)
1 cup sugar
2–3 teaspoons nutmeg
1 (14-ounce) can sweetened condensed milk
2 (12-ounce) cans evaporated milk
3 cups sugar
6 medium eggs
1–2 tablespoons vanilla extract
1 cup chopped pecans

Bake sweet potatoes. Mash and add one cup sugar and 2–3 teaspoons nutmeg. Cool.
In a large saucepan, combine sweetened condensed milk and evaporated milk. Add sugar and eggs and mix well. Heat, stirring constantly, until steam begins to rise from the custard. Do not allow mixture to boil. Remove from heat and add vanilla. Cool. Process custard in an ice-cream freezer according to manufacturers' directions. Just before the custard freezes completely, add 2 cups of the sweet potato mixture and the pecans. Continue processing until frozen.
Yield: 2 quarts.

Third Saturday in October

National Shrimp Festival, Gulf Shores, AL

With the arrival of October in Gulf Shores, Alabama, the tourist industry has subsided, giving the locals a chance to relax and enjoy themselves. At least that's the way it used to be when the Shrimp Festival first started. The center of town was blocked off, and a pickup truck with a band on the back was strategically parked. Folks would dance in the street, drink beer, and eat a whole lot of boiled shrimp and coleslaw. It wasn't long before the Chamber of Commerce saw the potential to promote the local shrimping industry in these goings-on. Today, the National Shrimp Festival hosts over a quarter of a million people over four days.

Musical entertainment abounds, ranging from gospel to jazz, Dixieland, blues, and Cajun. There's a boat show, a sailboat regatta, and a surfing contest, as well as an art show and arts and crafts vendors. But it's seafood, especially shrimp, that really pulls in the crowds.

On the Seafood Boardwalk, visitors purchase untold amounts of specialties like shrimp stir-fry, shrimp gratin, fried shrimp, shrimp po'boys, and even Cajun pistolettes (miniature rolls filled with shrimp). Many of the vendors participate in the Best of the Fest recipe contest. The competition gets fierce, and many winners are recorded in Joan States-Davidson's cookbook *The Shrimp Book*.

Shrimp-Artichoke Casserole

This recipe made Mrs. J. F. Dusenbury a winner in the 1972 cooking contest.

6½ tablespoons butter
4½ tablespoons flour
1 cup milk
¾ cup heavy cream
1 tablespoon Worcestershire sauce
Salt and pepper to taste
2 (14-ounce) cans artichoke hearts packed in water, drained and sliced
1 pound raw shrimp, shelled and deviened
¼ pound fresh mushrooms, cleaned and sliced
2 tablespoons butter
½ cup grated Parmesan cheese
Paprika

Melt the 6½ tablespoons butter and stir in flour. When blended, add milk and cream, stirring constantly. Sauce should be medium thick and smooth; if necessary, thin with additional milk. Season with Worcestershire, salt, and pepper.

Arrange artichoke hearts in the bottom of a buttered baking dish. Top with shrimp. Sauté mushrooms in remaining 2 tablespoons butter for 6 minutes; spoon over shrimp. Pour cream sauce over top and sprinkle with grated Parmesan and paprika. Bake in a preheated 375° oven for approximately 50 minutes or until shrimp is cooked and the casserole is browned and bubbly. Serves: 6.

Second Full Weekend in October

Peanut Butter Festival, Brundidge, AL

Brundidge, Alabama, is proud of the important part it played in pioneering the peanut butter industry of the Southeast. In 1929, Brundidge native J.D. Johnston recognized peanut butter as a tasty, inexpensive source of protein, so he set up a crude machine in a wood-frame building just off the town's Main Street and started one of the first peanut butter mills in the United States.

As the popularity of peanut butter spread, Johnston's mill flourished and soon he was shipping over two million jars a year. In the early 1930s, Grady and Oscar Johnson opened a competing mill and named it the Louis-Anne Peanut Butter Company after Grady's two children, Louis and Anise. These mills provided a huge economic boost to the Brundidge community and sustained it during the hard years of the Great Depression. Today, peanuts are the number one cash crop for Brundidge and surrounding Pike County, representing $12 million a year in business.

Thus it is that each fall, the town of Brundidge pays tribute to the peanut with a harvest and heritage celebration now known as the "Peanut Butter Festival." Antiques, arts and crafts, a street dance, and music and singing make this a truly fun event for the 10,000 folks who attend year after year. The Nutter Butter parade is characterized by its "nutty" participants, including "the biggest goober in Alabama."

Demonstration crafts include grinding peanuts into butter, basket making, and a quilting bee. There's also a fifty-year-old jar of peanut butter on display. And then there are the contests: goober rollin', hog callin', peanut shellin', hay pitchin', and cow chip throwin' number among the most popular.

A Saturday in October

The annual construction of the South's largest peanut butter and jelly sandwich, some fifty feet in length, is followed by free servings to the hungry crowd. Meanwhile, all you need is one half cup of peanut butter and a little creativity to enter the festival's recipe contest. Entrants make a sample for judging and several for sharing at the peanut butter TasteFest where the public gets to sample the entries.

For everyone, the order of the day is "chow down." The smokehouse breakfast begins at 6:00 A.M. at the Peanut Butter Barn. Peanuts, also known as "goober peas," are available boiled or fried, sweet or salty. Peanut butter and banana sandwiches, peanut butter and pickle sandwiches, pork chops, spare ribs, turnip greens, and sweet potatoes mark this as a true celebration of the Deep South. Sweets include peanut butter pie, cakes, cookies, and candies. It's all washed down with cider, "cane squeezins" or "goober cocktails" (cola garnished with peanuts).

Peanut Butter Chiffon Pie

Sonya J. Hubbard of Brundidge, AL, was a proud winner of the
Peanut Butter Festival's recipe contest with this pie.

1 cup dark corn syrup
½ cup super chunky peanut butter
½ cup water
1 envelope unflavored gelatin
3 eggs, separated
1 teaspoon vanilla
3 tablespoons sugar
1 prepared chocolate cookie piecrust
Whipped cream
Chopped peanuts

In a medium saucepan, stir together corn syrup, peanut butter, water, gelatin, and egg yolks until well blended. Stirring constantly, cook mixture over medium heat until well thickened. Stir in vanilla. Cool until mixture mounds slightly when dropped from a spoon.

In a small bowl with mixer at high speed, beat egg whites until soft peaks form. Gradually beat in sugar and continue beating until stiff peaks form. Carefully fold in peanut butter mixture. Chill until mixture mounds, about ½ hour—watch carefully so it doesn't set too firmly before placing in pie shell.

Pile filling into chocolate crust. Chill until firm. Garnish with whipped cream and sprinkle with chopped peanuts.

Note: The U.S.D.A warns that raw eggs have been found to contain salmonella bacteria and recommends eggs be cooked or that commercial egg substitutes be used.

Red Snapper Festival, Orange Beach, AL

There are over a hundred snapper species found in the world's tropical waters, and about a dozen of them are found in the Gulf of Mexico. The American red snapper is characterized by the brilliant red color of its skin, the firm texture of its meat, and a nutty sweetness that combines well with chilies, tropical fruits, and spice rubs. Chef Paul Prudhomme popularized red snapper nationally when he began serving blackened redfish at his New Orleans restaurant, K-Paul's, in 1979.

A full forty percent of recreationally caught red snapper from the Gulf of Mexico is landed along the Alabama coast. This fact was enough to convince the city fathers of Orange Beach to nickname their area "Red Snapper Capital of the World." With over two hundred artificial reefs off the state's coastline, snapper, grouper, and other saltwater species are abundant.

The Orange Beach Sports Association and the city fire department established the Red Snapper Festival as a way to simultaneously promote the local fishing industry and to raise funds for their organizations. Activities include a car show, arts and crafts, a silent auction, and music. Kids can enjoy a number of activities while parents swap fishing stories.

Attendance runs around 7,500. Some folks come for the bake sale, but everyone comes for the snapper fillets that are served either fried or grilled. Traditional Southern luncheon accompaniments include coleslaw, grits, and hush puppies (a deep-fried cornmeal dumpling).

The Saturday before Mardi Gras

Marinated Red Snapper

Bebe Gauntt of the Alabama Gulf Coast Convention and Visitors Bureau shared the following recipe for the local specialty.

Red snapper fillets
Teriyaki marinade
Salt
Butter
Toasted pecans

Marinate red snapper fillets in teriyaki marinade for 2–3 hours. Lightly salt the fillets and grill or pan fry on both sides until fish flakes.

Drizzle fillets with melted, almost browned butter and top with toasted pecans. Serve immediately.

Waldo Sorghum Sopping Days, Talladega, AL

It is thought that sorghum, an old world grain known for animal forage and for yielding sweet syrup, was brought to the United States from Africa around 1700. It wasn't an important crop until pioneer settlement moved into the great plains and forage was needed for sheep and cattle. Soon, sweet sorghum was made into sorghum molasses, an important sweetener throughout the nineteenth century. It declined in popularity after World War II when refined sugar became cheaper to mill and more generally available, but the grain is still grown in the southeastern area of the U.S. Sorghum syrup is used as a sweetener in breads, cakes, and cookies as well as a topping for pancakes.

In most areas, old-fashioned sorghum soppings are a vanishing part of Southern culture. But in 1974, the Waldo, Alabama Fire Department organized its first Sorghum Sopping Days which has since become an annual event. It takes place at the Waldo Town Hall just south of Talladega. Local citizens donate their labor to harvest and mill the sorghum cane. The juice is cooked in an open pan, producing a thick, amber syrup. The skimmings, once an important ingredient in moonshine, are today *officially* discarded.

Visitors have the opportunity to view sorghum making from cane to can, and many purchase some to take home. Hot biscuits, butter, and sausage with sorghum for sopping are served all day, both days. Many first time soppers eavesdrop on old time soppers reminiscing about bygone days of life on the farm. A craft show and live entertainment round out the event.

Saturday and Sunday on a Weekend in September

Sorghum Cake

The Waldo Sorghum Sopping Committee shared this traditional Southern recipe.

1 egg
¼ cup buttermilk
½ cup vegetable oil
1 cup sorghum syrup
2¼ cups flour
1 teaspoon baking soda
1 teaspoon cinnamon
1 teaspoon ginger

Preheat oven to 375°. Beat together egg, buttermilk, oil, and syrup. Mix together dry ingredients, add to liquid mixture, and mix well. Pour into a greased tube pan and bake for 35–40 minutes. Remove from oven, cool for 15 minutes, and unmold onto a wire rack.

Arkansas

Agriculture is the number one industry in Arkansas so, not surprisingly, the state ranks tenth in total U.S. agriculture receipts. Primary crops are rice, broilers, turkeys, and catfish, with Arkansas ranking first in the country for rice production and second for broiler. While that may account for chicken and rice being the traditional meal of choice among state residents, there's more to the story.

Nestled in the hills of western Arkansas, near the small town of Altus, lie Arkansas' commercial wineries, dating back to 1880. The specialty wine is that old Southern favorite, muscadine. And then there are the famous pink tomatoes, raised in Bradley County, an area known for its tall pines. The "Natural State," known for its scenic beauty, boasts not only five national parks but thirteen major lakes and over 9,000 miles of streams and rivers, making it a major destination for fishing enthusiasts.

Altus Area Grape Festival, Altus, AR

Altus, with hundreds of acres of vineyards, is billed as the "Wine Capital of Arkansas." Settled by German and Swiss immigrants, the region's winemaking dates to the 1880s. Grape festivals were an annual event until Prohibition took effect. The Arkansas wine industry recovered, and in 1984, the region was designated an official "Appellation of Origin" by the U.S. government. That was also the year that the Altus Area Grape Festival was revived. The Altus Viticultural Area encompasses some 12,000 acres in the scenic Arkansas River Valley; the sandy loam soil there is ideal for growing grapes.

The festival features all sorts of grape related contests and games, including public and celebrity grape stomps and an amateur winemaking contest. Everyone gets to sample free wine and juice, as well as fresh grapes. In 1997, the Great Grape Cuisine Contest was inaugurated. Entrants must use fresh grapes as a main ingredient in one of six categories covering brunch or breakfast, salads, jam, gelatin, "drink-it" (no wine, please), desserts, and main dish.

Great Grape Meatballs

Cindy Norton of Lone Grove, OK, won high praise for this winning entry in the Main Dish Division of the Altus Great Grape Cuisine Contest.

2 pounds ground beef
Vegetable oil
2 cups red seedless grapes
½ cup water
⅓ cup grape jelly
⅓ cup cocktail sauce or chili sauce
¼ cup soy sauce
1 tablespoon cold water mixed with
  1 tablespoon cornstarch
Salt and pepper to taste

Form ground beef into small meatballs and fry in vegetable oil; drain on paper towels. Boil grapes in water for 10 minutes; mash and put through a sieve, discarding grape skins. Mix sieved grape liquid with jelly, cocktail sauce or chili sauce, and soy sauce and heat. Whisk in water and cornstarch mixture, whisking constantly, for about 1 minute or until sauce thickens. Add meatballs and simmer.
Serves: 10–12 as an appetizer.

Friday and Saturday
of the Fourth
Weekend in July

Bradley County Pink Tomato Festival, Warren, AR

Bradley County is billed as the land of tall pines and pink tomatoes. The area supplies most of Arkansas' tomatoes for produce sale. The Tomato Festival was begun in 1957 to celebrate the pink tomato harvest season and to honor the farmers. It follows hard upon the heels of the Warren Tomato Market that opens the first weekend in June with buyers attending from all over the nation.

At the festival, visitors enjoy music, dancing, a parade, a quilt show, and numerous children's activities. Tomato packing and tomato eating contests are among the most popular spectator events for the 15,000–20,000 folks who annually attend the festival.

Typical food available from vendors includes corn dogs, onion blossoms, chicken or alligator on a stick, and bacon-and-tomato sandwiches. Everyone, it seems, looks forward to the All-Tomato Luncheon. This is a pretty laid-back affair, based on whatever the women of the Home Extension Club feel like making—as long as the dishes have tomato in them. But it's a given that they'll trot out traditional favorites like "Tomarinated" Carrots, Green Tomato Beans with Toasted Almonds, and Heavenly Tomato Cake.

Green Tomato Beans with Toasted Almonds

Thanks to the Bradley County Extension Homemakers, we can re-create this famous festival dish at home.

¼ cup slivered almonds, toasted
¼ cup butter
½ teaspoon salt
¼ cup chopped green tomatoes
4 cups green beans, hot, cooked, and drained

In a saucepan, cook almonds in butter over low heat to a golden brown, stirring occasionally. Remove from heat. Add salt and tomatoes to cooked beans. Cook 5 minutes longer. Mix almonds with beans and serve. Serves 8–10.

Felsenthal Bream Festival, Felsenthal, AR

The tiny town of Felsenthal, population 99, serves as the southern gateway to the Felsenthal National Wildlife Refuge. The confluence of various waterways makes the area a fisherman's haven where numerous freshwater sunfish, known as "bream," are much desired. Pronounced "brim" throughout the South, bream is a delicacy no longer found on restaurant menus but often served in home kitchens lucky enough to have a talented fisherman in residence.

Every Memorial Day Weekend, Felsenthal, known as the "Bream Capital of the South," bursts at the seams with the arrival of anywhere from 8,000–10,000 visitors who come for the bream fishing tournament and family-oriented festival.

Friday and Saturday of Memorial Day Weekend

Because bream is a controlled game fish, it cannot be sold. So Saturday's fish fry features another Southern favorite, catfish, served up with french fries, coleslaw, baked beans, hush puppies, and pickle and onion. Those successful in the fishing tournament, however, surely hold private banquets featuring the prized bream. Festival chairman Carol Lambert says that because bream are so small, they are wonderful cooked like shrimp, chilled, and served in the same manner as shrimp cocktail.

Felsenthal Mock Shrimp

Carol Lambert, Bream Festival chairman, is known far and wide for her creative cooking.

3 pounds bream, bass, or crappie, cut into
  4 x 2-inch strips
3 quarts water
2 teaspoons salt
1 tablespoon Zatarain's Crab and Shrimp Boil Seafood cocktail sauce

Bring water, salt, and shrimp boil to a rolling boil. Add fish strips and boil 5 minutes. Do not overcook. Drain immediately. Chill fish on a bed of ice. Serve with cocktail sauce. Serves: 12.

Felsenthal Fried Bream

Another winning recipe courtesy of Carol Lambert, Bream Festival chairman.

2 pounds bream fillets or 8 whole bream, cleaned (bass, crappie, or catfish may be substituted)
1 cup Louisiana hot sauce
2 cups yellow cornmeal
2 teaspoons salt
3 teaspoons Creole seasoning (more if desired)
Vegetable oil for cooking

Marinate fish in hot sauce for 30–60 minutes. Drain and discard marinade. Mix cornmeal, salt, and Creole seasoning. Roll fish in mixture. Quickly deep-fry fish in hot oil for about 3 minutes, turning once and removing promptly. Do not overcook. Drain on paper towels and serve. Serves 4.

Delaware (Delmarva Peninsula)

Every year, the Delmarva Chicken Festival is held in a different community on the peninsula comprised of Delaware, Maryland, and Virginia. This narrow strip of land covering 200 miles along the eastern shore is the 1923 birthplace of the commercial broiler industry. Today, over 11,000 broilers are sent to market weekly, accounting for approximately ten percent of total U.S. production.

Delmarva Chicken Festival

In 1948, a small group of area residents involved in the production of broiler-fryer chickens organized the first Delmarva Chicken Festival. The following year, the chicken cooking contest was born and has remained an integral part of the celebration. Other activities include a parade, crafts, a trade show, an educational display, sports events, a carnival, and plenty of musical entertainment.

Of course, the focus is on chicken, and there's plenty of it—barbecued chicken, chicken frankfurters, and most especially, fried chicken, produced in the festival's giant fry pan measuring ten feet in diameter. This mother of all frying pans requires 180 gallons of cooking oil and can cook 800 chicken quarters at a time. Over the two days of the festival, nearly 10,000 pieces of chicken are fried Southern-style and served up to the crowd.

Many flock to the cooking demonstrations—where participants can pick up some free recipes along with new tips and tricks—and home cooks from Virginia to Maine compete in the semiannual chicken cooking contest.

Chicken with Mushrooms and Fresh Sage Cream

Julie Fox of Annapolis, MD, won first place in the chicken cooking contest in 1996.

A Weekend in June

4 chicken breast halves, boned and skinned
2 tablespoons flour
¼ teaspoon salt
⅛ teaspoon freshly ground pepper
3 teaspoons olive oil
2 cloves garlic, minced
1½ cups sliced crimini or white button mushrooms
¾ cup chopped green onion
½ cup dry white wine
1 (8–ounce) package low-fat cream cheese, cubed
½ cup grated Parmesan cheese
¼ cup low-fat milk
1–2 tablespoons chopped fresh sage
4 cups hot, cooked linguine
Parmesan cheese
Fresh sage

Pound chicken to ¼-inch thickness. Mix flour, salt, and pepper, and add chicken, turning to coat all sides. In a large, nonstick fry pan, heat oil to medium-high temperature. Cook chicken, turning, about 8 minutes or until chicken is brown and fork tender. Arrange on a platter; cover loosely and keep warm.

To drippings, add garlic, mushrooms, green onions, and wine. Cook, covered, over low heat 3 minutes or until vegetables are tender. Add cream cheese, Parmesan cheese, milk, and sage; stir until cheeses melt and sauce is smooth. If sauce is too thick, add more milk or low-fat chicken broth. Place linguine on four plates and arrange chicken on top. Spoon mushrooms and sage cream over chicken. Pass additional Parmesan cheese and garnish with fresh sage. Serves: 4.

Note: Regular cream cheese and milk may be substituted for the low-fat versions.

Florida

Florida's Cuban heritage dates back to the 1500s when Cuba served as a base of operations for Spanish exploration of the New World, a chain of events spearheaded by the 1539 landing of Hernando de Soto in Tampa Bay. In the 1800s, Cubans immigrated to Key West and Tampa to develop the fledgling cigar industry that began in Cuba with the rise of tobacco farming. In 1869, Martinez Ybor, a Havana cigar manufacturer, moved his factory to what became known as Ybor City, then next door to Tampa. The arrival of Cuban exiles peaked in the years following Fidel Castro's ascension to power in 1959. With today's Cuban exile community numbering more than a million, Cuban heritage and traditions have made their mark on Florida's culture.

Fiesta Day, Tampa, FL

Cubans and Latinos celebrate their heritage every February with a fiesta held in Tampa's Ybor City. Other groups are honored as well, including African, Cuban, German, Italian, Jewish, and Spanish, all of whom participated in the 1886 settlement of Ybor City. Fiesta Day is held in conjunction with Tampa's Gasparilla Invasion, which commemorates the exploits of pirate Jose Gaspar. Cultural exhibits, a juried fine arts and crafts show, music, and fiesta food attract over 50,000 people.

Tradition dictates that out of towners be treated to a free cup of Spanish bean soup, Cuban bread, and café con leche. The garbanzo bean, potato, and chorizo sausage soup is served by the Columbia Restaurant, which sets up its giant ten-and-a-half feet paella pan, for the production of a few thousand servings of paella. Almost everyone enjoys a Cuban sandwich at Fiesta Day.

The festival continues to try to break the Guinness world record for the largest Cuban sandwich. A Cuban sandwich, or Cubano as it's known on the street, is a judicious layering of sliced ham, roast pork, Swiss cheese, salami, thinly sliced pickles, and mustard on Cuban bread, pressed and grilled. Authentic directions for a Cuban sandwich follow, courtesy of the Junior League of Tampa.

Silver Ring Cafe Cuban Sandwich

This is a famous heritage recipe from *The Gasparilla Cookbook*. It is from the Silver Ring Cafe in Tampa, a restaurant that is now closed.

1½ loaves Cuban or French bread
Mustard (such as Gulden's)
Butter
¾ pound baked ham, thinly sliced
½ pound barbecued or roast pork, thinly sliced
¼ pound thinly sliced Swiss cheese
¼ pound Italian salami, thinly sliced
Lengthwise slices of dill pickle

Cut bread in 6 pieces, each 8 inches long. Split pieces lengthwise and spread butter on one side, mustard on the other. Divide ham, pork, cheese, salami, and pickle, and arrange in layers on the bread. Wrap each sandwich in a napkin and secure with a toothpick. Flavor is improved by warming in the oven before serving. Serves: 6.

For authentic Cuban sandwiches, toast in a sandwich press until heated through and crispy outside. Or, place sandwich in a cast-iron skillet, weight it down with another, smaller skillet, and toast.

Note: If barbecued or roast pork is not available, thinly slice 3 thick pork chops into 12 slices. Sauté in butter, remove from pan, and brush lightly with barbecue sauce.

Georgia

   Most of us know Georgia as the "Peach State" and one of its
important crops is peaches, grown in—where else?—Peach County. As
preservation and storage methods have improved in support of wider
distribution, Georgia has become almost as well known for its sweet
Vidalia onions. In 1990, the Vidalia was recognized as the official state
vegetable, and growers have created numerous other products like salad
dressings, barbecue sauces, and relishes, all containing the prized onion
as an ingredient. A veritable cult has grown up around the Vidalia.
How long will it be before Georgia's license plates sport an onion
instead of the traditional peach?

Vidalia Onion Festival, Vidalia, GA

Georgia's official state vegetable is the guest of honor at the Vidalia Onion Festival, an event that attracts around 60,000 visitors annually. The Vidalia has assumed cult status as its fame has grown worldwide, with many folks claiming it is so sweet that it can be eaten raw and out of hand, just like an apple.

In 1931, a local farmer by the name of Mose Coleman discovered that the onions he had planted were sweet rather than hot. Mose was successful in selling his onions, and other area farmers began imitating his success. By 1940, the state had erected a farmer's market in Vidalia, crossroads for a number of major highways. In 1986, the Georgia legislature followed in the footsteps of the French government, giving the Vidalia a type of "appellation controlée" in order to protect it from imitation products. Strict geographic demarcations for the cultivation of Vidalias were established, and only onions grown within that region could bear the name "Vidalia." Marketing and public relations campaigns on behalf of the Vidalia onion have reached epic proportions, with the festival an offshoot of those efforts.

The festival's focus is on culinary events. Vidalia Onion Cooking School attendees learn how to use Vidalias in all sorts of creative ways. Those who tout the sweetness of the Vidalia may participate in the Onion Eating Contest, sure to test anyone's resolve. For those who have explored the versatility of this onion, there's the Vidalia Onion Cooking Contest that consistently delivers innovative recipes. Almost no one leaves the festival without at least one Vidalia onion taste treat: relish, pickles, sauce, salad dressing, or jelly. Lots of folks purchase the festival's *Vidalia Onion Cookbook*. Vidalia is a registered certification mark of the Georgia Department of Agriculture.

Thursday through Sunday of the Last Weekend in April

Bland Farms Vidalia Onions

No discussion of Vidalia Onions would be complete without mention of Bland Farms, the largest single producer of Vidalia onions, with some thirty-five percent of market share. This is a family operation, with everyone pitching in to help ensure a supply of Vidalias for an increasingly demanding worldwide market. Bland Farms has even installed the largest controlled-atmosphere storage facilities in an effort to meet year-round supply requirements. But even Bland sometimes runs a bit short—as they say, "There just simply are not enough Vidalias to satisfy everyone all the time!"

Bland Farms' thriving mail-order business resulted in the compilation of the *Vidalia Sweet Onion Lovers Cookbook,* which contains recipes collected from inventive customers all over the country. As they say at Bland Farms, "They only make you cry when they're gone!"

Roasted Vidalia Onion Soup

Banquet Chef Karl Krebs of the Ritz-Carlton—Buckhead in Atlanta, GA, is well known for his innovative use of local ingredients. You'll appreciate his generosity in sharing a recipe often requested by patrons and guests. Reprinted with permission from the *Vidalia Onion Cookbook*.

3 large (about 3 pounds) Vidalia onions, peeled and cut in wedges
3 tablespoons vegetable oil
1 teaspoon minced garlic
2 (13¾-ounce) cans chicken broth
1 tablespoon fresh thyme or 1 teaspoon dried thyme leaves, crushed
1 bay leaf
⅛ teaspoon ground red pepper
2 tablespoons chopped chives
⅓ cup heavy cream (optional)

Preheat oven to 425°. Place a 13 x 9 x 2-inch baking pan in oven for 5 minutes. Add onions and sprinkle with oil, stirring to coat. Bake, uncovered, until onions are very tender and golden, stirring twice, about 50 minutes. Stir in garlic; bake until garlic softens slightly, about 2 minutes. Add chicken broth, thyme, bay leaf, and red pepper; stir to combine. Cover tightly with foil and bake 20 minutes to blend flavors. Remove foil and bay leaf; cool slightly. Place half of mixture in the bowl of a food processor or in the container of an electric blender and process until onions are coarsely puréed. Repeat with remaining mixture. Serve hot, garnished with chives. Serves: 4–6.

Variation: *Cream of Roasted Vidalia Onion Soup:* Just before serving, stir ⅓ cup warm heavy cream into the puréed soup.

Note: Because this soup is very sweet, it is best served in small portions as a first course.

Vidalia Onion and Tomato Bake

Created by Mrs. Sterling Sasser of Austin, TX, this recipe is so good that it was chosen for inclusion in Bland Farms' *Vidalia Sweet Onion Lovers Cookbook*.

6 large Roma tomatoes
1 large Vidalia sweet onion
1 teaspoon fresh dill or ½ teaspoon dried
1 teaspoon fresh thyme or ½ teaspoon dried
¼ teaspoon salt
½ teaspoon black pepper
½ cup fresh bread crumbs
3 cloves garlic, diced
1 cup grated mozzarella cheese
¼ cup olive oil

Preheat oven to 350°. Butter a deep 8-inch casserole dish. Blanch tomatoes to remove skin and core and cut into wedges. Turn upside down on paper towel to drain. Peel and slice onion into ¼-inch rings. Mix herbs, salt, pepper, and bread crumbs together. Layer half of the tomatoes and onions in casserole dish and top with half the garlic. Sprinkle half the crumb mixture over tomatoes and onions along with half the cheese. Drizzle with half of the olive oil. Repeat procedure, ending with olive oil. Bake for 50 minutes or until bubbly. The onion should still be crisp and tender. Serves: 6.

Note: For a spicier dish, add ½ to 1 teaspoon red pepper flakes to herb/crumb mixture. If Roma tomatoes are not available, regular tomatoes may be substituted. Use 3 large or 6 small tomatoes, depending upon size.

Kentucky

The Bluegrass State is known for its champion racehorses and the world-famous Kentucky Derby. Kentucky also leads the nation in the production of bourbon whiskey, a most fortuitous circumstance given the number of mint juleps consumed during Derby Week. With farms occupying nearly three-fifths of the state, agriculture and livestock are important industries. Farmers raise broilers and hogs along with substantial corn crops used to feed all that livestock. It's no wonder that the country hams of Kentucky are so prized or that Colonel Harland Sanders ended up creating the most famous fried chicken in the world. The name of another famous Kentuckian, Duncan Hines, eventually ended up on a line of food products. Naturally, folks in Kentucky take a backseat to no one when it comes to barbecue. In the western part of the state, the old tradition of barbecuing mutton is becoming a bit of a lost art in the face of today's preference for pork, but Kentucky barbecue sauce, which often incorporates a goodly quantity of bourbon, is mighty popular.

Duncan Hines Festival, Bowling Green, KY

Many today think only of cake mixes when hearing the name Duncan Hines, and few know that there really was a gentleman by that name. Hines was a traveling salesman from Bowling Green, Kentucky, who kept detailed notes of restaurants he visited and meals he ate during his travels. Requests for recommendations from friends and strangers alike culminated in the publication of Hines' first book in 1936, *Adventures in Good Eating: A Directory of Good Eating Places Along the Highways of America.* The book was a compilation of homey descriptions of the dining establishments Hines recommended.

The guide was such a success that by 1938, Duncan Hines was traveling full-time, not as a salesman, but as a restaurant and hotel critic. *Adventures in Good Eating* went through forty-six editions, not discontinued until four years after his death in 1963. In addition to numerous magazine articles and a syndicated column, Hines also wrote *Adventures in Good Cooking and the Art of Carving in the Home, Lodging for a Night, Vacation Guide,* and *The Duncan Hines Dessert Book.* In the 1950s, he licensed his name to Proctor and Gamble; the firm still uses his name on baking mixes.

Today, the folks of Bowling Green pay tribute to Duncan Hines' achievements in the hospitality industry by staging the Duncan Hines Festival. In addition to numerous sporting events, there's a Duncan Hines Look-a-Like Contest and a Cake Carrying Race. Sadly, there is no cake-baking contest, but one year the festival incorporated a huge cake created especially for the celebration. Weighing in at 1,200 pounds, it was baked and constructed under the watchful eye of the indefatigable Romanza Johnson of the President's Club of South Central Kentucky. This giant confection consisted of 337 cakes, each measuring 13 x 9 inches and covered with frosting made from 170 pounds of vegetable shortening, 650 pounds of powdered sugar, 2 gallons of vanilla, and 24 packages of decorative sprinkles. Everyone got a free piece of cake to top off all that famous Kentucky barbecue, which is also available at the festival. Another year, the festival featured the world's biggest brownie, weighing in at 950 pounds.

Under the guidance of Mrs. Johnson, members of The President's Club have compiled a cookbook entitled *Still Cookin' After All These Years,* a compendium of local recipes, as well as several favorites of Mr. Hines.

A Weekend in June

Blackberry Jam Cake

A favorite recipe of Duncan Hines from *Still Cookin' After All These Years.*

1 teaspoon baking soda
1 cup buttermilk
1 cup butter
2 cups sugar
4 egg yolks, beaten
3 cups flour
2 teaspoons cinnamon
1 teaspoon nutmeg
1 teaspoon cloves
1 teaspoon allspice
1 teaspoon vanilla
1 cup blackberry jam
4 egg whites, beaten

Preheat oven to 300°. Dissolve soda in buttermilk. Cream butter and gradually add sugar; add egg yolks. Sift together flour and spices. Add to creamed mixture alternately with the buttermilk mixture. Add vanilla and jam. Fold in the beaten egg whites. Bake in a well-greased, deep 10-inch tube or Bundt pan in a 300° oven for
15 minutes, then at 350° for 15 minutes, and then at 360° for 30 to 40 minutes. Test with cake tester before removing from oven. Remove from oven, unmold cake to a rack, and cool.

International Bar-B-Q Festival, Owensboro, KY

As the second weekend in May opens, the aroma of hickory smoke fills the air over the Owensboro Riverfront, and it isn't long before the smell of true barbecue can be detected. It's the International Bar-B-Q Festival, an annual event held in Owensboro, located on the Ohio River in Western Kentucky. The event draws a crowd of over 70,000 to the "Mutton Capital of the World," and most of these folks have strong opinions about what constitutes real barbecue.

Around this part of Kentucky, the barbecue meat of choice is mutton. According to area experts, the tradition dates back to the Civil War, when many Daviess County pioneers raised sheep. Much of the population was Catholic, and when it came time for church picnics and political rallies, they cooked what they had, which was mutton. Today, the mutton is prepared over outdoor pits that, they claim in these parts, produce barbecue "a pit above the rest." Talk to the experts and they'll tell you that the real secret is in the dip, a delicately blended basting sauce that flavors and moistens the meat. The dip typically consists of Worcestershire sauce, vinegar, lemon, salt, pepper, and water, enhanced according to individual taste.

The major competition at the Bar-B-Q Festival involves teams who begin setting up their pits as early as the Thursday before the festival. By the wee hours of Saturday morning, the fires are lit and the cooking begins. Many of the teams still represent local Catholic churches, raising funds for parish projects. There are three main categories: mutton, chicken, and burgoo, another Kentucky specialty that is the subject of heated debate. The stew originally called for game, but in western Kentucky it has been replaced by mutton. Judging takes place in the afternoon, and then each team donates a required portion to the public serving line. Folks line up to claim their plates filled with mutton, chicken, potato salad, baked beans, sliced sweet onion, and a dill pickle. Back at the team-cooking sites, visitors can purchase their choice of individual entries.

There are plenty of other activities at the International Bar-B-Q Festival. Backyard chefs participate in the classic Cook-off,

The Second Weekend in May

where booth-decorating talent counts for almost as much as grilling abilities. The Pie Eating Contest has contestants seated with their hands behind their backs in a race to see who can be the first to finish eating a cream pie. Once that mess is cleaned up, the next contingent moves in to participate in the Mutton Eating Contest. The winner is the first to stuff and swallow a mutton sandwich. Other special events guaranteed to delight include a car show, sporting tournaments, and an arts and crafts show.

Vendors, many representing local churches and charitable groups, provide plenty of chow for the crowds. Festival officials report that more than 5,000 chickens, 10 tons of mutton, and 1,500 gallons of burgoo are consumed annually.

Visitors who miss the Bar-B-Q Festival need not despair. Indoor barbecue restaurants have a long history in the area, with the first credited to Harry Green around 1890. Today, Owensboro boasts so many barbecue joints that it has earned the nickname of "mutton heaven." Among those considered top-notch are Old Hickory Bar-B-Q and Moonlite Bar-B-Q Inn.

Moonlite's Mutton Dip

This is the original mutton dip used at the Moonlite Bar-B-Q Inn.

1 gallon water
1⅔ cups Worcestershire sauce
2½ tablespoons black pepper
⅓ cup brown sugar
1 teaspoon MSG
1 teaspoon allspice
1 teaspoon onion salt
1 teaspoon garlic
2 tablespoons salt
2 tablespoons lemon juice
1⅔ cups vinegar

Mix all ingredients. Bring to a boil. Use as a dip for chopped mutton and for cooked, sliced mutton. Yield: About 1 gallon.

Kentucky Bourbon Festival, Bardstown, KY

Bourbon is the only distinctly American spirit. The name comes from Bourbon County, originally in Virginia but now a part of Kentucky. Almost eighty percent of the world's bourbon is made in Kentucky. The area in and around Bardstown traces its distilling records back to 1776 and once boasted twenty-two operating distilleries. Today, Bardstown is recognized as the "Bourbon Capital of the World."

The Kentucky Bourbon Festival salutes the state's bourbon industry and attracts over 30,000 people who come to enjoy the musical entertainment, have fun, and learn about bourbon. Tours of the Oscar Getz Museum of Whiskey History and of various distilleries are supplemented by a bourbon heritage seminar. For those who desire a more hands-on approach, there's the Great Kentucky Bourbon Tasting and Gala, a black-tie affair, which requires reservations and costs a hefty admission.

The Food Court is a major attraction because of its bouron-related products. Bourbon candy, barbecue sauces, ice cream with bourbon fudge sauce, and marinated beef and pork dishes provide sustenance to visitors.

For inspiration, there's a minischool—Culinary Arts Bourbon Style—where chefs demonstrate recipes. Class opens with a bourbon whiskey sour and proceeds through the preparation of a multicourse meal. The

Bourbon Barbecue Cook-Off attracts competitors from throughout the United States, with everyone adding at least a touch of bourbon to their favorite concoction for the barbie. Cooks dedicated to the bourbon genre can even purchase a special apron commemorating the experience.

Bread Pudding with Bourbon Sauce

The Kentucky Bourbon Festival was most generous in sharing this famous recipe for a true Southern specialty.

Bread Pudding:
4 cups milk
2 cups sugar
3 eggs
1 teaspoon vanilla
10–12 slices of bread
2 tablespoons butter

Bourbon Sauce:
½ cup butter
½ cup water
2 cups sugar
1 egg, beaten
¾ cup Bourbon or to taste

Pudding: Preheat oven to 350°. Combine milk, sugar, eggs, and vanilla and mix well. Crumble bread and add to mixture. Let soak about 5 minutes. Melt the butter in a baking dish. Pour pudding mixture into a 15 x 9½-inch oval baking dish or equivalent. Bake for about 1 hour or until set and top is golden brown. Serve hot with bourbon sauce. Serves: 8–10.

Bourbon sauce: Bring butter, water, and sugar to a boil. Let cool and then slowly add beaten egg, stirring constantly. Add bourbon to taste and keep warm.

A Weekend in September

Kentucky Derby Festival, Louisville, KY

To many, the Kentucky Derby simply means the famous thoroughbred horse race that takes place every year on the first Saturday in May. But in Louisville, it's a different story entirely. The Kentucky Derby Festival is an enormous extravaganza resulting from the yearlong efforts of some 4,000 volunteers and attracts one and a half million people over a ten-day period prior to the race itself.

The festival opens with Thunder Over Louisville, the largest fireworks show in North America, witnessed by 500,000 spectators. Louisville has a community crazy about racing, and other major festival attractions are geared around such events. There's the Great Balloon Race, in which a maximum of fifty-one participating hot-air balloons launch into the sky in the early morning hours, and then there's the Great Steamboat Race that pits the Belle of Louisville against Cincinnati's Delta Queen. As many as 8,000 racers from all over the U.S. participate in the 13.1-mile minimarathon, as spectators cheer them on. Somewhat more tame by comparison, but impressive nonetheless, is the Pegasus Parade, consisting of around a hundred bands and floats and lasting up to two hours. Numerous sporting events and concerts round out a full roster of entertainment with something for everyone. All that activity is bound to make folks mighty hungry and this is where Louisville shines. An abundance of celebrations showcase regional foods and Kentucky's legendary hospitality. Propelled by the excitement of "Derby Fever," the mint juleps flow while barbecue pits are continually refueled.

According to those in the know, every Louisville hostess possesses what is referred to as a GRAM or "Generally Recognized As Mandatory" list of foods to be served at lavish Derby soirees. Kentucky ham, fried chicken, real Kentucky burgoo, corn pudding, and feather-light biscuits are familiar staples rounded out by innumerable delicacies presented by clever hostesses and restaurateurs alike. For out-of-towners lacking invitations to private parties, the Taste of Derby Festival provides an opportunity to check out the best food and spirits that Kentucky has to offer.

Begins Ten Days Prior to Derby Day, the First Saturday in May

Benedictine

CORDONBLUEGRASS, the cookbook of The Junior League of Louisville, contains dozens of recipes that can only be described as having a very distinguished pedigree. One such formula is that for Benedictine, developed and made famous by Jennie Carter Benedict in the 1890s. Miss Benedict, a civic leader and cookbook author, operated a tea shop in Louisville, and among her most popular items were dainty sandwiches made of Benedictine spread. Today, it remains a favorite sandwich spread of Louisvillians served on toast with bacon or tomato or both. It can also be thinned with milk or sour cream to make a beautiful vegetable or chip dip. Reprinted with permission from The Junior League of Louisville.

1 large cucumber
8 ounces cream cheese, softened
1 small onion, grated
¼ teaspoon salt
1 tablespoon mayonnaise
2–3 drops green food coloring

Pare, grate, and drain cucumber well, first in a colander and then on paper towels. Combine with remaining ingredients. Refrigerate until serving time. Yield: 1½ cups.

Note: Benedictine makes a marvelous sauce for pita bread sandwiches composed of stir-fried beef or lamb and topped with tomato, onion, and lettuce.

The origin of Kentucky's famous burgoo is somewhat vague, to say the least, but it most likely has its origins in frontier days as a hunter's stew featuring whatever was available. Gus Jaubert, a Frenchman who was known around the Louisville area for his fine cooking, was evidently the first to bear the appellation of "Burgoo King." Legend has it that Jaubert cooked thousands of gallons of this stew for General John Hunt Morgan and his Confederate raiders. Since Jaubert most likely referred to his concoction as a ragout, the name could very well have evolved into burgoo. However, an equally titillating story has it that a Union soldier with a speech impediment threw blackbirds into a pot and attempted to call it bird stew!

Supposedly, J. T. Looney, another Lexington cook who had developed quite a following among the racing crowd, inherited the crown of "Burgoo King" when Jaubert died. Colonel E. R. Bradley named a colt in honor of Looney, and in 1932, Burgoo King won the Kentucky Derby. No wonder, then, that this rich stew is a ubiquitous part of Derby entertaining.

Dead Heat Kentucky Burgoo

The Kentucky Derby Museum Cook Book provides the definitive recipe for this famous Southern specialty. Reprinted with permission from The Kentucky Derby Museum.

1 fat hen, at least 4 pounds
1–2 pounds lean stew meat (beef, veal, or lamb), cubed
6–8 cups water
1½ teaspoons coarsely ground pepper
½ teaspoon cayenne pepper
2 (8-ounce) cans tomato puree
12 medium potatoes
4 large onions, chopped
1 large head cabbage, finely chopped
6–8 medium tomatoes, peeled and chopped (or three 1-pound cans tomatoes)
2 (15-ounce) cans of corn or 6–8 ears of corn, cut off cob
1 pound fresh carrots, sliced
1–2 tablespoons salt
1 teaspoon pepper
½–1 cup Worcestershire sauce

Cook chicken and other meat in water with coarsely ground pepper and cayenne pepper until chicken leaves the bones and the meat is very tender (about 40 minutes). Remove bones, shred meat, and return to the liquid. Add tomato purée, potatoes, onions, cabbage, tomatoes, corn, and carrots. Season with salt, pepper, and Worcestershire sauce. Cook slowly for 2–3 hours, until consistency of a thick stew, stirring from the bottom to keep from scorching. Add water, if necessary, to keep from sticking. If you like additional vegetables, add 2 cups fresh cut butter beans, 2 cups fresh sliced okra, and/or 2 green peppers, finely chopped. Serves: 10.

Old Market Days and Barbecue on the River, Paducah, KY

If a spirit of hospitality and goodwill, accompanied by great barbecue, appeals to you, then you'll want to be in Paducah, Kentucky, during the annual Old Market Days. This charitable event, which helps support numerous nonprofit organizations throughout the area, includes a contest called "Barbecue on the River."

Almost everyone in Paducah and McCracken County has an opinion about barbecue where long, slow cooking over hickory is considered an art. Sauces are nearly always tomato-based, but with the addition of varying amounts of vinegar, brown sugar, and cayenne, the results run the gamut from hot-hot-hot to mildly hot and sweet.

Ro Morse, former restaurateur turned active civic leader and author of *Ro's Taste of Paducah,* decided to put all that local expertise to good use and kicked barbecuing into high gear when she served as Tourist Bureau Director. The result is an extravaganza that has surely earned Ro the title "Pride of Paducah."

The media cook-off on Friday night is open to regional newspaper, TV, and radio personnel who compete to produce the best backyard-type barbecue on typical outdoor grills. On Saturday, serious "amateur" barbecuers compete with offerings ranging from chicken to pork ribs or pork shoulder. Lately, a clever twist has been added to the promotion of this event that is now billed as the Barbecue Tournament and Pig Out. Hog-calling and chicken-clucking contests add to the ambience.

Commercial vendors open for business in the afternoon, selling typical Paducah-style barbecue platters, which include baked beans, coleslaw, and potato salad made with a mayonnaise-mustard base. In the midst of it all, everyone continues to debate the merits of one barbecue over another.

Kay's Friend, Pam's Bar-B-Que Sauce

Ro Morse, cook extraordinaire, author of *Ro's Taste of Paducah,* and an active civic leader, is a huge fan of this sauce for chicken and ribs that she describes as a "keeper."

¼ cup butter, melted
1 tablespoon Worcestershire sauce
2 tablespoons vinegar
1 teaspoon lemon juice
1 tablespoon prepared mustard
3 tablespoons brown sugar (light or dark), packed
1 teaspoon chili powder
1 teaspoon paprika
½ cup ketchup
Salt and pepper to taste

Combine all ingredients in a saucepan. Heat until mixture comes to a low bubbling boil or until the sugar melts. Yield: 1 cup.

Note: Cider vinegar and Hungarian paprika are recommended for depth of flavor.

Stanton Corn Festival, Stanton, KY

Eastern Kentucky's Powell County is a major producer of tobacco and corn, with most of the latter grown for grain. There's still plenty of sweet corn grown, however, and both corn crops provide the Stanton Tourism Action Committee with an excellent reason for a festival to attract visitors.

The annual Corn Festival in Stanton is a true celebration of corn. Overnight, some fifty ears of corn, each six feet in length, are painted on the streets. Visitors have only to follow the corn to reach the festival grounds in the Stanton City Park. Vendors sell handcrafted items like woven chairs, brooms, and hand-painted articles. Many can be seen demonstrating their crafts. There's a pageant on Saturday and a car show on Sunday. The regional Livestock Producers Association, specializing in beef, pork, and lamb, produces all the corn needed for the festival. That's a tall order, since over 18,000 attendees enjoy fresh sweet corn served boiled or roasted in shucks over charcoal. Those with a big appetite and plenty of courage sign up for the corn-eating contest. For the kids, there are butterscotch suckers in the shape of an ear of corn. Organizers claim that the festival cookbook entitled *Follow the Corn* includes a recipe for corn dodgers from Daniel Boone's wife Rebecca.

Corn Pudding

Eastern Kentucky has long been famous for its delectable corn pudding. This heritage recipe is from *Follow the Corn*.

Saturday and Sunday of the First Full Weekend in August

2½ cups canned corn
2 tablespoons butter
2 tablespoons flour
Heavy cream
¼ cup chopped green bell pepper
1 chopped fresh pimiento (or 3 ounces canned, drained pimiento)
2 egg yolks
¾ teaspoon salt
¼ teaspoon paprika
¼ cup crumbled, crisp bacon
2 egg whites

Preheat oven to 350°. Drain the corn, reserving the liquid. In a saucepan, melt butter. Stir in flour until well blended. Combine corn liquid with enough heavy cream to equal one cup. Add slowly to the flour mixture, stirring constantly. When the sauce is smooth and hot, stir in corn, green pepper, and pimiento. When the mixture boils, reduce heat. Beat the two egg yolks well and, off heat, pour part of the corn mixture over them. Beat and return all of the mixture to the pan. Stir and cook several minutes to permit the mixture to thicken slightly. Add salt and paprika and cook for 1 to 2 minutes. Add bacon and mix. Whip the egg whites until stiff but not dry and fold into the corn mixture. Pour into a buttered and floured 6-cup soufflé or baking dish and bake for about 30 minutes or until pudding has set. Serve hot.
Serves: 6–8.

Trigg County Ham Festival, Cadiz, KY

Trigg County runs along the eastern edge of the Lakes Recreation Area in south-western Kentucky. For years, many folks thereabouts have cured their own hams, a process involving a ritual soaking in salt for three weeks followed by smoking for around two weeks in a smokehouse with smoldering hickory chips. The ham is then hung, and a year and a half later, it's considered fit to eat.

While country hams, as they are known throughout the South, are held in high regard, northerners often wonder what all the fuss is about. Accustomed to relatively insipid commercially produced hams, they fear both the mold that encases such hams, as well as the fact that they don't have to be refrigerated. Country hams are also salty. The secret is to soak the ham in water, scrape off the mold, boil the ham to reduce the salt, and then serve it finely sliced, almost slivered.

In 1977, farmers around the Cadiz area got together and asked a local packing company to judge their hams. After years of haggling, it was agreed upon that an impartial judging was in order. This was the beginning of the Trigg County Ham Festival that is now held over three days and attracts some 80,000 locals and visitors. Country hams are displayed in all their glory, and there's still a formal judging of the hams along with a ham giveaway.

Trigg County is hog-raising country, so the hog-calling contest is an important event, as is the greased pig contest that measures prowess of a different order. Country and Western music, a car show, a carnival and parade, a horse and mule pull, fiddling, a "Kiss the Pig Contest," and a craft show round out the events.

A canning contest showcases local talent, and there's a baking exhibit. Many of the entrants are retirees who have hung onto the old ways and values. The world's largest ham and biscuit sandwich weighs in at over 500 pounds, making those offered by popular chains pale by comparison. Moved by forklift to the town square, it is cut into smaller portions and sold to the crowd. For those who still crave pork, vendors sell pork chop sandwiches.

Friday through Sunday of a Weekend in October

Robert Earl Fowler's Grand Champion Country Ham

Robert Earl Fowler, Cadiz, KY,
1992 Champion, Trigg County Ham Festival.

Soak a country ham in cold water for 24 hours. Add 1 cup vinegar and 2 cups brown sugar to water. Remove from water and brush and clean the ham. Put ham in lard stand and cover with cold water. Bring to a boil and boil 1 minute per pound. Take off heat. Wrap container in old quilts or blankets. Let stand 24 hours. Remove ham from water and remove skin. Make a mixture of pineapple, brown sugar, and cracker crumbs, spread on top, and bake until brown.

Sources for Country Hams

Ballance Country Hams
Route 1, Box 15
Oakland, KY 42159
(270) 563-3956

Broadbent's Hams B&B Food Products
6321 Hopkinsville Road
Cadiz, KY 42211
(800) 841-2201
(270) 235-5294
Fax: (270) 235-9601

D. L. Penn's Hams
8850 Liberty Road
Campbellsville, KY 42718
(270) 465-5065

World Chicken Festival, London, KY

In 1956, Colonel Harland Sanders, proprietor of a restaurant in Corbin, Kentucky, known for its delicious fried chicken, suffered a major setback. A new interstate highway by-passed his eatery, and business was reduced to a trickle. Despite having been made an honorary colonel for his contribution to the state's cuisine, Sanders was forced to look for another way to make a living. Undaunted, he packed up his famous seasoning mixture, consisting of eleven herbs and spices, along with his pressure cooker, and peddled franchises for his famous chicken. By 1964, he had over six hundred such franchises that grossed in excess of $37 million per year.

Today, the nearby town of London celebrates Sanders and his "Kentucky Fried Chicken" with the World Chicken Festival, attracting over 200,000 devotees of the dish that made chicken and Kentucky synonymous. The festival is held in the middle of town. There's a full lineup of activities ranging from continuous live entertainment, parades, thrill rides, magic shows, a circus, and volleyball tournaments to the Crowing, Strutting, and Clucking Contest complete with props and costumes. The Chick-O-Lympics attracts kids aged four to seven with an egg hunt, spoon race, egg toss, and chicken scratch contest. On Sunday, crowds are entertained by gospel singing. The Chicken Wing Eating Contest is a measured of who can eat the most wings clean down to the bone in a specified amount of time.

During the festival, some 8,000 chicken quarters are cooked in what organizers claim to be the world's largest skillet. It was made and donated to the festival by the London Bucket Company in 1991, and measures ten feet, six inches in diameter. Empty, it weighs in at a hefty 700 pounds. It can cook 882 chicken quarters at a time. Fried chicken is the festival specialty, and it's dredged before cooking in a mixture consisting of flour, salt, pepper, paprika, and the festival's special secret ingredient. Chicken dinners include potato salad, baked beans, and a roll.

Other favorite foods at the World Chicken Festival include grilled chicken, plenty of cornbread, and chicken and dumplings made by local nonprofit groups.

Thursday through Sunday During the Last Weekend in September

Many visitors to the festival make a pilgrimage to Corbin to visit the restored Harland Sanders Cafe and Museum, now on the National Registry of Historic Places. The establishment is complete with the original 1940s kitchen, vintage equipment, and furnishings.

Pan Fried Chicken

Based on a recipe featured in *Poultry in Family Meals: A Guide to Consumers* published by the U.S.D.A. in 1979 and as provided by Carol Benson, Laurel County, KY, Extension Agent for Home Economics, this is an example of a typical fried chicken recipe used by Kentucky cooks.

3 pounds mixed chicken fryer parts
Vegetable oil or shortening for frying

Coating mix:
1 cup flour
2 teaspoons salt
¼ teaspoon black pepper
Any or all of the following ingredients may be added to taste–remember, Colonel Sanders used "11 secret herbs and spices": paprika, thyme, dried parsley, basil, sage, celery salt, garlic powder, onion powder, savory, tarragon, and oregano. Suggestion: start by mixing in ½ teaspoon parsley and ¼ to ½ teaspoon each of all other spices.

Rinse and dry chicken pieces. Cut into serving pieces if needed. Place coating mixture in a large bag and shake two or three pieces of chicken in the bag at a time until all pieces are coated. Shake off excess coating.

In a heavy skillet, heat just enough oil to cover the bottom of the pan. Use moderate heat. Add meatier pieces first, but do not crowd the pan. Brown on one side, then turn and brown on the other side. Over reduced heat, continue to cook slowly, uncovered, until tender, turning frequently. Total cooking time will be 30 to 45 minutes. Remove chicken and drain on paper towels before serving.

Louisiana

To many Americans, southern Louisiana is the culinary capital of the country. The region has spawned so many famous restaurants, chefs, food festivals, and notable dishes that it's impossible to keep track of them all. Millions of tourists flock to the region to experience the history of such places as New Orleans' Vieux Carre and South Louisiana's Acadiana, and most folks have good eating at the very top of their agenda. Louisiana's culinary heritage is a unique blend heavily influenced by French, Spanish, and African hands. Creoles, descendants of the original Spanish and French settlers, and Cajuns, descendants of the French who were forced to flee Acadia in eastern Canada, have very distinctive cooking styles.

Of course, the abundance of great food is the result of Louisiana's prodigious agricultural and fishing resources. Rice, sugar cane, sweet potatoes, tomatoes, strawberries, peaches, and melons are all leading crops. The state's commercial fishing industry delivers shrimp, catfish, crayfish, and oysters. Food processing makes its contribution to the economy as well, delivering sugar, coffee, milled rice, and a host of hot sauces and condiments. Louisianans are mighty proud of their food traditions and are happy to share them with one and all.

Alligator Festival, Boutte, LA

St. Charles Parish is in the center of Louisiana's alligator harvesting grounds. On the last full weekend of September, the Alligator Festival is held in the Coronado Park Area on U.S. Highway 90 in Boutte, about twenty miles west of New Orleans. The event coincides with the annual September alligator hunting season, which lasts for thirty days. The festival was first held in 1980 by the St. Charles Parish Rotary Club as a fund-raiser and to promote the alligator industry.

While most people have long been familiar with the use of alligator skins in everything from wallets to footwear, many are just discovering alligator meat, the taste of which is described as a cross between fish and pork. It is considered especially delectable in a variety of regional dishes.

At the Alligator Festival, alligator cuisine is definitely something to celebrate, and it makes its appearance in the form of alligator sauce piquante, fried alligator, gator burgers, and gator po'boys. Folks not up to the likes of such dishes can opt for alternative Cajun delicacies like white beans and shrimp, crawfish étouffée, jambalaya, or gumbo. For entertainment, there's Cajun music, an arts and crafts display, and games for both children and adults.

Last Full Weekend in September

Alligator and Sausage Jambalaya

Alligator recipes in St. Charles Parish are treasured family secrets. The following recipe is based on one that was acquired with a great deal of subterfuge and no small amount of begging—along with an ironclad promise never to reveal the name of the creator.

4 pounds alligator meat (boneless, skinless chicken breast may be substituted)
Salt and pepper to taste
Hot sauce to taste
2 pounds beef sausage, sliced thin
¼ cup vegetable oil
4 large onions, chopped
4 medium green bell peppers, chopped
12 green onions, chopped
4 cloves garlic, finely chopped
18 cups chicken broth
2 cans cream of mushroom soup, undiluted
4 cups long grain rice
2–4 teaspoons cayenne pepper or to taste

In a 6-quart pot, combine alligator meat with enough water to cover. Season to taste with salt, pepper, and hot sauce. Boil meat until tender. Drain and debone, cutting meat into medium-sized chunks. Set aside. If substituting chicken, poach, cool, and cube.

Place sausage in a large pot with enough water to cover the bottom. Cook sausage until water evaporates. Remove sausage and set aside. Add oil to the drippings in pot, then add onion and bell peppers and sauté until tender. Add green onions and garlic and sauté a minute more. Add alligator meat or chicken, sausage, 4 cups of the broth, and mushroom soup. Cook for 45 minutes; most of the liquid will cook down. Add remaining 12 cups of broth, rice, and cayenne pepper to taste. Cover and cook over low heat until rice is tender, stirring frequently to keep from sticking. Turn off heat and let stand, covered, for 15 minutes. Serves: 10–12.

Allons Manger, Belle Rose, LA

According to the parishioners at St. Jules Catholic Church in Belle Rose, Louisiana, there are basically two kinds of people in this world: those who are Cajun and those who wish they were Cajun. They offer salvation for those in the latter category in the form of their annual festival, Allons Manger, which is designed to get you as close to being Cajun as possible without actually getting mud between your toes!

Here is Cajun cuisine the way it has been prepared in backyards and on the bayous for years. Local delicacies that can be enjoyed are crawfish, shrimp, oysters, alligator, turtle, fish fried and in stews, étouffées, gumbo, boudin, jambalaya, and sauce piquante. Brisket smoked, marinated, and then baked, served with a fabulous gravy made with ground beef, onions, celery, bell peppers, garlic, and tomato sauce on hot po'boy bread, is outstanding.

Homemade sweets of every description are served at the Sweet Booth, and pies like custard, coconut, and pecan are top-sellers, along with a feisty creation containing pecans, chocolate chips, and a healthy dose of bourbon.

Continuous live music plus games for children, bingo, raffles, and a crafts booth featuring handcrafted cypress woodwork indigenous to the area keep everyone moving, working up an appetite for another go at the food. Virtually no one leaves the festival without a copy of the cookbook *Allons Manger Avec Le Monde De St. Jules Et St. Martin,* which is a definitive guide to Cajun cooking today. Believe it or not, it even contains the recipes for festival specialties, allowing anyone with the strength to whip up brisket or a crawfish stew for 2,500 and jambalaya for 600.

Always the First Sunday after Easter

Lee's Fried Oysters

Here is Lee J. LeBlanc's famous recipe from *Allons Manger Avec Le Monde De St. Jules Et St. Martin*.

1 gallon peanut oil
1 gallon oysters
3 pounds Al's Seasoned Fish Fry Mix (recipe follows)
½ cup Tony Chachere's Creole Seasoning

Heat oil in a large, deep fryer to 350°. Wash oysters and drain. Mix seasoned fish fry mix with Creole seasoning. Coat oysters evenly with mixture, a few at a time. Fry until golden brown (approximately 3 minutes). Do not overcook. Drain on paper towels.
Serves: 15–20.

Note: This recipe can be reduced to serve 4 or 5 people by substituting the following quantities:

1 quart peanut oil
1 quart oysters
Al's seasoned fish fry mix (recipe follows) for 5 pounds of fish
2 tablespoons Tony Chachere's Creole Seasoning.
Proceed according to directions above.

Al's Seasoned Fish Fry Mix

Al "Coonie" Caillet's recipe from *Allons Manger Avec Le Monde De St. Jules Et St. Martin* is a must for Lee J. LeBlanc's fried oysters.

10 pounds yellow cornmeal
1 cup plus 2 tablespoons white pepper
6 tablespoons red (cayenne) pepper
6 tablespoons garlic powder
4 cups salt

Mix all ingredients. Use to coat oysters, fish, or shrimp before frying.

Note: For approximately 5 pounds of fish, use the following quantities:

1 cup yellow cornmeal
1 teaspoon white pepper
1 teaspoon red (cayenne) pepper
1 teaspoon garlic powder
2 teaspoons salt

Mix all ingredients. Coat fish with mixture and fry in hot oil quickly, just until golden, so fish doesn't overcook and dry out.

Andouille Festival, LaPlace, LA

Twenty-five minutes west of New Orleans, St. John the Baptist Parish encompasses the areas known to early Mississippi River navigators as the "German Coast" and the "Acadian Coast." In the late 1700s, French settlers brought their unique recipes for preparing and smoking a sausage known as andouille. The original recipes were adjusted to accommodate available indigenous herbs and spices. Descendants of those early settlers still make andouille sausage in the Old-World manner from treasured family recipes. Andouille is a sweet-spicy sausage made with pork and smoked using a special blend of wood. To celebrate their heritage and local product, the residents of St. John the Baptist Parish stage their annual Andouille Festival in LaPlace. Travelers new to the area can't miss the town's water tower that proudly proclaims the parish as the "Andouille Capital of the World."

Most of the food vendors sell such unique Cajun specialties as chicken and andouille gumbo, andouille po'boys, andouille pizza, red bean gumbo, fried corn on the cob, corn and shrimp soup, blackened chicken, jambalaya and white beans, and a spicy bayou pasta. Alligator is served in a variety of ways, including barbecued, fried, and with sauce piquant, a light tomato gravy.

The cooking contest includes all manner of andouille-enhanced dishes like gumbos, an andouille-stuffed chicken, and even an andouille spaghetti sauce, which won eight-year-old Dustin Root first place in the children's division.

Usually the Last Weekend in October

Pasta St. John

Dave MacDonald of Bull's Corner Restaurant in LaPlace, LA, created this recipe that has brought him fame and patrons from near and far.

1 pound boneless chicken, cubed
2–4 tablespoons butter
8 ounces smoked andouille sausage, cubed (or smoked beef sausage)
½ red bell pepper, cut into thin strips
½ teaspoon chopped garlic
¼ teaspoon crushed red pepper flakes
¼ teaspoon coarse black pepper
¼ teaspoon whole dry thyme
Pinch of salt
¼ cup dry white wine
2 cups heavy cream
¼ cup chopped green onions
8 ounces penne pasta, cooked and drained
½ cup freshly grated Romano cheese

Sauté chicken in butter until partially cooked. Add the andouille sausage and bell pepper and sauté until peppers are half cooked. Add the garlic and spices, stirring for one minute. Add the wine and simmer until liquid is reduced by half. Add the cream and simmer until liquid is again reduced by half. Add the green onions and pasta and fold into sauce. Add Romano cheese and fold into pasta mixture. Pour into a large serving dish. Serves: 4.

Breaux Bridge Crawfish Festival, Breaux Bridge, LA

Legend has it that the crawfish came to Louisiana with the Acadians. They were originally lobsters, but during the long and difficult trip into exile, they got smaller and smaller, so that by the time the lobsters arrived in Louisiana, they were only a few inches long.

Today, the crawfish is a recognized symbol of the Cajuns and their venerated foodways and culture, but this wasn't always the case. Old-timers recall when people were ashamed to eat crawfish and fishermen couldn't even give their catch away. In 1959, the Louisiana Legislature, in an effort to stimulate the economy, allocated funds to develop crawfish farming. Bob Angelle, Speaker of the Louisiana House of Representatives at the time, was from Breaux Bridge, and he wanted to do something for the town, then celebrating its hundreth anniversary. He convinced the legislature to declare Breaux Bridge "La Capitole Mondiale de l'Ecrevisse" or the "Crawfish Capital of the World," a title earned by the fact that the townsfolk had been commercially serving crawfish in local restaurants since the 1920s. But a market for crawfish outside Louisiana needed to be created.

The Crawfish Festival, which grew out of the Breaux Bridge Centennial, was first held in 1960 and sparked the commercial potential of the local crustacean. The festival garnered the attention of the media and brought in visitors from all over the United States to see Louisiana, experience Cajun culture, and to eat the then exotic crawfish. With the combined marketing of both tourism and crawfish, the festival grew to be the second largest in Louisiana, outdistanced only by Mardi Gras. This, in turn, created a huge demand that stimulated the crawfish industry. Today, Louisiana crawfish are shipped throughout the United States.

Hundreds of thousands journey annually to Breaux Bridge, a sleepy little town on the banks of the Bayou Teche, to enjoy the authentic Cajun celebration staged in Parc Hardy. There is plenty of Cajun music and dancing, along with traditional craft demonstrations of accordion, fiddle, and bonnet making. The crawfish race sparks good-humored competition, as does the

Always the First Full Weekend in May

crawfish eating contest, where the record is still held by Nick Stipelcovich for consuming fifty-five and three-quarters pounds in forty-five minutes. Local residents share their secret recipes with cooking demonstrations in the Cajun Heritage Tent.

For a true taste of Louisiana, festival visitors gather at the Crawfish Étouffée Cook-Off where cooks from all over the Acadiana region vie for titles. Once the judging is over, samples are available to one and all. Throughout the festival, thousands of pounds of crawfish are cooked by Cajun natives producing local specialties like jambalaya, crawfish boudin, crawfish pies, crawfish bisque, gumbo, and étouffée, as well as boiled and fried crawfish.

Stuffed with good Cajun food and lulled by the music and warm hospitality, most festivalgoers stop to pick up a copy of the *Breaux Bridge Crawfish Festival Cookbook,* which features a lexicon of great recipes. Those who have discovered a taste for Monsieur Ecrevisse are surely delighted with instructions for the preparation of such crawfish specialties as dip, cornbread, casseroles, bisque, étouffée, stew, and pie.

Crawfish Etouffée

Pat Huvel established a reputation as a fine cook with this once secret recipe from the *Breaux Bridge Crawfish Festival Cookbook.*

3 tablespoons cooking oil
1 large onion, diced
½ bell pepper, diced
1 pound crawfish tails
½ cup crawfish fat
¼ cup water
1½ cups rice, cooked separately

In a frying pan, heat the oil and sauté onion and pepper. Add crawfish tails and brown. Add fat and water, stir, and let boil one minute. Add salt and pepper to taste. Serve over hot rice. Serves: 4.

Cajun Heritage Festival, Cut Off, LA

"Come and pass a good time" say the folks at the Cajun Heritage Festival and from all accounts, everyone who attends does just that. It's certainly not your run-of-the-mill festival with music, food, and other sorts of entertainment, although that's also a big part of the fun.

For carvers and collectors, this is the place to be for the Cajun Heritage Decorative Lifesize Wildfowl Championship, the Louisiana and Bayou Championship Waterfowl Carving Competition, and the Miniature Boat Competition. Craft booths feature quality woodcrafts, needlecrafts, porcelain dolls, handmade boats and jewelry, and hand-carved ducks. The work of some of the finest carvers from New Jersey, Mississippi, and Louisiana appears in the decoy raffle. All proceeds from the festival go to benefit the Cajun Heritage Museum.

But because this is Louisiana and, in particular, Cajun country, the competition also extends into the realm of food with both a jambalaya cook-off and a gumbo cook-off. Patrons start out the day with hot coffee and beignets (deep-fried pastries), then progress to all the jambalaya they can eat. And that's before they dig into Ben Pierce's World Famous Seafood Gumbo that he has cooked at the festival every year since 1977. No wonder they have to work it off with a four-hour dance called the fais-do-do.

Ben Pierce's World Famous Seafood Gumbo

The Cajun Heritage Festival shares Ben's famous recipe.

First Weekend after Labor Day

½ cup vegetable oil
½ cup all-purpose flour
8 cups chicken broth or water
1 cup chopped onions
1 cup chopped celery
1 cup chopped green bell pepper
½ cup chopped parsley
½ cup thinly sliced green onions
1½ pounds (60–70 count) raw shrimp, shelled and deveined
4 cups shelled oysters with broth
1 pound crabmeat
1 teaspoon cayenne pepper
Salt and pepper to taste
Fresh gumbo filé powder
Cooked rice

First, make a roux. In a deep, heavy cast-iron pot, heat ½ cup vegetable oil until it starts to smoke. Add the ½ cup flour (about one-third of it at a time), whisking it in quickly. Constantly whisk the roux over low heat until it turns medium brown. If the roux burns, throw it out and start over—you want a nutlike flavor, not a burnt flavor, in your gumbo!

Slowly whisk in the chicken broth (for added flavor) or water. Boil slowly for 20 minutes, whisking occasionally. Add onions, celery, peppers, parsley, and green onions. Cook on low heat for 20 minutes. Add seafood and cayenne pepper and cook over low heat for 20 minutes. Salt and pepper the gumbo to taste. Add fresh filé powder last, when gumbo is cooked. Ladle the gumbo over cooked rice. Serves: 6–8 generously.

French Food Festival, Larose, LA

Friday through Sunday of the Last Full Weekend in October

Every year, a huge, 200-foot-long striped circus tent erected on the grounds of Larose Regional Park is the site of the French Food Festival, an old-fashioned celebration that features the best there is in Cajun cooking. This is French South Louisiana and lovers of Acadian cuisine from all over Louisiana flock to the event. Authentically decorated booths feature local cooking specialties, at least half of which are seafood dishes. Visitors delight in tasting such creations as shrimp boulettes, boucherie and white beans, fried crab claws, crawfish étouffée, seafood gumbo, alligator sauce picante, jambalaya, oyster po'boys, and fried fish. At the sweet shop, tarts, cobblers, pralines, and beignets bring connoisseurs back year after year. All of the food is prepared and sold by volunteers of the Larose Civic Center. The air is filled with the music of the old time "fais-do-do" and newer zydeco sounds. The Houma tribe provides insight into yet another culture of the South Bayou Lafourche area with demonstrations of dance, music, and native crafts. Locals demonstrate quilting, decoy carving, and cooking tart de bouille from a century-old recipe.

Shrimp Boulettes

Thanks to the folks at the Bayou Civic Club in Larose, LA, we can enjoy their famous boulettes any time of the year.

4 cups peeled, raw shrimp (1½–2 pounds unpeeled)
1 medium potato
1 medium onion
1 clove garlic
1 stalk celery
¼ cup finely chopped parsley
1 egg
Salt and pepper
Vegetable oil for frying
Optional: Cajun seasoning

Grind shrimp, potato, onion, garlic, and celery. Add egg, salt, and pepper. Mix until blended. Drop by tablespoonfuls into hot oil. Fry until golden brown. Drain on paper towels, sprinkle with Cajun seasoning if desired, and serve immediately. Yield: 36 puffs.

Boullie

For French Pudding, The Bayou Civic Club of Larose, LA, shares this Cajun heritage recipe.

¼ cup cornstarch
⅓ cup sugar
1 egg
2 cups whole milk
1 cup evaporated milk
2 tablespoons butter
1 teaspoon vanilla
½ teaspoon vanilla and butternut flavoring

With a wire whisk, mix together cornstarch, sugar, egg, whole milk, and evaporated milk. Cook over low heat until thickened. Remove from heat and add butter and flavorings. Stir until well mixed. Bouille can be poured into an unbaked pie shell as a pie filling or it can be used as a pudding or sauce for dessert.

French Market Tomato Festival (Creole Tomato Festival), New Orleans, LA

Locals try to keep the French Market Tomato Festival, also known as the "Creole Tomato Festival," a secret but it's doubtful that their efforts will bear fruit over the long term. Amid music from Louisiana and the Caribbean, the Creole tomato season and the diversity of the tomato is celebrated in the French Market's Dutch Alley, located between Dumaine and Decatur streets. From 3,000 to 5,000 locals and tourists converge on the area that is located in the heart of the historic district. New Orleans' French Market is the oldest public market in the country, dating from 1791. Today, it includes not only a Farmers' Market but a Butchers' Market, a Vegetable Market, a Bazaar Market, and renovated replicas of the Red Stores of the antebellum period.

Since the festival takes place coincident with the initial picking, the first official box of Louisiana's Creole tomatoes is auctioned off, and visitors can taste fresh Creole tomatoes. There are numerous arts and crafts dealers, as well as food vendors selling tomato-based specialties like jambalaya, shrimp Creole, stuffed tomatoes, stewed okra and tomatoes, tomato crawfish pies, and fried green Creole tomatoes. A highlight is the opportunity to view cooking demonstrations by dozens of well-known New Orleans chefs who generously pass out their recipes.

Crawfish Cannelloni with Basil and Ricotta Cheese in Creole Tomato Sauce

Chef Horst Pfiefer of Bella Luna has patrons waiting in line to order his signature dish.

Sunday of the First Weekend in June

Crawfish Cannelloni:
2 tablespoons olive oil
½ cup chopped onions
1 teaspoon chopped garlic
2 tablespoons fresh basil
2 teaspoons fresh parsley
8 ounces lump crabmeat
8 ounces peeled crawfish
12 ounces ricotta cheese
Salt and pepper to taste
12 sheets pasta (6 x 5 inches), precooked

Heat oil and sauté the onions and garlic; add chopped herbs, crab, and crawfish. Let it cool and mix in the ricotta cheese and season with salt and pepper. Split mixture in equal parts and roll up in pasta sheets. Reheat and top with hot Creole Tomato Sauce. Garnish with Parmesan cheese if desired.
Serves: 4–6.

Creole Tomato Sauce:
¼ cup olive oil
4 cups chopped onion
2 tablespoons chopped garlic
3 pounds red Creole tomatoes, chopped, (whole tomatoes may be substituted)
1 cup chopped fresh basil, oregano and rosemary
Salt and pepper to taste
Chili flakes to taste

Heat oil in a 2-quart saucepan; add onion and garlic and sauté until brown. Add tomatoes and seasonings and simmer over low heat for 30–45 minutes until sauce thickens.

Gueydan Duck Festival, Gueydan, LA

Deep in the heart of Cajun country lies the town of Gueydan, which bears the title "Duck Capital of America." That honor was bestowed by the Louisiana Secretary of State in 1977 at the urging of Les Dames de Gueydan, a local women's organization. Few people outside Louisiana realize the importance of ducks to the culture and foodways in this area, but the Gueydan Duck Festival Association aims to change all that. The Duck Festival, which also started in 1977, promotes duck season and has grown in size every year.

Activities include a skeet shooting competition, dog trials where retrievers show off their expertise, and a duck and goose calling contest. Decoy carvers exhibit their wares and provide demonstrations of their craft. A carnival, along with foot races, live bands, an arts and crafts show, and auctions, round out what has remained, despite growing crowds, a family event.

The annual cooking contests are a big draw for onlookers and participants alike. There are two, one for indoor cooking and the other for outdoor cooking, and contest categories are "Duck" and "Goose." Pot Roasted Teals and Duck and Guinea Gumbo are two of the winning recipes. Having worked up an appetite watching all that cooking, visitors make haste to the food concessions where all manner of duck specialties can be purchased, including duck jambalaya, duck gumbo, and Cajun duck fajitas. Many of the festival's winning contest recipes are printed in the annual program.

Usually the Weekend before Labor Day

Cajun Duck Fajitas

The Gueydan Duck Festival Association sells these prize-winning fajitas at the annual festival.

2 wild ducks
Salt and pepper
Butter
Chopped onion
Chopped green pepper
Shredded lettuce
Diced fresh tomatoes
Sour cream
Flour tortillas

Boil duck until tender. Skin and debone the duck, then cut into one inch pieces. Season to taste with salt and pepper. Brown duck in a small amount of butter over high heat for 5–8 minutes. Wrap flour tortillas in foil and heat in a preheated 350° oven for 5 minutes. Fill the tortillas with duck and add the onion, pepper, lettuce, and tomatoes. Top with a dollop of sour cream and serve.

Gumbo Festival, Bridge City, LA

On the west bank of the Mississippi River, directly across from New Orleans, lies Bridge City, Louisiana, "Gumbo Capital of the World." Each October, gumbo lovers from all corners of the globe flock to Bridge City for its famous Gumbo Festival, sponsored by Holy Guardian Angels Roman Catholic Church.

The dictionary defines gumbo as "a soup, usually thickened with okra pods." Whoever wrote this definition was obviously not from Louisiana, where gumbo is as ubiquitous as the all-American hamburger. Actually, gumbo is more like a stew, made from a fat and flour base called a "roux," which is cooked slowly until it turns a deep, rich mahogany color. Vegetables such as garlic, parsley, onions, celery, and green pepper are added to the roux and cooked a bit before stirring in fish, shellfish, sausage, poultry, or game. There are even richly seasoned all-vegetable gumbos, called "gumbo des herbes," popular during the Lenten season. Gumbos (an African term for this Southern favorite and from which the dish got its name) are thickened with the addition of okra or filé powder, made from the young leaves of sassafras trees growing along the Gulf Coast. Most cooks produce more than a touch of piquancy with the addition of hot peppers in one form or another. Gumbo is typically served with rice.

At the festival, Bridge City's world famous gumbo is cooked daily with over 2,000 gallons of both seafood and chicken and sausage gumbo served to visitors every year. Other Louisiana specialties available include jambalaya, New Orleans-style red beans and rice with sausage, funnel cakes, and a variety of homemade baked goods and candies. There's also a cooking contest where champion gumbo chefs are pitted against each other for top honors.

Always the Second Full Weekend in October

Once initiated into the glories of gumbo, there's no turning back. Those in the know grab a copy of the *Gumbo Festival Cook Book* that, along with a number of other Louisiana specialties, provides excellent recipes for the dish. Anyone wishing to invite a few of their closest friends in to enjoy gumbo will find salvation—the book includes a couple of recipes designed to produce 300 or 400 gallons of goodness.

Seafood/Sausage Gumbo

This prize-winning recipe is based on that used by John Noel, King Creole Gumbo VII.

½ cup vegetable oil
½ cup flour
8 cups chicken broth or water
1 cup chopped onions
1 cup chopped celery
1 cup chopped parsley
1 cup chopped green bell pepper
1½ pounds ground or sliced smoked sausage
2 pounds raw shrimp, peeled and deveined
1 pound crab meat
2–4 cups oysters with liquid
1 teaspoon cayenne pepper
Salt, Tabasco Sauce, and black pepper to taste
Gumbo filé powder (optional)
Cooked rice for serving

First, make a roux: In a deep, heavy cast-iron pot, heat ½ cup vegetable oil until it starts to smoke. Add the ½ cup flour (about one-third of it at a time), whisking it in quickly. Constantly whisk the roux over low heat until it turns medium brown. If the roux burns, throw it out and start over—you want a nutlike flavor, not a burnt flavor, in your gumbo!

Slowly whisk in the chicken broth (for added flavor) or water. Boil slowly for 20 minutes, whisking occasionally. Add onions, celery, parsley, and green pepper and boil slowly for 20 minutes. Add sausage, shrimp, crabmeat, oysters, and oyster water. Add cayenne pepper, salt, Tabasco, and black pepper to taste—don't be shy! Simmer for an additional 20 minutes. Turn off fire and let gumbo set for about 5 minutes. Skim off any excess fat and add filé powder if desired. Serve over rice. Serves: 8–10.

Note: If using filé powder as a thickening agent, remove gumbo from heat before adding it; filé becomes stringy if boiled or reheated.

Independence Italian Festival, Independence, LA

Always Friday through Sunday the Last Full Weekend in April

Louisiana's French heritage is well known but there's also a strong Italian heritage. Independence, located in Tangipahoa Parish about fifty miles north of New Orleans, is known as the "Little Italy" of Louisiana. Sicilian families searching for a place to settle in the 1880s were attracted by the thriving strawberry industry of the area. Independence slowly became a predominantly Italian community and today it's known for its excellent Italian cuisine and its annual Italian Festival.

Marked by a parade and a variety of entertainment, including authentic Italian music and special exhibits at the Italian Cultural Museum, it's the food that really attracts visitors to this event. The usual array of Louisiana specialties are available: catfish, crawfish étouffée, shrimp and oyster po'boys, boiled crawfish, and roasted pig sandwiches with dirty rice. But there's a definite Italian spin to this celebration with popular foods including Italian eggplant casserole, pizza, lasagna, spaghetti and meatballs, cannoli, shrimp fettuccini, meatball po'boys, and those famous Italian-inspired muffaletta sandwiches made so famous by New Orleans' Central Grocery.

Rose Sinagra Ingram, who grew up in Independence in an Italian immigrant family, has authored a cookbook entitled *Chesta e Chida* ("a bit of this and a little of that") that is sold in conjunction with the festival. The book is filled with recipes much beloved by those Sicilians who settled in Louisiana, made it their home, and became proud Italian-Americans.

Jujulaine Cookies

Rose Sinagra Ingram rose to celebrity for her fabulous cooking, and under a constant barrage of recipe requests, she compiled her own cookbook titled *Chesta e Chida*.

1 cup margarine
⅔ cup sugar
1 teaspoon vanilla
2 eggs, beaten
3½ cups flour
2 teaspoons baking powder
Milk
½ cup water or milk
½ cup sugar
Sesame seeds

Preheat oven to 350°. In a large bowl, cream margarine and sugar. Add vanilla and eggs and mix well. Sift flour and baking powder. Add to creamed mixture. Work with hands, adding enough milk to hold dough together. Roll out small pieces of the dough in ropelike fashion until they are the size of your little finger. The thinner the dough, the more crisp the cookie. Cut rope into pieces about 2 inches long. Combine water or milk and sugar and boil 3–5 minutes. Pour into a small bowl. In another bowl, place sesame seeds. Roll each cookie first in the water or milk and sugar mixture, then in the sesame seeds. Place cookies on greased cookie sheet and bake for 10–12 minutes or until brown. Cool completely and store in an airtight container.

Jambalaya Festival, Gonzales, LA

Competition is fierce at the Jambalaya Festival in Gonzales, Louisiana, the "Jambalaya Capital of the World." The Festival Association, chartered in 1967, bestows the coveted and prestigious title of World Champion Jambalaya Cook upon one person, who emerges after three days of cooking in three separate "heats."

Jambalaya is a Cajun-Creole dish made from meat, rice, and seasonings such as onions, pepper, and garlic. It is a favorite dish throughout Louisiana, where every cook has their own variation and where lively debates about the perfect jambalaya can erupt at any time. Jambalaya is so popular that it is commonly served at weddings, family reunions, and fund-raisers.

At the festival, jambalaya is cooked in thirty-gallon cast-iron pots over open wood fires. There's also a "Mini-Pot" cooking contest where jambalaya is cooked in pint-sized pots. As the delicious cooking aromas permeate the air, many head for the dining hall to enjoy what they came for—jambalaya. Others work up an appetite dancing the Gonzales-style jitterbug to a variety of music, including "swamp pop."

Byron Gautreau, World Champion Jambalaya Cook in 1992, 1994, and 1997, worked with the festival to come up with the following recipe for a stove top, from-scratch jambalaya, cooked in a five-quart black pot. It's a scaled-down version of those cooked in large pots at the festival.

Gautreau's World Champion Jambalaya

Byron Gautreau, Gonzales Jambalaya Festival World Champion Jambalaya Cook, 1992, 1994, and 1997 provided this winning recipe.

½ cup cooking oil
1 (4–5 pound) hen, cut up
1 teaspoon black pepper
3 medium onions, chopped
1 teaspoon garlic powder
8 cups water
2 tablespoons salt
1 more teaspoon garlic powder
½ teaspoon MSG, optional
1 more teaspoon black pepper
¼ teaspoon ground red pepper
1 teaspoon Tabasco Sauce or 1 tablespoon Cajun seasoning
4 cups long grain rice

Memorial Day Weekend

Pour the oil in the pot, season hen with 1 teaspoon black pepper, and brown over high heat. When oil clears, reduce heat to medium high and continue until the chicken is brown and the pot has a layer of brown. Add onions and the 1 teaspoonful of garlic powder. Sauté over low heat until the onions are translucent. Add water, stir, and bring to a full boil. Turn fire off and allow oil to rise. Skim off as much oil as possible without removing the gravy. Add the rest of seasonings, to taste, and bring to a boil again. Add rice and bring to a relatively vigorous boil, stirring to prevent sticking. Reduce heat to low, cover, and cook for 10 minutes. Remove lid and stir, allowing liquid to seep into rice. Replace lid and cook 20 minutes longer. Serves: 8.

Variation: Substitute 3 pounds of cubed boneless pork and 1 pound of sausage cut into 1-inch pieces for the hen.

Note: If less rice is preferred, reduce quantity to 2 cups.

Laurel Valley Village, Thibodaux, LA

Laurel Valley Village, at 230 Laurel Valley Road in Thibodaux, is a rural-life sugar plantation museum. Dating from the late 1800s, it is the largest surviving sugar plantation in the United States. Some seventy structures are still standing, and most are small, Acadian-style cabins complete with brick chimneys. Sugar cultivation has been the major agricultural activity in the area since the 1830s. Cotton, rice, and other crops are also under cultivation.

Laurel Valley was settled around 1790 by Etienne Boudreaux, an Acadian who obtained a Spanish land grant. In 1832, the land was sold to Joseph W. Tucker, who expanded the plantation to 3,200 acres. He built the mill and introduced sugar and slave labor. In 1873, Burch Wormald of New Orleans purchased the plantation and introduced a dummy railroad system to aid in the sugarcane harvest. The golden age was from 1893 to 1926, when an agricultural partnership to purchase the plantation was formed by Frank Barker Sr., and J. Wilson Lepine Sr. These men completely restructured operations, expanding mill production to three million pounds of sugar. At one time, there were over 300 workers living in the plantation's Quarter section. Disaster struck in 1926, when the mosaic disease destroyed the entire sugar crop of South Louisiana. It would take eighteen years for the plantation to recover.

The Friends of Laurel Valley Village direct the rural-life museum and have rehabilitated the country store and a dozen other structures since 1978. Visitors must register at the store for a guided tour. Fund-raising is paramount to the organization's efforts to preserve the heritage of Laurel Valley. The Country Store sells items made by residents of Bayou Lafourche. The Friends sponsor several activities during the year. Gourmet suppers featuring prominent chefs attract visitors and locals alike. Spring and Fall Heritage Festivals offer the opportunity to view antique cars and farming machinery, to enjoy Cajun food and music, and to buy local handmade crafts. Coffee and beignets are available for early morning arrivals, who quickly purchase a variety of the sweets made by volunteers.Everyone looks forward to lunch and the Friends' famous shrimp jambalaya, accompanied by white beans, fried fish, coleslaw, and French bread. In December, the Country Store is the site of the Christmas Open House. A Cajun Santa, dressed in blue jeans, holds court with children who receive free candy. Adults enjoy holiday eggnog while purchasing unique Christmas gifts for loved ones.

Spring Heritage Festival
Last Sunday of April
—
Fall Heritage Festival
Second Sunday of October
—
Cajun Christmas Open House
First Sunday of December

Apple Cake

Supporters of Laurel Valley are sure to buy sweets baked by Friends Volunteer Ruby Landry of Thibodaux, LA, who shares the recipe that established her reputation as one of the finest cooks in the area.

2 medium apples, peeled and chopped
⅔ cup pecans, chopped
2 cups self-rising flour
4 eggs
2 cups sugar
¾ cup vegetable oil
1 teaspoon vanilla

Preheat oven to 325°. Mix chopped apples and nuts with ½ cup of the flour and set aside. Beat together eggs and sugar. Add oil and vanilla. Mix in the remaining 1½ cups flour. Fold in apples and nuts. Mixture will be thick. Place mixture in a well-buttered and floured 10-inch Bundt pan and bake for one hour or until cake tests done. Cool on rack for 10 minutes, then remove cake from pan and complete cooling.

Laurel Valley Festival Shrimp Jambalaya

Friends Volunteer Robert Boudreaux of Thibodaux, LA, prepares his famous jambalaya at the annual fundraiser to benefit the Laurel Valley Museum.

1 cup vegetable oil
6 cups chopped onions
1 cup chopped celery
½ cup chopped green bell pepper
¾ gallon shrimp broth (recipe follows)
1 cup sliced mushrooms
1 tablespoon paprika
¼ cup soy sauce
2 cloves garlic, crushed
¼ cup Worcestershire sauce
Salt and pepper to taste
2 pounds raw shrimp, peeled and deveied
2 pounds long grain rice
¾ cup chopped shallots
½ cup chopped parsley

Heat vegetable oil, add onions, and cook over high heat until onions soften and begin to turn brown. Add celery and green pepper and sauté for 5 minutes. Add shrimp broth and stir. Add mushrooms, paprika, soy sauce, garlic, and Worcestershire sauce. Stir and add salt and pepper to taste. Cook over medium heat about one hour. Add shrimp and cook for about 5 minutes. Once sauce begins to boil, add rice, stirring constantly. As rice begins to swell, add shallots and parsley. After about one minute, cover and remove from heat. Rice will absorb all liquid in about 30 minutes. Serve immediately. Serves: 10–12.

Shrimp Broth: Preheat oven to 350°. Remove heads and shells from the 2 pounds of shrimp for the jambalaya and place in a buttered baking pan. Season with salt and pepper and bake for 30 minutes. Place baked shells in a pot filled with about one gallon of boiling water. Boil for 30 minutes and strain liquid. This shrimp broth provides a great deal of flavor to the jambalaya.

Louisiana Corn Festival, Bunkie, LA

Bunkie, Louisiana, population 5,044, lies midway between Lafayette and Alexandria. Like many other towns in the state, Bunkie, too, has its annual celebration and, folks in Bunkie unabashedly state that the Louisiana Corn Festival is to promote family fun. Adults enjoy sports tournaments, pirogue races, and corn shucking and eating contests. For the kids, there are lizard races, a carnival, and a corn creature contest. Visitors of every age take in the bands, street dances, and arts and crafts booths.

There's plenty of roasted corn for everyone. And then there are the Corn Cooking Contests with junior, individual, and team competitions. All recipes must, of course, include corn and after judging, the entries are available for purchase. In years past, the festival has produced *Aw Shucks— The Louisiana Corn Festival Cookbook*, a popular souvenir that has been issued in several editions.

Friday through Sunday of the Second Weekend in June

Fresh Corn Seafood Chowder

Vicki Ryland was a first-place winner of the Corn Cooking Contest and one taste of this chowder will tell you why.

6 slices bacon
5 tablespoons flour
2½ cups chicken broth
2½ cups half and half
2 tablespoons butter
½ cup finely chopped celery
1 cup finely chopped onion
1½ cups crawfish, scaled, deheaded and peeled, no fat
2 cups fresh corn, parboiled and cut off the cob
1 (12-ounce) can crabmeat
1½ cups fresh shrimp, peeled and deveined
1 teaspoon seafood seasoning or 3 teaspoons Cajun seasoning
Salt and pepper to taste

Fry bacon, crumble, and set aside. Add flour to the bacon fat, stirring with a wire whisk. Add broth and half and half, stirring rapidly with a whisk. Cook for about 10 minutes. In another pot, melt the butter and add celery and onions. Cook briefly until transparent. Add crawfish and smother for about 5 minutes. Add to half and half mixture. Add corn, crabmeat, shrimp, seafood or Cajun seasoning, and salt and pepper to taste. Simmer for about 10 minutes. If soup is too thick, thin with more half and half or chicken broth. Add crumbled bacon and serve. Serves: 6.

Note: If crawfish is not available, this soup is equally delicious made with a total of 1 pound crabmeat and 1 pound raw shrimp, peeled and deveined; add to celery and onion mixture. Frozen corn may be substituted for fresh corn.

Louisiana Shrimp and Petroleum Festival, Morgan City, LA

A somewhat incongruous name, the Louisiana Shrimp and Petroleum Festival honors two of the state's natural resources—shrimp and oil. With beginnings in 1936, it's now Louisiana's oldest state-chartered festival, attracting between 100,000 and 150,000 attendees annually.

Morgan City is located in the Atchafalaya Basin near the Gulf of Mexico, deep in Bayou Country. The area has long been synonymous with seafood. Catches from rivers, lakes, and bayous fed the Native Americans, as well as the first white settlers, and today fishing is a major industry in the area. All species of fish known to the Lower Mississippi and Atchafalaya are obtainable in the vicinity. This includes the large gulf shrimp that prompted the port of Morgan City to adopt the moniker of "Jumbo Shrimp Capital of the World" back in 1948.

The centerpiece of the festival is the Blessing of the Fleet and water parade. A local priest ceremoniously blesses elaborately decorated shrimp trawlers, pleasure craft, and some of the biggest "muscle" boats of the oil patch, followed by the parade circling Berwick Bay.

Music plays a big role in the festival with offerings encompassing Cajun, zydeco, zyde-Cajun, country, and pop. Over a hundred artisans from throughout the South showcase their crafts. In Lawrence Park, there's a Children's Village guaranteed to entertain kids of all ages. A large parade is held in the downtown historic district. There's also a bass fishing tournament, boat tours of the harbor, fireworks, and square dancing.

The Shrimp Cook-Off attracts individuals and corporate teams from throughout the Tri-City area of Berwick, Patterson, and Morgan City, who vie for bragging rights of having "the best shrimp dish around." Celebrity chefs do the judging and visitors get to taste the winning recipes.

The Cajun Culinary Classic, held Saturday through Monday, consists of more than two dozen food booths, sponsored by local, nonprofit groups featuring traditional, home-cooked Cajun food. There's a showmanship award for the best decorated booth. But the real show is the food itself which includes shrimp, crawfish and fish po'boys, shrimp and crawfish étouffée, barbecued shrimp, boiled shrimp, shrimp Creole, gumbos and stews, jambalaya, crawfish pie, seafood-stuffed bread and potatoes, crawfish and shrimp fettuccine, barbecued and fried chicken, meat pies, smoked meats, seafood pistollettes, boudin, fried fish, alligator—and more.

Friday through Monday of Labor Day Weekend

Herbal Seasoned Shrimp and Crawfish

Keith J. Leonard of Catered Affairs in Berwick, LA, reveals one of the recipes that built his reputation as a chef par excellence.

¾ to 1¼ cups olive oil
1½ cups chopped celery
1½ cups chopped onion
2 tablespoons minced garlic
½ cup chopped sun-dried tomatoes
1 cup sliced fresh mushrooms
1 cup sliced artichoke hearts
¾ pound raw shrimp, peeled and deveined
¾ pound raw crawfish tails
1–2 tablespoons sweet basil
1–2 tablespoons oregano
1 tablespoon Creole seasoning
½ cup chopped green onions
¼ cup chopped fresh parsley
Pasta of choice or 2 loaves of thin, baguette-style French bread
Swiss cheese, sliced

In a large pan, sauté the celery and onions in olive oil over medium heat until edges begin to brown. Add minced garlic, sun-dried tomatoes, mushrooms, and artichoke hearts and cook 3–4 minutes over medium heat. Add additional olive oil as needed. Add shrimp and crawfish, season with basil, oregano, and Creole seasoning and cook for 3 minutes over high heat. Add green onions and parsley and cook 2–3 minutes over medium heat. Serve over pasta of choice, mixing cooked pasta with mixture in pan while still on heat. Serves: 4–6.

Variation: The shrimp and crawfish mixture can be served as an appetizer by spreading it on top of sliced French bread, topped with Swiss cheese, and baked or broiled until the cheese melts. Drizzle the bread with olive oil before adding topping and be generous with the Swiss cheese. Serves: 8–10 as an appetizer.

Note: If dehydrated sun-dried tomatoes are used, soak in warm water for one hour before chopping. If crawfish is not available, substitute with a total of 1½ pounds of shrimp.

Louisiana Sugarcane Festival and Fair, New Iberia, LA

As the luxuriant growth of succulent sugarcane reaches its pinnacle in late September, the air fills with excitement—it's time for the annual Louisiana Sugarcane Festival and Fair, a big, lusty, fun-filled celebration held every year since 1937, except during World War II.

Jesuit priests introduced sugarcane to Louisiana where, early on, it was found that the state's semitropical climate provided ideal growing conditions. When a young Frenchman, Etienne DeBore, discovered the secret of granulated sugar, making large-scale sugar production possible, the entire economy of Southern Louisiana changed. There are seventeen parishes that make up the state's "Sugar Bowl," producing twenty-five percent of U.S. cane sugar on some 300,000 acres. An estimated 20,000 people are employed in the industry. By the way, Louisianans take their sugar seriously—a telephone call to the Sugar Cane Festival office is answered with a resounding, "Hi Sugar!"

The festival formally opens with a mass and blessing of the crop at the Louisiana Sugar Cane Festival Building. Events and activities include a livestock show, street fair, parades, a "fais-do-do," or street dance, concerts, and flower, photography, and art shows. A boat parade down the Bayou Teche commemorates the fact that, in earlier years, the waterway was the main means of transportation for the export of sugar. King Sucrose is chosen by his peers based on his contribution to the sugar industry and Queen Sugar, chosen from among sugar-producing parish contestants, reigns by his side. An important part of Louisiana's sweetest festival is the Sugar Cookery Contest. Many of the affairs during the festival feature delicious Cajun foods and sweets that could only be produced in Louisiana, a state where caution over calories is thrown to the wind.

Pecan Pie Cake

Sylvia Dugas of Sylvia for Catering, New Iberia, LA, finds her services in great demand during the festival, and she was kind enough to share the recipe for one of her famous confections.

1 (18¼-ounce) box yellow cake mix
½ cup butter, softened
1 egg
1½ cups light corn syrup
½ cup brown sugar, packed
3 eggs
1½ cups chopped pecans

Preheat oven to 350°. Remove ⅔ cup of the cake mix and set aside. Cream butter and beat in the egg. Add remaining cake mix and blend until smooth. Pat evenly into a greased 13 x 9-inch pan. Bake for 20 minutes. Cool.

Mix together corn syrup, brown sugar, 3 eggs, and the remaining ⅔ cup cake mix; stir in pecans. Pour over cooled crust and bake at 350° for 45–60 minutes, until center is set. Cool thoroughly, running a knife around outside edges while still warm. Cut into squares.

Louisiana Yambilee, Opelousas, LA

The Sweet Golden Yam, Louisiana's sweet potato, was discovered around 1687 by the first French settlers in the area. Native American tribes cultivated the yam and it rapidly became a favorite food item of both French and Spanish settlers who arrived in the Opelousas District. These early settlers and their successors devoted a great deal of time and effort to making the golden yam a prime crop.

Louisianians call their particular brand of sweet potato a "yam," from the Senegalese word "nyami" (to eat), to distinguish it from other varieties of sweet potatoes. According to locals, the Louisiana yam is sweeter, moister, and more nutritious than ordinary sweet potatoes.

The first Louisiana Yambilee was held in 1946. Because yams are harvested in late summer and early fall, a celebration in the last week of October is considered ideal. The Yambilee is, after all, designed to honor and promote a local industry. The Yambilee King is chosen in recognition of his achievements and success in the yam industry and/or service to the Yambilee. Mr. Yam or Mrs. Yam are also selected on the basis of a significant contribution to the development and growth of the sweet potato industry.

Exhibits in the Yamatorium showcase the yam industry and include fresh sweet potatoes and "Yam-I-Mals," oddly shaped yams decorated to resemble insects, birds, fish, or animals. Naturally, there is a Sweet Potato Auction. In addition to arts and crafts, a flower show, and the Grand Louisyam Parade, there is a cooked food contest with junior and adult divisions. Guidelines require that the sweet potato flavor predominate in each dish entered, and classes include ten categories such as yam pones, pies, cakes, cookies, and candies. Prize-winning entries are displayed in the Yamatorium.

Usually the Last Full Weekend in October

Praline Glazed Yams

Pam Stelly was the 1996 overall winner of the Yambilee Cooked Foods Show and the Louisiana Yambilee when she entered her favorite recipe.

2 pounds yams, cooked, peeled and cut up
1 cup packed light brown sugar
3 teaspoons cornstarch
A pinch of salt
⅛ teaspoon ground cinnamon
¼ cup hot water
1 tablespoon butter
¼ cup chopped pecans

Preheat oven to 350°. Place yams in an 8-inch square pan or 8-inch pie plate and set aside. In saucepan, combine brown sugar, cornstarch, salt, cinnamon, and hot water. Bring to a boil, stirring constantly. Once boiling, cook and stir 2 minutes more. Remove from heat. Stir in butter and pecans. Pour over yams. Bake, uncovered, for 15–20 minutes or until heated through. Serves: 5–6.

Mandeville Seafood Festival, Mandeville, LA

Mandeville, Louisiana, is strategically located on the north shore of Lake Pontchartrain, directly across from the city of New Orleans. The Fourth of July holiday brings thousands of people streaming across the causeway to Mandeville for the Seafood Festival held at Lakefront Harbor.

The festival features top musical entertainment, an arts and crafts show, and a special children's entertainment area. The annual fireworks show over the lake is the best of its kind.

Then there's the food, and because this is Louisiana, it's mainly based on seafood that is conspicuous in both quantity and variety. Bill Dobson, President of the Greater Mandeville Seafood Association, says it's all just too much to describe. His solution? "Come on down!"

Always Weekend of Fourth of July

Shrimp Fettuccine

Pat's Seafood of Mandeville, LA, provided this recipe for a famous Mandeville specialty.

½ cup butter
1 cup chopped shallots or sweet onions
½ cup chopped celery
4 medium cloves garlic, finely chopped
2 cups half and half
Salt and pepper to taste
2 pounds fresh shrimp, peeled and deveined
1 pound fettuccine
3 ounces grated Parmesan cheese
3 ounces grated Romano cheese

In a medium pot, sauté butter, shallots, and celery until tender. Add garlic and sauté for one minute. Add half and half and salt and pepper to taste. Cook over low heat about 10 minutes. Add shrimp and continue cooking 2–3 minutes or until shrimp turn pink and are cooked through.

Meanwhile, cook fettuccine, until tender, in boiling, salted water. Drain and return fettuccine to cooking pot. Fold in grated cheeses. Pour sauce over pasta and mix well. Serve immediately. Serves: 8.

Note: If your preference is for a generous amount of sauce on pasta, add 2 cups of heavy cream along with the half and half. You may also wish to double the amount of Parmesan and Romano cheese, stirring half into the sauce until it is smooth and adding the rest to the hot pasta.

Mayhaw Festival, Marion, LA

Small mayhaw trees grow throughout the river bottoms in the southern United States, yielding a fruit that looks like a tiny pink apple. In Marion, Louisiana, locals gather mayhaws to make a delicious jelly. In 1982, the Jaycees established a festival and based it around the mayhaw. Now administered by the Marion Activities Committee and the Marion Fire Department, the celebration attracts around 1,500 visitors. Many visitors check out Lynn Creek Vineyard & Winery, which produces wines made one hundred percent from Louisiana grown fruits and grapes. Their flagship product is Sabine, made from Louisiana mayhaws. Bill Lynn describes the flavor as one that will "recall those butter-drenched biscuits and fresh mayhaw jelly" favored by locals. The festival gets underway on Friday evening with a live band and dancing. On Saturday, there's a parade and a quilt show, and crafts vendors are a big draw. Saturday morning, it's time to get down to business with the Mayhaw Cooking Contest, divided into two categories: jellies and baked goods. The latter covers creations like mayhaw cobbler, mayhaw cake (a pound cake made with mayhaw pulp), and mayhaw pie, filled with a delicious custard made from the fruit. Visitors can buy fresh mayhaws as well as mayhaw jelly and butter to take home.

Mayhaw Cake

Gail Durbin of Marion seems to have unlocked the secret of winning the Mayhaw Baking Contest. With this recipe, she won first place in 1995 and 1997.

Second Friday and Saturday in May

Cake:
1 box spice cake mix
1 box butter recipe yellow cake mix
1 small French vanilla instant pudding mix
2 cups water
½ cup vegetable oil
½ cup butter, softened
1 cup mayhaw butter
6 eggs, separated
1½ cups walnuts, chopped

Frosting:
2 (8-ounce) packages cream cheese, softened
½ cup butter, softened
1 cup mayhaw butter
½ teaspoon cinnamon
4 pounds powdered sugar
1½ cups walnuts, finely chopped

Preheat oven to 350°. Mix together the dry spice cake mix, yellow cake mix, and pudding mix. Add water, oil, and butter. Mix well and add mayhaw butter. Mix for 4 minutes on medium speed of electric mixer. Add egg yolks and mix well. Stir in walnuts by hand. In a separate bowl with clean beaters, beat egg whites until almost stiff. Fold egg whites into cake mixture by hand. Pour batter into two greased and floured 13 x 9-inch pans and bake for about 35–40 minutes. When cakes have cooled, make the frosting by creaming together the cream cheese and butter. Beat until fluffy, then add mayhaw butter and cinnamon. Slowly mix in the powdered sugar. Stir in walnuts and frost cakes. Yield: 2 cakes.

Plaquemines Parish Fair and Orange Festival, Buras, LA

Most people don't know that Louisiana is considered one of the oldest and best orange-growing regions in the United States, much of it centered in Plaquemines Parish. It is believed that oranges were first introduced into Louisiana by Jesuit priests who brought in stock from southern Spain over 200 years ago. In 1860, Florentine Buras planted the first documented orange grove in Plaquemines Parish. Eventually, orange groves proliferated throughout the area with many of the growers concentrating their efforts on cultivation of a navel orange called "Bahia," discovered in the city of the same name in Brazil. With the evolution of various species and varieties of oranges, the term "Louisiana Sweet" is now applied to all oranges grown in the state, and navels from the district are characterized by their deep orange color, excellent flavor, and heavy juice content.

The first Plaquemines Parish Orange Festival was held in 1947 in order to promote cultivation and marketing of Plaquemines' citrus crop. Unfortunately, parish orange groves have suffered from the periodic and devastating consequences of both hurricanes and severe frosts, at first resulting in the cancellation of the Orange Festival for some years. But folks in Plaquemines Parish are a hardy, determined lot who simply turned the event into a celebration of all local industry, including fishing and oystering.

Today, as the annual orange harvest gets into full swing in early December, festival visitors enjoy all sorts of entertainment, as well as local seafood delicacies and citrus treats and exhibits. The festival is held at historic Fort Jackson in Buras, Louisiana. Fair activities include seafood contests, such as shrimp peeling and deheading, catfish skinning, and oyster shucking. Kids enjoy pie-eating and orange-rolling contests. Some years have even featured a recipe contest and several winning recipes can be found in the festival's official cookbook, *Plaquemines Parish Fair and Orange Festival Special Edition Cookbook Celebrating Our 50th Anniversary.*

First Full Weekend in December

And then there's the food: fresh oysters on the half shell, shrimp and oyster po'boys, Louisiana specialties like Cajun pistolettes, gumbo, jambalaya, citrus candy, lots of fresh orange juice, and much, much more. Those with stamina are urged to try a Toko Toddy, a unique local drink devised by Croatian immigrants that's made from a lemon and sugar mash mixed with water and plenty of Bourbon. Paula Cappiello, dedicated secretary and treasurer for the festival, warns, "You can usually drink one or two Toko Toddies with no problem but it's the third one that gets you!"

Fresh Citrus Cake

The *Plaquemines Parish Fair and Orange Festival Special Edition Cookbook Celebrating Our 50th Anniversary* features this old-fashioned layer cake recipe that won first place in the cooking contest for Doris LeBoeuf in 1972 and 1973.

Cake:
3 cups sifted flour
2 teaspoons baking powder
½ teaspoon salt
¾ cup soft vegetable shortening
1½ cups sugar
3 eggs
1 tablespoon grated orange rind
½ cup orange juice
⅔ cup milk

Preheat oven to 350°. Grease and lightly flour two 9-inch cake pans. Sift flour, baking powder, and salt onto waxed paper. Reserve. Combine shortening, sugar, eggs, and orange rind in large bowl of mixer. Beat at high speed 3 minutes. Sift in flour alternately with orange juice and milk, beating after each addition until batter is smooth. Pour batter into prepared pans. Bake for 30–40 minutes or until center springs back when lightly pressed with fingertip and top is lightly browned. Cool layers in pan on wire rack for 10 minutes. Loosen around edges with a knife. Turn out onto wire racks. Cool completely. Cut each layer in half. Fill between layers with orange filling, then frost with orange lemon icing. Once frosted, the cake should be refrigerated in hot weather.

Golden Orange Filling:
¼ cup flour
¾ cup sugar
½ teaspoon salt
1 cup boiling water
2 egg yolks
1 cup orange juice

1 tablespoon butter
Rind of 1 lemon
Rind of 1 orange
Few drops of orange food coloring

In medium saucepan, combine flour, sugar, and salt. Add water and cook over medium heat until thickened, whisking constantly. Add egg yolks, slightly beaten, to a little of the hot mixture and blend. Add to hot mixture. Simmer for 2 minutes, stirring constantly. Blend in remaining ingredients. Refrigerate until cold before spreading on cake.

Orange Lemon Icing:
2½ cups sifted powdered sugar
¼ cup butter
1 (3 ounce) package cream cheese
1 egg yolk (optional–see note below)
Grated rind of 1 lemon
Grated rind of 1 orange
2 tablespoons orange juice
1 tablespoon vegetable shortening (optional)

Combine sifted powdered sugar, butter, cream cheese, and egg yolk and blend well. Stir in rinds and juice. Beat until light and fluffy. You may add one tablespoon vegetable shortening; it will make your icing fluffier. Spread on cake.

Note: The U.S.D.A warns that raw eggs have been found to contain salmonella bacteria and recommends eggs be cooked or that commercial egg substitutes be used.

Rayne Frog Festival, Rayne, LA

Many people consider frog legs a delicacy, and various preparations are based specifically upon the legs of three distinct species of frogs found in the United States. The majority of the catch is from Florida or Louisiana. At one time, Rayne was the leading U.S. exporter of frogs. Though that's no longer the case, Rayne still retains its title of "Frog Capital of the World." Frogs continue to be memorialized in the frog-themed murals painted on the sides of the town's buildings, as well as by the Frog Festival that attracts 40,000 visitors.

Everyone, it seems, goes frog-wild during the festivities. In addition to Cajun, zydeco, and country music, there's a parade honoring M'sieur Jacques, Rayne's favorite frog, a carnival, arts and crafts, and a Cajun folklore tent. Older residents reminisce about being taught as children how to handle a gig, a device used to capture bullfrogs, and how to skin and clean a frog.

Cajun food abounds, with fried frog legs and frog sauce piquant taking the spotlight. For those who prefer something more traditional, there are meat pies, jambalaya, seafood pistolettes, blooming onions, and barbecue. The festival's cooking contests garner the attention of many. The Barbecue Ribs and Rice Dressing Contest delivers ribs basted with the entrant's secret spices and seasonings, as well as delightful variations on that Southern favorite, rice dressing. There's also a general cooking contest with entries in numerous divisions including vegetables, meats, and desserts. The Frogs-n-Rice Cooking Contest brings out the best in the area's restaurant chefs whose work is taste-tested by celebrity chefs such as John Folse. Each year, the *Rayne Independent* publishes a cooking supplement with the winning recipes from the contests.

Fantastic Frog Puffs

Antonia T. Hoffpauir was a first-place winner in the Frog Festival Cooking Contest with this recipe that is reprinted with permission from the *Rayne Independent*.

1 cup flour
2½ teaspoons baking powder
1 teaspoon salt
½ teaspoon black pepper
½ teaspoon onion powder
2 eggs, separated
¾ cup milk
1 tablespoon vegetable oil
2 cups frog meat from legs (or use chicken)
2 cups cooked rice
¼ cup minced green onion tops
Dash of Tabasco
Oil for frying

Sift together dry ingredients. Beat egg yolks, milk, and vegetable oil until blended. Add to dry ingredients and beat until blended. Stir in frog meat, rice, and green onion tops. Beat egg whites until stiff. Fold into batter. Add Tabasco to taste. Drop by tablespoons into oil heated to 375° in a deep fryer. Fry until golden and puffy, 3–4 minutes, turning once. Drain on paper towels. Serve piping hot.

Roberts Cove Germanfest, Roberts Cove, LA

About five miles north of Rayne, Louisiana, lies Roberts Cove, a small German settlement with roots sunk firmly into this predominantly Acadian area. The town was founded in the early 1880s when Father Peter Leonard Thevis, pastor of Holy Trinity Church in New Orleans, founded the parish and sent word to families in Germany to come establish homes.

Today, the residents of Roberts Cove celebrate their German heritage with an annual festival begun in 1995. Dancers travel from near and far to dance the polka in traditional German costumes. Tents throughout the grounds house German heritage exhibits and demonstrations such as the making of sausage, sauerkraut, and the accordion.

At the food pavilion, visitors are overwhelmed with the tantalizing choice of foods. There are no commercial vendors here—everything is prepared by folks in the community. Wurst, or sausage, served on a bun or stick and sauerkraut are favorites for some, while others prefer chewy, freshly baked pretzels. There are hundreds of German cookies like *spekulatius* (spice cookies), and *platzkas* (sugar cookies) along with homemade apple *kuchen*, or cake. Few can resist the temptation of the festival's delicious potato stew flavored with sausage.

Recipes and Remembrances is a delightful cookbook produced by the ladies of Roberts Cove in honor of their German heritage and forebears. The book is a composite of traditional German recipes presented alongside Cajun specialties and just plain American fare, a culinary portrait of Roberts Cove itself set amid the diversity of Southern Louisiana.

Saturday and Sunday of the First Full Weekend in October

Kartoffell Wurst Schmoren
Potato Sausage Stew

Featured in *Recipes and Remembrances*, this recipe was contributed by Antonia Thevis Hoffpauir, a cook whose creativeness also garnered her first place in the Rayne Frog Cooking Contest.

2 pounds smoked sausage
1 cup water
1 large onion, diced
10 large red potatoes, cubed
2½ cups water
¼ cup chopped green onion tops
¼ cup chopped parsley
Salt and pepper to taste

Slice sausage into one-inch pieces and put in a large pot with one cup of water. Boil until the water evaporates and sausage browns in its own grease. Add chopped onions and sauté until transparent. Add the cubed potatoes and 2½ cups water. Bring to a boil, then reduce heat. Add onion tops and parsley. Cover and simmer for about 45 minutes or until potatoes are tender, stirring frequently to prevent sticking. Serves: 6–8.

Tee Mamou-Iota Mardi Gras Folklife Festival, Iota, LA

The old Bourgeois General Store, built in 1914, still stands on Main Street in Iota, Louisiana. Today, it is the American Legion Hall, but it still bears a symbol of times past with its mural of a long-ago Tee Mamou Mardi Gras scene. Revived in the 1950s, the roots of this street festival date to medieval times, and every effort is put forth to retain the old Mardi Gras, or Fat Tuesday, traditions. Tee Mamou Mardi Gras groups, some one hundred strong, arrive at the festival with everyone wearing colorful handmade screen masks, *capuchons* (hats), and costumes. Onlookers thrill to the spirited singing of their 400-year-old chant in French. On the main festival stage, the singing and dancing continues in this last of the totally traditional Prairie Cajun Mardi Gras celebrations. The Cajun Ladies are seniors dancing in full Cajun dress, including bonnets. Various zydeco dancers and the Cajun French Music Association's Cajun Dance Troupe are featured. Louisiana folk-craft demonstrations include the construction of musical instruments, Cajun cooking, quilting, costume making, and duck callers. The food is pure old-line Cajun produced by locals. There's no room for fast food here. No one misses it with a menu consisting of boudin, gumbo, sauce piquant, crawfish étouffée, jambalaya, boiled crawfish, fried alligator, cracklins (thin slices of salt pork or fat back cooked until crisp), pralines, cane syrup pies, and Cajun doughnuts. The official cookbook of the Tee Mamou Mardi Gras Folklife Festival was compiled by the alumni of St. Francis School in Iota. It is filled with many of the traditional Prairie Cajun dishes enjoyed at the festival and, like the celebration itself, represents an effort to preserve the best of the past while enjoying the benefits of the present.

French Market Beignets

From the *St. Francis School Alumni Cookbook* comes this renowned Louisiana recipe contributed by Judy Doucet Breaux.

1½ cups warm water
1 package active dry yeast
½ cup sugar
1 teaspoon salt
2 large eggs
1 cup undiluted evaporated milk
7 cups flour
¼ cup vegetable shortening
Oil for frying
Powdered sugar

Mix warm water and yeast in a large bowl and stir until dissolved. Add sugar, salt, eggs, and evaporated milk. Gradually stir in 4 cups flour and beat until smooth and blended. Beat in shortening and add rest of flour, ⅓ cup at a time. It will get too stiff to stir, so work in with your hands. Cover with plastic wrap and refrigerate overnight. Dough keeps for a week. Roll out on floured board to a thickness of ⅛ inch. Cut rectangles 2½ inches by 3½ inches with a sharp knife. Heat oil to 360° and deep-fry the beignets. They are done when puffed out and golden brown. Sprinkle with powdered sugar. Serve hot.

The Great Louisiana BeerFest, Covington, LA

When the Mystic Krewe of Brew Club of Mandeville, Louisiana decided to hold an annual beer tasting festival, they cast about for a worthy nonprofit organization to host and sponsor the event. From among the many contenders, they chose the St. Tammany Humane Society. This organization works tirelessly in its efforts to provide shelter for homeless animals and to fund low-cost sterilization and vaccination programs for the pets of St. Tammany Parish. As a "no kill" shelter, all animals remain residents of the shelter until they are adopted into good homes.

A few thousand people annually crowd the Northpark Corporate Center near Covington to try out new brews and help their furry friends. All proceeds from The Great Louisiana BeerFest are donated to the St. Tammany Humane Society. In its first year, thirteen thousand dollars was raised. Tickets are sold in advance or at the door.

Accompanied by live entertainment, attendees stroll from station to station, hosted by craft breweries, microbreweries, and brew pubs, tasting their choices from a selection of over one hundred ales and beers. Those with an adventurous nature check out the home-brewing kits, which are demonstrated, while others purchase BeerFest T-shirts and posters.

Local restaurants sell specialty foods, including such Louisiana favorites as beer-battered catfish or jambalaya. Beer, of course, is a featured ingredient for many of the dishes like baked eggplant and barbecued crab claws that have become popular with festival attendees. For those who insist upon a doggie bag, there are dog biscuits to go.

Changes Yearly— Usually Late October or Early November

BBQ Crab Claws

Abita Beer in Abita Springs, LA, provided this medal-winning recipe.

For each serving:
1 tablespoon unsalted butter
1 teaspoon finely chopped garlic
1 teaspoon Creole seasoning blend
4 dashes worcestershire sauce
1 sprig fresh rosemary
¼ pound crab claws
2 ounces shrimp stock
2 ounces amber beer
1 tablespoon unsalted butter

In a saucepan, place 1 tablespoon butter, garlic, Creole seasoning, Worcestershire sauce, and rosemary. Place over high heat and when the butter melts, add the crab claws and sauté. Deglaze with shrimp stock and beer and reduce sauce. Remove from heat, allow to cool slightly, and add remaining butter to make a smooth sauce. Serves: 1.

World Championship Crawfish Étouffée Cook-Off, Eunice, LA

Cajun culture is at the heart of the World Championship Crawfish Étouffée Cook-Off held every year in Eunice, Louisiana. Musicians from throughout the state provide Cajun and zydeco music as the perfect backdrop to the friendly competition of this event that is held at the Northwest Community Center.

Teams compete to produce the best crawfish étouffée in amateur, professional, and club or organizational categories, walking off with both bragging rights and unique trophies decorated with popular symbols of Louisiana, such as rice or the crawfish itself. All participants are asked to use only Louisiana-grown crawfish, and most go so far as to use homegrown rice as well. No other food is sold until judging is completed and all teams have sold their étouffée. Attendees get a great bargain, buying as many different samples as they want for only a dollar a cup. With no admission fee, it's likely that this is one of the best buys in Louisiana.

Betty's Crawfish Étouffée

Armed with this unique recipe, Betty Pousson of Eunice, LA, is always a hands-down winner of étouffée contests.

2 large onions, chopped
1 clove garlic, chopped
½ cup butter
1 can cream of mushroom soup, undiluted
1 can cream of celery soup, undiluted
1 (10-ounce) can RO*TEL tomatoes
2 pounds shelled crawfish
1 bunch green onion tops, chopped
1 bunch of parsley, chopped
Cooked rice

Sauté onion and garlic in butter until tender. Add soups and RO*TEL tomatoes and simmer for 30 minutes. Add remaining ingredients and cook no more than 30 minutes longer. Serve over rice. Serves: 6–8.

The Last Sunday in March Except Easter Sunday When Festival is Moved Up One Sunday

Maryland

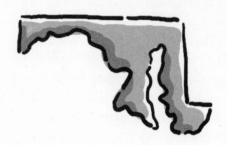

Although industrial growth has tied Maryland economically to the northeastern states, it is firmly rooted in the South when it comes to food and cooking. Maryland's coastal waters, accessed by over 3,000 miles of shoreline that comprise the arms and inlets of Chesapeake Bay, deliver blue crabs, clams, oysters, shrimp, and a plethora of fish. The livestock industry produces poultry, as well as hogs that supply the famous smoked hams. Historic restaurants and food festivals serve up plenty of Southern cuisine based on time-honored and traditional recipes handed down through families for hundreds of years. Food and entertaining here is Southern hospitality with the unique stamp of Maryland.

Crab Days and Oysterfest, St. Michaels, MD

The village of St. Michaels, Maryland, is located on a spit of land that juts from the Delmarva Peninsula far out into the waters of the eastern portion of Chesapeake Bay. It is home to the Chesapeake Bay Maritime Museum, which preserves and honors the area's rich seafaring heritage.

In an effort to educate the public on nature's rich bounty, the museum holds two annual festivals: Crab Days and Oysterfest. Nominal admission fees are charged for both events, which are a satisfying combination of food, fun, and education.

America's favorite crustacean is shrimp, closely followed by crab. In the eastern part of the United States, crabs from Maryland's Chesapeake Bay are the most revered. According to John Mariani in *The Encyclopedia of American Food and Drink*, crab cakes, a dish now featured throughout the United States, were first mentioned in print in Crosby Gaige's 1939 *New York World's Fair Cook Book*, where they were called "Baltimore Crab Cakes," no doubt an indication that they had long been enjoyed throughout communities along Maryland's shores.

Crab Days features crab potting demonstrations, boat rides, musical entertainment, and children's activities. The Best-Ever Crab Recipe Contest

calls for advance recipe submissions in categories of appetizers, soups, salads, and main courses. Three are chosen for preparation at the festival. Attendees can ward off hunger induced by fresh Bay breezes with steamed crabs, crab cakes, Maryland crab soup, and soft-shelled crab sandwiches.

Mariani also notes that oysters were a staple in the diet of the Native Americans, and early European explorers were awestruck when confronted with oysters up to a foot in length. Oyster cultivation became an early occupation among immigrants to the Chesapeake Bay region. Since 1632, Maryland and Virginia have waged "oyster wars" over offshore beds.

For decades, it was considered fashionable to consume prodigious quantities of oysters. Diamond Jim Brady, a wealthy financier of the late nineteenth century, has perhaps gone down in history as much for his consumption of three to four dozen oysters a day as for his financial expertise. Today's Oysterfest continues to extol the virtues of the mollusk, though perhaps on a more modified scale. Activities include

Crab Days
the First Weekend
in August
—
Oysterfest
the First Saturday
in November

tonging and nippering for oysters, boat rides with simulated oyster purchases, educational presentations by the museum's curator, carving demonstrations, and an oyster-shell stripping contest. Raw and steamed oysters are served along with oyster fritters, fried oysters, and oyster stew.

At both festivals, the Chesapeake Bay Maritime Museum sells copy after copy of its cookbook *From A Lighthouse Window*, a publication filled with seafood recipes including those for crab and oysters.

The Classic Crab Cake

From *A Lighthouse Window*, reprinted with permission from the Chesapeake Bay Maritime Museum.

1 egg
2 heaping tablespoons mayonnaise
1 heaping teaspoon prepared yellow mustard
1 tablespoon cream
Salt and pepper to taste
1 slice bread, toasted and crumbled
1 teaspoon chopped fresh parsley
½ teaspoon Worcestershire sauce
1 pound fresh crabmeat
Cooking oil

Mix all ingredients except crab. Stir in crab and form into patties. Fry in oil until golden brown, 5 minutes on each side. Serves: 2.

Oyster-Artichoke Pan Roast

From *A Lighthouse Window*, reprinted with permission from the Chesapeake Bay Maritime Museum.

1 (14-ounce) can artichoke hearts, drained and quartered
¼ cup butter
1 cup chopped scallions
½ cup chopped onion
1 clove garlic, minced
3 tablespoons flour
1 quart (4 cups) fresh oysters with their liquor
½ cup chopped fresh parsley
1 teaspoon Worcestershire sauce
1 tablespoon lemon juice
¼ teaspoon Tabasco sauce
½ teaspoon salt
2 tablespoons butter or margarine
1 cup fresh bread crumbs

Preheat oven to 350°. Cover artichoke hearts with water and bring to a simmer. Keep warm. Heat ¼ cup butter in medium skillet and sauté scallions, onions, and garlic until tender. Sprinkle on flour and sauté another 3 minutes to cook flour. While vegetables are cooking, poach oysters in their liquid, adding water if necessary, until edges curl and they plump up. Drain oysters, reserving liquid. Add 1–1½ cups of oyster liquid to vegetables. Add parsley, Worcestershire sauce, lemon juice, Tabasco sauce, and salt. Simmer until thickened. Place oysters and artichokes in a shallow casserole and cover with sauce. Melt 2 tablespoons butter in skillet and toss with bread crumbs until coated. Sprinkle over casserole. Bake for 15–20 minutes until crumbs are browned and sauce is bubbly. Serves: 4.

Note: Dish can be produced with half the oysters.

J. Millard Tawes Crab and Clam Bake, Crisfield, MD

The approach to Crisfield, located on Maryland's Eastern Shore, is clearly marked by its water tower that sports a bright red crab. Indeed, this tiny town of around 2,500 bills itself as the "Softshell Crab Capital of the World." Before World War II, Crisfield was connected by rail to major cities like New York and Philadelphia and was home to numerous industries ranging from oystering to beef processing. As trucks replaced railroads and Chesapeake Bay oysters were eradicated by disease, Crisfield found itself isolated and dependent upon seasonal crabbing as its major occupation. Crisfield is credited with the birth of the soft-shell crab industry, begun in the nineteenth century. To promote the crab industry and celebrate its seafood heritage, Crisfield hosts two festivals each year, the J. Millard Tawes Crab and Clambake in July, and the National Hard Crab Derby on Labor Day Weekend. The Crab and Clambake was begun in 1979 to help fund the J. Millard Tawes Museum. Tawes was the fifty-fourth Governor of Maryland and a Crisfield native. In true political tradition, the event is attended by numerous Maryland politicians, especially during a campaign year, who come to shake hands with potential supporters. Sponsored by the Crisfield Area Chamber of Commerce, the J. Millard Tawes Crab and Clam Bake is a somewhat exclusive event. Admission is by advance reservation only and limited to 5,000, who shell out thirty dollars per ticket. But its an "All You Can Eat" feast with steamed crabs, corn on the cob, fresh fried fish, onion rings, french fries, and steamed, raw, and fried clams. Serving is 1:00 to 5:00 P.M. Helen Avalynne Tawes, wife of the governor, was born and raised in Crisfield. An accomplished cook, she extolled the virtues of Maryland food and earned a reputation for serving elegant dishes at the governor's mansion. Her recipes are preserved in *My Favorite Maryland Recipes*, published at the insistence of Bennett Cerf.

Chesapeake Bay Soft-Shell Clam Fritters

From *My Favorite Maryland Recipes* by Helen Avalynne Tawes. Copyright 1964 by Helen Avalynne Tawes. Used with permission from the publisher.

2 cups clams, fresh or canned
2 eggs
½ cup milk
1½ cups flour
2 teaspoons baking powder
Salt and pepper to taste
Dash of cayenne

The Third Wednesday in July

Drain clams and chop them. Beat eggs until light, add milk; sift flour and baking powder, and beat into the eggs and milk. Add chopped clams, then add seasonings. Drop mixture into deep, hot fat and fry until golden brown. Drain and serve. Serves: 8.

St. Mary's County Oyster Festival, Leonardtown, MD

A drive south from Maryland's current capital of Annapolis leads to Southern Maryland and the charming western shore of the Chesapeake Bay. Travelers come to tour the waterside towns, as well as historic St. Mary's City, the original state capital. Come October, nearly everyone is headed for the annual Oyster Festival held at the county fairgrounds south of Leonardtown. This event celebrates the opening of the Chesapeake's fall oyster season.

Established in 1967 as a country festival, the event has grown over the years and now attracts about 25,000 guests over two days. Two stages keep everything lively with continuous entertainment, including orchestra, bluegrass, popular, and jazz music. Kid's rides, carnival games, a huge flea market, and local arts and crafts offer something for everyone. There are exhibit buildings and a farm museum building with memorabilia. Free oyster-shucking lessons are provided by men and women who make their living oystering, crabbing, and fishing the waters of the Chesapeake Bay and its tributaries.

Oystermania prevails with Maryland oysters found in every possible form— fried, stewed, and nude. A local favorite is scalded oysters. There is also a choice of fried and steamed clams, crab cakes, a lovely softshelled crab sandwich, shrimp, fried catfish, and a tangy seafood chowder.

The National Oyster Shucking Championship Contest is held both days with skilled champions from ten oyster-producing states competing for the national title. Cash prizes are awarded to the six finalists in both men's and women's divisions. A final battle ensues when the women's finalist competes against the male finalist for the grand prize consisting of cash and an all-expenses-paid trip to Galway, Ireland, to represent the U.S. as national champion.

Saturday and Sunday of the Third Weekend in October

On Saturday, the National Oyster Cook-Off features nationwide finalists competing for prizes in four fresh-oyster cooking contests: main dish, hors d'oeuvres, soups and stews, and outdoor cooking and salads. The top winners in each category are judged for the best overall recipe. Early visitors to the cook-off have the opportunity to taste-test contestant's dishes. Often, past winners and renowned chefs are on hand to demonstrate and prepare their favorite oyster dishes.

Volunteers from local nonprofit organizations sell regional specialty dishes including barbecued chicken, beef, and pork. Foremost among such offerings are sandwiches made with St. Mary's County stuffed ham, a savory preparation unique to the area. For over 300 years, special country cured, or corned, hams have been stuffed with greens and flavored with red pepper, then presented as the traditional centerpiece on holidays. Some believe the preparation was brought to America by English colonists in the 1600s. Others believe that it originated at a Jesuit retreat known as St. Inigoes Manor, where it was created as an Easter dish for the priests.

Stuffed hams are serious business in this part of the country, where a contest is held annually at the St. Mary's County Fair. It is said that folks can tell from what part of the county one hails simply by sampling a slice of stuffed ham. According to experts, upper-county folks stuff their hams with kale while those in the lower county prefer cabbage. Terri Taylor, wife of Oyster Festival Administrator David Taylor, judiciously uses a mixture of both. The Taylors have produced a video series entitled *The Traditions Cooking Series,* which documents the technique for stuffed ham as well as other historic regional fare based on oysters and crabs. The videos are available by mail. Corned hams are produced by Esskay, a commercial packing house in Baltimore. The annual cookbook, *Award Winning Recipes from St. Mary's County National Oyster Cook-Off,* as well as the *Special 20th Anniversary Cookbook,* are available through the festival office.

Fiesta Oyster 'N Corn Chowder Olé

Shirley DeSantis of Bethlehem, PA, was the 1988 Grand Prize Winner of the National Oyster Cook-Off and St. Mary's County Oyster Festival.

4 cups milk
1 (3-ounce) package cream cheese, cubed
1 (15-ounce) can cream-style corn
6 strips bacon, diced
1 onion, chopped
4 medium potatoes, cooked, peeled, and diced
1 (4-ounce) can chopped green chilies, drained and divided
½ teaspoon seasoned salt
⅛ teaspoon cayenne pepper
1 quart (4 cups) oysters
½ cup sour cream

Place milk in a large saucepan and slowly bring to a boil; lower heat. Add cream cheese cubes and corn. Cook, stirring often, over low heat until cream cheese has melted. Set aside.

In a small skillet, cook bacon and onions until bacon is crisp; drain off excess bacon fat and discard. Add bacon, onions, and potatoes to milk mixture. Reserve 2 to 3 teaspoons green chilies for topping. Add remaining green chilies to milk mixture along with seasoned salt and cayenne pepper. Heat through. Taste and adjust seasonings if necessary.

Drain the oysters, add to hot soup, and cook just until edges of oysters curl. Ladle soup into bowls. Top each serving with a dollop of sour cream and scatter reserved chilies over sour cream. Serves: 6–8.

Southern Maryland Stuffed Ham

Terri Taylor of Phocus Videotape Productions, Lexington Park, MD, has devoted enormous time and effort to preserving the traditional cooking and foodways of Maryland. Her research uncovered this treasured recipe.

3 medium cabbages
4–5 pounds kale (or 8 boxes frozen, chopped
  kale, thawed and drained)
3 bunches green onions
3 pounds yellow onions
1 bunch celery
3 tablespoons crushed red pepper
1 tablespoon ground red pepper
2 tablespoons mustard seed
2 tablespoons celery seed
1 tablespoon ground mustard
4 tablespoons salt
1 (20-pound) corned ham

If using all fresh vegetables, you may parboil them for a couple of minutes and drain. Chop the vegetables into small pieces. Mix spices together. Combine all ingredients except ham in a large bowl.

Cut slits into the ham, piercing almost all the way through the ham. Stuff the dressing into the holes, packing in as much as possible without rupturing the slits. Place any remaining dressing on top of the ham. Wrap securely in cheesecloth.

Place the wrapped ham in a very large pot of hot water and bring to a boil. Simmer for 20 minutes to the pound. Alternatively, wrap the stuffed ham in cheesecloth, then in heavy-duty foil. Place in a preheated 350° oven and bake for 20 minutes to the pound or about 7 hours.

Mississippi

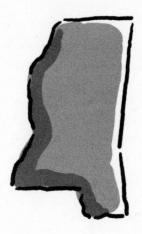

  Mississippi has worked hard to diversify its prominently agricultural economy. It has successfully added manufacturing, services, and communications industries to an ever-increasing roster. But farmland covers half the state, and in Mississippi's alluvial plain along the western edge of the state, an area known as the Delta, farmers have found a new use for their land. Cotton fields have been converted into catfish farming ponds, and around 91,000 acres are devoted to the business. Mississippi catfish farming, which produces seventy-two percent of the nation's catch, has spawned new jobs and new businesses. No wonder that Mississippians are constantly heard boosting their favorite fish. Sales slogans like "It's good eatin' and good for you!" are bolstered by state license tags bearing the message "Eat More Catfish." The Catfish Institute is quick to point out that "You don't have to fry it to love it" and lists numerous methods of preparation. Even Mississippi catfish paté is now marketed. Higher in protein than most meats, farm-raised catfish are described as tasting sweet, like pecans, and are rated as far superior to their muddy river cousins.

World Catfish Festival, Belzoni, MS

Anyone who has done even a modest amount of traveling in the South most likely has memories of seeing solitary individuals or even entire families quietly fishing the lakes, rivers, and streams. Some folks fish from the waters' edge, others dangle poles from high atop a bridge, and still others head out to deeper water via pirogue, canoe, or even a fancy powerboat. Although a great variety of fish are to be found in southern waters, it's a "good mess of catfish" that is commonly on the day's agenda.

Long considered "Southern food," catfish have begun to appear regularly in grocery stores and seafood markets throughout the United States—all thanks to the efforts of one J. B. Williams, who dug his first catfish pond in Humphreys County, Mississippi, back in 1965. At that time, Humphreys County was just another economically blighted area in the Mississippi Delta. Williams and those who followed his example could only hope that their efforts would turn a modest profit.

With guidance and assistance from the Mississippi Cooperative Extension Service and other far-sighted agencies, the fledgling catfish farmers

quickly established themselves as leaders in an exciting new industry that was to transform the economy of the area by literally giving birth to the farm-raised catfish business. Within just ten years, Humphreys County became the site of more acres of catfish ponds than anywhere else in the country, and in 1976, the area was aptly named "The Catfish Capital of the World." Today, the region lays claim to the title of global leader in the production of farm-raised catfish. In addition to sales throughout the United States, entry into European and Asian markets has made catfish a worldwide commodity.

And every year, come April, the folks down in Belzoni, Mississippi, "In the Heart of the Delta," hold their World Catfish Festival. Even when compared to the high standards set by the festival's organizers and the area's catfish farmers, this is a big deal, attracting some 30,000 visitors who come to learn, have fun and, of course, to eat catfish.

The South's Largest Catfish Fry is a sight to behold, featuring a deli-

First or Second Saturday in April, Depending upon Easter

cious lunch of fresh pond-raised and pan-fried catfish, golden hush puppies, and coleslaw the likes of which you can only obtain in Mississippi. And as they say down in Belzoni, "If you're hungry for a little competition, you can even throw your napkin into the ring at the Catfish Eating Contest." Each contestant is given three pounds of fried catfish and challenged to plow through as much as possible in ten minutes. The record to date is three pounds in only eight minutes!

Anyone not up to the rigors of the contest will find lots of other entertainment, including the crowning of the Catfish Queen, catfish farming displays, and a visit to the Catfish Capitol Museum. There, the Catfish Women of America, a group of hardworking catfish farmer's wives, can be found performing the duties of official hostesses and serving up samples of—what else?—catfish. Several bands provide musical entertainment, and over 200 arts and crafts booths provide shopping opportunities. The Catfish Institute holds a Celebrity Chef's Cook-Off from 11:00 A.M. to 1:00 P.M., where cooks can learn creative ways to prepare their favorite fish.

Once visitors discover the delights of catfish, the festival's cookbook is a must. Loaded with Southern delights, it includes a chapter on cooking catfish. It was compiled with recipes from past patrons and winners of Catfish Cooking Contests.

Catfish Lafitte

Chef Michael Marcello of the Downtown Grill in Oxford, MS, created this award-winning recipe recognized by the Catfish Institute.

Oil for frying
1 cup flour
1 teaspoon salt
½ teaspoon cayenne pepper
1 egg blended into ½ cup milk
4 catfish fillets

Sauce:
12 uncooked deveined shrimp (3 per fillet)
4 tablespoons melted butter
2 teaspoons chopped garlic
24 strips of ham (6 per fillet) (optional)
¼ cup dry vermouth
2 cups heavy cream
5 tablespoons chopped green onions
5 lemon wedges
Salt to taste
4 teaspoons cayenne pepper (or less, to taste)
4 sprigs parsley

Heat oil in deep fat fryer to 360°. Combine flour, salt, and cayenne in a bowl. Dredge fillets first in flour, then in the egg wash and then in the flour again. Drop fillets one or two at a time into hot oil and fry until golden brown, about 5–6 minutes per side. Keep cooked fillets warm in oven.

While frying catfish, sauté shrimp in butter until light pink on both sides (do not overcook). Add garlic, ham, and vermouth and bring to a boil. Add heavy cream, 1 tablespoon of the green onions, and squeeze in juice from 1 lemon wedge. Add salt and cayenne pepper to taste Continue to boil for 1–2 minutes or until cream is reduced. Place each catfish fillet on a plate and arrange 3 shrimp in a row on top. Place ham strips in gaps between shrimp. Spoon sauce over fish and sprinkle remaining green onion on top. Garnish with lemon wedges and a sprig of parsley. Serves: 4.

North Carolina

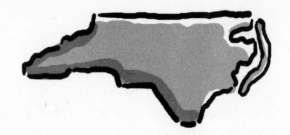

North Carolina's turkey industry, one of the largest in the country with production at some forty-one million turkeys, brings in $475 million annually. The state's seafood production pales in comparison with a value of around $100 million, but that is not a figure to take lightly. Shellfish and fish which account for that figure include valuable catches of blue crabs, clams, and shrimp. North Carolinians are so proud of these two important industries that they hold festivals honoring both the turkey and seafood.

North Carolina Seafood Festival, Morehead City, NC

Friday through Sunday of the First Weekend in October

The North Carolina Seafood Festival just keeps growing and growing. First organized in 1987, it is now the second largest festival in the state. Not bad for a festival that depends upon the efforts of more than 1,500 volunteers from civic, nonprofit, and church organizations in Carteret County to make it happen year after year.

The Seafood Festival was established to recognize the importance of the fishing industry in eastern North Carolina and to promote the wide variety of seafood indigenous to the area's coastline. Without Carteret County's fishing fleet, the availability of fresh fish and shellfish in grocery stores and restaurants throughout the state, as well as the country, would be greatly impacted. With this in mind, the festival serves as a tribute to the men and women who risk their lives to make a living from the sea. The emotional Blessing of the Fleet, held on Sunday morning at the North Carolina State Port waterfront, recognizes the many who have given their lives in their occupation and thanks those who continue in the industry today.

Education is a major facet of the Seafood Festival that provides interactive exhibits and demonstrations. The heritage of North Carolina's coast is carried on by a host of craftsmen who demonstrate skills of yesterday and today, including boat building, net hangers, crab-pot makers, decoy carvers, and oar makers. Top entertainment is featured on three stages with both country and pop music. A special treat is the traditional music of the Menhaden Chanteymen, the rugged sailors who worked the seas pulling nets filled with the day's catch aboard the first commercial fishing boats. Ship tours, arts and crafts, rides, street dances, and a host of sporting events round out the activities.

Seafood sampling is a major form of recreation at the festival. On Friday night, the traditional fish fry prepared by the Crystal Coast Habitat for Humanity is held. Saturday and Sunday feature nearly seventy booths sponsored by restaurants, civic groups, and nonprofit organizations, all featuring their own interpretation of North Carolina's best bounty from the sea. Some of the offerings are common and others are for the more adventuresome. Choices range from "Down East" clam chowder, shrimp burgers, oyster fritters, fresh clams, soft crab sandwiches, and charcoal mullet to calamari, marinated eel, and sea urchin on a stick.

Beaufort Bisque

This recipe is traditional in Beaufort, North Carolina, a town near Morehead City. Its historic waterfront and excellent seafood are a major tourist attraction. Recipe courtesy of North Carolina Seafood Festival.

8 ounces scallops
8 ounces shrimp, peeled and deveined
1 tablespoon lemon juice
1 small onion, finely chopped
½ rib celery, chopped
3 tablespoons butter
3 tablespoons flour
3 cups fish stock or light chicken stock, heated
¼ teaspoon ground fennel seeds (optional)
Salt and pepper to taste
1 cup milk, light cream or heavy cream, heated
¼ cup sherry
½ teaspoon sweet Hungarian paprika
1 tablespoon chopped parsley

In a large skillet, combine the scallops, shrimp, and lemon juice with water to cover. Cover with waxed paper. Bring to a boil and remove from heat. Let stand for 1 minute. Remove seafood with a slotted spoon, straining and reserving the cooking liquid. In a saucepan, sauté onion and celery in butter for 4 minutes. Sprinkle with flour and cook for 1 minute, stirring constantly. Whisk in the stock and reserved cooking liquid. Season with fennel, salt, and pepper. Cook for 8 minutes over low heat, stirring constantly. Stir in the hot milk. Simmer for 3 minutes. Add seafood and simmer for 2 minutes. Stir in sherry and simmer for 2 minutes longer. Ladle into serving bowls and sprinkle with paprika and parsley.
Serves: 4–6.

Note: To make fish stock, place shrimp shells in a saucepan and cover with water. Simmer for 20 minutes and strain broth before using.

North Carolina Turkey Festival, Raeford, NC

In 1984, the residents of Hoke County, North Carolina, held their first festival, the Hoke Heritage Hobnob. Evaluating the results of that first event, someone came up with the suggestion that they ought to be honoring the turkey, which is one of North Carolina's largest commodites. Surprisingly enough, no one else had capitalized upon the idea even though there was a turkey cooking contest held every year in Raleigh. With Raeford located smack in the middle of turkey country, the theme was overwhelmingly adopted. Today, the festival serves as a major promotional instrument for America's number one culinary bird as the center of feasts other than Thanksgiving.

The local citizenry are assisted in their efforts by volunteers from nearby Fort Bragg who supply a lot of the muscle power required to pull off the event that attracts some 60,000 people over three days. The festival is family-oriented and includes numerous activities for children like story telling, pony rides, and a petting farm. Adults are attracted by the musical entertainment, a car show, and an arts and crafts show. Even man's best friend gets to participate—the Humane Society holds a dog show in the park on Saturday morning followed by a military dog show later in the afternoon. Sporting events like the Turkey Bowl Football Game draw a big crowd.

When it comes to food, everyone's talking turkey. Smoked turkey, barbecued turkey, turkey dogs, and turkey sausage all have their loyal fans. Some hold out for the Stuffin' and Stompin' Turkey Dinner and Dance held on Friday night.

The Turkey Cooking Contest, sponsored by the North Carolina Poultry Association, attracts the best cooks in the state, each of whom assumes control of a mini-kitchen in which to prepare what is hoped to be the winning dish. Previous winning recipes have included Carolina Turkey Calzones and Turkey-n-Vegetable Lasagna. The *North Carolina Turkey Festival Cookbook* contains recipes entered in the Turkey Cook-Off from 1985 to 1996. It is a testimonial to the versatility of turkey.

Having launched the cooking competition, the audience flocks to the Turkey Hoagie Brunch, an event inaugurated in 1997. Diners enthusiastically gobble up the featured entrée, "Tar Heel" marinated turkey breast steaks grilled to perfection.

Thursday through Saturday of the Third Full Weekend in September

Tar Heel Turkey Hoagies

Developed by Emmie Whitley, Marketing Home Economist, N.C. Poultry Federation and the North Carolina Turkey Festival, this is the world-famous specialty of the festival.

1½ pounds turkey tenderloins

Marinade:
½ cup lite soy sauce
¼ cup vegetable oil
2 teaspoons sugar
1 teaspoon ground ginger
1 teaspoon ground mustard
2 cloves garlic, minced
Hoagie rolls
Accompaniments such as lettuce, tomato, and
   onion
Dijonnaise dressing (optional)

   Cut tenderloins in half lengthwise. Place in a self-closing plastic bag. Combine marinade ingredients and mix well. Pour marinade over tenderloins and seal bag. Refrigerate at least 1 hour but no longer than 10 hours, turning occasionally. Drain and discard marinade.

   Oil or vegetable-spray the grill. Grill tenderloins five inches above hot coals for 3–5 minutes per side. For gas or electric grills, use a medium-high temperature. Turkey is done when thickest part is no longer pink or internal temperature is 160°. Do not overcook. Turkey will be juicy. Serve in hoagie rolls with accompaniments of choice such as lettuce, tomato, and onion. Serves: 6.

   Note: This sandwich is terrific served with Dijonnaise dressing made by combining ½ cup mayonnaise with 2 tablespoons Dijon mustard.

South Carolina

South Carolina boasts the only tea plantation in the contiguous forty-eight states. The Charleston Tea Plantation on Wadmalaw Island produces American Classic Tea. While no festival celebrates South Carolina tea, numerous events celebrate the state's agricultural heritage. In the 1920s, fruits and vegetables grown in South Carolina were thought to contain significantly higher quantities of iodine than those grown elsewhere. Thus, the state became known as the "Wonderful Iodine State." Capitalizing on this nickname, the call letters of WIS radio and WIS-TV stem from "Wonderful Iodine State." South Carolina grows many of the South's favorite foods, including okra and watermelon, ranking fifth in production nationally for the latter. Although non-Southerners may think that grits grow on trees, this Southern breakfast staple is actually coarsely ground corn. Corn that is grown in South Carolina often ends up at one of the old-time mills still in operation in the state that produce stone-ground grits.

Hampton County Watermelon Festival, Hampton County, SC

All of Hampton County gets involved in the annual Watermelon Festival, even though activities are mainly centered in the towns of Hampton and Varnville. Having started way back in 1939, it's the oldest continuing festival in South Carolina, celebrating the county's position as one of the state's top watermelon producers.

People from all over come to enjoy the Southern hospitality of the friendly people in the South Carolina Low Country where, for a week in June, King Watermelon reigns supreme. There's a huge, two-hour parade with over 200 marching units that begins in Varnville and winds its way to Hampton, two miles away. There's a watermelon-eating contest, plus a melon contest from which champion melons are chosen. There's also a decorated melon contest.

A Taste of Hampton County showcases more than a hundred specialty items prepared by cooks countywide. Recipes for representative dishes are annually gathered into a festival cookbook that generally sells out at the celebration itself. For watermelon lovers, free ice-cold watermelon slices are passed out on Saturday afternoon, and those with money to spend can purchase watermelon preserves and pickles.

Watermelon Salsa

Featured in *A Taste of Hampton County Recipes*, festival committee member Joyce Horres developed this recipe that has since become a popular regional specialty.

2 cups watermelon, seeded and coarsely chopped
2 tablespoons chopped onion
2 tablespoons chopped water chestnuts
2–4 tablespoons chopped chili peppers
2 tablespoons vinegar
¼ teaspoon garlic salt

Combine all ingredients and mix well. Refrigerate at least one hour. Serve with crackers. Yield: 2 cups.

Sunday through Sunday of the Last Full Week in June

Irmo Okra Strut, Irmo, SC

Irmo, South Carolina, is located just outside of Columbia, the state capital, and plenty of okra is grown in the area. In 1974, the Lake Murray/Irmo Women's Club needed to raise money for a branch library. When someone came up with the idea of an okra festival, a local disc jockey started joking about the "ancient Irmese" who would have survived on a diet of okra. Then a song called the "Okra Strut" was dredged up out of musical archives and the festival had its official name. The event now draws over 60,000 attendees.

Kicked off with the Okra Strut Golf Tournament on Thursday before the festival, things begin to heat up in a hurry. The Friday night street dance is followed by a Saturday morning parade, an arts and crafts show with vendors from all over the Southeast, and entertainment on two stages. The Irmo Dam Run has folks running across the Lake Murray Dam. For kids, there's an area called "Okryland."

With a distinctly Western theme, the Okra Corral offers all types of food, including specialties like boiled and fried okra. The okra-eating contest calls for a great deal of courage—not only is one expected to consume a truly respectable amount of the vegetable—the okra has been frozen and thawed, resulting in a plate filled with what one festival organizer refers to as "cold slime." Nevertheless, okra is a delicious and nutritious vegetable, and veteran attendees of the festival and its okra cooking contest say they are continually amazed by the different ways that contestants dream up for cooking okra. Although there is no festival cookbook, winning recipes are published by the local press.

Okra Crab Cakes with Cayenne Mayonnaise Appetizer

Mickey Clark has received repeated accolades for her winning entry in the okra cooking contest.

Cayenne Mayonnaise:
1 cup mayonnaise
1 teaspoon cayenne pepper
1 teaspoon horseradish

Okra Crab Cakes:
1 cup okra, sliced thin
Cornmeal
1 (8-ounce) can crabmeat
3 tablespoons mayonnaise
1 teaspoon chopped onion
5 crackers, crushed
¼ teaspoon Old Bay Seasoning
¼ teaspoon dry mustard
Salt and pepper to taste
Corn oil

Friday and Saturday during the Last Weekend in September

Mix all ingredients for mayonnaise and chill until Okra Crab Cakes are ready to serve.

Roll okra in cornmeal and brown in a nonstick skillet with no oil. Combine okra with rest of ingredients except corn oil and form into small cakes. Sauté the cakes in a few tablespoons corn oil until golden brown on both sides. If desired, cakes can be rolled in flour before they are sautéed. Serves: 2.

World Grits Festival, St. George, SC

Grits have been newly discovered. They are the darling of trendy restaurants who dress them up and charge exorbitant prices for dishes that invoke sighs of appreciation from initiates. But grits are nothing new to the folks of St. George, South Carolina, where, it is claimed, the population of around 2,000 consumes more grits per capita than anywhere else in the world. According to resident Nell Bennett, the local grocery store was once provisioned by no less than four major purveyors of grits, and while there are now only two such suppliers, sales have remained consistently high. Annual attendance at the World Grits Festival, ranging between 45,000 and 55,000 over the three days, offers further proof that the South stands by its traditional devotion to grits.

The World Grits Festival raises funds that are used to provide college scholarships for deserving students who have to work extra hard in their studies. It's well known as a fun, family-oriented event with activities that appeal to everyone: a parade, crafters, a carnival, puppet shows, street dances, clogging, square dancing, and gospel music. Competitions include corn tossing, corn shelling, and the Rolling in the Grits contest. The grits-eating contest requires that each entrant eat a measured amount of grits, which may be flavored with a choice of condiments such as honey, peanut butter, or ketchup. When done, each contestant holds the bowl over his or her head. The grits are specially cooked by Nell Bennett to insure that there are no lumps and that the grits are cooled enough to eat. Enthusiastic diners have never complained.

Visitors, however, don't have to enter the contest to enjoy grits at the festival. A tasting booth is set up where grits are cooked all day long and free samples of plain or cheese-flavored grits are passed out. The American Legionnaires serve breakfast, which consists of grits and sausage, grits and ham, grits and scrambled eggs, or grits with biscuits and red-eye gravy, made from ham drippings and flavored with coffee, and named for the "red eye" which appears in the middle of the reduced sauce. For lunch and dinner, grits again make their appearance, served alongside homey fried chicken, fish, or country fried steak and tomato gravy. The latter is a specialty of Southern mountain cooking and is based on a white sauce flavored with tomato juice. Home-ground grits are a favorite souvenir of the World Grits Festival.

Friday through Sunday on a Weekend in April, Depending upon Easter

Nell McKinnon's Cajun Grits Creole

Recipe reprinted with permission of Martha White®.

12 ounces bacon
½ cup chopped onion
½ cup chopped celery
½ cup chopped green pepper
½ pound raw shrimp, cleaned and deveined
1 (14½-ounce) can chopped tomatoes, undrained
1 (4-ounce) can chopped mushrooms, drained
1 teaspoon sugar
1 teaspoon Worcestershire sauce
½ teaspoon salt
½ teaspoon chili powder
¼ teaspoon garlic powder
Dash or more of hot sauce, to taste
2 tablespoons Martha White® All-Purpose Flour
2 cups water
½ cup Martha White's Jim Dandy Quick Grits®
½ teaspoon salt

Preheat oven to 350°. Cook the bacon, drain, and crumble. Sauté the onion, celery, and green pepper in 2 tablespoons of the bacon drippings. Add shrimp and cook just until pink. Remove from heat and drain. Add tomatoes, mushrooms, half of the bacon, sugar, Worcestershire sauce, ½ teaspoon salt, chili powder, garlic powder, hot sauce, and flour.

Bring water to a boil in a saucepan. Slowly stir in grits and remaining ½ teaspoon salt. Cook 4–5 minutes, stirring occasionally. Combine the grits and shrimp mixture. Pour into a greased 2-quart baking dish and bake for 25 minutes. Garnish with remaining bacon and serve.
Serves: 6–8.

Tennessee

The lush flatlands of Western Tennessee, created by the Mississippi River's ancient floodplains, support row-crop agriculture. Lauderdale county is known for its tomatoes. Producers have long raised their own plant seedlings, and varieties are selected based on their positive impact upon establishing and keeping markets. And those markets stretch from Ann Arbor, Michigan, to Dallas, Texas, with plenty held back for local enjoyment. Predominant varieties include Mountain Fresh, Mountain Pride, Mountain Spring, and Mountain Supreme. In the eastern part of Tennessee, fertile river valleys are home to dairy farms and related agricultural production. Here, corn is raised primarily for feeding livestock, but plenty of sweet corn is grown for local consumption. Throughout the state, homage is paid to cornbread, the traditional "bread of the South."

Lauderdale County Tomato Festival, Ripley, TN

In 1984, the first Tomato Festival was held to salute the Lauderdale County tomato industry. The event now attracts about 7,000 visitors who come from Memphis and throughout West Tennessee. Growers show off their tomatoes, all of which are commonly known as "Ripley tomatoes," and attendees can taste and purchase their favorites to take home.

In 1994, the Tennessee Association for Family & Community Education (FCE) held its first Tomato Tasting. It has been such a success that organizers have found it necessary to relocate to larger quarters. For the price of a ticket, tomato lovers can taste a variety of tomato dishes prepared by the Extension Service of the University of Tennessee. Old favorites like Tennessee Cornbread Salad and Garlic Tomato Creamies make their appearance annually and are augmented by new dishes. To create additional interest, green tomatoes are fried on site, and the "garlic creamies" are made to order. Another traditional favorite is Green Tomato Pie, which was created by Terry Ford, editor of *The Enterprise*—folks claim it tastes just like apple pie! Two excellent cookbooks, *Lauderdale County Recipes Featuring Ripley Tomatoes—Volumes I and II*, compiled by the FCE Club, feature loads of interesting recipes.

Garlic Tomato Creamies

Jane H. Connell, University of Tennessee Extension Agent, created the recipe for this famous festival treat.

4 small, ripe tomatoes
16 rounds of crustless bread (tomato-slice size), toasted
1 cup mayonnaise
4 garlic cloves, minced
Chopped chives
8 slices crisply fried bacon, drained and crumbled

Core and cut each tomato into four slices. Put a slice on each piece of toast. Mix mayonnaise with garlic. Spread one tablespoon of the mixture on each tomato. Broil for 3 minutes or until browned and bubbly. Sprinkle with chives and bacon and serve immediately. Serves: 4.

Tennessee Cornbread Salad

Created by District 1 Extension Agents, this popular Tennessee dish is enjoyed by one and all at the festival.

1 (8-ounce) package white cornbread mix, prepared according to package directions
3 cups chopped tomatoes
½–1 cup chopped green peppers
1 cup chopped onions
½ cup chopped sweet pickles
12 strips bacon, cooked crisp and crumbled
1 cup mayonnaise
¼ cup sweet pickle juice

Crumble half the prepared cornbread into the bottom of a large serving bowl. In another bowl, combine tomatoes, green peppers, onions, pickles, and bacon. Spoon half of mixture over cornbread. Stir together mayonnaise and pickle juice. Spread half the dressing over vegetables. Repeat layers. Garnish as desired. Cover tightly and chill 2–3 hours before serving. Serves: 8.

National Cornbread Festival, S. Pittsburg, TN

Tennessee is cornbread country and some 22,000 folks from all over the United States have shown up each year since 1997 to check out what's cookin' in South Pittsburg.

Martha White®, the well-known Tennessee producer of flour and cornmeal, cosponsors the cornbread cook-off on Saturday. Ten finalists are chosen to cook their main dish cornbread recipes under a tent set up in the middle of town. Cook-off cosponsor Lodge Manufacturing, a South Pittsburg-based manufacturer of cast-iron cookware and the oldest such producer in the United States, ensures an ample supply of cooking vessels for contestants. As most everyone knows, it's preferable to bake cornbread, among a host of other dishes, in cast-iron and the folks at Lodge have gotten together with Chef John Folse to produce a wonderful cookbook, *Black Magic—100 Years of Cast Iron Cooking*.

The festival also showcases other traditional Southern fare with the likes of pinto beans, turnip greens, and the local fire department's famous barbecue providing the perfect accompaniments to cornbread. In addition to music, a car show, clowns, and magicians, several renowned artisans registered with Southern arts and crafts associations proffer their wares. A must-see is the working grist mill grinding corn.

Last Weekend in April or First Weekend in May

Chicken and Dressing Skillet Bake

Sue Gulledge of Springville, AL, won first place in the National Cornbread Festival Cook-Off with this recipe.

1 cup chopped celery
1 cup chopped onion
1/4 cup butter
1 tablespoon vegetable oil
2 cups buttermilk
2 eggs, beaten
1 (81/2-ounce) can cream-style corn
2 cups Martha White® Self-Rising Cornmeal Mix
2 teaspoons poultry seasoning
3 cups chopped, cooked chicken, seasoned with salt and pepper

Preheat oven to 450°. In a 10½-inch cast-iron skillet, cook celery and onion in butter until tender, about 10 minutes. Remove vegetables from skillet and place in a large bowl. Pour oil in same cast-iron skillet and place in oven to heat for about 5 minutes. Add remaining ingredients to vegetables in a large bowl; blend well. Pour cornbread batter into hot cast-iron skillet. Bake for 25–35 minutes or until golden brown. Cut into wedges. The dressing may be garnished with fresh sage leaves and served with quick chicken gravy (recipe follows). Serves: 6.

Note: If you like a more moist consistency, increase celery and onion to 2 cups each, sautéed in 6 tablespoons butter, and substitute 1 (14½-ounce) can cream-style corn. Bake in a 10½-inch cast-iron stew pot at 450° for 25 minutes; lower oven temperature to 375° and continue baking for 30 minutes or until center is firm and top begins to brown.

Quick Chicken Gravy

2 (14½-ounce) cans chicken broth
⅓ cup cold water
⅓ cup cornstarch
Gravy browning and seasoning sauce to taste
Salt and pepper to taste

Heat chicken broth to boiling. Mix together water and cornstarch and whisk into boiling broth. Bring back to a boil, lower heat to medium, and cook, stirring, for 2 minutes. Add gravy seasoning and salt and pepper to taste and simmer for another 3 minutes.

Virginia

Since 1980, the population of Virginia has increased sixteen percent, and three-fourths of the residents live in eight of the state's largest metropolitan areas. Millions of tourists annually swell the population even further and make a substantial contribution to the economy. The result is a very cosmopolitan consumer base that frequents the large number of restaurants, specialty food shops, and food festivals that have sprung up in recent years. Virginia has a diverse population and many of its ethnic groups, like African Americans and Lebanese, celebrate their heritage at annual festivals. Vegetable and fruit cultivation can be found throughout the state, and many growers are diversifying as a result of Virginia's alternative crop research. An increasingly large variety of garlic is an example of that new production.

Karla's Great Cheesecakes Open House, Fredericksburg, Virginia

In 1985, Karla Seidita, a former restaurateur and home economics teacher, established Karla's Great Cheesecakes with a tiny stand at the Old Town Farmer's Market in Alexandria, Virginia. Today, Karla operates a thriving wholesale and retail business, selling her famous cheesecakes from her country bakery in Fredericksburg to locals as well as throughout the country via mail order.

At one time, Karla held an annual Cheesecake Festival that started by accident. Operating as a wholesale outlet, Karla's bakery was located off the beaten path on an unpaved country road. When people started knocking at the door, insisting they be allowed to buy cheesecake, presto, she was in the retail business. One Saturday in October, when business was unusually slow, Karla put up a handwritten sign along the roadside that said "Cheesecake—Free Samples!—Drive In!" and the festival was born. It quickly grew from an initial attendance of twelve happy tasters to thousands of guests who came throughout the month of October to sample and to buy Karla's cheesecakes that include both sweet and savory categories.

Sadly, and to the disappointment of her many fans, Karla has had to cancel her Cheesecake Festival. It was just too successful, and Karla's little cottage on a third of an acre couldn't withstand the crowds. But, as always, Karla had a solution.

Although the majority of her business these days is wholesale, she throws open the doors of her cheesecake cottage to the general public during the holiday season that extends from the day after Thanksgiving right up to just before Christmas. From Tuesday through Saturday, adoring fans and newcomers can taste samples and purchase specialty cheesecakes, Karla's unique Cheesecake Truffles, and other homemade candies. Cheesecake flavors run the gamut from Creme Sickle, Pink Squirrel, and Lemon Creme to Cheddar and Herb, Spinach and Garlic, and Sun-Dried Tomato Pesto. Loaded down with delicious holiday treats, few people leave the shop without a copy of *Just Desserts*, a compendium of many of Karla's cheesecake and dessert recipes.

Karla's Great Cheesecakes is located at 41 Cool Springs Road, Fredericksburg, Virginia. The shop is open to retail customers year round on Thursdays and Fridays only from 10:00 A.M. to 4:00 P.M. From the day after Thanksgiving until just before Christmas, retail customers are welcomed to the weekly holiday open house Tuesday through Saturday.

Call (540) 371-3754 for hours.

> Tuesday through Saturday, Beginning the Day After Thanksgiving until Just before Christmas

White Chocolate Cheesecake

Karla Sedita, the undisputed queen of cheesecake, says this is her most-requested recipe.

12 ounces white chocolate
1¼ cups vanilla pound-cake crumbs (recipe follows)
1½ pounds cream cheese, softened
1 cup sugar
2½ teaspoons vanilla
1 tablespoon apricot brandy
2 cups sour cream

Melt white chocolate. Preheat oven to 350°. Prepare pound-cake crumbs by using a food processor. Distribute pound-cake crumbs evenly over bottom of a buttered 9-inch springform pan. Press crumbs down lightly. Set aside.

In a large bowl, cream together the cream cheese, sugar, vanilla, and apricot brandy with an electric mixer for at least five minutes or until very smooth. Add the melted white chocolate and blend another five minutes. Add the sour cream and mix to combine. Pour into crumb-lined pan and bake for 30–40 minutes, just until top begins to take on a light golden hue. Cool, then chill overnight or at least 8 hours before serving. The cheesecake will firm up in refrigerator.

Plain Good Vanilla Poundcake

¾ cup butter
1½ cups sugar
1 teaspoon vanilla
1½ cups flour
5 eggs

Preheat oven to 350°. Grease a 9-inch square pan. Using an electric mixer, in a large bowl cream together butter or margarine, sugar, and vanilla. Alternately add flour and eggs. After the last addition, beat at high speed for five minutes. Spread into prepared pan and bake for 40–50 minutes, until cake tests done. Cool in pan five minutes before removing.

St. Anthony's Lebanese Food Festival, Glen Allen, VA

This is the place for great Lebanese food. The ladies of St. Anthony's Maronite Church prepare a huge variety of authentic dishes. While many work up a healthy appetite dancing to Lebanese tunes, others attend cooking demonstrations by parish members. Specialties include shawirma—strips of marinated beef or chicken broiled over an open flame and served with tahini sauce on pita; bubbaghanooge-baked eggplant; stuffed squash—a festival favorite; and a huge array of Middle-Eastern sweets such as zalabia-fried strips of spiced dough served with a special syrup. After tasting the delights of this ancient cuisine, most attendees are determined to enjoy it year round and thus pick up a copy of *Favorites of the Lebanese Food Festival and Lebanese Cuisine.*

Shawirma with Tahini Sauce

This is a traditional Lebanese dish that has become a hands-down favorite at the Lebanese Food Festival. Reprinted with permission from *Favorites of the Lebanese Food Festival and Lebanese Cuisine.*

2 pounds beef (such as London broil) or lamb
½ cup vinegar
1 cup water
1 teaspoon salt
½ teaspoon ground cardamom
¼ teaspoon allspice
Pita bread
Chopped parsley
Chopped onions
Chopped tomatoes
Tahini sauce (recipe follows)

Always the Friday, Saturday, and Sunday after Mother's Day

Mix vinegar, water, and spices. Marinate meat in the mixture, refrigerated, overnight. Broil, basting with the juice. When meat is cooked, slice very thin and serve on a bed of rice or serve in pita bread with chopped parsley, onions, and tomatoes topped with Tahini Sauce.

Tahini Sauce
2 cloves garlic
1 teaspoon salt
½ cup tahini (ground sesame seeds)
½ cup water
½ cup lemon juice

Mash garlic and salt. Add tahini, mixing well. This will thicken. Gradually add water, blending thoroughly. Add lemon juice and mix well. The consistency of the sauce can be thicker or thinner by simply adjusting the amount of water and lemon juice accordingly. Let set for an hour or two before serving if possible.

Note: Tahini is found in the international section of supermarkets or in Middle-Eastern import shops.

Staunton's Annual African-American Heritage Festival, Staunton, VA

In 1989, a group of dedicated and determined volunteers got together to launch the first festival in western Virginia's Shenandoah Valley that celebrates African-American heritage.

The African-American Heritage Festival takes place in Gypsy Hill Park with most activities held outdoors under tents. Exhibits, music, and dance performances are supplemented by children's activities and arts and crafts vendors.

Breakfast and lunch are served with a variety of foods available, including many dishes traditionally associated with African-American culture. Popular items include country ham sandwiches, biscuits, chitterlings (small pieces of hog intestine coated and deep-fried), peanut pie, fried plaintains, fried chicken, various fish dishes, and hot dogs and hamburgers for less adventurous souls. Brunswick Stew, said to have originated at a political rally in Brunswick County, Virginia, in 1828, is favored by many.

Festival organizers are continuously adding attractions with both a cookbook and a cooking contest in the works.

Staunton Peanut Pie

Sergei Troubetzkoy of the Staunton Convention and Visitors Bureau provided the recipe for this festival specialty.

½ cup dark brown sugar, packed
1½ cups dark corn syrup
¼ cup butter
¼ teaspoon salt
3 eggs, well beaten
¼ teaspoon freshly grated nutmeg
1 tablespoon vanilla
1½ cups coarsely chopped, roasted Virginia peanuts
1 deep 9-inch piecrust, unbaked

Preheat oven to 400°. Combine brown sugar, corn syrup, butter, and salt. Bring mixture to a boil over low heat. Remove from heat and allow to cool for 5 minutes.

Stirring constantly, slowly add hot syrup to the beaten eggs. When completely blended, the mixture should be thick and smooth. Stir in nutmeg, then allow mixture to cool for a few minutes.

Add vanilla and peanuts and mix thoroughly. Pour mixture into the unbaked piecrust. Bake for 10 minutes at 400°, then reduce oven temperature to 375° and bake for an additional 40 minutes. Allow the pie to cool thoroughly before serving.

Note: The amount of filling in this recipe requires a very deep 9-inch pie crust.

Always Saturday and Sunday of the Third Weekend in September

Virginia Garlic Festival, Amherst, VA

A panoramic view of the Blue Ridge Mountains provides the perfect backdrop for the Virginia Garlic Festival. It was started in 1991 when a group of Virginia garlic growers got together and asked Richard and Ella Hanson of Rebec Vineyards to sponsor the event.

Amid a relaxed and fun atmosphere, families from other countries and dozens of states come to the Garlic Festival to enjoy special garlic foods and wines served up by vendors and five participating wineries. The "Most Odiferous Royalty of the Stinking Rose," otherwise known as the "King and Queen of Garlic," preside over their "stinking subjects."

In addition to music and nearly a hundred arts and crafts booths, there are herbal products and lots of garlic and garlic specialty foods for sale. The festival also features a garlic-eating contest, garlic games for kids, and a garlic cook-off with foods that include garlic as a major ingredient. Those folks who take their garlic seriously can attend an elaborate dinner and seminar on Saturday evening. Most attendees go home with a souvenir copy of *Virginia Wine & Garlic Gourmet—The Official Virginia Garlic Festival Cookbook* by Meg and Bill Hibbert.

Second Saturday & Sunday in October

Roast Garlic and Sun-Dried Tomato Bruschetta

Lanaux Hailey of Lynchburg, VA, was a winner in the Garlic Cook-Off with this creative entry. Reprinted with permission from *Virginia Wine & Garlic Gourmet—The Official Virginia Garlic Festival Cookbook* by Meg and Bill Hibbert.

3 ounces sun-dried tomatoes, steamed over boiling water for 3 minutes to rehydrate
⅓ cup olive oil, plus extra for brushing
6 large cloves elephant garlic
1 medium head regular garlic, plus 4 cloves
3 tablespoons fresh parsley
¾ teaspoon sugar
Black pepper to taste
1 loaf crusty bread
3 ounces goat cheese
2 tablespoons grated Parmesan cheese

Preheat oven to 350°. Cut the tops off the elephant garlic cloves and the whole head of garlic, leaving on the outer skin. Drizzle the olive oil over the garlic and place either in a terra-cotta garlic roaster or in aluminum foil. Bake for 40–50 minutes. Let cool so that you can handle the garlic. Squeeze the garlic pulp out of skins and discard skins. Place the garlic in a food processor bowl fitted with a steel blade. In the processor, purée the garlic with sun-dried tomatoes, the ⅓ cup olive oil, the parsley, sugar, and pepper.

Slice bread lengthwise and brush with olive oil. Finely chop the 4 remaining cloves of raw garlic and sprinkle on bread. Bake in a preheated 350° oven for 10–15 minutes. Remove from oven and spread with sun-dried tomato mixture. Crumble goat cheese over top. Sprinkle with Parmesan cheese and return to oven for 5 minutes, just to heat through.

Washington, D.C.

In 1829, a British scientist named James Smithson bequeathed his fortune to the United States for the purpose of establishing an organization for "the increase and diffusion of knowledge." The result was the Smithsonian Institution in Washington, D.C., a federally chartered, nonprofit organization composed of sixteen museums and galleries, as well as several research facilities in various locations around the globe.

The Smithsonian's Center for Folklife and Cultural Heritage researches folklife traditions in America and around the world in order to present the various facets of individual cultures from an educational perspective and to preserve such records for future generations. At the annual Folklife Festival held on the National Mall, artists, craftspeople, and musicians demonstrate their skills and artistry.

Festival of American Folklife, Washington, DC

Initiated in 1967 by the Smithsonian Institution, the Festival of American Folklife attracts millions of visitors to the National Mall. Visitors discover "a museum without walls" where they can become acquainted with the folkways, music, dancing, arts, and crafts of other nations as well as regional America and the ethnic diversity that makes up our country.

Each year's festival focuses on specific themes—a country, region, state, or a particular cultural group. In 1997, the Mississippi Delta and African Immigrant Folklife in Washington, D.C., were featured. In 1998, the state of Wisconsin, rich in ethnic makeup and foodways, was chosen. Anyone interested in cooking and food will be well rewarded. Ethnic and regional cooks abound, preparing specialties in live demonstrations and interweaving their instructions with anecdotes and stories that deliver a bit of living history. After sampling the various dishes, most visitors purchase traditional lunches, snacks, and dinners offered by vendors chosen to reflect the celebrated cuisines.

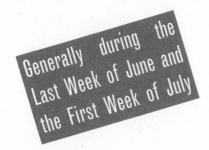

Generally during the Last Week of June and the First Week of July

Gouda Fondue with Beer or Wine

Shelley and Randy Krahenbuhl, both master cheesemakers, are the owners of Prima Kase, Inc., a cheese plant located in Monticello, WI. Shelley created this recipe, which was featured in the 1998 *Smithsonian Folklife Festival Cookbook*, and incorporates Prima Kase's 1998 World Champion Gouda Cheese.

Fondue:
1 pound Gouda cheese, cubed
3 tablespoons flour
1 garlic clove, halved
1 (12-ounce) can beer or 1½ cups wine (a dry white wine is recommended)
1 tablespoon spicy brown mustard (optional)

Dippers:
Unsliced rye bread, cut in 1-inch cubes and toasted
Blanched broccoli florets
Blanched cauliflower florets
Small red potatoes, cooked and halved or quartered

Blanch broccoli and cauliflower florets in a small amount of boiling water for 3 minutes or until tender but still crisp. Drain and rinse with cold water. Prepare potatoes.

Combine cheese and flour in a mixing bowl; toss to mix. Rub bottom and sides of a heavy saucepan with cut surface of garlic; discard garlic. Add beer or wine to the saucepan. Heat over low heat just until warm. Gradually add small amounts of the cheese and flour mixture, stirring constantly over low heat until all is melted. Stir in mustard, if desired. Transfer hot cheese mixture to a fondue pot and keep warm over the fondue burner. Serve immediately with dippers; swirl as you dip. If cheese mixture thickens while standing, stir in a little warm beer or wine. If you don't have a fondue pot, serve fondue in a casserole. Serves: 8.

West Virginia

The rugged terrain of West Virginia created great hardships for early settlers, resulting in a long history of poverty and isolation. Nearly two-thirds of the state residents still live in rural areas, and many still harvest the same foods used by the mountain folk for decades. A large variety of timber covers much of the state, and black walnut trees provide an abundance of the greatly prized nuts. With the march of housing developments and industry, the highly odiferous ramp that has always grown rampant in rural ravines is now becoming a bit harder to find. The easternmost part of West Virginia is recognized as one of the best apple-growing regions in the United States. These foodstuffs all provide the basis for festivals celebrating generations of life in the mountains with its unpretentious yet delectable foods.

Apple Butter Festival, Berkeley Springs State Park, Berkeley Springs, WV

Every Columbus Day weekend, thousands of folks converge on the small town of Berkeley Springs, West Virginia, to share in the magic of the annual Apple Butter Festival. There's plenty of great mountain cooking, like country ham, chicken, and homemade ice cream. Purchases of fall produce, baked goods, and fresh apple cider are brisk.

According to local experts, cider making in West Virginia has changed little over the past century. The best sweet cider is made from a blend of both sweet and tart apples. At Applejack Orchard in Berkeley Springs, the apples are washed, ground into a mash called a "pomace," then pressed between layers of cloth-covered wooden plates. The juice is strained and jugged with no additives or pasteurization.

But it's the slowly simmered apple butter, cooked over open fires for hours and hours, that's the star of the festival. Old-timers reveal the secret of how to make the best apple butter, and they'll even let visitors take a stir or two. Local experts like Jeanne Mozier say that apple butter must be made in copper-lined kettles using a long-handled stirrer with a spoon-bill head usually made from poplar. Hardwood fires, which produce coals rather than flames, are preferred. The addition of sugar is called "putting in the money." Apple butter, many claim, should never be made alone. It's a group project calling for the participation of family, friends, or strangers passing by the kettles at the festival. Mozier says, "There is something about the tradition of making apple butter that brings people together in a spirit of warmth and cooperation. There is love in every sticky bite!" After looking in on the Apple Baking Contest and the Apple Butter Contest, both sponsored by the West Virginia Extension Club, most folks buy a few jars of dark, spicy apple butter to enjoy over the winter or to dole out as prized Christmas gifts.

Always Columbus Day Weekend

Marge's Cider Barbecue

Jeanne Mozier of Berkeley Springs, WV, has won recognition as an expert cook with this recipe.

To prepare Apple Cider Syrup, boil fresh (not pasteurized) apple cider for 8–10 hours over a low flame until dark and thick. It can be stored, unprocessed, in the refrigerator, for months or canned by a simple water-bath process.

1 onion, chopped
1 clove garlic, finely chopped
2 tablespoons butter
1½ cups ketchup
2 teaspoons prepared mustard
2 tablespoons lemon juice
4 tablespoons apple-cider syrup
Salt and cayenne pepper to taste

Sauté onion and garlic in butter until clear. Add rest of ingredients and simmer for 20 minutes. Use on chicken or ribs.

International Ramp Cook-Off and Festival, Elkins, WV

While the National Ramp Association may be headquartered in Richwood, West Virginia, folks in Elkins, about sixty-five miles north as the crow flies, are also ardent fans of the ramp. Here, the International Ramp Cook-Off and Festival is held in an effort to promote the virtues of the ramp and draw tourism into Randolph County.

For potent taste and strong smell, no modern food surpasses the ramp. West Virginians view it as better than a spring tonic and acknowledge the ability of the wild leek to excite taste buds and open sinus cavities after a long, cold winter. According to festival organizers, "eating ramps is part tradition, part bravado, and sometimes self-defense."

The festival at Elkins City Park is kicked off on Friday night with a traditional ramp dinner: ham, fried potatoes, cornbread, beans, and ramps. For those who still haven't gotten their fill, Saturday offers a whole new ramp world to conquer. Vendors even sell ramp candy.

Over at the ramp cook-off, public tastings of the creations of entrants follows judging. There's plenty of strong (smelling) competition in both civic and professional divisions, and prizes are awarded for best recipe, best booth decorations, and taster's choice. Winning recipes from "ramp champs" have been compiled into the *International Ramp Cook-Off Cook Book*.

Hot and Spicy Stir-Fried Duck

Andy Pordy and Sara Baird of Pete's Place, Elkins, WV, won first place in the Professional Division of the Ramp Cook-Off with this creative entry.

4 (8–10-ounce) skinless duck breasts, cut diagonally into ½-inch strips
2 tablespoons sunflower or corn oil
8 scallions, cut into one-inch lengths
2 carrots, cut into matchsticks
Ramps to taste, cut into 1-inch lengths
½ pound snow peas
7 ounces canned water chestnuts, drained, rinsed, and sliced

Marinade:
2 teaspoons dark soy sauce
2 teaspoons red wine vinegar
1-inch piece of fresh ginger, peeled and grated
2 fresh red chilies, cored, seeded, and coarsely chopped
Grated zest and juice of one orange
1 teaspoon sesame oil
1 teaspoon cornstarch
1 teaspoon sugar
Salt and pepper

For the marinade: In a large bowl, combine all ingredients and mix well.

Toss the duck strips in the marinade, cover, and let stand 10 minutes. Lift duck strips out of marinade and drain on paper towels, reserving the marinade. Heat oil in a large wok or skillet. Add the duck and stir-fry over high heat for 5 minutes or until browned all over. Add scallions, carrots, and ramps and stir-fry for 2–3 minutes. Add snow peas and stir-fry for 1 minute. Pour marinade into wok and stir-fry for 2 minutes longer or until the duck is just tender. Stir in the water chestnuts, heat through, and season to taste. Serves: 6–8.

Friday and Saturday of the Last Weekend in April

The Feast of the Ramson, Richwood, WV

The Feast of the Ramson has been going strong in Richwood, West Virginia, since 1938. For the uninitiated, ramps are a wild leek and a member of the lily family commonly found in spring in parts of Europe and in the United States throughout the southern Appalachians.

The name "ramsom" is derived from the Zodiac sign of Aries that heralds the arrival of spring and which, in Arabic, means "ram." Because nature had provided an equally strong and powerful plant, it was called "Son of the Ram," or "Ramson." As Maxine Folk Corbett of Richwood points out, "Without question, we are talking the King of Stink here, folks!" The tart, snappy taste of ramps leaves a pungent odor on one's breath that lingers for days, delaying the time when a ramson eater can safely reenter society.

However, that doesn't seem to deter anyone in Richwood, population 2,808, known as the "Ramp Capital of the World." Every year, after gathering more than a ton of the little stinkers, the National Ramp Association, headquartered in Richwood, holds its Feast of the Ramson for some 1,200 diners who come from near and far.

The festival includes more than sixty artisans who sell handcrafted items and demonstrate their art. There's also mountain music and dancing. But it's the authentic Appalachian mountain food that's the big attraction. Along with ramps that have been parboiled in a gigantic skillet, diners are served bacon, ham, fried potatoes, brown beans, corn bread, and sassafras tea made from freshly dug roots from the surrounding forests.

Annually on a Saturday in April

Ramps may be served in a variety of recipes ranging from soups to salads to casseroles. A Richwood restaurant serves up its own specialty, ramp pizza. Natives insist the best way to serve ramps is over an open fire, fried in bacon grease in an iron skillet, with fried potatoes, bacon, and eggs. But it doesn't stop there. Norene Facemire of Richwood has written the ultimate guide to cooking with ramps entitled *Ramps A Cookin'*—bound to be a bestseller in West Virginia.

Ramp Soup

Norene Facemire of Richwood is an enthusiastic ramp cook and has shared a collection of wonderful recipes in her book *Ramps A Cookin'*.

6 medium potatoes
2 small onions
3 cups water
2 teaspoons salt
½ teaspoon black pepper
1 cup diced ham
1 cup chopped ramps
2 cups milk
3 tablespoons flour
Butter

Peel and dice potatoes and onions. In a kettle, combine potatoes, onions, water, salt, pepper, ham, and ramps. Cook until potatoes are tender. Add milk and bring mixture to boiling point. Thicken with the flour and a little milk. Add a bit of butter and serve. Serves: 6.

Note: Use ramps while the bulbs and leaves are tender. You may use 1 cup dehydrated ramps in place of fresh ramps.

Ramp Quiche

Another selection from *Ramps A Cookin'* by Norene Facemire, this recipe illustrates the versatility of the ramp.

4 eggs
1½ cups milk
12 slices bacon, cooked and crumbled
1 cup grated Swiss cheese
1 small can mushroom pieces, drained
1 cup chopped ramps
1 (9-inch) pie shell, unbaked

Preheat oven to 350°. Combine the eggs and milk and beat well. Add the remaining ingredients. Pour into unbaked pie shell. Bake for 45 minutes. Remove from oven and let pie stand 10 minutes before serving.

West Virginia Black Walnut Festival, Spencer, WV

The Black Walnut Festival has its roots in the year 1954 when Henry Young sold two million pounds of his black walnuts. That sale of a local product got a member of the Little Kanawha Regional Council to thinking. It was determined that black walnuts could be successfully developed into a cash crop for local farmers. Then a few civic-minded folks got to talking and they decided that a festival promoting the black walnut was definitely in order.

The first event was held in 1955 and today, the town of Spencer annually hosts some 50,000 visitors. No mean undertaking, local officials launch "Operation Walnut" in order to pull off the tremendously successful festival that takes place year after year. While many of the events, like a carnival, flea market, parade, the local Black Walnut Bowl high-school football game, and a crafts show, are definitely in tune with the times, others date back to an earlier era. History buffs are thrilled with the Civil War Encampment and artillery display as well as the firing of a Civil War cannon and a black-powder shoot. In recent years, Sergeant Mills has demonstrated the grinding of corn on old granite stones and visitors often purchase an entire year's worth of quality cornmeal. There's also a quilt show and tours of a one-room school.

For those with an appetite, Saturday features an old-fashioned ox roast. Over 1,000 pounds of meat are served up in the form of sandwiches with not a morsel left over. The traditional Black Walnut Bake-Off is also held on Saturday and the festival sells the *Black Walnut Festival Cookbook,* a wonderful compendium of many years of award-winning recipes.

Thursday through Sunday the Second Weekend in October

Black Walnut Swirl Bread

Mrs. Grace Price was a 1981 winner of the Black Walnut Bake-Off with this recipe.

Bread:
4½–4¾ cups all purpose flour
2 packages active dry yeast
1 cup milk
½ cup granulated sugar
½ cup butter
1 teaspoon salt
2 eggs

Filling:
2 cups finely chopped black walnuts
¾ cup honey
⅓ cup packed brown sugar
1 teaspoon cinnamon
1 teaspoon nutmeg

Glaze:
1 cup powdered sugar
1 tablespoon butter
2 tablespoons milk
Dash of salt

In a large mixer bowl, stir together 2 cups of flour and the yeast. Blend milk, sugar, butter, and salt in a saucepan and heat until warm (115–120°), stirring constantly until butter is almost melted. Add to dry ingredients, then add eggs. Beat at low speed for ½ minute. Beat 3 minutes at high speed. By hand, stir in enough remaining flour to make a moderately soft dough. Knead on a floured surface until smooth. Place in a greased bowl. Cover and let rise 1¼–1½ hours or until double in bulk.

Preheat oven to 350°. Divide dough in half. Cover and let rest for 10 minutes. On a lightly floured surface, roll half the dough to a 14 x 8-inch rectangle. For filling, stir together black walnuts, honey, brown sugar, cinnamon, and nutmeg. Spread half the filling over the dough to within ½ inch of edges. Starting from the long side, roll up in jelly-roll fashion. Pinch edge to seal. Cut in 1-inch slices. Arrange 2 layers of pinwheels, cut-side down, in a greased 10-inch tube pan, staggering layers. Repeat with remaining dough and filling to make a total of 4 layers. Cover and let rise 45–50 minutes or until double in size. Bake for 40–50 minutes. Let stand 10 minutes. Remove from pan and cool. Mix ingredients for glaze until smooth and drizzle over bread. Yield: one loaf.

Chapter 3

The Midwest

Illinois | Indiana | Michigan | Minnesota
Missouri | Ohio | Wisconsin

Illinois

Chicago, the largest city in Illinois, is an important center of industry and transportation. The commercial importance of the state has its roots in the 1600s, when fur trade with the Native Americans was big business. As settlers moved west, eventually establishing Illinois as part of the great Midwestern Corn Belt, numerous immigrant groups, including Swedes and Scots, made the area their home. Today their descendants celebrate their heritage with various festivals.

Manufacturing processed foods in Illinois ranks second in value in the manufactured goods category. Several of America's largest food processing companies are in Illinois. Apples are the most valuable fruit crop, but it's the high quality of Illinois horseradish that attracts most of the attention. More than two-thirds of all horseradish root is grown in Madison and St. Clair Counties. The world's highest concentration of horseradish production is at the American Bottoms, near Collinsville.

Bagelfest, Mattoon, IL

A Bagelfest, you ask? Absolutely! Mattoon is home to Lender's largest bagel factory, so a festival seemed a good way to promote the town. In 1986, the festival began as a bagel breakfast on Saturday morning, and it has bloomed into a full week of events. The celebration has become big in a lot of other ways. Over 50,000 people attend the "World's Largest Bagel Breakfast," where free bagels are handed out at a three-block-long picnic table in midtown Mattoon. And then there was the "World's Biggest Bagel," produced in 1996, weighing in at 563 pounds.

In addition to musical entertainment, games, and the Bagelfest parade, there is plenty of food. Bagels with cream cheese and jelly are supplemented by barbecued ribs, pork burgers, and corn dogs.

Wednesday through Saturday of the Last Full Week in July

Peachy Pineapple Bagels

At one time there was a cooking contest featuring bagels as an ingredient. Lois Love of the Mattoon Chamber of Commerce was a frequent winner in those days and says that the contest may soon be revived.

¼ cup butter, melted
1 (15- or 20-ounce) can crushed pineapple in syrup, undrained
1 (21-ounce) can peach pie filling
1 cup butterscotch chips
6 plain bagels
⅓ cup chopped nuts
Whipped topping or ice cream

Preheat oven to 400°. In a medium saucepan, combine 2 tablespoons of the butter, pineapple, peach pie filling, and butterscotch chips. Heat until hot and bubbly. Pour the hot fruit mixture into a 8-x 12-inch baking pan. Cut the bagels in pieces and dip in the remaining melted butter. Arrange over the hot fruit mixture. Sprinkle with nuts. Bake for 15 minutes, until golden brown and bubbly. Serve warm or cooled with whipped topping or ice cream. Serves: 10.

Fall Festival of Spoon River Scenic Drive, Fulton County, IL

The arrival of fall in western Illinois heralds the annual Fall Festival of Spoon River Scenic Drive. This countywide event involves eighteen picturesque villages that spare no effort to produce a festival with a distinct country flavor. Over 100,000 visitors and locals journey from one town to another, crisscrossing the foliage-flanked Spoon River, which meanders its way throughout Fulton County.

Highlights of the festival include musical entertainment in each village, exhibitions of arts and crafts, antiques and quilts, vintage autos, and steam engines, as well as flea markets. Pioneer and Civil War encampments along Spoon River are major attractions. Lewistown, the 1890s home of Edgar Lee Masters, famous poet and author of *Spoon River Anthology*, attracts those with a literary bent.

Hosts dressed in period costumes demonstrate traditional crafts like blacksmithing and the making of lye soap. Beloved specialty foods of the Midwest abound, including apple butter at London Mills, apple dumplings at Farmington Park, Astoria's famous cinnamon rolls, Smithfield's chicken and noodles, and Amish foods at the Tarvin Horse Farm. Elephant ears—fried bread sprinkled with cinnamon and sugar—are available, along with caramel apples, caramel corn, and homemade pies. County roadsides are dotted with fresh produce stands.

Each year, the Spoon River Valley Scenic Drive organization compiles and sells a booklet of the area's specialty recipes.

The First Two Full Weekends in October

Caramel Baked Apples

Joan Johnson's recipe was among the delicious regional specialties to be included in *Heritage Recipes from the Spoon River Valley Scenic Drive Associates*.

6 tablespoons butter, softened
2 teaspoons ground nutmeg
6 red baking apples, cored
¼ cup water
1 (10-ounce) package caramels
2 tablespoons water
½ cup heavy cream

Preheat oven to 350°. In a small bowl, combine the butter and nutmeg. Fill the center of each apple with 1 tablespoon of the mixture. Place apples in a baking pan and add ¼ cup of water to the bottom of the pan. Bake 30–35 minutes. In a heavy pan over low heat, melt caramels with 2 tablespoons of water, stirring occasionally. Remove from the heat and stir in the cream. To serve, pour the caramel mixture over the baked apples. Serves: 6.

International Horseradish Festival, Collinsville, IL

Madison and St. Clair Counties in Illinois are literally horseradish heaven. Here seventy-five percent of all horseradish is grown, earning Collinsville the title "Horseradish Capital of the World."

A two-story-high balloon in the shape of a horseradish root floats over the town throughout the weekend, and there's plenty of competition on the festival grounds below: root golf, root volleyball, a root toss, and a root-sacking contest provide contestants with ample opportunity to work up an appetite, while bystanders "root" them on from the sidelines.

Then it's on to the Horseradish Eating Contest, where contestants dig into frankfurters piled high with—you guessed it—horseradish. There are also contests for the biggest and most unusual horseradish roots grown.

Finally, there's the ever-popular Horseradish Recipe Contest. A few years ago, organizers introduced a festival cookbook entitled *Horseradish Recipes,* containing many winning entries from the contest. It has been a runaway best-seller in Madison and St. Clair Counties.

Hot Reuben Dip

Doris Chiste was the 1993 first-place winner of the Horseradish Recipe Contest.

1 cup mayonnaise
1 (16-ounce) can Bavarian sauerkraut, drained, squeezed, and dried
1 small onion, finely chopped
2 cups shredded Swiss cheese
4 (2½-ounce) packages dried corned beef, finely chopped
2 tablespoons prepared horseradish

Preheat oven to 350°. Mix all ingredients in a 1½-quart casserole dish. Bake for 30–40 minutes. Serve with toasted rye bagel chips or party rye bread. Yield: About 5 cups.

First Weekend in June

Jubilee Autumn Harvestfest, Jubilee College State Historic Site, Brimfield, IL

For a look at early frontier life up through the Civil War period in Illinois, there's no better place than the Jubilee Autumn Harvestfest. Jubilee College was established in 1840, and the festival honors Jubilee's founder, Bishop Philander Chase, who also established Kenyon College in Ohio.

The festival, which started in 1981, features a farmers' market, a buckskinners' camp, a Civil War encampment, a Kickapoo Indian medicine show, a black powder muzzle-loaded firing contest, and period crafts.

There is also plenty of food, including stone-oven breads, herbal teas, and black kettle popcorn. A delicious Indian corn stew, based on a mid-1700 recipe, is made in huge cast-iron kettles. The buckskinner and Civil War groups prepare turkey, beef, and buffalo dinners.

The first Autumn Harvestfest offered a small booklet of apple recipes and the formula for Indian Corn Stew. Under the direction of Jim Tuminelli, historic site manager for Jubilee College, a new cookbook entitled *Jubilee College Autumn Harvestfest* has been compiled. It incorporates recipes from the original cookbook, plus instructions for many additional items.

Indian Corn Stew

This heritage recipe was provided by the Jubilee College State Historic Site.

2 tablespoons butter
1 pound ground beef
1 onion, finely chopped
1 clove garlic, finely chopped
1 green bell pepper, coarsely chopped
3 cups corn, fresh or frozen
3 ripe tomatoes, skinned and coarsely chopped
1 tablespoon Worcestershire sauce
2 teaspoons sugar
1½ teaspoons salt

Melt the butter in a large skillet. (A cast-iron Dutch oven imparts the best flavor.) Add the beef and sauté over high heat until brown. Stir in the onion, garlic, and bell pepper and cook about 5 minutes. Add the corn, tomatoes, Worcestershire sauce, sugar, and salt. Cover and simmer gently for about 30 minutes. Serves: 4–6.

Second Weekend in September

Morton Pumpkin Festival, Morton, IL

Pumpkins are big business in Morton. Home of Nestle/Libby's pumpkin-packing plant, Morton is billed as the "Pumpkin Capital of the World." The town has been celebrating its annual Pumpkin Festival since 1967.

Shop windows and pumpkins are decorated, and there is a giant pumpkin contest. The entertainment consists of sporting events, parades, live entertainment, a flower and garden show, arts and crafts, and a carnival. The Punkin' Chuckin' Contest, inaugurated in 1996, attracts thousands who come to witness machines designed and built by participants hurl 8- to 10-pound pumpkins as far as possible.

The food tent draws visitors with butterfly pork chop sandwiches and bratwurst, not to mention pumpkin chili. In the Pumpkin Delights tent, folks try pumpkin praline cheesecake, pumpkin cookies, pumpkin fudge, and pumpkin pie as well as pumpkin ice cream made from a secret recipe. On Saturday, there's an all-you-can-eat pumpkin pancake breakfast. The Pumpkin Cookery Contest, sponsored by Nestle/Libby, calls for the use of at least ½ cup of Libby's processed pumpkin in a broad range of categories.

Pumpkin Party Spread

Scott and Natalie Weer took the 1996 grand prize in the Pumpkin Cookery Contest.

12 ounces nonfat cream cheese
½ cup canned pumpkin
2½ tablespoons packaged taco seasoning mix
⅛ teaspoon garlic powder
½ (2-ounce) jar sliced dried beef, finely chopped
⅓ cup chopped green bell pepper
⅓ cup chopped red bell pepper
⅓ cup chopped black olives
1 (7-inch) round loaf pumpernickel bread
Corn chips, crackers, or vegetables, to serve

Blend together the cream cheese, pumpkin, taco seasoning, and garlic powder. Add the dried beef, peppers, and olives and mix well. Scoop out the center of the bread and fill with dip. Serve with corn chips, crackers, or fresh vegetables. The front of the bread can be decorated as a pumpkin face with cheese slices. Yield: About 3 cups.

Wednesday through Saturday During the Second Week of September

Old Settler's Day, Jordbruksdagarna (Agricultural Days), Julmarknad (Christmas Market), Lucia Nights, Bishop Hill, IL

In 1846, Swedish immigrants seeking religious freedom founded the colony of Bishop Hill under the leadership of Eric Jansson. Bishop Hill was a communal society that quickly grew and prospered until Jansson was murdered in 1850. Mounting dissension resulted in the colony's dissolution in 1861.

Bishop Hill today has been preserved and maintained as a national historic landmark, and it's also listed as a historic district in the National Register of Historic Places.

Old Settler's Day began as a fiftieth anniversary reunion of the original settlers of Bishop Hill in 1896 and continues as a celebration of the colony's founding, attended by descendants of the founders and a host of interested visitors. The Old Settler's Association serves a noon dinner of chicken, potatoes, vegetables, bread, pies, and, in true Swedish style, lots of coffee.

Jordbruksdagarna, or Agricultural Days, highlights the agrarian life of this immigrant settlement. Visitors view such chores as cane pressing and cooking, cheese making, and cider pressing and can taste Bishop Hill Colony Beef and Barley Stew, hard tack, kettle popcorn, and rice pudding.

The annual Christmas Market, or Julmarknad, provides a wonderful alternative to a more traditional seasonal activity. Shoppers purchase unique crafts while enjoying nineteenth-century holiday decorations, music, and Swedish folk characters roaming the village. The Cookie Walk, held on selected days, provides an opportunity to purchase Christmas cookies.

During Lucia Nights every window is illuminated by candles, and the museum and shops serve coffee, hot cider, and a dessert such as cookies, rusks, or Lucia Buns. The voices of carolers rise in song, and a local church holds a soup and chili supper.

Varsågod—Bishop Hill Heritage Cookbook is a recent collection of recipes, including many from the families of original Bishop Hill settlers, compiled by the Bishop Hill Heritage Association. It is an excellent resource on Swedish culinary traditions. Collectors may want to search for two earlier cookbooks. In 1936, the Ladies Aid Society of the Bishop Hill Methodist Church compiled a cookbook of their favorite recipes. Many of those recipes were again featured in the *Bishop Hill Heritage Cookbook*, compiled by Carol Nelson and published by the Bishop Hill Heritage Association in 1975.

Old Settler's Day
Usually the Second Saturday in September
—
Jordbruksdagarna
Always the Last Full Weekend in September
—
Julmarknad
Thanksgiving Weekend and the Following Weekend
—
Lucia Nights
Always the Weekend Closest to St. Lucia Day on December 13th

Christmas Rice Pudding

Contributed by Karen Johnson DeRouin, this heritage recipe is from *Varsågod—Bishop Hill Heritage Cookbook*.

Rice pudding:
¾ cup uncooked rice
2 cups milk
1½ cups sugar
½ teaspoon salt
2 cinnamon sticks
Dash of nutmeg
1 cup half and half
3 eggs, beaten
1 teaspoon vanilla
2 tablespoons butter

Kram:
4 cups grape juice
½ cup sugar
2 tablespoons cornstarch mixed with ¼ cup water

Preheat oven to 350°. Put the rice in an ovenproof pot, cover with water, bring to a boil, and cook for 5 minutes. Drain rice and add the milk, sugar, salt, cinnamon sticks, and nutmeg. Stir well and bake for 1 hour. Add the half and half to eggs. Slowly add some hot rice mixture to the egg mixture, stirring constantly. Then add egg mixture to rice mixture along with vanilla and butter. Mix well. Bake half an hour longer. Combine all ingredients for kram. Bring mixture to a boil and cook until thickened. Serve over cooled rice pudding. Serves: 6–8.

Pepper Nuts

This traditional cookie, served during Lucia Nights, was contributed by the 1882 Poppy Barn Colony Handwovens and Brooms to *Varsågod—Bishop Hill Heritage Cookbook*.

10–11 cups flour
1 teaspoon ginger
1 teaspoon cloves
1 teaspoon allspice
2 teaspoons black pepper
1 cup butter
1 cup sugar
1 cup lard
1¼ teaspoons baking soda
1 cup sour milk
2 eggs
1 cup sorghum molasses

Preheat oven to 375°. Mix first 5 ingredients together. Cream together butter, sugar, and lard. Add baking soda to sour milk. Add eggs and sorghum molasses to milk mixture, then add to dry ingredients. Mix well. Refrigerate overnight. Roll dough into small balls and place 1 inch apart on cookie sheet. Bake until slightly brown, about 7–10 minutes. Cool on wire racks. Yield: 250 cookies.

Springfield Highland Games and Celtic Festival, Springfield, IL

Scottish immigrants to America gave their surnames to places like Dallas, Houston, Albany, Cooperstown, and Scottsdale and were assimilated so early into American society that they eventually became what historians term "undistinctive." Some estimates say that twenty-five percent of the U.S. populace owes some genetic influence to Scottish ancestors, hence the Scottish-American saying "Scratch almost any American, you'll find a Scottish grandmother just about skin deep!"

Folks of Scottish heritage are drawn to the Highland Games and Celtic Festival at the Illinois State Fairgrounds every May. A family oriented event, the festival features competitive highland dancers, a dog show and animal exhibition, clan tents, Scottish athletic games, and a *ceilidh*, or big party and dance.

Of course, there are hundreds of kilt-wearing bagpipers. Bagpipes date back to 1500 B.C., but their actual origin has not been identified. The Roman infantry had pipers and probably introduced bagpipes throughout the empire. Certainly, all Celtic countries have a long history of bagpipe music. The only older instruments found in Celtic culture are the *bodhran* (drum), *clarsach* (harp), and *feadan* (whistle or flute).

There are plenty of savory Scottish treats to enjoy such as meat pies called "briddies," sausage bangers (sausage links in hot dog buns), fish and chips, shortbread, and scones. There's also haggis, a distinctive Scottish dish often mentioned by the poet Robert Burns, which is certainly not for the faint of heart!

Traditional Haggis

Dave Campbell of the Springfield Highland Games and Celtic Festival provided this heritage Scottish recipe.

1 pound lamb's liver
1 large onion, chopped
2 pounds dry oatmeal
1 pound suet
2½ cups stock
½ teaspoon cayenne pepper
Jamaica pepper and salt to taste
1 sheep's pluck (stomach bag)

Boil liver and parboil onion, then mince them together. Lightly brown the oatmeal. Mix together all ingredients except the sheep's pluck. Fill the pluck with the mixture, pressing it down to remove all the air, and sew up securely with thread. Prick the pluck in several places so that it does not burst. Place in boiling water and boil slowly for 4–5 hours. Serves: 6–8.

Indiana

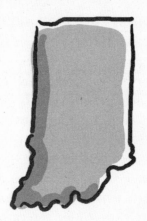

Following the exploration of Robert Cavelier, Sieur de La Salle in 1679, French fur traders pushed into what is now known as Indiana. By the 1720s, they had constructed fur-trading posts in Ouiatenon and Miami. The British eventually defeated the French and took control of the region in 1763.

Today, Indiana is a leading agricultural state, with corn one of its major products. Corn is used to manufacture marshmallows, so Indiana is also home to one of the world's major marshmallow-manufacturing facilities. So popular are marshmallows in Indiana that residents jokingly call them a major food group. Residents also satisfy their sweet tooth with the annual maple syrup production. Although Indiana is at the southern edge of maple syrup country, it still manages to produce approximately 10,000 gallons a year.

Blueberries are another important crop and account for 40 percent of U.S. cultivation. With the arrival of October's hard frosts, southern Indiana residents harvest prized persimmons. Although most of the persimmons are used to make the traditional fall and Thanksgiving persimmon puddings, some end up as persimmon table wine, a libation perhaps unique to Indiana.

Feast of the Hunter's Moon, Fort Ouiatenon Historic Park, W. Lafayette, IN

Indiana's first fortified European outpost, Fort Ouiatenon, was founded by the French in 1717. Following England's victory in the French and Indian War, it was taken over by the British in 1763. Ouiatenon and the adjacent Indian villages were destroyed in 1791 by order of President Washington.

The Feast of the Hunter's Moon, which attracts tens of thousands of people, is a re-creation of an eighteenth-century trade gathering of French and Native Americans along the Wabash River. With over 8,000 costumed participants, the festival serves as a window to the past, featuring the fort's history, along with Native American culture and civilian life. Also featured are the voyageurs, the hired canoemen who brought trade goods, news, and mail to Ouiatenon and carried out the heartland's precious furs. Traditional crafts are demonstrated, and many of the products can be purchased.

More than sixty different French and Native American foods are available, prepared over open fires and served by costumed participants. Specialties include voyageur stew, persimmon pudding, giant smoked turkey legs, roasted ears of corn, voyageur pea soup, jerky, fry bread, hominy soup, a sweet fritter called *Croquignoles,* and French marble cake. The foods are prepared by local service organizations with proceeds supporting year-round projects.

The Tippecanoe County Historical Association, the feast's sponsor, offers an excellent cookbook, *Ouabache Potpourri,* which contains recipes based on French and Native American dishes, adapted to modern ingredients and palates. The book contains a good bibliography for further reading on early American foods.

French Marble Cake

This heritage recipe is reprinted from *Ouabache Potpourri.*

A Weekend in October

1 scant cup butter
2 cups sugar
4 eggs, separated
3 cups cake flour, sifted
3 teaspoons baking powder
Pinch of salt
1 cup milk
1 teaspoon vanilla
1 teaspoon lemon flavoring
½ teaspoon freshly grated nutmeg
1 square (1-ounce) bitter chocolate, melted

Preheat oven to 350°. Cream the butter and sugar until light and fluffy. Add the egg yolks. Sift the flour, baking powder, and salt together and add to the butter mixture alternately with milk. Add the vanilla, lemon flavoring, and nutmeg. Beat the egg whites until stiff and fold in. Pour one-third of the batter into a separate bowl and add the melted chocolate. Spoon batters alternately into a greased and floured 10 inch tube pan. Pull a knife through gently to create marbling. Bake for 45 minutes. Cool cake on wire rack and remove from pan.

Ligonier Marshmallow Festival, Ligonier, IN

For forty years, the annual Labor Day Festival in Ligonier was known as the "Strawberry Valley Day Festival," but when the area's wild strawberries began to disappear, townspeople felt it was time to change the name. Choosing that new name wasn't difficult. Noble County, in which Ligonier lies, is the world's largest producer of marshmallows, so the new title "Marshmallow Capital of the World" seemed perfect.

Marshmallows date back to around 2000 B.C., making them one of the world's oldest candies. Egyptians extracted a sweet sap from a wetlands plant known as the "marsh mallow" and combined it with honey. The resulting confection was reserved for royalty. By the mid-1800s, French candy vendors were sweetening and whipping the mallow sap into a fluffy treat sold in tins as penny candy. Today, the mallow sap has been replaced by gelatin combined with sugar, cornstarch, corn syrup, and vanilla. Egg whites can be added, but the major component, accounting for eighty percent of the confection, is air.

There's plenty of both fluff and substance at the festival, which attracts about 20,000 people and has craft and merchant tents, art and car shows, and parades. Everything is marshmallow related, from the Marshmallow Olympics to marshmallow skits and a marshmallow roast.

In 1995, the festival produced the "World's Largest Marshmallow." Weighing in at 2,973 pounds, it squashed 1993's paltry 671-pound puff.

The Marshmallow Festival is paradise for kids as they devour s'mores, a traditional camp snack made from roasted marshmallows, graham crackers, and chocolate bars. Even adults get into the swing of things with the cook-off. Marshmallows are a required ingredient in categories ranging from cookies and candies to cakes, salads, and pies. After judging, all entries are auctioned off.

Labor Day Weekend

Joyful Almond Cake

Judy Cunningham of Ligonier, IN won first place in the Cakes Division of the Marshmallow Cook-off.

1 box milk chocolate cake mix
1 cup evaporated milk
1 cup sugar
24 large marshmallows
1 (14-ounce) package shredded coconut
½ cup butter
½ cup evaporated milk
½ cup sugar
1 (12-ounce) package semisweet chocolate chips
½ cup slivered almonds, toasted

Preheat oven to temperature indicated on the cake mix box. Prepare the cake mix according to directions and bake in a 16 x 10 x 2-inch pan.

While cake is baking, mix 1 cup evaporated milk with 1 cup sugar, bring to a rapid boil, and remove from heat. Add the marshmallows and stir until melted. Add coconut and mix well. As soon as the cake has finished baking, remove from the oven and spread the marshmallow mixture over the top.

In a saucepan, combine the butter, ½ cup evaporated milk, and ½ cup sugar. Bring to a rapid boil and remove from heat. Stir in the chocolate chips, mixing until melted. Spread over coconut layer. Cover top with almonds. Cool thoroughly, then refrigerate for easier serving and slicing.

Marshall County Blueberry Festival, Plymouth, IN

Blueberries star in what has become the largest three-day festival in the entire Midwest. The Marshall County Blueberry Festival attracts around 600,000 visitors, and there's something for everyone on the huge roster of events. Top-notch entertainers perform on two sound stages, and there's a wide range of sporting events. The Blueberry Parade lasts around two hours, and there's a giant fireworks display. With 500 craft booths, shoppers are in heaven.

Over a hundred food vendors sell blueberries in everything from sundaes to pies, ice cream, and cheesecake. The Plymouth Optimist Club holds a Blueberry Pancake Breakfast on Sunday morning. A festival favorite is the thirst-quenching blueberry drink called "Blue Witch's Brew." Anyone suffering from blueberry overload can indulge in perennial Midwestern favorites like pork chops and chicken. There's even alligator and ostrich! While the festival doesn't feature any culinary contests centered around the luscious blueberry, organizers anticipate the compilation of a blueberry cookbook in the near future.

Blue Witch's Brew

The Marshall County Blueberry Festival provided this recipe for its popular festival libation.

2½ cups fresh or frozen, thawed blueberries
1¼ cups apple juice
1 cup vanilla ice cream
¼ cup milk
¾ teaspoon ground cinnamon

Whirl all ingredients in a blender until smooth. Serve immediately. Serves: 4.

Saturday through Monday of Labor Day Weekend

Parke County Maple Syrup Festival, Rockville, IN

The Last Weekend in February and the First Weekend in March

When European immigrants arrived in the New World, the Native Americans introduced them to the virtues of the sugar maple. It wasn't long before maple syrup and sugar were adopted by settlers as cost-effective substitutes for sugar from the West Indies. Maple sweeteners became even more popular with the passage of the 1764 Sugar Act, which imposed high duties on imported sugar. Maple products remained the principal sweeteners well into the nineteenth century. Today, Vermont and New York produce more than two-thirds of the 1.1 million gallons in the United States annually.

Indiana is the sugar maple's western limit, and the high concentration of growth in the Parke County area is unique. The entire region looks like a bit of New England transposed to the Midwest. The county, in west-central Indiana, is dotted with thirty-two historic covered bridges along winding country roads. Its villages boast antique shops and art galleries, as well as an old grist mill and an 1880s roller mill. The county's sugar camps, ranging from primitive to modern, are fired up each year for the production of maple syrup, and many can be visited during festival season.

Rockville is the self-proclaimed "Capital of Covered Bridge Country" and is the focal point for activities during the Maple Syrup Festival. Group tours depart from festival headquarters for the sugar camps and covered bridges. A dining area in the main festival building is where the maple syrup really flows. Meals of "Whole Hog Sausage" and all the pancakes you can eat, drenched in maple syrup, are served during the festival. Throughout the county, visitors purchase gallons and gallons of maple syrup, maple candy, maple cream, maple doughnuts, maple cookies, sausage, bacon, and ham.

Maple Syrup Doughnuts

Florence Williams generously shares her recipe for a long-time festival favorite.

1 cup maple syrup
2 eggs
3 teaspoons shortening
⅔ cup sour cream
4 cups flour (approximate)
½ teaspoon salt
½ teaspoon nutmeg
1 teaspoon baking soda
1 teaspoon baking powder
Vegetable oil for frying

Combine the syrup, eggs, shortening, and sour cream and beat well. Sift the flour with the salt, nutmeg, baking soda, and baking powder. Add to the liquid mixture and combine well. Roll the dough out on a floured board and cut with a doughnut cutter. Fry doughnuts in hot oil until golden brown. Drain on paper towels and serve. Yield: About 18 doughnuts.

Persimmon Festival, Mitchell, IN

When the Persimmon Festival began in 1946, the focus was on pudding. The festival has grown and changed, but persimmon pudding still plays a central role.

Persimmon trees are native to the southeastern United States and grow wild throughout much of southern Indiana. The fruit is a delicacy for eating out of hand or for use in many dishes. Persimmons are harvested from mid-September to late October and should be fully ripened before eating or they will be a bit sour. Festival visitors can enjoy fragrant persimmons in an endless number of ways including persimmon ice cream, pies, cookies, cakes, and—dare we say it?—pudding.

Events include a candlelight tour of the Pioneer Village in Spring Mill State Park, a parade and carnival, various sporting events, and a juried arts and crafts show.

There's also plenty of substantial Hoosier cooking such as chicken and dumplings, steak sandwiches, pork dinners, a fish fry, barbecued chicken, and ham, beans, and cornbread. A two-division persimmon cooking contest is held, one for pudding and the other for "novelty desserts." It is said that the key to winning is not only in the recipe and the prowess of the cook, but also in what tree the persimmons came from. Recipe-related inquiries are referred to Mrs. Dymple Green, the resident expert on persimmons. Dymple founded a thriving business processing and selling persimmon pulp in addition to compiling the definitive book on cooking with persimmons. She explains that persimmon pudding should be served warm or at room temperature. Folks who prefer a more concentrated taste of persimmon should omit seasonings.

Dymple's Delight Persimmon Pudding

Dymple Green is probably the best-known persimmon cook in America. This is one of her most famous dishes, and it is reprinted from Dymple's cookbook *Persimmon Recipes*.

2 cups persimmon pulp
2 cups sugar
2 eggs, beaten
1 teaspoon baking soda
1½ cups buttermilk
1½ cups flour
1 teaspoon baking powder
1 teaspoon cinnamon
¼ cup heavy cream
1 tablespoon honey
¼ cup melted butter

Preheat oven to 350°. Mix the persimmon pulp and sugar in a large mixing bowl. Add the beaten eggs. Add the baking soda to buttermilk and set aside. Combine the flour, baking powder, and cinnamon and add to the persimmon mixture alternately with the buttermilk mixture. Add the cream and honey and mix. Add the melted butter and mix. Pour into a buttered 13 x 9-inch glass baking dish and bake for 1 hour. Serve warm or at room temperature, topped with whipped cream, if desired.

Wakarusa Maple Syrup Festival, Wakarusa, IN

A short distance outside South Bend, Indiana, is the tiny town of Wakarusa. According to Lois Meissner of the chamber of commerce, Wakarusa is as good as it gets when it comes to maple syrup.

The Maple Syrup Festival has all the trappings of a true country get-together. Folks can visit a maple sugar camp or learn how maple syrup is made in the middle of downtown Wakarusa. A quilting demonstration and quilt sale attract well-heeled buyers. Crafts, antiques, baked goods, maple syrup and other maple products, and a used book sale complete the shopping venue. The Historical Museum throws open its doors for the festivities, and an antique tractor show draws crowds.

On Friday, free popcorn made in an open kettle tantalizes the crowds all day. Also sold—by the ton!—are big, black jelly beans. At last count, 8,500 pounds of them sold out in a few hours.

On both days, serious hunger can be slaked with barbecued chicken, pork sandwiches served with ham and beans cooked in an open kettle, sausage sandwiches, or pancakes and sausage. Elephant ears provide a fitting dessert.

Saturday, there's a Maple Syrup Baking Contest in which the talented Wakarusa cooks vie for recognition and prizes.

Maple Fruit Bread

Enid Rogers of Wakarusa, IN, provided this winning recipe, which continues to earn praise for her creative use of maple syrup.

2 tablespoons melted shortening
1 cup maple syrup
1 egg, well beaten
Grated rind of 1 orange
2½ cups flour
3 teaspoons baking powder
½ teaspoon baking soda
½ teaspoon salt
¾ cup chopped nuts
¾ cup orange juice

Preheat oven to 350°. Blend together the shortening, maple syrup, egg, and orange rind. Sift together the flour, baking powder, baking soda, and salt. Blend into maple syrup mixture. Mix in the nuts and orange juice. Bake in a greased loaf pan for 1 hour. Bread is best the day after baking.

Friday and Saturday on a Weekend in March

Michigan

Michigan's diverse population reflects the numerous immigrant groups who journeyed to America, including the Dutch, who settled in the western part of the state. In 1847, Dutch immigrants seeking religious freedom and a better life established what would become the city of Holland. Those early Dutch settlers helped to build the agricultural economy of Michigan, which remains significant in this state primarily known for automobile production.

Today, most of the state's vegetable and fruit farming is done in the Lower Peninsula, where tart red cherry production accounts for seventy-five percent of the national crop and sweet cherry production, twenty percent. Most of the cherries are processed, with the tart variety going into jams, juices, and pie fillings, while the sweets are mainly used for maraschino cherries.

Michigan is home to the largest baby-food plant in the United States and is a leader in the production of cucumbers for pickling. Michigan's forests provide fertile ground for many wild mushroom varieties, including the highly prized morel. The mania for morels has resulted in the formation of the National Morel Mushroom Hunter's Association, an assortment of other clubs, and businesses offering guided hunts for the novice. Northern Michigan's famous black morels are at their peak during the last week of April and the first couple of weeks in May.

Christmas Pickle Festival, Berrien Springs, MI

It's surprising to discover that many people don't know about the tradition of the Christmas Pickle, but if the folks of Berrien Springs, Michigan, have their way, this omission will soon be rectified.

It all began in the tiny town of Lauscha, sixty miles north of Nuremburg, Germany, birthplace of a thriving cottage industry that supplied nearly all blown-glass Christmas tree ornaments from the 1840s until just before World War I. These nineteenth-century Germans considered the pickle a very special Christmas tree ornament. It was always the last ornament hung on the tree on Christmas Eve, with parents hiding it deep among the boughs. When allowed to view the tree on Christmas morning, the children would gleefully search for the pickle ornament, and whoever found it would receive a special gift left by St. Nicholas.

Berrien Springs is in the heart of southwest Michigan's cucumber-growing region, which produces between four and six million bushels of cukes annually. The area has a pickling plant and relish plant, so it's only natural that the Pickle Promotion Board sponsors the festival. Michigan is also a major supplier of pine trees for the Christmas market, so the combination of pickles and Christmas makes even more sense to folks in the Berrien Springs area. The Pickle Packers International organization has formally recognized Berrien Springs as the "Christmas Pickle Capital of the World."

Entertainment includes a Pickle Fling, with contestants competing for the longest throw of a pickle. Muhammed Ali, a resident, has been known to participate in the competition, but he doesn't hold the world record. The Dillmeister campaign is an election in which candidates can buy votes, since constituents vote by placing money in

First Weekend in December

pickle jars. The festival is kicked off with a parade led by the Grand Dillmeister, who passes out pickles along the route.

Among the many pickled delicacies available at the festival are chocolate-covered sweet pickles, Polish pickle sausage, and deep-fried dill spears. A popular souvenir is the festival's special pickle relish packed in Christmas jars. Visitors often purchase traditional hand-blown glass pickle Christmas tree ornaments made from original molds, and even gherkin earrings have become popular.

Unable to wait a full year for the Christmas Pickle Festival, Berrien Springs residents also hold a pickle smash and pickle recipe contest over the Fourth of July, when Sun Pickles are especially in vogue.

Sun Pickles

The recipe for this regional favorite was provided by Richard Schinkel, Berrien Springs, chairman, Pickle Promotion Board.

In a half-gallon jar, layer pickling cucumbers, from which the ends have been trimmed, with dill from 2 whole plants, or to taste. Add 2 or 3 cloves of garlic, peeled and cut in half, and
1 teaspoon pickling spice.
Combine ¼ quart of vinegar and ½ quart of water. Add 4 heaping teaspoons of salt and ¼ teaspoon alum and mix. Pour over pickles. Cover and place in the sun for two days.
Yield: ½ gallon of pickles.

Fall Mushroom Mania, Walloon Lake, MI

Joe Breidenstein is maniacal about mushrooms, a fact that pretty much explains why he started Fall Mushroom Mania, a series of organized mushroom hunts at Springbrook Hills Resort in Walloon Lake, Michigan. The state is known for its morel mushrooms, which sprout all over the place in spring. Little known is that in the fall, forest floors in northern Michigan literally explode with hundreds of varieties of wild mushrooms like the Stumper or Honey Mushroom, Chanterelles, and the Shaggy Mane.

Of course, not all mushrooms are edible, and many are fatal. That's why Breidenstein organizes the weekend mushroom packages for individuals, couples, and families, who are taken on formal hunts by experienced guides. Royal Olsen and Larry Hildreth, who bring over fifty years of experience to the venture, lead the hunts and provide an unparalleled mushroom education.

In addition to the hunt, there's a seminar on mushrooms and plenty of mushroom cuisine. Cooking authorities like food writer and cooking teacher Annabel Cohen, and Ruth Johnston, chef and author of *The Buffalo Cookbook,* are on hand to demonstrate the preparation of mushroom specialties. It's not unusual for guests to get into the act, producing their own favorite dishes. Breidenstein notes that the weekend is also filled with camaraderie, joking, and a lot of tall mushroom stories. No one goes away hungry, and all are richer for the experience.

Late August through September

Sautéed Chicken with Dried Cherry and Morel Mushroom Sauce

Food writer and cooking teacher Annabel Cohen of Bloomfield Hills, MI, is well known for her culinary contributions and development of recipes using ingredients indigenous to Michigan. This recipe combines two of the state's most famous crops: cherries and morel mushrooms.

2 pounds boneless, skinless chicken breasts
  (about 6–8 halves)
Salt and pepper to taste
¼ cup butter

Sauce:
1 cup dry white wine
1½ ounces dried morel mushrooms, reconstituted
  and sliced thin
½ cup dried cherries, soaked in water and drained
½ cup chopped pecans, toasted for 5 minutes in
  a 350° oven
1 cup cream
1 tablespoon lemon juice
Salt and pepper to taste
Small handful chopped fresh parsley
½ teaspoon sweet Hungarian paprika

Place chicken breasts, one at a time, into plastic wrap and pound gently until they are about ½-inch thick. Season with salt and pepper. In a large skillet over medium heat, heat the butter until it is melted and just bubbles. Add the chicken breasts and sauté until golden on both sides. Remove the breasts to a baking dish and keep warm while you make the sauce.

Add wine to the skillet and cook about 3 minutes, until wine is reduced and slightly thickened. Add morels, cherries, and pecans and cook for 3 minutes more. Stir in the cream and cook another minute before adding the lemon juice, salt, pepper, parsley, and paprika. Place chicken on individual plates or a serving platter. Pour sauce over the chicken and serve.
Serves: 4–6.

Note: If morels or cherries are not available, Annabel suggests substituting any dried fruit or berry and other wild mushrooms.

Holland Dutch Winterfest, Holland, MI

For the sight, sound, taste, and smell of a traditional Dutch yuletide season, there's no place like Holland—Holland, Michigan, that is. In part this event is designed to reenact the so-called Christmas Days of the Low Countries, as well as the Feast of Sinterklaas, observed on December 6 for centuries in the Netherlands.

The very Dutch town of Holland is at its best, exuding holiday charm along its brick-lined streets. In typical Dutch fashion, all traces of snow have been removed from Main Street. In Centennial Park, 23,000 lights create fanciful images evocative of every child's dream of Christmas. Historic buildings and Holland's one-of-a-kind shops are decked out in holiday trimmings, as locals and visitors alike attend special holiday theater productions, historic home tours, and holiday teas, or purchase gifts and decorative greens. The open-air Kerstmarkt consists of quaint wooden booths that line the brick pathways of Centennial Park, and visitors flock to the area in search of unique gifts and foods for the holidays.

Everyone enjoys the very Dutch foods, such as hot pea soup, pigs in a blanket, *Oliebollen* (fruited doughnut balls), and chocolate *Letterbanket.* The latter is a renowned Dutch pastry, usually made of puff pastry with an almond paste filling, traditional on both Sinterklaas Eve and at Christmas. For Sinterklaas, the *Letterbankets,* or "Dutch letters," are shaped into the family initials; at Christmas, they're shaped into wreaths and decorated with glacéed fruit. On St. Nicholas Eve, Sinterklaas arrives atop his white horse and passes out *Speculaas,* a traditional cookie, or Spicy Sinterklaas Cake.

Two cookbooks from the Holland Junior Welfare League contain wonderful Dutch recipes: *Eet Smakelijk,* the group's first cookbook, and *Dawn to Dusk: A Taste of Holland,* which won the 1996 Tabasco Community Cookbook Midwest Award.

Erwtensoep (Dutch Pea Soup)

This heritage recipe was contributed to the Holland Junior Welfare League's *Eet Smakelijk* by Mrs. Ken Kleis.

1 pound dried peas
1 medium pork hock, shoulder pork, or metworst
3 quarts water
Salt and pepper to taste
1½ cups celery, diced
3 medium onions, chopped
3 potatoes, diced
2 carrots, diced
Parsley
1 cup milk

The Day After Thanksgiving Through the Third Sunday in December

Cover peas completely with cold water and soak overnight. Drain. Cook the peas and meat in water for 2 hours. Add the salt, pepper, celery, onions, potatoes, and carrots and cook for 1 hour. Add the parsley and milk and cook for 10 minutes longer. Serves: 8–10.

Morel Mushroom Festival, Boyne City, MI

An organized search for "the elusive morel" has been going on in Boyne City, Michigan, since 1961 under the guise of the Mushroom Festival, recently renamed the "Morel Mushroom Festival." The celebration starts with an educational seminar for both the novice and the experienced hunter, along with samples of morel soup, followed by a guided practice hunt designed to show novices the ropes.

The big day is Saturday, when visitors and competitors can enjoy the "Morel Cookbook Breakfast," in which a local chef prepares one of the morel recipes in the *Taste of Boyne* cookbook. Then it's off to the National Morel Hunting Championship, where approximately 450 participants compete to see who can gather the most morels in ninety minutes.

Back in town, everyone heads for "A Taste of Boyne," where area restaurants offer specialties made with their favorite fungi, as well as wild leeks and wild asparagus. Those who wish to take a few morels home attend the morel auction.

Cheese-Stuffed Mushrooms

Rebecca Andrews of Boyne City developed this winning recipe reprinted from *A Taste of Boyne*.

1 cup flour
Salt and pepper to taste
9 ounces beer (add more if necessary)
String cheese (enough to stuff 20–25 mushrooms)
20–25 medium to large morels, whole, or medium button mushrooms
3 cups vegetable oil for frying
Salt

Whisk together the flour, salt, pepper, and beer to make a thickened batter. Stuff very thin, short strips of cheese into the base of each mushroom until full. Heat the oil in a saucepan. Dip mushrooms in batter and deep-fry until light brown and crisp. Do not overfry. Drain on paper towels and salt to taste. Serve immediately. Yield: 20–25 mushrooms.

Thursday through Sunday of the Third Weekend in May

National Baby Food Festival, Fremont, MI

Fremont, Michigan, home to Gerber Products, is known as the "Baby Food Capital of the World," and the National Baby Food Festival promotes and celebrates the local industry. This is a family-oriented event, with activities including a bed race, an executive tricycle race, and a baby crawl race. In the baby food-eating contest, adult entrants attempt to eat five jars of baby food as quickly and neatly as possible.

The Baby Food Cook-Off makes the point that baby food isn't just for babies. Each recipe must include baby food as an ingredient. The contest has delivered so many excellent recipes that the National Baby Food Festival, in conjunction with the Fremont Chamber of Commerce, produced a cookbook. The *National Baby Food Festival Cook-Off Cookbook* contains recipes for main dishes, salads, vegetables, breads, cookies, and desserts.

Third Week in July

Blueberry Buckle Pastry Bread

Pat Glancy of Fremont, MI, entered this bread and walked off with the grand prize at the 1995 National Baby Food Festival Cook-Off.

½ cup warm milk (105°–115°)
1 package active dry yeast
1 tablespoon sugar
3 egg yolks
1 cup heavy cream
3½ cups all-purpose flour
¼ cup sugar
1 teaspoon salt
½ cup firm butter
2 jars Gerber Blueberry Buckle (Third Foods)
1½ cups fresh or frozen blueberries
Powdered sugar for garnish

Combine the milk, yeast, and 1 tablespoon sugar. Mix in the egg yolks and cream. Set aside for 10 minutes. Blend flour, ¼ cup sugar, and salt in mixing bowl. Cut in butter until the pieces are the size of small beans. Pour the yeast mixture over the flour mixture. Fold just until ingredients are mixed. Do not overmix. Cover with plastic wrap. Refrigerate for 4 hours or overnight.

Turn dough onto a lightly floured board. Divide into three portions. Dust each with flour. Roll one portion at a time to make a rectangle. With a knife, make 4-inch cuts on each long side on the diagonal, leaving four inches in the middle uncut. Spoon ⅓ of the Gerber Blueberry Buckle down the center and then cover with ½ cup blueberries. Crisscross strips over filling to simulate a braid. Repeat with remaining dough.

Place braids on greased cookie sheets. Let rise until almost double in size (1–2 hours). When rising is almost complete, preheat oven to 375°. Bake loaves for 25–30 minutes or until golden brown. Sprinkle with powdered sugar. Yield: 3 loaves.

National Cherry Festival, Traverse City, MI

Peter Dougherty, a Presbyterian minister, planted the first cherry orchard in 1852 on Michigan's Old Mission Peninsula, and others soon followed suit. By 1900, the tart cherry industry was booming. Today, there are over two million cherry trees in the region, earning Traverse City the title "Cherry Capital of the World." About three-fourths of the U.S. tart cherry crop is produced here. The primary variety is the Montmorency, perfect for pies, preserves, jellies, and juices.

A spring ceremony called the "Blessing of the Blossoms" started in 1924 and has become the National Cherry Festival. Held in July and attracting a half million visitors annually, the Cherry Festival includes an array of activities—air shows, parades, sporting events, concerts, children's events, a juried arts and crafts fair, and a giant midway.

Those who come for the cherries are not disappointed. After touring a cherry farm or two, most visitors purchase fresh cherries to take home. There are also lots of packaged products for sale, such as cherry mustard, cherry fudge sauce, cherry salsa and barbecue sauces, cherry pastries, and dried cherries. An entire meal prepared with cherries is the focal point of the Very Cherry Luncheon Buffet. And, of course, there's the Cherry Pie Eating Contest.

Glazed Pork Roast

A winning recipe from *Cherry Creations— The Ultimate Cherry Cookbook* by Dr. Myles H. Bader.

One 4-pound boneless pork loin roast, rolled

Sauce:
12 ounces cherry preserves
2 tablespoons light corn syrup
¼ cup red wine vinegar
¼ teaspoon salt
¼ teaspoon cinnamon
¼ teaspoon nutmeg
¼ teaspoon cloves
¼ cup slivered almonds, toasted

Sauce: In a saucepan, combine the cherry preserves, corn syrup, vinegar, salt, cinnamon, nutmeg, and cloves. Cover and cook on low heat for about 4 minutes. Remove cover, stir, and cook for 2 minutes more. Add almonds.

Assembly: Preheat oven to 325°. Insert a meat thermometer into the center of the thickest muscle of pork loin. Roast the loin, fat-side up, until the meat thermometer reads 150°. Glaze with cherry almond sauce and continue cooking until meat thermometer reads 170°. Or simply roast the pork at 350° for 30 minutes per pound. Serve remaining sauce with the roast.
Serves: 6–8.

Note: You may want to increase the amount of sauce by fifty percent or even double it—it's that good!

Begins on the First Saturday After the Fourth of July and Runs for Eight Days

Pig Gig Rib Fest, Bay City, MI

No wonder folks in the Midwest are partial to pork: Iowa leads the way in U.S. pork production with other Midwest states contributing as well. Shortly after the Civil War, Chicago became a meatpacking center with the establishment of facilities by such industry luminaries as Armour and Swift. So abundant was pork that "Chicago" remained a slang term for pork meat well into the twentieth century.

The Pig Gig, held in Bay City's Veterans Memorial Park, is the Midwest's championship rib cook-off. The contest was the brainstorm of Billy Bones, former city manager and rib competitor, and grows more popular every year. Lots of fun activities are based on the theme of pigs: pig racing, pig calling, the Kiss a Pig Contest, an "Oink Oink" contest, and a comedy called "Come Tickle Your Ribs." There are also plenty of musical entertainment, a Paul Bunyan Lumberjack Show, and a jalapeño-eating contest.

The rib cook-offs are serious business at the Pig Gig. National contenders battle Michigan's best "ribbers" for the first place trophy and the title Best in the Midwest. Radio, TV, and political celebrities compete in the Celebrity Rib Challenge. Everyone in attendance gets to vote for the People's Choice Award.

Johnny Burke's "For Crying Out Loud" BBQ Sauce

Johnny Burke of WHNN Radio in Saginaw, MI, has won the celebrity rib contest on numerous occasions and modestly says that his rib sauce "is pretty darn good."

1 cup ketchup
½ cup prepared yellow mustard
½ cup honey
¼ cup whiskey
¼ cup Louisiana cayenne pepper sauce (more if desired)
2 tablespoons brown sugar
2 tablespoons red wine vinegar
1 tablespoon soy sauce
1 tablespoon teriyaki sauce
2 teaspoons chili powder
1 teaspoon onion salt
1 teaspoon dry mustard
1 teaspoon Worcestershire sauce
1 teaspoon ground black pepper
½ teaspoon minced garlic
½ teaspoon cayenne pepper
½ teaspoon salt
¼ teaspoon liquid smoke

Thursday through Sunday During the First Weekend in August

Mix all ingredients in a large saucepan, bring to a boil over medium heat, then lower heat and simmer, uncovered, for ½ hour. Use as you would any favorite BBQ sauce. It is wonderful for barbecued ribs and chicken. Yield: 2½ cups.

Johnny says, "This recipe is very spicy to most people, but some are real gluttons for punishment (count me in that crowd!), so for extra spiciness, you might try adding your favorite jalapeño salt, chopped red jalapeño peppers, ground Scotch bonnet pepper, or other favorite hot spices."

Minnesota

The British assumption of control over the early fur trade paved the way for increasing settlement of Minnesota, first by savvy Yankees and then by German and Scandinavian immigrants beginning in the early 1800s. By the late 1800s, the state's lucrative dairy industry was well established, and the proliferation of flour mills and dairy products earned the state one of its nicknames, the "Bread and Butter State." Lumbering, begun during the 1830s, attracted other pioneers, who came to work in the logging camps that were the forerunners of Minnesota's still flourishing timber industry.

Many people associate Minnesota with its famous wild rice, officially recognized as the "state grain." Production of wild rice is closely regulated, and it must be harvested in the traditional way from a canoe, using only a pole for power and sticks with which to beat the rice into the canoe. Minnesota also has significant potato production and a populace that likes its pie. The traditional Danish afternoon coffee ritual, known as *eftermiddagskaffen,* has so greatly influenced Minnesotans that pie and coffee are practically a state institution.

Aebleskiver Days, Tyler, MN

Since 1963, folks in Tyler, Minnesota, have gotten together to celebrate Aebleskiver Days. The festival was originally begun by the town's businessmen to show their appreciation to the community, and it serves to highlight Danish heritage as well. The festival is so popular that Tyler, population 1,257, temporarily quadruples in size.

On Friday evening, there's a kiddie parade and float competition as well as a Junior Miss program. Saturday features volleyball and softball tournaments, an artfest, Danish dancers, and Danish craft demonstrations. At night, there's a parade followed by a dance under a giant tent.

There's plenty of traditional cuisine on Saturday. Spearheaded by the ladies of the Danebod Church, *aebleskiver* are served throughout the day, and adventurous visitors can even try their hand at frying the round Danish pancakes. From 11:00 A.M. until 3:00 P.M. on Saturday, a mouthwatering array of open-faced Danish sandwiches is available. Made from roast pork, salmon loaf, sliced eggs, *vullepolse* (spiced cold meat), and Havarti cheese, the sandwiches are prepared on homemade rye bread baked in tall round cans, then beautifully garnished with red cabbage, potato salad, lettuce, radishes, cooked prunes stuffed with cream cheese, orange slices, olives, and green pepper.

At the sweet shop, visitors can select a variety of cookies and Danish coffee cakes served with milk and coffee. Many recipes are in the cookbook *Danish Recipes: Greetings from Tyler,* compiled by the Danebod English Ladies Aid.

Friday and Saturday of the Weekend Following Father's Day in June

Danish Kringle (Coffeecake)

A heritage recipe from *Danish Recipes: Greetings From Tyler*, compiled by
Danebod English Ladies Aid, Tyler, MN.

Cakes:
1 cup lard
Pinch of baking soda
1 package dry yeast
¼ cup warm water
2 tablespoons sugar
2½ cups flour
2 teaspoons salt
½ teaspoon crushed cardamom
2 egg yolks, beaten
1 cup milk
Soft butter
Powdered sugar
Thick cream
Rum extract
Unblanched sliced almonds

   Beat the lard and baking soda until fluffy.
Dissolve the yeast with warm water and sugar.
Combine flour, salt, and cardamom. Combine the
lard, yeast mixture, eggs, and milk and add to
flour mixture. Mix well, forming a soft dough.
Refrigerate several hours or overnight.
   Roll dough out into two large or three small
strips. Spread the center of each strip with soft
butter and prepared filling of choice (see below).
Fold dough over from both sides, pinching to seal
well. Place on cookie sheets and let rise for
2–3 hours.
   Preheat oven to 350°. Before baking, spread
each strip with a frosting made from powdered
sugar, thick cream, and rum extract. Make
frosting just thick enough to spread easily. If too
thin, it will run off during baking. Sprinkle with
unblanched sliced almonds. Bake for 20–30
minutes, until lightly browned. Yield: 2 or 3
loaves.

Filling 1:
¾ cup brown sugar
1 teaspoon cinnamon
¾ cup sugar

   Mix all ingredients together.

Filling 2:
½ teaspoon ground cardamom
¼ cup soft butter
2 cups sifted powdered sugar
2 tablespoons cream
1 cup light raisins

   Mix together cardamom and butter, then
gradually stir in remaining ingredients.

Filling 3:
1 can almond filling (Solo is recommended)
½ cup sugar
½ cup water
¾ cup crushed rusks or zwieback
1 teaspoon almond extract

   Heat almond filling, sugar, and water until
blended. Add rusk or zwieback crumbs and
extract.

Bean Hole Days, Pequot Lakes, MN

Pequot Lakes, Minnesota, is in the heart of the state's lake country along the Paul Bunyan Trail. It's the home of "Bunyan's Fishing Bobber"—a giant red and white water tank that towers over the city.

Those in the know equate Pequot Lakes with its annual Bean Hole Days, a local tradition rooted in the logging camps of yesteryear, when camp cooks buried kettles of beans to cook overnight in coal pits, unearthing them the following day to feed small armies of hungry lumberjacks. The Pequot recipe, passed down from one generation of "Bean Holers" to the next, is a closely guarded secret that dates back seventy to a hundred years, depending which legend you believe.

For the festival, nearly 500 pounds of made-from-scratch beans are cooked in six immense cast-iron kettles, lowered into the cooking pits the night before with the help of a trusty backhoe. At noon the next day, the beans are raised from the hot coals, stirred with the traditional canoe paddle, and served free of charge to over 2,000 hungry people in Pequot's Wayside Park. Lemonade, made from another secret recipe, and buns are the traditional accompaniments. For those who need a little something extra, the local Lions Club serves bratwursts.

Meanwhile, the women of Our Savior's Lutheran Church hold their annual bazaar and bake sale, and they demonstrate the Scandinavian art of making *lefse,* a traditional flatbread. Hot-off-the-grill *lefse* is sold along with fresh fruit pie and ice cream, the perfect finale to a Bean Hole meal. A flea market and live music add to the day's events.

The Bean Hole Days Recipe Contest offers two categories—main dishes and miscellaneous. Judging is based fifty percent on taste, twenty percent on ease of preparation, twenty percent on originality, and ten percent on appearance. Despite low ratings for the appearance of the beans, folks are urged to take a "looky looky" at the beans before judging in order to get new ideas for summer picnics.

Tuesday and Wednesday Following the Fourth of July

Black Bean Chalupas

This entry won Joe Hallbeck first place in the Bean Hole Days Recipe Contest.
Reprinted with permission from Echo Publishing.

1 pound dried black beans
2 quarts ham stock*
1 cup diced celery
1 cup diced onion
1 cup diced red bell pepper
¼ cup vegetable oil
2 tablespoons chopped garlic
2 tablespoons chili powder
1 tablespoon dried oregano
1 teaspoon ground cumin
2 teaspoons white pepper
1 cup mixed wild and white rice, or 1 cup white rice, cooked
Prepared salsa
1 package flour tortillas (jumbo, red-pepper tortillas are recommended)
2 cups shredded cheddar cheese

Toppings: shredded lettuce, diced tomatoes, black olives, and avocado
Sour cream and additional salsa

Bring the black beans to a boil in ham stock, then simmer until tender. Soaking overnight will reduce cooking time, but allow 1½–2 hours. Sauté the celery, onion, and bell pepper in oil until tender. Add the garlic and spices and simmer a little longer.

Preheat oven to 400°. Mix together the beans, vegetables, and rice. Spread the desired amount of salsa on tortillas, then top with equal measures of bean mixture and shredded cheddar cheese. Bake until cheese is melted and edges of tortilla are turning golden brown. Slice baked tortilla into wedges with pizza cutter and sprinkle with toppings. Serve with sour cream and additional salsa. Serves: 10–12.

*Ham stock: Add 2–3 tablespoons ham or beef base to boiling water. Add dashes of Tabasco and Worcestershire sauces to taste.

Note: If the beans have been soaked overnight, they can be successfully cooked in 3 (15-ounce) cans beef broth spiced to taste.

Braham Pie Day, Braham, MN

It should be no surprise that a day devoted to pie can be found in America's Heartland. Some 5,000 people flock to Braham, one hour north of the Minneapolis-St. Paul area, every year to celebrate Braham as the "Homemade Pie Capital of Minnesota." Begun in 1990, Braham Pie Day "married its sweetheart, the Isanti County Historical Society's Ice Cream Social, in 1992, creating a perfect union between soul mates."

Pies are everywhere. Performing artists put pie into their repertoires, and there's even a r^2 math challenge. A pie race, an art show, artisans, and a quilt show provide plenty of entertainment.

Braham's official motto is "Pie for Strength." Two pie-eating contests challenge those with an appetite for America's favorite dessert. Those who lack a competitive spirit can buy their pie by the slice, selecting from hundreds. Fruit and berry pies are served outdoors, and two local restaurants serve cream, chiffon, and custard pies. Every slice is available á la mode, and the Pie Day song is "Remember the Alamode."

The pie-baking contest attracts the very best talent from miles around. There are two categories—fresh fruit and baked fruit—for both adults and children. Following the judging and presentation of special pie plates to the winners, all pies are auctioned off to the highest bidders. For a more lasting souvenir of the festival, visitors can purchase a copy of *Braham's Pie Cookbook*.

Fruit 'n' Nut Cherry Pie

At the age of 12, Rose Arrowsmith of Braham, MN, won Best Overall Pie with this entry in the Braham Pie Baking Contest.

1 (21-ounce) can cherry pie filling
1 (20-ounce) can crushed pineapple, undrained
¾ cup sugar
2 tablespoons cornstarch
1 teaspoon red food coloring (optional)
4 medium, firm bananas, sliced
½ cup chopped pecans or walnuts
2 (9-inch) pie shells, baked and cooled
Whipped cream for garnish

In a saucepan, combine the pie filling, pineapple, sugar, cornstarch, and food coloring. Bring to a boil over medium heat, stirring constantly. Cook and stir for 2 minutes. Cool. Fold in the bananas and nuts. Pour filling into the cooled pie shells and chill in the refrigerator for 2–3 hours. Garnish with whipped cream and refrigerate. Yield: 2 pies.

Heritagefest, New Ulm, MN

In 1683, the first German immigrants came to America. Eventually, Germans made their way to Minnesota and established the town of New Ulm.

Heritagefest is all about keeping old traditions alive, and there is plenty to celebrate. Thousands of visitors come to the festival for German music and family entertainment, including Tuba Mania, in which hundreds of tubas serenade the crowd with German tunes. The *Narren,* or masked characters, are a composite of everyday people who give color and life to communities everywhere. Characters like Fritz the Sausagemaker, Rosa the Baker, and Tilly the Feather Lady roam the festival. The masks come from Germany. For shoppers, there's the Bavarian-style gift shop with oodles of imported items, and there's also the arts and crafts exhibit featuring handmade items and traditional folk crafts.

A large selection of German beverages is available, including imported beer and *radlers,* beer mixed with lemon-lime soda. Favorites like bratwurst, *Landaeger* (a smoked German dinner sausage made with pork, beef, and mustard seed), sauerkraut, spaetzle, German potato salad, *pfannekuchen* (miniature doughnuts), apple strudel, and *schmierkuchen* (a delicious coffeecake) are especially popular.

Es Schmeckt Gut, a cookbook developed by the ladies of New Ulm for the city's centennial celebration in 1983, is a great souvenir for visitors who want to learn more about German cooking.

Friday through Sunday During the Second and Third Weekends in July

Schmierkuchen (Coffeecake)

A heritage recipe from Es Schmeckt Gut.

Dough:
1 package dry yeast
¼ cup warm water
1 cup milk
3 tablespoons plus 1½ teaspoons sugar
2 eggs, beaten
1½ cups flour
3 tablespoons soft shortening (lard)
2 cups flour

Filling:
1½ pounds small curd cottage cheese
½ cup cream
¾ cup sugar
2 tablespoons flour
1 teaspoon salt
2 eggs, beaten

Topping:
1 pound prunes
¼ cup sugar
1 teaspoon cinnamon
½ teaspoon nutmeg
Sugar
Cinnamon

Dough: Dissolve yeast in warm water. Let stand for 10 minutes. Scald the milk and pour over the sugar. Let it cool down to lukewarm. Then add the yeast to the milk mixture, and stir in 2 beaten eggs. Add 1½ cups flour. Stir until very smooth. Add the lard and beat until smooth. Add the 2 cups of flour and stir until the dough forms a rough ball. If needed, add a little bit more flour. Grease bottom and sides of a bowl and also grease the ball of dough. Set dough into bowl, cover, and set in a warm place until dough doubles in size.

Filling: Mix all ingredients.

Topping: Cook prunes until tender; drain and mash. Add rest of ingredients and mix.

Preheat oven to 350°. Divide the dough into 4 (9-inch) pie pans. Make a well in the center of each piece of dough and work it up the edges of the pan. Fill each dough-lined pan with a quarter of the filling. Dot each with a quarter of the topping. Sprinkle with a little more sugar and cinnamon. Bake for 30–35 minutes.
Yield: 4 coffee cakes.

Hopkins Raspberry Festival, Hopkins, MN

Years ago, the town of Hopkins, just outside Minneapolis, was known as "America's Raspberry Capital." A local civic group decided to capitalize on the raspberry crop, and the first big berry bust was held in 1935 to spotlight the superiority of Hopkins' red raspberries. Some 20,000 people turned up at that first festival and proceeded to have a wonderful time.

Today, the Raspberry Festival hosts over 200,000 people, although only a few berry farms remain in the area. The festival has a Raspberry Cook-Off. Vendors trot out delicious raspberry specialties like raspberry lemonade. There's also a Raspberry Pie-Eating Contest. Other events include an enormous parade, loads of sporting events, and an impressive arts and crafts show. Those who choose to honor the raspberry seek out a copy of *Raspberry Delights*, a cookbook compiled by the Hopkins Community Center and filled with old-fashioned, mouthwatering recipes.

Ten Days in July, Always Ending on the Third Sunday

Fresh Raspberry Encore

Florinda K. Buntrock created this recipe and took the grand prize in the 1981 Raspberry Cook-Off.

Crust:
¼ cup butter
2 tablespoons brown sugar, packed
½ cup wheat germ
½ cup crushed vanilla wafers
½ cup flaked coconut
¼ cup finely chopped walnuts

Filling:
1 (3-ounce) package raspberry-flavored gelatin
2 tablespoons sugar
1 cup boiling water
¾ cup ice cold water
2 cups fresh raspberries

Topping:
30 large marshmallows
⅓ cup milk
1 cup heavy cream
¼ cup reserved crust mixture

Crust: In a saucepan, melt the butter over low heat. Add the brown sugar and stir until dissolved. Remove from heat and add rest of ingredients. Reserve ¼ cup of mixture for topping. Press remaining mixture evenly and firmly over the bottom of a 11 x 7-inch pan. Chill in freezer for 10 minutes, then transfer to refrigerator.

Filling: In a bowl, mix the gelatin and sugar. Add boiling water and stir until gelatin and sugar are dissolved. Add cold water and raspberries and stir to combine. Chill until almost set but still spreadable. Spread over crust and refrigerate while preparing topping.

Topping: In a heavy saucepan over low heat, melt marshmallows with milk, stirring until smooth. Cool but do not refrigerate. Whip the cream and fold into the cooled marshmallow mixture. Spread over the filling. Sprinkle with the reserved crust mixture. Cover and chill for several hours before serving. Serves: 12.

Variation: Subsitute black raspberry gelatin and black raspberries.

Isanti County Potato Festival, Cambridge, MN

Isanti County, just north of Minneapolis, is an area long connected with potatoes. On the last Saturday of September, students, assisted by parents, community residents, the Cambridge Chamber of Commerce, newspapers, and the Isanti County Historical Society, celebrate local potato production.

Home to folks of Scandinavian descent, Isanti County ties its event to a potato festival in Sweden. Everything is geared to the noble spud. A potato obstacle course and the couch potato race provide amusement for energetic souls, while performing artists put the potato in their repertoire. The coronation of King and Queen Spud from seventh- and eighth-graders is as popular as the Potato Pancake and Potato Sausage Breakfast. Potato sausage is a Swedish delicacy prepared by a local packing plant.

Visitors snack on other regional favorites, including *lefse* (Scandinavian flatbread), baked potatoes with various toppings, fried potato chip swirls, deep-fried onion rosettes, potato soup, and Cornish pasties filled with potatoes. Those with a competitive spirit enter their favorite potato dish in the Great Potato Bake-Off.

Cheesy Potato Slices

Kathryn Stavem's recipe made her a winner in the Great Potato Bake-Off at the Isanti County Potato Festival.

Last Saturday in September

6 medium, unpeeled russet potatoes
¼ teaspoon salt
⅛ teaspoon black pepper
½ teaspoon rosemary leaves
½ teaspoon thyme leaves
½ teaspoon chives (fresh or dried)
¾–1 cup butter
½–1 cup grated cheddar cheese
¼ teaspoon paprika

Preheat oven to 425°. Scrub potatoes well and slice very thin. Spread in layers in a lightly greased 13 x 9-inch or larger pan. Sprinkle with salt, pepper, rosemary, thyme, and chives and dot with butter. Bake, covered with foil, for 15–30 minutes. Sprinkle with grated cheese and paprika. Bake another 10–12 minutes or until potatoes are tender-crisp and cheese is melted. Serves: 4–6.

Lake Vermilion Wild Rice Festival, Tower, MN

Saturday and Sunday of Labor Day Weekend

Tower is located on Lake Vermilion in the heart of the lake district of northeastern Minnesota. This is tall pine country, and nearby Soudan Underground Mine State Park serves as a reminder that it's also a former mining area. Many people in and around Tower work in the production of wild rice, a major export of the state.

Wild rice isn't really rice. It's an aquatic grass that grows wild in lakes and rivers. Today's commercial production takes place in artificial paddies. French explorers discovered the rare wild grain in 1650 in northern Minnesota. They raved over the new taste sensation and called it *folle ovoine,* or "wild oats." Native Americans in the lake region, mostly Chippewa and Sioux, also revered the tall aquatic grass. For nearly two centuries, they waged tribal wars for control of the shallow waters where wild rice flourishes. Chippewa Indians still paddle their canoes out onto Lake Big Rice or Lost Lake, not far from Tower, to harvest wild rice.

Several thousand people attend the Lake Vermilion Rice Festival, where they learn about the grain's rich history. A voyageur encampment and rendezvous demonstrations illustrate the old trading days, and many visit the Sisu Heritage Log Cabin, an authentic Finnish abode. Plenty of tall mining tales from the 1880s are told during the storytelling sessions.

Each day the festival opens with a wild rice pancake breakfast. Afternoons are reserved for the ice-cream and pie social and a fish fry put on by the Native Americans. One of the most popular events is the Wild Rice Sampler held by the Women's Civic Improvement Club of Tower. They prepare specialties from their *Wild Rice Cookbook,* and for just one dollar, visitors can taste five different dishes.

Wild Rice Pancakes

A festival favorite from *Tower Women's Club Wild Rice Cookbook.*

1 cup flour
1 tablespoon sugar
¼ teaspoon salt
1 tablespoon baking powder
1 egg
1 cup milk
2 rounded tablespoons sour cream
2 tablespoons butter, melted
½ cup cooked wild rice

Combine and sift the flour, sugar, salt, and baking powder. Combine the egg, milk, and sour cream and beat. Pour into dry ingredients and beat until smooth. Add the butter and rice. Preheat and lightly grease a griddle. Drop batter by tablespoons and cook pancakes until golden on each side. Yield: 10–12 pancakes.

Missouri

   Early German immigrants to the United States settled with everyone else in the eastern colonies, primarily in New York, New Jersey, and Pennsylvania. As America's population moved westward, so did German immigrants, with the vast majority settling in the Midwest.

   In 1824, a German businessman named Gottfried Duden arrived in Missouri's Lake Creek Valley and began writing what would become a series of eighteen letters home describing the new land in glowing terms. So influential were his letters, later published as a volume entitled *A Report on a Journey to the Western States of North America*, that Duden's book was described as "the most important piece of literature in the history of the German immigration." As a result, German immigrants poured into Missouri seeking land and opportunity. In the 1840s, Warren County, Missouri, continued its growth as a German-American settlement. Although Gottfried Duden had returned to his homeland in 1827, German settlement in the area was largely due to his influence.

Deutsch Country Days, Luxenhaus Farm, Marthasville, MO

Always Saturday and Sunday of the Third Weekend in October

The glory of the fall foliage blanketing the hills around Marthasville, Missouri, provides the perfect backdrop for Deutsch Country Days, a re-creation of the area's early German life, which was first celebrated at Luxenhaus Farm in 1982. Over 10,000 people flock to this festival, attracted by the opportunity to learn about German immigrant history and culture, try their hand at various old-time crafts, and eat great food.

Luxenhaus Farm was established by Bob and Lois Hostkoetter, who realized in 1970 that many of Missouri's historic buildings were disappearing. This was the beginning of what became a Herculean effort to salvage nineteen log buildings and a covered bridge, relocate them to a rocky wooded hillside near Marthasville, and restore each structure to its former glory. All the buildings and the bridge were originally built between 1800 and 1860. Today, Luxenhaus Farm, *platt Deutsch* for "log house farm," is a testimonial to the determination of one family to preserve nineteenth-century German heritage, traditions, and folkways.

The farm can only be visited during Deutsch Country Days, and visitors from all over the world make their plans early. The uniqueness of the event is underscored by the sheer number of exhibits, conducted by juried artisans, who re-create the trades and lifestyle of early German immigrants. There is something for every member of the family in the seventy-two skills exhibited. Women are drawn to hand quilting, loom weaving, *scherenschnitte*, German *fraktur,* goose feather trees, *kloppolei* (bobbin lace), and Moravian paper stars, while men generally head for exhibits on gunsmithing, the crafting of Windsor chairs, log hewing, rail splitting, wood carving, and blacksmithing. Kids seem fascinated by every detail. For cooks, there are wonderful exhibits on butter churning, apple pressing, sausage stuffing, apple butter cooking, canning and preserving, root beer brewing, and open-pan sorghum making.

Visitors are rewarded with German cuisine, available from the *Essen Haus* (Eating House), the *Landschaft Küche* (Countryside Kitchen), and the *Kirche Küche* (Church Kitchen). The food is pure German goodness, with bratwurst or frankfurters accompanied by German potato salad, plenty of sauerkraut, and those wonderful German gherkins (pickles). Most folks cannot resist the festival's famous kettle cooked beef. Funnel cakes, caramel apples, German *keks* (cookies), freshly baked pretzels, Amish candy, and peanut brittle are favorite sweets, and nearly everyone returns home with a loaf of freshly baked bread, along with a few jars of native honey or homemade jellies and preserves.

Anyone interested in German heritage cooking will find *Deutsch Country Days Old German Cookbook* indispensable. Lois Hostkoetter carefully researched the recipes, gleaning them from old cookbooks and updating them for modern kitchens. All recipes date from the late 1700s to the late 1800s.

Kettle Beef

A traditional recipe uncovered by Lois Hostkoetter in her research of authentic German culinary traditions, this is the prized dish served at Deutsch Country Days, where a full quarter of beef is cooked in an enormous cast-iron kettle. Once cooked, the beef is pulled apart, warmed in gravy, and served on sandwich buns. The recipe is from *Deutsch Country Days Old German Cookbook*.

1 (5-pound) beef rump roast or brisket
¼ cup bacon drippings
1 teaspoon ground ginger
2 teaspoons salt
¼ teaspoon ground pepper
3 bay leaves
5 whole cloves
1 large onion, minced
5 cloves garlic, minced
1 cup water or beef stock

Have roast tied so it holds its shape. Heat bacon drippings in a heavy iron kettle. Season with ginger, salt, and pepper and sear well on all sides. Add the bay leaves, cloves, onion, garlic, and stock. Cover tightly and simmer 4–5 hours or until tender. Cool, pull meat apart, and reheat in gravy. Serves: 10–14.

Japanese Festival, St. Louis, MO

The Japanese Garden, surrounding a 4½-acre lake at the Missouri Botanical Garden, is the perfect setting for the annual Japanese Festival. The Japanese Garden is the largest traditional garden of its type in North America. More than 30,000 visitors come to experience a broad range of Japanese cultural events staged by the Missouri Botanical Garden and Japanese-American organizations in the St. Louis area.

Concerts of Japanese folk music and spectacular performances of *taiko* drums attract the interest of many, while others take part in traditional dancing or martial arts demonstrations. Formal Japanese tea ceremonies are held throughout the weekend on Teahouse Island. Demonstrations of *ikebana* (flower arranging), bonsai, origami, *raku* pottery making, and a host of other activities introduce viewers to Japanese crafts and art forms.

Exquisite Japanese cuisine is demonstrated by local restaurateurs, and in the food court, the Japanese America Society's *Seinen* (Young People's Committee) prepares other culinary delights, such as *yaki soba* (fried noodles).

Saturday through Monday of Labor Day Weekend

Tempura

Hiroshi Seki of Seki's Japanese Restaurant in St. Louis is known for his authentic preparation of Japanese specialties and is often asked to demonstrate his culinary skills at the festival.

Tempura batter:
1 whole egg
1 cup ice cold water
1 cup cake flour
Oil for frying

Shrimp, shelled and deveined
Flounder or other white fish, filleted and cut into pieces
Eggplant, mushrooms, green beans, and asparagus, cleaned and cut into pieces

Additional cake flour

Dipping sauce:
4 cups water
Bonito fish flakes
1 cup mirin (sweet rice cooking wine)
1 cup soy sauce
½ teaspoon sugar
½ teaspoon salt
Pinch of minced daikon (Japanese radish)
Pinch of grated fresh ginger

Batter: Mix egg with water. Add the cake flour, taking care not to overmix; there should be some lumps in the batter.

Fill a deep-fry pan ⅔ full with vegetable oil and heat to 350°. Coat each piece of shrimp, fish, and vegetable with additional cake flour, then dip into batter and deep fry until a light golden brown in color. Tempura ingredients will come to the top of the oil when done. Do not overfry. Serves: 3–4.

Dipping sauce: Bring water to a boil and add one bunch of bonito fish flakes. Let sit for 30 minutes. Drain fish flakes and add the mirin, soy sauce, sugar, and salt. Mix all ingredients and bring to a boil. Reduce heat to very low and keep warm. Just before serving, add the daikon and ginger.

Ohio

Ohio, at one time the "Gateway to the West," is populated by many people claiming Irish, German, Polish, and Swiss heritage. In the 1880s, Poles left an area of their homeland then ruled by Germany, founding the Cleveland community of Warszawa. Now known as "Slavic Village," its population was increased by subsequent waves of Polish immigrants between 1880 and 1921. Following World War II, Poles and other Europeans, left homeless by the ravages of war, arrived. Today the populations of Ohio cities like Cleveland and Columbus are growing with the arrival of new immigrants from Asia and India.

One of America's most populous states, Ohio is known for its manufacturing, including food processing. But, it's still an agricultural state that boasts substantial truck crops, especially in counties bordering Lake Erie and along the Ohio River. Troy, on the Miami River, is home to Fulton Farms, the largest producer of strawberries in the Midwest. Many farmers are diversifying into pumpkin production to round out the harvest season, and Ohio now ranks sixth in the country for this crop. Ohioans celebrate crop diversity, even embracing the dandelion, which is not a weed but a wild vegetable packed with nutrients. Even the honeybee plays a major role in the state economy, producing millions of dollars in revenue from beeswax and honey and pollinating vegetable and fruit crops. Folks in Ohio also love chocolate, and nearly everyone eats their annual share of those famous Ohio Buckeyes, cookies made from chocolate and peanut butter.

Asian Festival, Columbus, OH

The Asian Festival began in 1995 and attracted 18,000 visitors to Columbus' Franklin Park. Today, attendance is around 40,000. Thirteen Asian countries, under the auspices of the International Center's Asian American Community Service Council, seek to educate the general public on Asian culture and traditions. Visitors enjoy a showcase of music, dance, and food from such countries as Cambodia, China, India, Japan, and Vietnam.

Other events include a parade, martial arts demonstrations, storytelling, and a Japanese tea ceremony. Craftspeople demonstrate Japanese origami, Chinese calligraphy, and Indonesian palm weaving and toy making.

In addition to food booths with all sorts of Asian specialty foods, cooking demonstrations are held throughout the festival, and a marketplace abounds with flowers, fruits, vegetables, and spices.

Saturday and Sunday of Memorial Day Weekend

Chole (Garbanzo Bean Stew)

Manjula Sankarappa of Delaware, OH, is frequently asked to demonstrate the preparation of this traditional dish from India.

7 cans garbanzo beans
2 teaspoons tamarind paste
5–6 tablespoons vegetable oil
4 medium onions
7 green chili peppers
1 rounded tablespoon coriander powder
4 rounded tablespoons chane ke masala
1 heaping teaspoon chili powder
1 rounded teaspoon cumin
3 large tomatoes, cut into large cubes

Beans: Put the garbanzo beans in pressure cooker, cover with water to ¼ inch above the beans, and cook for about 3 minutes to soften. Add the tamarind paste and mix until it has melted into the garbanzo beans and water.

Gravy: In a separate pot, heat the vegetable oil on high. Sauté the onions and peppers until the onions are transparent, making sure there is enough oil to keep the onions from sticking. Add coriander powder and cook and stir for about 15 minutes. Add chane ke masala and stir; add more if desired—more can be added for flavor at end of cooking time. Add the chili powder and cumin. Add the tomatoes and mix well. Cook on low heat for about 10 minutes. Add beans and cook on low heat for 5 minutes. Remove from heat and let beans soak in gravy for about 20 minutes before serving. Serves: 6.

Note: Tamarind paste and chane ke masala may be purchased from Asian or Indian food markets.

Chocolate Festival, Lorain, OH

One-stop shopping for a vast array of Easter goodies draws a big crowd to the annual Chocolate Festival in Lorain, Ohio, which benefits the area chapter of the American Red Cross. Three local candy companies serve as major sponsors of the event, and admission entitles attendees to a free sample from each vendor. If you're looking for chocolate, it's here at the festival.

Entertainment includes an Oreo-stacking contest for both children and adults, as well as a Double Your Chocolate trivia game. At one booth, young and old have their picture taken with the Easter Bunny. Chocolate-flavored coffee and other chocolate drinks fortify shoppers, and sales of such goodies as chocolate-covered strawberries, pretzels, and gummy worms are brisk. Other favorites include chocolate truffles, brownies, cakes, and cookies. The *Chocolate Lover's Cookbook*, compiled by the Lorain County Chapter of the American Red Cross, contains may of these decadent recipes.

Fourth Friday Before Easter

Mike James' Red Ribbon Award-Winning Chocolate Peanut-Butter Chip Cookies

The late Mike Whitmore was a well-known radio personality whose stage name was Mike James. Nobody could have been more proud of having a red ribbon than Mike, and his recipe is featured in the *Chocolate Lover's Cookbook*.

1 cup butter, softened
¾ cup granulated sugar
¾ cup brown sugar, packed
1 teaspoon vanilla
2 eggs
¼ cup chocolate syrup
2½–3 cups unsifted flour
1 teaspoon baking soda
½ teaspoon salt
1 cup peanut butter chips
1 cup chocolate chips
1 cup chopped pecans or walnuts (optional)

Preheat oven to 375°. Cream butter with the granulated sugar and brown sugar. Add the vanilla and eggs. Beat well. Mix in the chocolate syrup. Combine the flour, baking soda, and salt. Add gradually to creamed mixture, then beat well. Add more flour as necessary to make a firm dough that begins to leave the sides of the bowl; this will produce a fat, soft cookie that won't spread out thin as it bakes. Stir in the chips and nuts. Drop by spoonfuls, 2 inches apart, onto ungreased baking sheets. Bake for 8–10 minutes, until edges are lightly browned. Yield: approximately 5 dozen cookies.

Circleville Pumpkin Show, Circleville, OH

Billed as "The Greatest Free Show on Earth," the Circleville Pumpkin Show is Ohio's largest festival, pulling in around 400,000 visitors annually. It's also the oldest festival in the state, conceived in 1903 when Mayor George Haswell invited area farmers to display the fruits of their harvest on the streets of town. The event was only postpond during the two World Wars.

With over fifty tons of pumpkins, many of gargantuan size, folks in Circleville say, "You really must see it to believe it!" Displays of home arts and crafts, fruits and vegetables, canned goods, and baked goods vie for attention with "The World's Largest Pumpkin Pie," which is five feet in diameter and weighs 350 pounds. Of course, there's a pumpkin pie-eating contest and a baked goods competition.

Nearly every visitor can be seen munching on one of the many delectable pumpkin goodies: waffles, fudge, pie, bread, brittle, taffy, ice cream, pancakes, doughnuts, and cotton candy. Those wanting to duplicate their favorites at home will be sure to buy a copy of *Pumpkin Recipes*, compiled by the Crusaders Sunday School Class of the Calvary United Methodist Church.

Pumpkin Fudge

The recipe for this famous festival favorite appears in *Pumpkin Recipes*.

1 cup granulated sugar
1 cup brown sugar, firmly packed
2 tablespoons light corn syrup
1 cup evaporated milk
⅓ cup canned pumpkin
¼ teaspoon cinnamon
⅛ teaspoon allspice
Pinch of nutmeg
Pinch of cloves
1 tablespoon butter
1 teaspoon vanilla
Chopped pecans (optional)

In a heavy saucepan, combine the sugars and corn syrup. Gradually stir in the evaporated milk. Cook and stir to soft ball stage (236°). Remove from heat. Mixture will be curdled. Stir in pumpkin and spices; add butter and vanilla. Place pan in cold water to cool to 100°. Beat mixture vigorously until thick, about 15 minutes. Fudge will be very thick, but curdling will disappear. Drop from spoon onto a greased cookie sheet or let stand a while, then shape into 2 logs and roll in pecans. Chill until firm. Slice logs.
Yield: Approximately 3 dozen pieces.

Begins the Third Wednesday in October for Four Days

Dandelion MayFest, Dover, OH

Anyone who thinks that the dandelion is nothing more than a pesky weed should talk to Anita Davis at Breitenbach Wine Cellars in Dover, Ohio. For over twenty years, Breitenbach has produced wine with dandelions picked by local Amish families. It wasn't long before those same folks began bringing her treasured family dandelion recipes. That was when it was decided to hold a dandelion festival to promote the health benefits and culinary uses of this member of the daylily family.

Dandelion MayFest visitors get to tour the winery and see how dandelion wine is made, and many participate in the 5K Dandelion May Run. The National Dandelion Cookoff lets amateurs and professionals compete for top honors and cash in divisions covering appetizers, soups, salads, main dishes, and desserts. A panel consisting of food writers and Ohio chefs does the judging, and prizes are awarded.

Plenty of dandelion food, based on Swiss, German, Italian, and Amish recipes, is served at the festival. Breakfast features sausage, omelettes, bread, and coffee, all of which include dandelions. A jelly tasting attracts many attendees. For lunch, there is dandelion soup, dandelion pierogies, dandelion pizza, and dandelion root ice cream. A dandelion dinner includes dandelion salad with bacon dressing, dandelion gravy over mashed potatoes, and a bit of dandelion wine to wash it all down. Those who remain unconvinced about the glories of dandelions can take home a copy of *The Great Dandelion Cookbook,* which provides 127 pages of delicious recipes.

Friday & Saturday of the First Weekend in May

Dente di Leone Polenta Lasagna (Dandelion and Polenta Lasagna)

Bocca Grande Restaurant in Canal Fulton, OH, walked off with first-place honors for this creation in the Professional Division of the National Dandelion Cookoff.

Polenta:
2½ cups boiling water
½ teaspoon salt
1 cup cold water
1 cup yellow cornmeal
2 tablespoons butter
¼ cup ricotta cheese
¼ cup grated mozzarella cheese

Meat sauce:
4 cups of your favorite marinara sauce
⅓ pound each ground veal, pork, and beef,
   browned and drained of fat

Dandelion greens:
2 pounds dandelion greens, thoroughly cleaned

White sauce:
6 tablespoons unsalted butter
6 tablespoons flour
3½ cups milk
¾ teaspoon nutmeg
¾ teaspoon salt

1¼ cups freshly grated Parmesan cheese

Polenta: In a 4-quart pot, bring 2½ cups water to a boil. Add salt. Mix the cold water and cornmeal together, then slowly add the mixture to the boiling water, stirring constantly. Lower heat and continue cooking, stirring constantly, for 15 minutes. Add the butter and mix well. Add the ricotta and mix well. Add the mozzarella and mix well. Remove from heat and pour into two 4½-inch bowls. Allow to cool thoroughly, uncovered. Cover and refrigerate at least 1 hour.

Meat sauce: Combine marinara sauce with cooked meats and simmer 20 minutes.

Dandelion greens: Blanch dandelion greens in a large pot of boiling water. Drain and immerse in ice water to retain color. Squeeze out excess water and chop finely. Set aside.

White sauce: In a large saucepan, melt the butter. Add the flour and mix well. Meanwhile, bring milk to a boil and then whisk it slowly into the butter and flour. Add seasonings and cook until thick. Remove from heat.

Assembly: Preheat oven to 350°. Remove the polenta from the bowls and cut into ¼-inch-thick slices. Spread some meat sauce over the bottom of a large baking pan. Make little lasagnas as follows: place a slice of polenta on the sauce and add more meat sauce and then white sauce. Top with a layer of dandelion greens and some of the Parmesan cheese. Repeat this layer. The third layer is polenta, white sauce and Parmesan cheese. Repeat procedure for other lasagnas. Bake for 25 minutes or until bubbly. Let stand 10 minutes before serving. Serves: 6.

Ohio Honey Festival, Oxford, OH

Ohio was buzzing with delight in 1967, the year of the first Honey Festival. Then-governor, James A. Rhodes, had proclaimed the fourth week in August as "Ohio Bee and Honey Week," in honor of Ohio's 15,000 beekeepers who have a multimillion-dollar business. The governor recommended that all citizens treat themselves to a royal breakfast of biscuits and honey that week.

The first festival was held in Lebanon, inaugurated with a press luncheon at the historic Golden Lamb. Unfortunately, no biscuits and honey were served, so, as the story goes, the governor "marched into the second-floor service area, found his biscuits, and began serving them to the newspeople." After twenty-three years, the Honey Festival was moved to Hamilton to accommodate growing crowds of more than 100,000 visitors.

In 1998, it was moved to its last location in Oxford, home of Miami University, to improve attendance and local involvement. The festival has been canceled in recent years, although the folks in Oxford-Hamilton vow to resurrect it.

The festival included a crowning of the Queen Bee, an auto and truck show, a grand parade, country music and clogging, and an arts and crafts show. Honey extraction demonstrations were held throughout the festival. The biggest draw was the Living Bee Beard performance in which some 10,000 live, swarming bees were enticed onto the chin of a brave (and caged) volunteer. According to bee experts, the secret is to fatten up the bees so they can't bend at the waist, which they must do to sting. At the conclusion of the performance, the bees were removed by a special bee vacuum.

Glorious honey confections were plentiful. Perhaps the biggest seller was the honey ice cream, made from raw honey by an Ohio ice cream manufacturer especially for the event. Other popular dishes included chicken, lemonade, waffles, and honey-crust pizza. For those with a sweet tooth, there was fresh baklava. Souvenirs included fresh honey in a variety of flavors, honey in the comb, cream honey spread, and tasty honey candy.

Not Currently Held—May be Rescheduled

Honey Lemon Cheesecake

Courtesy of the National Honey Board, this recipe is a winner for every honey lover. September is annually celebrated as National Honey Month.

Crust:
1½ cups broken vanilla wafer cookies
½ cup slivered almonds, toasted
¼ cup butter, melted

Filling:
11 ounces cream cheese, softened
1½ cups milk (divided into 1¼ cups and ¼ cup)
¼ cup fresh lemon juice
2 teaspoons freshly grated lemon peel
1 envelope unflavored gelatin
½ cup honey (such as orange blossom, sage, or tupelo honey)

Topping:
Honey for drizzling
Fresh fruits, such as raspberries, blueberries, and/or strawberries

Honey whipped cream:
1 cup heavy cream
¼ cup honey

Crust: Place the cookies and nuts in blender or food processor and process until coarse crumbs are formed. Add the butter and process until blended. Pour the crumb mixture into a buttered 9-inch springform pan, spread, and press evenly onto the bottom and up the sides of the pan, to form a crust. Freeze while preparing the filling.

Filling: Using an electric mixer, beat the cream cheese until smooth. Slowly add 1¼ cups milk, mixing until smooth and well blended. Beat in the lemon juice and peel; set aside. In a small saucepan, sprinkle gelatin over remaining ¼ cup milk; let stand 1 minute. Stir over low heat until gelatin is completely dissolved. Stir in the honey and whisk to blend. Add to the cheese mixture, mixing until well blended. Freeze for 15 minutes, then whisk the partially set mixture until smooth. Pour into prepared crust and refrigerate for at least 2 hours before serving.

Topping: Drizzle with honey and add fresh fruit on top. If desired, prepare honey whipped cream by beating heavy cream until soft peaks form; add ¼ cup honey and beat until stiff peaks form. Top cheesecake with the whipped cream or add a dollop to individual servings.

Ohio Swiss Festival, Sugarcreek, OH

Sugarcreek lies nestled in Ohio's Tuscarawas Valley, an area settled by German-Swiss immigrants, as well as the Amish. The Swiss Festival was begun in 1956, when locals realized that their major industry, making Swiss cheese, was languishing. The result was a celebration of Swiss culture that successfully promotes the wonderful Swiss cheese still produced by local cheese factories. Today, at least eight such businesses are in the immediate area surrounding Sugarcreek.

With residents decked out in authentic Swiss costumes, visitors to the festival enjoy Swiss and polka music, parades, and Swiss athletic events like *Steintossen* (stone throwing) and *Schwingfest* (Swiss wrestling). Along with grilled bratwurst served up with a good helping of kraut, there are tons of delicious Swiss cheese for immediate consumption, as well as to take home.

Fourth Friday and Saturday After Labor Day

Swiss Cheese Pie

Although the Swiss Festival doesn't produce a cookbook, Patricia Kaser of the Ohio Swiss Festival Committee graciously shared her recipes for two traditional Sugarcreek favorites that are guaranteed to win raves.

1 (9-inch) unbaked pie shell
3 eggs
1¾–2 cups milk
1 teaspoon salt
Dash of pepper
½ pound Swiss cheese, grated

Preheat oven to 400°. Thoroughly chill the pie shell. Beat the eggs and add the milk, salt, and pepper. Unless you use a very deep pie dish, you will need only 1¾ cups of the milk. Sprinkle the cheese into the pie shell. Pour the egg mixture over the cheese. Bake pie 10 minutes, then reduce heat to 350° and bake 25–40 minutes more, or until a knife inserted in center of the pie comes out clean and top is golden brown. Let set for 10 minutes before slicing. This is also excellent served cold.

Roesti

Courtesy of Patricia Kaser, Ohio Swiss Festival Committee.

3 medium potatoes (1 pound)
¼ cup finely chopped onions
½ teaspoon salt
Dash of pepper
2 tablespoons butter
½ cup grated Swiss cheese

Boil the potatoes with skins on until tender but still firm. Cool and peel the potatoes, then shred them. Mix with the onion, salt, and pepper. Melt butter in a skillet and add potatoes, frying until golden brown and stirring often. Just before serving, add the Swiss cheese and heat until cheese is melted. Serve immediately. Serves: 4.

Slavic Village Harvest Festival, Cleveland, OH

Southeast Cleveland's Fleet Avenue, between E. 55th and E. 65th Streets, is transformed into a lively street fair for one weekend every August. The historic Warsawa neighborhood is known as "Slavic Village" and was originally settled by Polish and Czech immigrants who came to work in the steel-rolling mills. Until the 1970s, it was a thriving ethnic enclave.

Today, Slavic Village is an old-world market district where sausage-makers still use secret family recipes. Although their numbers have dwindled, the sausage-making community remains tightly knit, even borrowing ingredients from each other in a pinch. Former residents retain a discriminating taste when it comes to sausage, and they return to the village to buy kielbasa flavored with garlic, stuffed into natural casings, and smoked over fruit wood. The shop owners strive to keep their food traditions alive by providing other Polish treats like *placki karlotlane,* or potato pancakes, and smoked sausage rods called *kabanosy.*

The Slavic Village Festival runs from 4:00 P.M. to midnight on Saturday and noon to 9:00 P.M. on Sunday. Nevertheless, attendance is one of the largest draws in Ohio.

The festival features polka bands and ethnic dancers. Vendors offer Polish folk art, European handicrafts, and collectibles, while local merchants sell souvenirs and pass out product information. The Slavic Village Historical Society sponsors a wonderful photographic display tracing the early history of the area.

Ethnic delicacies available from over forty vendors include kielbasa, cabbage and noodles, stuffed cabbage, pierogi, dumplings, strudels, Slovenian nut rolls called *potica,* duck soup, and Bohemian pastries known as *listy.* Sauerkraut is served alongside the sausage and pierogi. At least one vendor offers unusual potato pancakes flavored with garlic. All this is supplemented by traditional street foods like hot dogs, onion rings, Italian sausage, and corn on the cob.

Every vendor selling kielbasa is automatically entered in the annual Kielbasa Cook-Off, where TV and radio personalities judge the sausage on taste and presentation.

Ron and Josephine Altman own a thriving photography business in Slavic Village, and Josephine is an accomplished cook. She has spent the last forty years gleaning and perfecting some five hundred recipes. The result is the publication of her cookbook, *In My Mother's Kitchen,* filled with instructions for many old world dishes.

Saturday and Sunday of the Third Weekend in August

Potica (Nut Roll)

A Slavic heritage recipe from *In My Mother's Kitchen* by Josephine Altman.

Dough:
1 package dry yeast
1 tablespoon warm water
½ teaspoon sugar
3½ cups flour
3 tablespoons sugar
½ teaspoon salt
½ cup butter
3 eggs
½ cup sour cream

Nut filling:
1 pound finely chopped nuts
1 cup packed brown sugar
1 teaspoon vanilla
Milk to moisten

1 beaten egg

Dissolve the yeast in warm water; stir in the ½ teaspoon sugar, and set aside. Sift the flour, 3 tablespoons sugar, and salt into a mixing bowl. Cut in the butter until mixture is crumbly. Beat the eggs with the yeast mixture and sour cream and add to flour mixture. Mix until blended. Turn onto a floured surface and knead a few minutes until dough is smooth.

Divide dough into four equal parts. Roll each into a quarter of an inch-thick rectangle. Spread nut filling on dough and roll up like a jelly roll. Place on greased baking sheets, cover, and let rise in a warm place about 1½ hours. Preheat oven to 350°. Brush tops of rolls with beaten egg. Bake for 25–30 minutes or until golden brown. Yiled: 4 rolls.

Filling: Combine nuts, brown sugar, and vanilla, adding enough milk to bind mixture together.

Troy Strawberry Festival, Troy, OH

The Troy Strawberry Festival, held in a pristine setting on the levee along the banks of the Miami River, is one of the best festivals in the Midwest. It put Troy on the map, showcasing the Miami Valley of southwestern Ohio and the local strawberries. Troy produces roughly 7.2 million pounds of strawberries annually.

Begun in 1977, the Strawberry Festival is a family-oriented event that attracts around 250,000 visitors each year. Highlights include sporting events, dances, and over 260 high-quality arts and crafts exhibitors. There is no longer a cooking contest, but the pie-eating contest is very popular. With more over 70 nonprofit organizations offering strawberry food items, berry lovers are in their glory. Visitors can enjoy strawberry shortcake, cheesecake, fudge, funnel cakes with strawberry topping, pies, bagels with strawberry cream cheese, and various beverages. The more unusual items include strawberry burritos and pizza. Few can resist a jar or two of homemade strawberry jam as a sweet remembrance. For those who can't get their fill of berries, there's *The Official 25th Anniversary Troy Strawberry Festival Cookbook.*

Saturday and Sunday of the First Full Weekend in June

Strawberry Burritos

Kay Hamilton, business manager of the Troy Strawberry Festival, provided this recipe for a festival favorite.

Large flour tortillas
Powdered sugar
Fresh sliced strawberries, sweetened with sugar
Real whipped cream, sweetened with vanilla and powdered sugar

Lightly spray flour tortillas with water, using a spray bottle. Dust both sides of the tortillas with powdered sugar. Fill with strawberries and fold tortillas into a pocket just as you would with a burrito, leaving one end open. Top with whipped cream. Messy and sticky—but absolutely delicious!

Strawberry Chocolate Pizza

The recipe for this festival specialty is from an earlier festival cookbook *Strawberry Delights—The Cookbook for the Strawberry Lover.*

1 (18-ounce) package refrigerated sugar cookie dough
⅓ cup sifted powdered sugar
⅛ teaspoon orange extract
1 (12-ounce) container whipped cream cheese
½ quart fresh strawberries, cleaned and halved
2 (1-ounce) squares semisweet chocolate, melted

Preheat oven to 350°. Slice cookie dough into ¼-inch slices and pat out onto a greased cookie sheet into an 11-inch circle. Bake 10–20 minutes or until golden brown. Cool. Stir the sugar and orange extract into the cream cheese. Spread over the cooled cookie crust to within ½ inch of edge. Lay the strawberries, cut side down, onto the cream cheese mixture. Drizzle chocolate over the strawberries. Cut into wedges or squares.

Wisconsin

Wisconsin has long been a state of great ethnic diversity. In the 1800s, Wisconsin established an immigration office in New York, where the state was actively promoted to new immigrants. Germans, who arrived primarily between 1845 and 1890, make up Wisconsin's largest ethnic group. They were joined by Poles, the second-largest ethnic group, and then by Italian immigrants. English, Scandinavian, and other groups from Europe created a cultural mix enriched today with Asians, whose numbers in the state have been soaring in recent years.

With more than half the population of Wisconsin claiming German heritage, it is not surprising that one of the major foods produced is sausage. Most popular and perhaps the best known is the Sheboygan bratwurst, which, in the form of a "double bratwurst on a hard roll, with the works," was named in 1997 by the Wisconsin legislature as "the ultimate state sandwich." Around the same time, plans were formulated for the Bratwurst Hall of Fame in Plymouth.

Wisconsin, "America's Dairyland," is the top cheese-producing state in the United States, producing more than two billion pounds annually, or nearly one-third of all U.S. cheese. The state is also an important producer of vegetables and fruits. Highly prized are rutabagas, also called "swedes." Cranberries are the top fruit crop. Wisconsin now boasts a Cranberry Highway that winds through the central part of the state. Travelers can snack on every imaginable cranberry concoction along the way, including cran-jack cheese and chocolate-covered cranberries.

Asian Moon Festival, Milwaukee, WI

Over 30,000 people attend the Asian Moon Festival held on Milwaukee's Summerfest Grounds on the shores of Lake Michigan. The symbol of the moon is used because many Asian celebrations revolve around the lunar calendar. Thirteen different cultures are represented at this festival, which seeks to share their rich diversity and preserve them as a valuable piece of American society.

This huge affair has a broad range of music and dance and features participants in traditional costumes. Martial arts and other sports are demonstrated, as are flower arranging, bonsai, Chinese brush-painting, Hmong needlework, and henna hand-painting. The Asian marketplace offers exquisite clothing, art, and jewelry.

Anyone interested in learning more about Asian cuisine is well advised to begin here, since the Asian Moon Festival provides as broad an overview as you'll ever find in one place. At the Chef's Corner, chefs from local Asian restaurants prepare their favorite dishes and share the recipes. Food is everywhere, tempting even finicky eaters to be more adventurous. Just a tiny sampling elicits such dishes as Filipino *Turon* (Saba banana, sugar, and jackfruit wrapped in a Filipino-style egg roll wrapper), Vietnamese *Bun Thit Nuong* (grilled pork, rice, noodles, vegetables, and fish sauce), Thai spring rolls, and Japanese sushi.

Usually Friday through Sunday of Father's Day Weekend in June

Norma C. Clemente's Pork and Chicken Adobo

Norma Clemente is a longtime member of the Wisconsin Organization for Asian Americans and an active supporter of the Asian Moon Festival.

2–3 pounds pork, sliced in 2½ x 2-inch pieces about ½ inch thick
3 pounds of chicken, cut up
6 cloves garlic, crushed
3 bay leaves
1 tablespoon ground black pepper or whole peppercorns
1 cup vinegar
1 cup soy sauce

Rinse pork and chicken well. Place ingredients in a 6-quart covered flameproof casserole or cooking pot in the order listed. Cook on high for about 30 minutes without mixing. Remove cover and mix carefully so meats soak well in sauce. Reduce heat and simmer for 15 minutes or until sauce dries up. Serves: 8–10.

Norma notes: "Some people like this recipe dry and cooking in its own oil, but I prefer it with a little bit of sauce to top my steamed rice or to dunk bread into the sauce. *Masarap* (delicious)! Adobo is one of many favorite dishes in the Philippines and among many Filipinos who migrated to other countries. Now it also has quite a reputation among Americans, who love garlic with vinegar and soy sauce. Adobo is of Spanish origin, but Filipinos have adapted their own variations in different islands of the Philippines. This recipe is so popular because it is easy to prepare. Adobo means cooking with vinegar and spices; any kind of meat can be used: beef, pork, and/or chicken. Some even use fish or, for vegetarians, vegetables alone."

Bratwurst Days, Sheboygan, WI

Sheboygan jokingly bills itself as the "Wurst City of the World," and indeed it is, since it's also known as the "Bratwurst Capital of the World." Bratwurst, a spicy pork sausage of German origin, is at the heart of Bratwurst Days, which began as German Days to celebrate Sheboygan's sesquicentennial. The festival, begun in 1953, attracts 50,000 visitors annually.

To say that Sheboygan's festival honors a major culinary tradition is perhaps an understatement. The city has eleven meat markets, all specializing in bratwurst. It's also the headquarters for the Johnsonville Company and the Old Wisconsin Sausage Company. It's only natural, then, that the festival's guest of honor is the sausage fondly known in these parts as "the brat."

Bratwurst Days is held in two locations, both featuring musical and theatrical entertainment. Alcohol-free Fountain Park is favored by families, while Kiwanis Park hosts the primary food and beer pavilions. Both locations have plenty of bratwursts. The traditional favorite is a grilled "double brat" on a crusty roll with mustard, onions, and pickles.

Much of the thousands of pounds of bratwurst consumed at the festival is devoured by entrants in the Bratwurst Eating Contest. The current record is seven and a half double brats on Sheboygan hard rolls with ketchup, mustard, pickles, and onions consumed in fifteen minutes. The contest was recently changed to require contestants to eat as many "naked brats" (with no roll or condiments) as possible in five minutes.

The bratwurst has been deployed in increasingly eclectic ways at the festival. Bratxotica Avenue features bratwurst in pizza, tacos, pitas, egg rolls, nachos, and heros. One local restaurant has a stand that features a bratwurst gyro complete with a secret cucumber sauce. Carol Sturgill and her family, of Tejanos Mexican-American Restaurant, conduct a brisk business selling their specialty, Bratwurst Tacos, which are so popular that over 350 pounds of brats are used to make them, per year.

Bratwurst Tacos

Carol Sturgill of Tejanos Mexican-American Restaurant in Sheboygan created these very special tacos for Bratwurst Days. Carol and her family are huge supporters of their community, and they have participated in Bratwurst Days every year since the festival was established.

1 (8-inch) flour tortilla
1 hot, spicy-style bratwurst, grilled
Grated cheddar cheese
Shredded lettuce
Chopped onion
Chopped tomato
Salsa

Warm the flour tortilla and add a grilled brat. Add cheese, lettuce, onion, and tomato and top with salsa. Serve immediately.

Chocolate Fest, Burlington, WI

Well over 100,000 chocoholics gather annually at the Burlington Festival Grounds for the Chocolate Fest, which boasts over 238 million calories worth of chocolate. Home of a Nestle Chocolate plant, Burlington is known as "Chocolate City USA." Everyone at the festival receives a free chocolate bar, and each year, a new chocolate creation is featured, such as O'Henrietta, a lifelike, 2,000-pound cow carved out of chocolate in 1992. The biggest-you-can-buy-anywhere chocolate bar is ten full pounds sold each year by the Burlington Kiwanis Club.

The Taste of Chocolate is a popular festival event where vendors and local fund-raising groups offer samples of everything from chocolate-frosted eclairs to fudge and chocolate cheesecake. The Annual Chocolate Cookoff attracts serious contenders, who prepare mouth-watering recipes that focus on the rich taste of chocolate in categories such as cakes, pies, candy, cookies, and desserts. In the past, the *Burlington Standard Press* issued an annual compendium of the year's winning recipes, and festival organizers are in the process of compiling a cookbook.

Chocolate Turtle Cheesecake

Stephanie Maass of Waterford, WI, walked off as first-place cake winner in the First Annual Chocolate Cook-Off.

2 cups vanilla wafer crumbs
6 tablespoons butter, melted
1 (14-ounce) bag caramel squares
1 (5-ounce) can evaporated milk
1 cup chopped pecans, toasted
2 (8-ounce) packages cream cheese, softened
½ cup sugar
1 teaspoon vanilla
2 eggs
½ cup semisweet chocolate chips, melted
Maraschino cherries (optional)

Preheat oven to 350°. Combine crumbs and butter; press into bottom and sides of a 9-inch springform pan. Bake for 10 minutes. In a 1½-quart heavy saucepan, melt the caramels with evaporated milk over low heat, stirring often, until smooth. Pour over crust. Top with pecans. Combine the cream cheese, sugar, and vanilla, mixing at medium speed with an electric mixer until well blended. Add eggs one at a time, mixing well after each addition. Blend in melted chocolate morsels. Pour over pecans. Bake for 40–50 minutes. Loosen the cake from rim of pan. Cool before removing. Chill. Garnish with maraschino cherries if desired.

Friday through Sunday of the Weekend Following Mother's Day

Eagle River Cranberry Festival and Fitness Weekend, Eagle River, WI

In Eagle River, Wisconsin, someone got the idea of selling local fresh cranberries and cranberry baked goods in a parking lot in 1980. Today, the folks in Eagle River mark the cranberry harvest with a full-fledged festival at the county fairgrounds.

The Cranberry Fest features cranberry bog tours, winery tours, a bridge tournament, an arts and crafts sale, and a Cranberry Fitness Walk, Run, and Bike Tour. After all, cranberries are good for you!

The main event is still a bake sale where attendees can purchase fritters, nut pies, cheesecakes, doughnuts, breads, muffins, and cookies, many featuring cranberries. Hot cranberry cider and cranberry sauerkraut meatballs top the list of specialty items at the festival. There's also a Cranberry Bake-Off that has resulted in the publication of a festival cookbook, *The Best Cranberry Recipes from the Eagle River Cranberry Fest.*

Saturday and Sunday of the First Full Weekend in October

Cranberry Sauerkraut Meatballs

This winning recipe was created by Marilyn Dunphy and featured in The Best Cranberry Recipes from the *Eagle River Cranberry Festival.*

2 pounds ground beef
2 eggs
1 envelope onion soup mix
½ cup water
1 cup finely crushed cracker crumbs
Salt and pepper to taste
Vegetable oil for frying meatballs
1 (16-ounce) can sauerkraut, drained and snipped into short pieces
1 (8-ounce) can cranberry sauce, whole or strained
¾ cup chili sauce or ketchup
2 cups water
⅓ cup brown sugar, packed

Preheat oven to 325°. Mix together the ground beef, eggs, onion soup mix, water, cracker crumbs, salt, and pepper. Shape into meatballs and brown in a skillet. Mix together the remaining ingredients to make the sauce. Pour half of the sauce in a 13 x 9-inch baking dish. Arrange the meatballs on the sauce. Pour remaining sauce over meatballs. Cover with foil and bake for 1 hour. Remove foil. Bake another 30–40 minutes. Serve hot over noodles or rice or serve as an appetizer. Yield: About 40 meatballs.

Great Wisconsin Cheese Festival, Little Chute, WI

In 1989, the village of Little Chute, Wisconsin, decided to challenge Rome, NY, home of the New York State Museum of Cheese, located in a reconstructed 1800s cheese factory. The New York cheeses took first and second places at the cheese competition in New York, while Wisconsin entries were relegated to third, fourth, and fifth positions. So Little Chute arranged to hold its own competition in the heart of Wisconsin's dairy industry. Wisconsin, of course, emerged as the victor over rival New York.

While the cheese wars have continued to rage, Wisconsinites generally thumb up their nose at any other state's cheese. More than 15,000 folks annually attend the Great Wisconsin Cheese Festival. Sporting events and the Big Cheese Parade are supplemented with a host of activities centered around cheese and dairy products. Entertainment includes events like Model Your Own Milk Mustache and cheese curd-eating contests. Cheese-carving demonstrations attract a major following, as does the free cheese tasting. There is a Dairy Social with free samples and a Sunday morning breakfast with cheesy omelettes. Vendors sell cheeseburgers, cheddar-wursts, and cheese curds that have been battered and deep-fried.

Cheesecake lovers are in their glory with the Cheesecake Contest. Past entries include such confections as Bailey's Irish Cream Cheesecake, Banana Split Cheesecake, Chocolate Turtle Cheesecake, and Piña Colada Cheesecake. Once judging is over and prizes are awarded, the cheesecakes are sold by the slice.

The First Full Weekend of June

Black Forest Cheesecake

Created by Brenda Walby of Greenville, WI, this was a first-prize winner in the Cheesecake Contest.

Chocolate crust:
1¼ cups finely crushed chocolate graham crackers
3 tablespoons sugar
¼ cup butter, melted

Black Forest filling:
3 (8-ounce) packages cream cheese, softened
¾ cup sugar
5 teaspoons cornstarch
3 eggs
1 egg yolk
1 cup semisweet chocolate chips, melted and cooled
¼ cup cherry schnapps or 2 tablespoons cherry brandy
2 teaspoons vanilla extract
⅔ cup fresh Bing cherries, pitted, chopped, and drained

Chocolate cherry topping:
½ cup sugar
2 tablespoons cornstarch
2 cups fresh or canned cherries with juice (add 2–3 tablespoons of water with fresh cherries)
1 teaspoon lemon juice
½ teaspoon almond extract
Chocolate ice cream topping

Garnish:
Hand-dipped chocolate-covered cherries

Crust: In a small bowl, stir together crumbs and sugar. Add melted butter. Stir until well combined. Press crumb mixture evenly onto the bottom of a greased 9-inch springform pan. Set aside.

Filling: In a large bowl, combine the cream cheese, sugar, and cornstarch. Beat with an electric mixer until smooth. Add eggs and egg yolk, one at a time, beating well after each addition. Beat in melted chocolate, schnapps, and vanilla. Stir in cherries.

Topping: In a small saucepan, stir together the sugar and cornstarch. Add the cherries and lemon juice. Cook and stir until thickened and bubbly. Stir in the almond extract. Cool slightly.

Assembly: Preheat oven to 350°. Pour filling into crust. Bake for 15 minutes, then lower oven temperature to 225° and bake for 1 hour and 10 minutes more, or until center no longer looks shiny. Turn oven off and leave cake in the oven for an additional hour. Remove from oven and complete cooling on a rack. Chill cheesecake in refrigerator for several hours or overnight before adding topping. When cheesecake has cooled, pour topping over cheesecake. Chill until serving time. Garnish with chocolate-covered cherries.

Holiday Folk Fair International, Milwaukee, WI

The celebration of cultural and culinary diversity in the United States reaches its zenith every year in Milwaukee with the annual Holiday Folk Fair. Originally launched in 1944, the fair is now the largest indoor multiethnic festival in the country. Over sixty ethnic groups participate, and the celebration hosts nearly 65,000 visitors.

In some years, the festival honors individual countries, and in other years, more general themes are chosen. In addition to ethnic dress, music, and dancing, there are cultural booths showcasing ethnic handiwork and history. The marketplace, filled with unique folkware, serves as a shopper's gateway to the world.

And then there's the food. Over thirty cafes, each operated by a distinct ethnic group, feature typical specialty foods in what amounts to a worldwide feast. This is the place to taste the lesser-known cuisines like Arab, Egyptian, Filipino, Hmong, Jamaican, and Pakistani. There are also African-American, Bavarian, Donauschwaben, Greek, Hungarian, Japanese, Scandinavian, Polish, Spanish, and Thai cafes, to name just a few.

Always the Weekend Before Thanksgiving

Finally, there's a cooking demo area. Each year, a certain food category is chosen, and local restaurant chefs demonstrate ethnic recipes using the highlighted food or ingredient. Recommended are the International Institute's *Holiday Folk Fair Cookbooks,* each of which contains outstanding recipes.

Oven Roasted Kalua Pig

Bruce Buege of the Maile Lei Dancers contributed this updated Polynesian heritage recipe to *The Fiftieth Anniversary Holiday Folk Fair Cookbook*.

"Kalua" means "to bake in the ground." Traditionally, the Polynesians bury a whole pig with hot rocks and banana leaves in an underground oven, or *imu*, and slow-roast it for half a day. Today, a simplified, more convenient method is used.

4–5 pounds fresh pork butt
1 tablespoon liquid smoke
2½ tablespoons coarse sea salt, divided

Preheat oven to 325°. Rub pork with liquid smoke and 1½ tablespoons of sea salt. Wrap and seal the pork tightly in aluminum foil. Place in a roasting pan and roast it in the oven for 5 hours. Remove pork from foil, shred the pork, and sprinkle with the remaining sea salt. Serves: 10–12.

Braised Pork Chops in Paprika-Dill Sauce

Linda Weissgerber of the Milwaukee Donauschwaben contributed this heritage recipe to *The Fiftieth Anniversary Holiday Folk Fair Cookbook*.

Linda says, "My mother immigrated to the United States from Vienna, Austria, in 1955, and she brought this Austrian-Hungarian recipe with her. She still makes it today."

8 ¾-inch-thick pork chops
Salt and freshly ground pepper
Flour
3–4 tablespoons lard or butter
1½ cups finely chopped onions
½ teaspoon finely chopped garlic
3 tablespoons Hungarian sweet paprika
1–2 cups chicken stock
⅓ cup heavy cream
⅓ cup sour cream
2 tablespoons flour
3 tablespoons finely chopped fresh dill or
    1 tablespoon dried dill

Season the chops with salt and pepper; dip in flour. Heat lard or butter in frying pan on medium high; brown chops and transfer to platter. Add onion to fat and brown; add garlic last 1 minute of cooking. Remove from heat and add paprika, coating onions and garlic. Return to heat, add chicken stock, and bring to a boil. Return the chops to pan; cover and simmer on low heat for 1 hour. Remove the meat. Combine heavy cream and sour cream in a bowl and, with a wire whisk, beat in flour. Add mixture to pan. Stir constantly for 2–3 minutes until sauce is smooth and thick. Add dill and taste for seasoning. Serve sauce over pork chops. Serves: 4–6.

Pepper Festival, North Hudson, WI

Because of its location, midway between the steamy equator and the chilly North Pole, August weather conditions in North Hudson, Wisconsin, have been known to fluctuate. Despite the temperature, however, everything heats up during the town's Pepper Festival.

A celebration of Italian heritage, the Pepper Fest started in the late 1800s, when Italian immigrants settled in North Hudson. The town, once part of the St. Croix River bottom, has long been known for its sandy soil, which produces quality peppers and watermelons. Each year, Italian families would gather their garden harvests for a community picnic.

The Pepper Festival was begun in 1954 and continues today as a hometown celebration. A parade, various races, talent and fishing contests, live music, and a Wisconsin beer garden are all part of the festivities. The spaghetti- and hot pepper-eating contests on Saturday night are a big attraction. In a relay type of event, each participant in five-member teams is required to consume a pound of spaghetti or peppers, one by one. After a team member inhales the food and shows the judge an empty mouth, the next is signaled to begin.

Visitors are drawn to the festival for its homemade Italian fare produced from heritage recipes. Ravioli, spaghetti and meatballs, stuffed green peppers, and a spiced meatloaf type of sandwich, affectionately known as a "Hot Dago," are all served up. An Italian cooking contest is open to the imaginations of amateur chefs, but entries in all three categories—appetizer, entree, and dessert—must contain some type of pepper.

Usually Friday through Sunday the Third Weekend of August

Cat A Loni

Mark "Cat" Madsen of North Hudson, WI, is a first-place winner of the Pepper Festival Cooking Contest.

Pasta:
1¾ cups pasta flour
1 teaspoon salt
2 extra large eggs

Filling:
1 clove garlic, minced
1 shallot, minced
2 teaspoons extra virgin olive oil
¾ pound ground pork
½ package frozen spinach cooked according to directions and chopped
¼ pound prosciutto (Italian ham), sliced paper thin
½ cup whole milk ricotta cheese
1 pound shredded mozzarella cheese

White sauce:
4 tablespoons butter
1 shallot, minced
2 cups heavy cream
1 cup grated Parmesan cheese

Ragu:
1 onion, finely chopped
2 tablespoons extra virgin olive oil
3 cloves garlic, minced
½ pound ground beef
½ pound hot Italian sausage
1 cup dry white wine
9 medium tomatoes, skinned, seeded, and chopped
½ teaspoon hot red pepper flakes
1 cup milk

Pasta: Mix all ingredients until dough forms a ball. Knead the dough by running it through a pasta machine on the thickest setting, folding it in thirds and running it through again. Do this 8 to 10 times, until dough becomes elastic. Cut the dough into quarters. Roll each piece of dough out into a thin sheet about 30 inches long and 5 inches wide. Cook in a large pot of salted, rapidly boiling water for about 2 minutes. Remove and place in cool water. Lay out on a towel and pat dry.

Filling: Over medium high heat, sauté the garlic and shallot in olive oil. Add the pork and brown. Remove to a bowl and mix in spinach. Reserve remaining filling ingredients.

White sauce: Over medium heat, brown butter slightly to give it a nutty flavor. Add the shallot and sauté 1–2 minutes until golden. Add half the cream and allow it to lightly boil; reduce it by a third. Add the rest of the cream and bring it to a light boil. Turn off the heat and add cheese, whisking until smooth. This sauce can be made ahead of time and kept in the refrigerator. (It also makes a great Alfredo sauce.)

Ragu: Over medium heat, sauté the onion in olive oil until translucent. Add garlic. Cook for 1–2 minutes (don't burn the garlic). Add the meat and brown. Add wine, tomatoes, and pepper flakes. Cook on medium low until wine is completely boiled off. Add milk and cook until reduced. Lower heat and simmer 2 more hours, being careful not to burn the ragu. (This is much better if made two or three days ahead of time and reheated at least once.)

Final assembly: Preheat oven to 325°. Lay out cooked noodles. On one end, place 2 or 3 slices prosciutto. Add 3 to 4 tablespoons of filling. Add 2 tablespoons ricotta. Spread a couple handfuls of mozzarella along the whole length of the noodle. Roll up noodle and slice in half at a 45-degree angle. Place the canneloni in a glass or ceramic baking dish. Cover with white sauce. Bake for 20 minutes. Top with dollops of ragu sauce and bake an additional 10 minutes, or until white sauce develops a light golden crust. Yield: 4 main courses or 8 side dishes.

Polish Fest, Milwaukee, WI

Poles have been emigrating to the United States since before the American Revolution. Today, more than eleven million Americans belong to Polish-American organizations, and millions more claim Polish roots.

Polish Fest, held every year at Summerfest Grounds on Milwaukee's lakefront, is the largest Polish festival in the country, attracting 40,000 to 50,000 attendees annually. Poles and non-Poles alike come to celebrate Polish pride and traditions. The Folk Stage features polka and folk dance troupes, while the Cultural Stage offers nonstop polka bands. The Williamsburg area is filled with shops and vendors selling authentic toys and clothing. In the Cultural Village, breathtaking displays tell the story of Polish history and long-held traditions. Polish folk art demonstrations include *pisanki* (Easter egg decorating), *wycinanki* (paper cutting), weaving, embroidery, and Christmas ornamentation.

However, the major attraction of Polish Fest is the food. It is everywhere, and it is delicious. There's a fish fry on Friday.

Kielbasa, a pork sausage flavored with garlic, is prepared on a forty-five-foot grill. Pierogi, plump, tasty little dumplings are sold by the thousands. They have a variety of fillings, such as cheese, potato, or ground meat. Fresh potato pancakes make an excellent accompaniment to the roast pork. Dill pickle soup, mushroom soup, and *czarnina*, or duck's blood soup, are ethnic favorites. Others opt for big bowls of hunter's stew, called *bigos*, an intoxicating mixture of smoked and fresh sausage, beef, sauerkraut, and mushrooms.

Sweet treats are plentiful. Jumbo cinnamon buns are practically a meal in themselves. Many claim that the perfect dessert is *paczki*, a doughnut filled with prune purée, then dusted with powdered sugar. *Nalesniki*, traditionally served at Christmas, are crepes filled with a mixture of creamed cottage cheese, raisins, and nuts, then topped with sour cream. Finally, there are *knes*, made from mashed potatoes mixed with flour and eggs to form a dough, which is broken off in pieces and deep-fried, then topped with sour cream.

Cheese-Filled Pierogi

While the vendors at Polish Fest understandably won't share their trade secrets, the following recipe is a traditional family favorite used for years by Nancy Hager and her family of Buffalo, NY. It is guaranteed to deliver the true taste of Polish Fest.

Cheese filling:
1 pound farmer's cheese
3 ounces cream cheese
1 egg
Heavy cream

Dough:
6 cups sifted flour
1 teaspoon salt
¼ pound butter, melted
½ cup milk
3 eggs
1 cup sour cream

Filling: Mix together the cheeses and the egg. Add heavy cream a little at a time until mixture holds together. Let it rest while you make the dough and cut it out.

Dough and assembly: Sift flour and salt into a bowl and add butter, milk, eggs, and sour cream. Mix to a soft dough that is easy to handle, knead a few minutes, and divide in half. Roll dough thin and cut into circles with a large biscuit cutter. Place a small spoonful of filling a little to one side of the center of each circle. Moisten edges with water, fold over, and press edges together firmly, being sure to seal them well. Drop pierogi into boiling, salted water and cook for 3–5 minutes. Lift out gently and drain.

To serve: Fry pierogi in plenty of melted butter (and perhaps a little chopped onion) until they are heated through and golden brown. Sour cream is a popular topping. Yield: Approximately 6 dozen pierogi.

Note: Pierogi freeze well for up to 3 months.

Rutabaga Festival, Cumberland, WI

According to the people of Cumberland, "Wisconsin's Beautiful Island City," the rutabaga is a vegetable to celebrate. The first Cumberland Rutabaga Festival was held in 1932 and was sponsored by the Cumberland Business Men's Club to show appreciation to area farmers. Since then, the festival has become a local institution.

In Cumberland's early days, it was discovered that rutabaga grew well there. The "bagas," as they are called locally, grew especially well on newly broken and rather rough ground, which made them popular when new farms were being established. The rutabaga industry was, and still is, an important part of Cumberland's heritage.

The Rutabaga Festival has a carnival, a parade, a basketball shoot-out, plenty of live entertainment, the Rutabaga Olympics, and an arts and crafts show. There's also a hot pepper-eating contest that has resulted in a friendly battle between teams from Cumberland and nearby North Hudson, home of the Pepper Festival. The Baga Cook-Off offers cooks the opportunity to show off their culinary skills, along with the diversity of the rutabaga.

Always the Weekend Preceding Labor Day Weekend

Rutabaga Bread

Dorie Chartraw of Cumberland, WI, is a grand champion winner of the Baga Cookoff.

1 package dry yeast
2 tablespoons warm water
1 cup cooked, mashed rutabaga
⅓ cup warm milk
¼ cup butter, softened
1 egg
3 tablespoons brown sugar, packed
¼ teaspoon salt
3½–4 cups all-purpose flour

Glaze:
1 egg, beaten
1 Tablespoon water

In a bowl, dissolve yeast in warm water. In a large mixing bowl, combine the rutabaga, milk, butter, egg, brown sugar, and salt. Mix well and add the yeast mixture and 1½ cups flour. Mix well and add enough remaining flour to form a soft dough. Knead dough until smooth and elastic. Place in a greased bowl, cover, and let rise in a warm place until doubled, about 1 hour.

Divide dough into thirds and roll each third into an 18-inch rope. Place on a greased baking sheet and braid ropes together, pinching ends to seal. Cover and let rise until nearly doubled, about 30 minutes.

Preheat oven to 350°. Combine glaze ingredients, brush over braid, and bake for 25 minutes or until golden brown. Remove from baking sheet and cool on rack.

Warrens Cranberry Festival, Warrens, WI

The Warrens Cranberry Festival began in 1973 to raise funds for the improvement of life in this village of 400 people. The festival has often been voted the number one community event in the state by subscribers of *Wisconsin Trails* magazine, and Warrens has been designated the "Cranberry Capital of Wisconsin." Over 100,000 people flock to the event, which features 350 vendors in its antique and flea market and over one hundred vendors of fall produce in its popular Farmers' Market.

Cranberries, of course, are the focus of attention. On Saturday, guests can tour a cranberry marsh. The Catholic Church serves a sunrise pancake breakfast with its famous cranberry syrup, and the Baptist Church offers cranberry pies. Cranberry goodies are everywhere: jelly beans, taffy, honey, mustard, jams and jellies, and fresh cranberry juice.

After eating one of the famous barbecued pork sandwiches, most attendees opt for a dessert of the festival's equally famous cranberry cream puffs. There's always heated competition among entrants in the Wisconsin Cranberry Recipe Contest. Every year, the contest is based on a theme and has two divisions, one for fresh cranberries and the other for processed cranberries. Recipes are published in an annual cookbook, *Best of the Cranberry Festival Recipes*.

Crustless Cranberry Pie

Helen Marr of Madison, WI, is a first-place winner of the Wisconsin Cranberry Recipe Contest. Her recipe is reprinted from *Best of the Cranberry Festival Recipes*.

3 cups (12 ounces) fresh cranberries
¾ cup coarsely chopped walnuts
½ cup firmly packed light brown sugar
1 teaspoon grated orange peel
1 teaspoon ground cinnamon
¾ cup snipped apricots (dried or very well-drained canned apricots)
2 large eggs
½ cup butter, melted
1 cup granulated sugar
¼ cup sour cream
1 teaspoon vanilla extract
1 cup all-purpose flour
Whipped cream for serving

Preheat oven to 325°. Butter a deep 10-inch pie plate. Toss the cranberries, walnuts, brown sugar, orange peel, cinnamon, and apricots in prepared pie plate until well mixed. Spread evenly. In a medium bowl, whisk together the eggs, butter, sugar, sour cream, and vanilla until thoroughly blended. Gradually stir in flour until smooth. Pour evenly over cranberry mixture. Bake 55-60 minutes until browned on top and fruit bubbles. Serve plain or with whipped cream. This makes an excellent holiday dessert.

Friday through Sunday of the Third Weekend in September

Chapter 4

The Great Plains

Iowa | Kansas | Nebraska | North Dakota
Oklahoma | South Dakota

Iowa

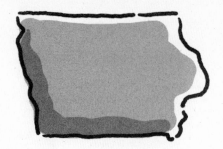

Iowa was first explored, if only briefly, by Frenchmen Louis Joliet and Father Jacques Marquette in 1673, but settlement of the region did not begin in earnest until the 1800s with the arrival of German immigrants. By 1850, most of the land in the midwestern states had been claimed, prompting settlers from the East Coast and newly arrived immigrants to move on to Iowa and other plains states. Hard upon the heels of the Germans were Dutch immigrants, who first established the town of Pella in 1847, Norwegians, who founded Decorah in 1849, and a host of people from other Scandinavian countries. Around the same time, Bohemians, Moravians, and Slovaks began arriving from the volatile and ever-shifting countries of Eastern Europe, adding a strong Czech presence to the fabric of Iowa.

Today, Iowa is one of America's greatest agricultural states, built on the backs of those immigrant farmers, who faced tremendous hardships in turning the unyielding prairie sod into the rich soil that would sustain major crops for generations to come. Iowa farmers produce somewhere around seven percent of our nation's food supply. Among the descendants of Iowa's original settlers, there remains a remarkable commitment to tradition and ethnic heritage, resulting in numerous annual historical reenactments and festivals.

Founders Day Communal Meal, High Amana, IA

In July 1842, a religious group, the Community of True Inspiration, was prompted by a prophecy to seek a new homeland. The persecuted worshipers, from such places as Germany, Alsace, and Switzerland, packed up their belongings and headed for the New World and religious freedom. They founded Ebeneezer, NY, near the city of Buffalo, but as their ranks grew, the cost of land also soared, limiting their ability to expand the community. When tuberculosis broke out, the community decided to head west, where land was cheap along the Iowa River. In 1855, they constructed Amana, the first of seven villages that would eventually grow to include West Amana, South Amana, High Amana, East Amana, Homestead, and Middle Amana. Here, the communal life of the Amana colonies flourished until 1932, when it was disbanded in favor of a less restrictive mode of living.

Today, under the direction of the Amana Arts Guild, the Amana colonies host visitors from all over the world who come to study and to gain an appreciation for the Amana people. One of the most important events of the year is the Founder's Day Communal Meal, which celebrates the establishment of the Amana colonies. Held in the first community church built in the colonies in 1858, the dinner is based on original recipes from the communal kitchens. For the first such celebration in 1992, women who worked in those kitchens prior to 1932 prepared the meal. While the menu varies from year to year, the cooks always try to outdo the previous year's meal, which is served at long tables in the traditional Amana manner. Diners are charged a nominal fee.

Seasons of Plenty: Amana Communal Cooking is a fascinating documentary of the foodways of the Amana colonies. Written by lifelong resident Emilie Hoppe, the book was compiled as a project of the Amana Arts Guild. It is filled with recipes for the hearty, delicious dishes based on foods long prepared in the Old Country and which still grace the tables of the members of the Amana Church. It is an enduring souvenir of a visit to the colonies, as well as a way to re-create the dishes served at the Founder's Day Communal Meal. Collectors may want to locate *A Collection of Traditional Amana Recipes,* compiled in 1948 by the Ladies Auxiliary of the Homestead Welfare Club, Homestead, Iowa.

The Second Saturday of November

Corn Relish

This heritage recipe, submitted by Connie Zuber, appears in *Seasons of Plenty: Amana Communal Cooking* by Emilie Hoppe and is reprinted with permission from the publisher.

12 ears of corn
1 quart cucumbers, peeled and chopped
2 quarts tomatoes, peeled
1 quart peeled and chopped onions
1 or 2 green bell peppers, coarsely chopped
4 cups sugar
1 tablespoon ground mustard
½ quart vinegar
1 tablespoon celery seed

½ cup salt
½ tablespoon turmeric
10–15 pint jars, sterilized, with lids and seals

Cook corn and remove kernels from cobs. In a very large kettle, boil all ingredients 45 minutes. Pour into hot, sterilized pint jars, leaving ½ inch at the top of the jar. Process in a boiling water bath for 15 minutes. Yield: 10–15 pints.

Herb Festival, Greene, IA

Every year since its inception in 1995, attendance at the Herb Festival in Greene, Iowa, has doubled. Word of the event, held on the banks of the Shell Rock River, has spread quickly, and no wonder—even the vendors call it the "feel good" festival.

This event is the brainstorm of Rita Barth and Juliene Bramer, who decided it would be fun to introduce others to their favorite pastime, growing and using herbs. Patty Woodley, proprietor of the Paddle Inne Restaurant, volunteered to host the festival. The first year, preparations were made for 100 visitors, and 300 showed up. The next year, attendance was 600, and it nearly doubled again the following year and has continued to grow.

With harp music in the background, visitors attend classes and demonstrations, which explain and promote the culinary, medicinal, and decorative use of herbs. Vendors sell an array of herbs, spices, vinegars, jams, jellies, and breads, and most serve free samples. Others offer wreaths, garlands, dried arrangements, potpourri, garden accessories, books, and plants.

Favorite goodies include lavender cookies, dill herb bread, lemon balm cookies, and lemon verbena bread, plus the free samples of delicious Parmesan-garlic popcorn. In addition to sack lunches, visitors can enjoy a light lunch aboard the docked Spirit of Greene paddleboat. Future plans include publication of an herbal cookbook.

Parmesan-Garlic Popcorn

The Under the Spell Herb Shop in Greene, IA, is well known as a resource of creative and delicious recipes using herbs.

Last Sunday in July

Popcorn spice:
½ cup grated Parmesan cheese
2 teaspoons salt
1 teaspoon dried tarragon
1 teaspoon garlic powder
1 teaspoon parsley flakes

To serve:
¼ cup melted butter
1 tablespoon popcorn spice
3 cups popped popcorn

Combine all ingredients for the popcorn spice. To serve, combine melted butter and 1 tablespoon of the spice mixture, pour over the hot popcorn, stir, and serve. Store the rest of the popcorn spice in an airtight jar.
Yield: 3 cups popcorn.

Herbal Cream Cheese Spread

Courtesy of Under the Spell Herb Shop, Greene, IA.

Chopped fresh herbs of your choice: basil, chives, sage, oregano, garlic, and/or thyme
1 (8-ounce) package cream cheese, softened
¼ cup olive oil (optional)

Chop herbs in a blender or cut finely with scissors. Combine with cream cheese. If a smoother, softer spread is desired, mix in the olive oil. Chill and serve with crackers. As an alternative, the spread may be further thinned and mixed with pasta salad. Yield: 1 cup.

Honey-Walnut Classic, Allerton, IA

Sponsored by The Inn of the Six-Toed Cat in Allerton and The Log Chain Apiary in Corydon, the Honey-Walnut Classic is a fun event held as part of the Allerton World Fair. The "Classic" is a food preparation competition requiring the use of two local products, honey and walnuts. It also honors the historic Iowa-Missouri Honey War, which raged from 1838 to 1841.

The Honey War began as a border dispute involving a twelve-mile-wide tract of timberland between the two states. While an 1816 survey had established the "Sullivan Line" as the northern boundary of Missouri, in 1837 another surveyor named Brown claimed the actual boundary was further south, putting the timbered area with its bee trees full of honey solidly in Missouri territory. Iowa settlers wanted nothing to do with becoming part of Missouri; they didn't believe in slavery and were afraid of losing their farms. When a Missouri sheriff tried collecting taxes from the Iowa folks, they refused to pay and decided to kidnap the sheriff. Then some Missourians cut down three honey trees, an inflammatory act. As the Missouri militia set out to rescue their sheriff, the Iowa militia responded to a call to arms. Fortunately, Congress intervened, and, before the "Honey War" began in earnest, both militias were ordered home. Although it took nearly two years and the intervention of the Supreme Court to rule that the Sullivan Line was the legal boundary, the dispute left its "sting" on the locals. After all, this was a time when honey was the only available source of "sweetnin'", and both sides coveted it for household use.

There's plenty of honey to go around these days, and loads of delicious foods are entered in the various divisions of the cooking contest. Following judging, the foods are sold or auctioned off, and many attendees head over to the Log Chain Apiary, a honey farm, where they quench their thirst with real honey lemonade. At the apiary, visitors can also purchase liquid and comb honey.

Always the Second Weekend in September

Honey Lemonade

Ann Garber of the Log Chain Apiary in Allerton, IA, knows her honey, and those seeking innovative uses for it can count on Ann for information and winning recipes.

3¾ cups lemon juice
3 cups honey
2 gallons water

Mix all ingredients well and serve ice cold. Yield: 2½ gallons.

Houby Days, Czech Village, Cedar Rapids, IA

Houby Days is a Czech festival—but with a twist—because it honors the *houby*, or mushroom. Staged by the Czech Village Association in Cedar Rapids, this celebration of Czech heritage includes lots of music, a parade, and a 5K run. A children's mushroom hunt challenges participants. Then there's a mushroom contest in which folks enter their most unusually shaped morel mushroom discoveries.

Food is everywhere, and the feasting begins with a scrambled egg and mushroom breakfast. Then it's on to a huge variety of Czech food, from the simplest brats to that beloved Czech favorite, *kolache*. No visitor misses a stop at Sykora Bakery, famous for its Czech delicacies made from scratch with no artificial preservatives. Built at the turn of the century, the building was first used as a bottling plant for Dubuque Beer. In 1903, it became the home of C. K. Kosek Bakery, which, in 1927, became Sykora Bakery.

Saturday and Sunday of the Weekend After Mother's Day

Koblihy (Doughnuts)

The Kolacky-Koblihy Cookbook is a wonderful source for Czech heritage recipes, including this one for lip-smacking good doughnuts made the old-fashioned way.

1 package dry yeast
¼ cup warm water
3 egg yolks
3 tablespoons melted butter
3 tablespoons warm milk
1 tablespoon dark rum
3 teaspoons sugar
1 teaspoon salt
1 teaspoon grated lemon rind
3 cups flour, sifted
Apricot jelly
Oil for frying
Powdered sugar

Soften the yeast in the warm water and let rise. Combine the egg yolks, butter, milk, rum, and sugar and beat slightly. Add the raised yeast, salt, and lemon rind. Sift the flour onto a board, add the first mixture, and knead until very smooth and air bubbles form. Place in a bowl, cover, and let rise until double in bulk.

Roll dough out into a square or oblong ⅜ inch thick. With a cutter, mark outlines of doughnuts on half of rolled-out dough. Put ½ teaspoon thick apricot jelly in the middle of each outline. Fold other half of dough over the marked doughnuts and jelly mounds so that every one is well covered. Press dough firmly around the jelly mounds and cut out doughnuts. Let rise again on both sides. Fry in 1½ inches of fat, covering the pan while the first side cooks and then turning the doughnuts and frying the other side uncovered. Place on paper towels to drain and, when cool, sprinkle with powdered sugar.

Today the bakery is operated by Don and Sheila Janda, who have retained the authentic fixtures and antiques, to create a real Old World atmosphere. Their products, including *koblihy* (doughnuts), *zelniky* (cabbage-filled buns), *babovka* (poppyseed- or fruit-filled coffee rings), and much more, are based on recipes brought over from Czechoslovakia in the late 1800s. The *Kolacky-Koblihy Cookbook*, filled with 106 Czech pastry recipes from Lester Sykora and John Kuba, is sold at the bakery and by mail order.

Mushroom Tarts

Elaine Brejcha, Czech Village coordinator, agreed to divulge her celebrated recipe for these lovely morsels.

Crust:
8 ounces cream cheese, softened
½ cup margarine, softened
1½ cups soft flour (Southern soft flour is recommended)

Filling:
1 large onion, chopped
3 tablespoons butter
½ pound chopped mushrooms
2 tablespoons flour
1 teaspoon salt
¼ cup sour cream
¼ teaspoon marjoram
¼ teaspoon grated orange peel
1 egg, beaten

Crust: Mix the cream cheese and margarine, then mix in flour to form a smooth, soft dough. Wrap in plastic and refrigerate for 1 hour.

Filling: Sauté the onion in butter about 5 minutes then add the mushrooms and sauté 5 minutes longer, cooking off some of the juice. Mix the flour, salt, sour cream, marjoram, and grated orange peel, then blend into the mushroom and onion mixture.

Assembly: Preheat oven to 450°. On a pastry cloth or floured board, roll dough out to ⅛ inch thick. With a cutter, cut 3-inch circles. Place a spoonful of filling in the center of half of the circles. Wet edges, cover with a second circle, and crimp edges with a fork. Brush tops with the beaten egg. Bake for 15 minutes or until tarts are a light golden color. Yield: about 24 tarts.

Note: Lovely open tarts can be made by lightly pressing the circles of dough into minimuffin pans; fill each with mushroom mixture. Bake the tarts at 400° for 30 minutes or until crust browns lightly and filling is hot and bubbly. Yield: 36 tarts.

Le Festival de L'Heritage Francais, Corning, IA

French-born Etienne Cabet founded the Icarian movement in the last half of the nineteenth century. The Icarians left France in search of Utopia in 1848. After a disastrous attempt to settle in Texas' Red River Valley, various groups established settlements in Missouri, California, and Iowa. The Icarians were the longest-lasting non-religious, pure communal experiment in American history.

In Corning, Le Festival de L'Heritage Francais celebrates the culture and contributions of the Icarians to Adams County and Iowa from 1852 to 1898. The Icarians were known far and wide for their apple and cherry orchards, vineyards, and the Percheron horses, which they brought from France. They introduced strawberries, rhubarb, asparagus, lilacs, and irises to the Corning area and, despite rugged conditions, produced skilled musicians, artists, painters, and craftsmen.

The festival highlights Icarian accomplishments through heritage tours, skills demonstrations, French folk dancing, and music. The big parade is followed by flower, quilt, china, and art shows. For the kids, there are storytellers, puppeteers, mimes, and a spelling bee.

Lunch offers a French picnic with croissant sandwiches; dinner's French cabaret offers a five-course meal that features a different French province each year. The local bakery offers creme puffs, eclairs, raspberry and almond pastry sticks, and a variety of French breads. A French wine seminar and sampling is a popular attraction, and the pie and tart contest, with a separate category for rhubarb, recalls the Icarian cultivation of the "pie plant" in a garden measuring 120 x 10 feet.

Souffle Froid au Chocolat (Cold Chocolate Souffle)

Saundra Clem Leininger of Le Festival de L'Heritage Francais researches and tests the authentic French heritage recipes used to prepare festival cuisine.

1 envelope unflavored gelatin
3 tablespoons cold water
2 squares (2 ounces) unsweetened chocolate
½ cup powdered sugar
1 cup milk
¾ cup granulated sugar
1 teaspoon vanilla
¼ teaspoon salt
2 cups heavy cream

Soften gelatin in cold water. Melt chocolate over hot, not boiling, water. When completely melted, add the powdered sugar and stir well. Heat the milk until a film forms on the surface, being careful not to boil it. Slowly and thoroughly, stir the milk into the chocolate mixture. Cook over hot water, stirring constantly, up to the boiling point but do not boil. Remove from the heat and stir in the softened gelatin, granulated sugar, vanilla, and salt. Chill until slightly thick. Beat until light and airy. In a separate chilled bowl, beat heavy cream until it holds its shape. Fold the two mixtures together and pour into a 2-quart serving dish or individual dishes. Chill 2–3 hours before serving. Serves: 6–8.

Nordic Fest, Scandinavian Food Fest, Norwegian Christmas, Decorah, IA

Vesterheim was a term that Norwegian immigrants used when referring to their new western home in America. The Vesterheim Norwegian-American Museum in Decorah, Iowa, established in 1877, documents the history of those immigrants and plays a highly active role in preserving the many aspects of Norwegian culture. Much of this effort is accomplished through Vesterheim's support of events that provide a living history environment to all who come: the Nordic Fest in July, the Scandinavian Food Fest in October, and the Norwegian Christmas Celebration in December. Each of these festivals has demonstrations of Norwegian folk arts, including rosemaling, woodcarving, weaving, knife making, and several fiber arts.

Norwegian food is plentiful, delivering a true taste of Norway. Nordic Fest is known for its cooking demonstrations and subsequent samplings of a crayfish boil, Scandinavian style; pastries like *krumkaker*, *kringla* and Norwegian wedding cake called *kransekake*; cookies known as *sandbakkles* and *rosettes*; *lefse*, a Norwegian flatbread; and *aebelskivers*. Various dinners and smorgasbords feature a full array of Norwegian cuisine.

The Scandinavian Food Fest offers many Norwegian foods and provides a classroom environment for those who wish to learn to prepare such specialties as *rosemaled* cookies, a little-known Norwegian tradition that involves painting frosted cookies.

The Vesterheim year winds up with the Norwegian Christmas, where guests are served, among other festive foods, *Rommegrot*, a traditional Norwegian Christmas Eve treat.

Highly recommended for anyone interested in Norwegian cooking is *Rosemalers' Recipes*, a publication of the Vesterheim Museum that includes the recipes for Norwegian foods served at the festivals.

Nordic Fest
Always the Last Thursday,
Friday, and Saturday in July

Scandinavian Food Fest
Always the First Saturday
in October

Norwegian Christmas
Always the First Saturday
and Sunday in December

Goro (Wafer Cookies)

From *Rosemalers' Recipes* comes this recipe with a long tradition in Norwegian cuisine.
The goro is a rich, flavorful, and crisp Norwegian cookie wafer made in a special goro iron.
The goro is similar to a small waffle iron that presses a fancy design into the wafer. Goro irons
may be purchased from the Vesterheim Gift Shop.

1 cup butter, softened
1 cup margarine, softened
2 cups granulated sugar
½ cup evaporated milk
1 whole egg, slightly beaten
3 egg yolks
26 whole cardamom pods, peeled and crushed,
  or 1 teaspoon ground cardamom
2 tablespoons cognac
3½ cups flour
2½ cups flour

Blend the butter, margarine, and sugar well; add milk, then the egg and egg yolks. Add the cardamom, cognac, and 3½ cups flour and mix well. Stir in the other 2½ cups flour by hand. Divide dough into 5 x 1-inch rolls, cover, and refrigerate at least 2 hours. Remove only one roll of dough at a time from the refrigerator and slice roll into six sections. Roll each slice out as thin as possible on a floured pastry board. Place a cardboard template (the same size as the iron) on the rolled dough and trim around edges with a knife. With a wide spatula or the template, move the goro rectangle onto waxed paper for storage in freezer. Stack rolled-out rectangles on top of each other and store in the freezer for several hours. It works best to roll out dough on one day and bake on the next day.

Baking goro: Heat the goro iron until water spatters on the surface. Brush with peanut oil for the first cookie only. Remove goro rectangles, six at a time, from the freezer. One by one, peel off waxed paper and position carefully on the iron. Close iron and cook a few minutes, turn iron on opposite side, and bake until golden in color, about 1 minute. With a wide spatula, remove cookie to a breadboard. Trim edges to separate one wafer from another while warm. Cool on cookie racks. Stack and store in an airtight container. Yield: about 5 dozen three-section cookies.

Orange City Tulip Festival, Orange City, IA

In 1870, seventy families of Dutch heritage in central Iowa moved to the area now called Orange City to establish a community where they could preserve their traditions and religious beliefs. Their new home was named after the leader they had left behind, William of Orange. But as time passed into the early twentieth century, the settlers and their descendants became increasingly Americanized. From 1933 to 1935, the descendants of Dutch immigrants in and around Orange City held a tulip show and contest, an event that grew out of their concern that they were losing touch with their heritage. In 1936, the first full-blown Tulip Festival was held, attracting 3,500 people. Today, the event draws nearly 150,000 visitors annually.

The Tulip Festival is like a voyage back into nineteenth-century Holland. Authentically costumed volunteers are everywhere, and the architecture is reminiscent of that of 1800s Netherlands. A flower show features gorgeous tulips and explains why the bulbs were once a much-prized form of currency. Horse-drawn Dutch trolley rides provide a relaxing excursion through town, allowing visitors to enjoy Dutch folk arts and crafts like wooden shoe making, the quilt show, and the puppet theater. People toting buckets and brooms scrub the streets in preparation for the arrival of the queen and her court. There are two daily parades with bands and floats. At the *Straat Feest*, visitors witness a parade of Dutch provincial costumes, *Klompen* (wooden shoe) dancers, and Dutch folk dancing.

Thursday through Saturday of the Third Weekend in May

At the *Straatmarkt*, a Dutch open-air market, visitors can purchase imported Dutch gift items. Specialty foods are available in stands inspired by Dutch architecture. The array of Dutch delicacies is tempting: imported Dutch cheese, bologna, home cured dried beef, pea soup, and *saucijzenbroodjes* (pigs in the blanket, a traditional meat pastry) provide substantial fare, followed by mouthwatering *gebak* or pastries such as *poffertjes* and *banket*. The popularity of these pastries is said to have developed along with the tradition of the bridal shower. According to Dutch legend, the bridal shower originated in the seventeenth century when a father refused to provide a dowry for his daughter. Friends stepped in, showered her with gifts, and all enjoyed the small pastries served for the occasion. The banket recipe is also used to make Dutch Letters, pastries formed in the shape of one's initials and much loved by Dutch children.

Banket (Dutch Almond Pastry)

The Orange City Tulip Festival generously shared this famous heritage recipe.

Pastry:
1 pound cold butter
4 cups flour
1 cup cold water

Filling:
1 pound prepared almond paste
1 teaspoon vanilla or almond extract
3 eggs
2 cups sugar

Beaten egg white
Sugar

Pastry: Prepare pastry in the manner of piecrust by cutting the cold butter into the flour. With a fork, stir in cold water until mixture comes together. Chill dough.

Filling: Combine all ingredients and beat well.

Assembly: Preheat oven to 400°. Divide dough into 10 or 12 equal parts. Roll each part into a thin 14 x 4-inch strip. Spread filling down the center. Fold one side of dough over the filling, then fold the other side over. Pinch ends shut. Place pastry strips seam side down on baking sheets. Brush tops with beaten egg white and sprinkle with sugar. Prick with a fork every two inches to allow steam to escape. Bake for 30 minutes.

Note: Dutch Letters are made by shaping the almond rolls into initials before baking.

Tivoli Fest, Elk Horn, IA

The Danish villages of Elk Horn and Kimballton, Iowa, represent one of the largest rural Danish communities in the United States. After a trip to Denmark in 1975, Harvey Sornson, a son of Danish immigrants, determined that the town of Elk Horn needed something Danish as a tribute to its roots. The citizens of Elk Horn agreed, and money was raised to purchase a windmill built in Denmark in 1846. The mill was moved from Norre Snede, Denmark, and its 30,000 pieces were reassembled by 300 volunteers. It was the last mill the Danish government allowed to leave Denmark.

Today, the mill houses a gift shop and serves as an official Iowa Welcome Center. It's also an important part of Elk Horn's annual Tivoli Fest.

Elk Horn's residents generously share their Danish heritage and hospitality with visitors to Tivoli Fest. The aroma of fresh rye bread, made from an original Danish recipe, wafts out from The Danish Bakery. The bakery is also a popular stop for coffee and offers a full range of Danish sweets, with many available by mail order.

Some visitors buy wheat and rye flour freshly ground by the 2,000-pound millstone at the Danish Windmill, which also offers Danish cheeses, meats, and jellies. *Aebleskiver* pans and other Scandinavian cookware, along with a full line of ethnic cookbooks and Iowa products, can be found at the mill.

At the Danish Immigrant Museum, visitors enjoy a taste of life on a Danish farm and explore the arts and culture developed by the Danes in their new American communities. The General Store Museum provides a look back in time. The store is housed in a building erected by Danish immigrants in 1913 and is listed on the National Register of Historic Places.

Festival activities include a craft fair, Danish folk dancing, handicraft demonstrations, and quilt displays, along with more modern attractions like a parade and carnival. Danish foods, as pleasing to the eye as the palate, are available throughout the festival and at local restaurants, which set up Danish buffets, or smorgasbords. Visitors can sample Danish *aebleskiver*, open-faced sandwiches, havarti and other Danish cheeses, pickled herring, kringle, and candy. Danish specialties include delicious slices of pressed chicken, a rolled, brined beef known as *rullepolse*, dried beef, and *medisterpolse,* or meatballs.

The *Better Elk Horn Club Cookbook* incorporates Danish heritage recipes with American favorites such as traditional Danish cookies, kringles, puddings, breads, meatballs, soups, and vegetables.

Saturday and Sunday of Memorial Day Weekend

Rullepolse (Danish Meat Roll)

This Danish heritage recipe has been preserved for future generations in the *Better Elk Horn Club Cookbook.*

2 sides veal or lamb breast or beef flank steak
2 tablespoons minced parsley
2 tablespoons salt
½ teaspoon pepper
¼ teaspoon cloves
¼ teaspoon allspice
1 tablespoon grated onion
½ teaspoon saltpeter

Brine:
2½ quarts boiling water
2 cups salt
½ teaspoon saltpeter
¼ cup sugar

Remove any bones and sinew from meat and wash thoroughly. Sew pieces together to form a large square or rectangle. Flatten and sprinkle remaining ingredients over the entire surface. Roll tightly. Hold together with meat fork while sewing ends and sides. Tie around with cord, securing tightly.

Mix ingredients for brine, add meat, cover, and place in refrigerator. After 5–10 days, remove meat from brine and cook slowly in water to cover. Cook 1–2 hours or until meat is tender when pierced with a fork. Remove from water, drain, and press between two flat surfaces until cold. Slice thinly for sandwiches.

Kansas

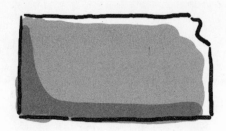

Kansas, more than any other state, embodies the romance of the Old West. The Kansas City area was once the jumping-off point for wagon trains headed west over the Oregon and Santa Fe Trails. When the railroads came in the late 1860s and 1870s, Texas cattle ranchers drove their herds of longhorn cattle over the Chisholm and Western Trails to the state's railroad towns. The railroads also brought new settlers to Kansas, aided by the Homestead Act, in which the federal government granted 160 acres of land to any individuals who stated their intent to become a citizen. Easterners and immigrants from Germany, Switzerland, and Belgium poured into the state, followed by Bohemians and Czechs in 1876. The first wheat harvests were often lost due to insects and drought, until the arrival of the Russian Mennonites in the 1870s, who brought with them a variety of wheat called "Turkey Red." Planted in the fall and harvested in early summer, Kansas' wheat crops were spared the earlier ravages of summer weather. Since 1894, wheat has been the number one crop in Kansas and the catalyst for the establishment of flour mills throughout the state. Known as "America's Breadbasket," Kansas is also a leading producer of beef.

After Harvest Czech Festival, Wilson, KS

Czech heritage is alive and well in Wilson, Kansas, where it has been celebrated every year since 1961 with the After Harvest Czech Festival. The town of Wilson even once sent a few representatives to Topeka, the state capital, on a special mission. They wanted Wilson to be named the "Czech Capital of Kansas," and they were so persuasive that the title was granted.

There's no better place to learn about Czech heritage and have fun, Czech style, than Wilson. Accordion and polka music and dancing abound on both festival days. Presentations are given on the Czech history of Wilson, and there's a museum at the Opera House where Czech cookbooks, dolls, and artwork are sold. A parade, various sporting events, a flea market, a beer garden, and an arts and crafts show round out the offerings.

For some visitors, the best way to become acquainted with Czech culture is through its food. *Kolaches* are available everywhere. At St. Wenceslaus Parish, there is a Czech-style cafeteria and a country store with various specialties. The opportunity to enjoy a Czech meal at the Opera House, built in 1901, is not one to miss. Mrs. Laverne Libal, the semiofficial ambassador of Wilson, presides. There is roast pork served with Libal's homemade sauerkraut and raised dumplings. Green beans, fresh sliced tomatoes, and creamed cucumbers accompany the entrée. Incredibly, it's all followed by poppyseed cake and kolaches.

The official festival cookbook, *Dobre Chutnani, or Good Eating from Wilson,* is a classic for anyone seeking authentic Czech immigrant recipes.

Friday and Saturday of the Last Full Weekend in July

Makovy Dort (Czech Poppyseed Cake)

Laverne Libal of Wilson, KS, is so famous for her cooking and baking that she is considered the best single resource in town for winning heritage recipes.

Cake:
¾ cup poppyseeds
¾ cup milk
1½ cups sugar
¾ cup shortening
2 cups flour
2 teaspoons baking powder
1 teaspoon vanilla
4 egg whites, beaten

Filling:
½ cup sugar
1½ tablespoons cornstarch
Pinch of salt
2 egg yolks, well beaten
1 cup scalded milk
1 teaspoon vanilla
½ cup chopped nuts
½ cup coconut

Frosting:
2 cups sugar
¾ cup cream

Cake: Soak the poppyseeds in milk for 5–6 hours or overnight. When soaking is complete, preheat oven to 375°. Cream the sugar and shortening. Add the soaked poppyseeds, flour, and baking powder. Beat well and add vanilla. Fold in the egg whites. Bake in two layer cake pans for 25 minutes, or until toothpick comes out clean. Cool.

Filling: Mix dry ingredients and add egg yolks. Stir in scalded milk. Cook for 15 minutes, stirring constantly. Remove from heat and cool. Add vanilla, nuts, and coconut. Spread between cake layers.

Frosting: Combine the sugar and cream and boil to the soft ball stage. Remove from heat and beat until thick enough to spread on cake. Frost cake.

Beef Empire Days, Garden City, KS

Because beef still reigns supreme in the Kansas economy, the annual Beef Empire Days was established in 1968. A group of folks created an educational event that included judging, discussion, and awards for those in the beef industry.

Beef Empire Days has evolved into a ten-day spectacle featuring rodeos and other sporting events, concerts, and cowboy poetry, in addition to the Cattle Feeders Symposium. Most events are held at the Finney County Fairgrounds.

There's plenty of food, especially beef. Those holding rodeo tickets can participate in the Hamburger Feed, Cowboy Breakfasts, and free barbecue, where brisket and corn on the cob are served.

For organizations and companies with a competitive spirit, Chuck Wagons in the Park is a perfect venue to showcase a combination of talent and quality. Attendees go to Stevens Park to sample the competitive entries. In 1997, one big feed was produced, and 3,000 people eagerly consumed over 2,000 pounds of beef steak fajitas, carrying home a souvenir copy of the recipe.

Beef Steak Fajitas

Garden City, KS, Beef Empire Days shared the winning recipe for this festival favorite.

Usually the First Two Weeks in June

¼ teaspoon cayenne pepper
½ teaspoon black pepper
¼ teaspoon cumin
½ teaspoon Tabasco sauce
¼ teaspoon dry beef bouillon
½ teaspoon Worcestershire sauce
½ cup water
1 pound boneless beef round
5 flour tortillas

Toppings of choice: lettuce, tomato, onion, hot sauce

To make the marinade, combine the peppers, cumin, Tabasco sauce, and beef bouillon with Worcestershire sauce and water. Chill beef for 5 minutes in freezer. Slice meat crosswise into ⅛- to ¼-inch-thick slices. Pour marinade over meat, cover, and refrigerate for 8 hours or overnight. Remove the meat from the marinade. Stir-fry beef in a nonstick frying pan for 2–3 minutes, stirring constantly. Fill tortillas with meat and toppings of choice. Yield: 5 fajitas.

Optional: Serve meat-filled tortillas with strips of green pepper and onion that have been stir-fried in oil. Pass the hot sauce.

For grilling: Marinate the whole steak, unsliced. Remove steak from marinade. Place on a grid over medium, ash-covered coals and grill 12–14 minutes for medium rare, turning once. Carve steak crosswise into thin slices.

Country Threshing Days, Goessel, KS

The whistle of a steam engine, the klip-klop of a mule team, the carving of a rocking horse, and the smell of funnel cakes—these are the sights, sounds, and smells of Country Threshing Days in Goessel, Kansas. The festival, established in 1974, honors the rural culture of the Goessel community and draws several thousand visitors from all over the United States and Canada.

Mennonites settled the Goessel area in the 1870s. They had received word of rich American acreage available at bargain prices from the Santa Fe Railroad. Kansas beckoned to these hard-working farm families who were seeking a place to live and worship in peace. Soon after their arrival, the Mennonites planted a Russian strain of winter wheat known as "Turkey Red," a crop so successful that it soon supplanted corn as the state's major crop and established Kansas as one of the world's largest producers of wheat.

Country Threshing Days is sponsored by the Mennonite Heritage Museum and The Wheat Heritage Engine and Threshing Company and is a major effort to preserve the old methods of farming and living. The festival has demonstrations of antique threshing machines, steam engines, saw mills, and quilting, spinning, weaving, and rug making.

Children learn historic games, and on both days, ladies gather to test their prowess in the rolling-pin–throwing contest. The Mennonite version of zwieback, a soft, buttery roll, is prepared and baked in a grass oven replicated from those of Russia circa 1875.

First Full Weekend in August

An integral part of this delightful celebration is food, mostly based on the Low German Netherlands cooking. Classic Mennonite turnovers or meat pies called *bierocks*, filled with a seasoned mixture of ground beef, cabbage, and cheddar cheese, top the list of tasty treats. Sandwiches, made from a variety of smoked meats, sausage, or ham, are served alongside generous helpings of coleslaw. At the Goessel

Grade School, diners enjoy a meal of *Verenike*, a type of ravioli filled with curd cheese and topped with ham gravy, country sausage, coleslaw, and zwieback. Cherry moos, a creamy, milk-based soup, is served as part of the Low German meal and throughout the festival. Homemade ice cream is as popular as New Year's Cookies, a variety of deep-fried doughnuts and fritters traditionally served at Mennonite or Low German New Year's celebrations.

The Mennonite Heritage Museum has compiled a cookbook, *From Pluma Moos to Pie*. Pluma, or plum moos, is representative of Old Country cooking, while Mennonites adopted pie as a favorite food shortly after migrating to Kansas. An entire chapter is devoted to peppernuts, spicy cookies traditionally associated with Christmas, and another chapter to New Year's Cookies.

Cherry Moos

Laura Schmidt contributed this recipe to the cookbook *From Pluma Moos to Pie* to preserve an important Mennonite culinary tradition.

5 cups water
1 quart fresh or canned sour cherries, pitted
1 cup sugar
½ cup flour
¼–½ cup sugar
½ teaspoon salt
3 cups milk

Add water to cherries. If using fresh cherries, cook until skins crack. If using canned cherries, heat until boiling. Add 1 cup of sugar during the last minute of boiling. Make a paste of the flour, ¼–½ cup sugar, salt, and milk. Slowly add thickening to fruit, stirring constantly until mixture comes to a boil and starts to thicken or coats a spoon. If soup seems too thick when cooled, add a small amount of water. Moos should have the consistency of medium-thick gravy. It is usually served cold but may also be served hot. Serves: 6–8.

Lenexa Spinach and Trails Fest, Lenexa, KS

Lenexa's recognition as the "Spinach Capital of the World" spanned the 1920s through the mid-1940s. Truck farms, operated by Belgian immigrants, raised and sold more spinach than anywhere else in the country. The restored Lenexa train depot, now located in Sar-Ko-Par Trails Park, site of the Spinach Festival, was the center for shipping spinach to canneries in the 1930s. One area farmer was awarded the title "Spinach King" by a local newspaper after producing an astonishing 41,000 pounds of spinach from just one acre of land.

Proud of its spinach heritage, Lenexa throws the Spinach and Trails Fest every year for over 10,000 visitors. The festival celebrates Lenexa's Belgian and agricultural heritage and has plenty of family activities, including Belgian pigeon racing, frog racing, a zoo, and an arts and crafts show. The community also celebrates the part it played in the settlement of the West. Located in the Kansas City area, Lenexa's connection with the Oregon and Santa Fe Trails is commemorated with such events as an authentic cattle drive and reenactments of 1800s life.

Although the Spinach Recipe Contest was discontinued several years ago, the Lenexa Historical Society still sells a cookbook, *Spinach Thyme*. And the Chamber of Commerce prepares "The World's Largest Spinach Salad," made from 400 pounds of spinach, 200 cloves of garlic, 32 jars of bacon bits, 200 cups of red wine vinegar, 130 cups of salad oil, 80 teaspoons of salt, and 28 teaspoons of pepper. Volunteers dressed as Popeye and Olive Oyle stir the whole concoction with green-and-white candy-striped pitchforks and serve it from a large children's wading pool.

Usually the First Saturday in September

Spinach Mediterraneanne

Judy Rose created this dish and won first place in the Spinach Recipe Contest in 1985.

½ pound ground beef
¼–½ pound ground sausage (Italian is recommended)
1 medium onion, diced
15 ounces ricotta cheese
8 ounces mozzarella cheese, grated
1 (10-ounce) package frozen, chopped spinach, thawed and squeezed dry
8–10 sheets of phyllo pastry
¼ cup butter, melted

Preheat oven to 350°. Brown beef, sausage, and onion. Drain off fat. Mix in a large bowl with ricotta and mozzarella cheeses and the spinach. Set aside. Place a sheet of phyllo dough in a deep 9-inch pie plate and brush with melted butter. Place another sheet over the first, staggering corners slightly, and brush with more butter. Continue until all the phyllo sheets are used. Turn the meat-cheese mixture into the phyllo-lined pie plate. Fold the overhanging edges of each sheet over the mixture until the top is completely enclosed. Brush with any remaining butter. Bake for 1 hour, or until golden brown. Serves: 6 (more if served as an appetizer).

Note: For a spicier version, add salt and crushed red pepper flakes to taste. Oregano or basil may also be added to taste.

Nebraska

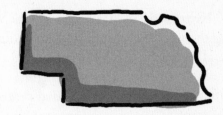

Once considered part of the "Great American Desert," Nebraska's settlement was influenced by three important factors: the Kansas-Nebraska Act in 1854, which established these regions as territories and opened them up for settlement; the Homestead Act of 1860, granting 160 acres of free land to settlers; and, in 1865, the arrival of the railroad in Nebraska and its promotion throughout the East and in Europe. Although most homesteaders were German, significant numbers came from Sweden and Czechoslovakia. In the early 1860s, Swedish immigrants established the town of Stromsborg, and many others followed when famine struck Sweden in the late 1860s. Czechs were also arriving in Nebraska, and the town of Wilber was founded in 1865.

Nebraska's treeless prairies created many challenges for the pioneers, not least of which was the need to build homes from blocks of sod ruefully referred to as "Nebraska marble." Settlers soon discovered that northern Nebraska was inhospitable to farming and turned to cattle ranching, while in the west, wheat was cultivated. Diversified farming arose in eastern Nebraska, and by the late 1920s, the area had earned a reputation for its fruit, which is still economically important. Although not widely distributed, Nebraska has a fledgling wine industry, and apples are processed into cider and other products.

Applejack Festival, Nebraska City, NE

Nebraska City has long been recognized as the hub of Nebraska's apple industry, and in the 1930s, children enjoyed a city holiday to celebrate the annual harvest. In 1968, two young men decided that a new promotion was needed to attract more people to the town. A revival of the 1930s festival was in order, but what would they name it? When one of the committeemen turned to his friend Jack Brewster and said, "Why not call it apple, Jack?" the problem was solved. "Applejack" became the official festival name, even though the event has nothing to do with the commercially distilled brew called Applejack.

The event attracts some 30,000 people yearly and includes an Applejam (music) Fest, marching bands, and apple-seed–spitting and apple-peeling contests. This roster is fleshed out with an antique car show, exhibits of quilts and other crafts, historic demonstrations and tours, and a football game called the "Apple Bowl."

The area's three commercial apple orchards sell an enormous variety of apple-based foods, in addition to fresh produce. Pies, fritters, caramel apples, and apple slushies tempt visitor's sweet tooths.

The Apple Pie Baking Contest is open to all cooks, and the only rule is that the pies must be made of apples. Contestants for Mr. Applejack, who reigns over the festival with Miss Applejack, serve as judges. It's no wonder that there is never a shortage of candidates!

Saturday and Sunday of the Third Weekend in September

Pecan Apple Dip

This festival winner is from a brochure entitled *Recipes for Nebraska City Apples.*

8 ounces cream cheese, softened
¾ cup light brown sugar
1 teaspoon vanilla
1 cup chopped pecans
Sliced apples
Orange juice
Pecan halves for garnish

Blend cream cheese, sugar, and vanilla. Stir in pecans. Dip apple slices in orange juice and arrange on a plate with dip in center. Garnish with pecan halves. Yield: About 2½ cups.

Clarkson Czech Festival, Clarkson, NE

Some 100 miles or so north of the "Czech Capital of the United States," also known as Wilber, Nebraska, lies the town of Clarkson. This region of eastern Nebraska, heavily settled by Czech immigrants, is known as the "Bohemian Alps." Here, too, folks have proudly celebrated their Czech heritage every year since the early 1960s.

The Nebraska Czech Queen Contest is hosted as part of the Clarkson Czech Festival. There is also a rodeo, stage entertainment, a parade, Czech music and dance groups called *beseda,* and special Czech church services. Young girls perform the Maypole dance, while elders dance the waltz and polka in the streets, taverns, and at the Opera House. Old World traditions are preserved in demonstrations of lace making, rug weaving, fine needlework, wool carding, and the making of pastry brushes from goose feathers.

There's lots of wonderful food. Local churches hold Czech dinners, and festival attendees can purchase dumplings and sauerkraut, wedding sausage sandwiches, and sandwiches of roast pork, sauerkraut, and cheese called *Czeska buchta.* There's also a full array of Czech pastries: apple strudel, kolaches, *koblihy nadivane* (filled doughnuts), *rohilky* (horn rolls), and *vdolky* (fried donuts). Local cooks conduct Czech cooking and pastry-making demonstrations and sell the pastries they make.

Houska (Christmas Braid)

Although there is no direct connection with the festival, those in the know will search out a copy of a small cookbook compiled by the GFWC Clarkson Woman's Club in 1989. It's an invaluable source of Czech recipes and includes instructions for many festival favorites.

3 packages dry yeast
⅓ cup warm water
½ cup sugar
⅓ cup butter or duck lard
1 whole egg plus 1 egg yolk, beaten
2½ teaspoons salt
2 cups milk, warmed and then cooled
5½ cups all-purpose flour, unsifted
½ cup almonds, chopped
½ cup white raisins
½ cup dark raisins
1 egg beaten with 1 tablespoon water

Fourth Full Weekend in June

Dissolve yeast in warm water. Cream sugar and butter. Add beaten egg, egg yolk, and salt. Stir in milk. Add yeast mixture, then 2 cups of the flour. Beat until smooth. Let rise about ½ hour. Add nuts and raisins and mix well. Add rest of flour to make a soft dough. Knead until smooth. Place in a bowl and let rise until double in bulk.

Divide dough into five elongated strips. Braid thre strips and place on a greased baking sheet. Twist the remaining two strips and place on top of the braid. Pinch ends together. Brush with egg beaten with water. Let rise 45 minutes. When rising is almost complete, preheat oven to 350°. Bake braid for 45 minutes. May be iced with confectioners' sugar icing.

Nebraska Czech Festival, Wilber, NE

Wilber, Nebraska, is a quiet, pastoral community with a population of 1,600. In early August, Wilber's numbers swell to nearly 30,000 when people come to the annual Nebraska Czech Festival, celebrating the town's ethnic heritage dating back to 1865, when the first Czech settlers arrived. The town has made a successful effort to preserve its roots, and in 1987, President Ronald Reagan signed a proclamation naming Wilber "The Czech Capital of the United States."

While there are a variety of activities, the food seems to be the biggest draw. Local cooks produce traditional Czech dinners of roasted corn-fed duck, sauerkraut made from home-grown cabbage, and baking powder and potato dumplings. Pork dinners and sandwiches, sausages, rye bread, and plenty of desserts round out the menu.

A walking tour of downtown Wilber will lead to Karpisek's Market, home of the "Wilber Wiener" and purveyor of *jelitka* (black sausage) and *jitrnice* (white sausage). The fragrance of smell baked goods lures visitors to the Wilber Bakery, specializing in Wilber rye bread, as well as *houska*, a raisin and nut-filled strudel, and kolaches—traditional Czech pastries. Those who have the necessary fortitude can take part in the kolache-eating contest, where the winner is determined by whoever can first chew and swallow a kolache, then whistle!

Kolaches

Lynne Paulsen and Jim Lisec of Wilber organize the concessions at the Czech Festival. Lynne says, "When you get used to a recipe like us good Czech cooks, you won't even have to measure your ingredients, as we instinctively know what the texture of this dough should be—one of the fine qualities of a true Czech!" Her winning recipe for kolaches follows.

First Friday, Saturday, and Sunday of August

2 packages dry yeast
¼ cup warm water
1 teaspoon sugar
½ cup lard or shortening
½ cup sugar
1 tablespoon salt
2 cups milk
4–5 cups flour (enough to make a soft dough)
2 eggs

Soak yeast in ¼ cup warm water and 1 teaspoon sugar; let stand. In a separate bowl, mix lard or shortening, ½ cup sugar, and salt. Scald the milk and pour over these ingredients to dissolve, then cool. Add 2 cups of the flour and beat well. Add the eggs and beat. Add the yeast mixture and beat. Add another 2 cups of flour or more—whatever is required to make a soft dough. Place dough in a large, greased bowl, lightly grease the top of the dough, cover, and let rise in a warm place until doubled in size, about 1–1½ hours. Make balls of dough a little bigger than a walnut and place on greased cookie sheets. Grease the tops of the kolaches, cover, and let rise again. Make impressions in the kolaches using two fingers and fill with cherry, poppy seed, apricot, apple, or prune fillings. Let kolaches rise again for a short while. When rising is almost done, preheat oven to 400°. Bake kolaches until lightly browned, about 20–25 minutes. Remove from baking sheets and cool on wire racks. Yield: About 8 dozen.

Swedish Festival, Stromsburg, NE

In 1953, descendants of Swedish immigrants established a festival to honor their heritage in Stromsburg, long acknowledged as the "Swede Capital of Nebraska." Now a three-day event, the festival is characterized by parades, sporting events, a band concert, and Swedish dancers. A Swedish craft show and sales bring out shoppers in droves.

The Swedish Festival offers specialty foods for sale in Grandma's Kitchen and plenty of Swedish pancakes to go around. On Friday evening, there is a chicken barbecue. Saturday is the legendary Smorgasbord, which is held in the high school gymnasium and requires advance reservations. Diners are greeted by a panorama of food, all prepared by local volunteer cooks. One recent menu listed seventeen appetizers, including pickled herring, pickled tongue, summer sausage, farmer cheese with caraway, and beets in vinegar. An abundance of Swedish breads can be found, such as hearty Swedish rye, as well as coffee rings and rusks. Baked salmon, Swedish meatballs, baked ham, and Swedish potato bologna called *Svenski potatiskorv* provide a taste of tradition. The meal is brought to a sweet ending with Swedish cheese, grape juice, or rice pudding accompanied by *spettekaka*, *pepparkaka*, *spritz*, and *rosette* cookies.

Food Favorites of the "Swede Capital" of Nebraska is a compilation of Swedish heritage recipes, as well as other beloved dishes found throughout America's heartland. It can be purchased at the festival or by mail order.

Friday Through Sunday of the Third Weekend in June

Swedish Almond Rusks

The late Mrs. Charles Walgren contributed her famous recipe to *Food Favorites of the "Swede Capital" of Nebraska.* According to Geraldine Rystrom, nearly every cook in Stromsburg uses the same basic recipe and then adds her own individual touch. Mrs. Rystrom likes to add a cup of sour cream and an extra cup of flour.

1 cup butter
2 cups sugar
2 eggs
1 teaspoon almond extract
3–4 cups flour
1 teaspoon baking soda
Pinch of salt
1 cup almonds, finely ground

Preheat oven to 350°. Cream butter and sugar. Beat in eggs and almond extract. Mix 3 cups of flour with baking soda, salt, and ground almonds, add to creamed mixture, and blend well. Add enough additional flour to make a stiff dough. Roll dough out into three long rolls as thick as two fingers. Place rolls on a baking sheet and bake for about 30 minutes, or until done and light brown. Remove rolls from oven and cut diagonally into slices ½ inch thick. Place on baking trays, cut-side up. Place rusks in oven, turn oven off, and leave until dry. Turn rusks once during this process.

North Dakota

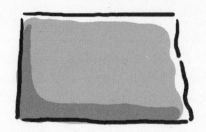

Six tribes of Native Americans were the first residents of North Dakota. Along the Missouri River resided the Mandan, Arikara, and Hidatsa tribes, while the Chippewa were located in the northeast, the Yankton Sioux lived in the Cheyenne and James River Valleys, and the Lakota Sioux were in the southwestern part of the state. The Native Americans' fierce protectiveness of their homelands in North Dakota discouraged early pioneers, even though the U.S. government offered them free land. It was not until Sitting Bull, the great Sioux leader, surrendered in 1881 that peace was finally achieved and settlers began pouring into the region.

The courageous and determined people who settled North Dakota came from the United States, Canada, and several European countries, including Germany, the Ukraine, Czechoslovakia, Poland, and Norway. Through sheer hard work, they established the wheat farms and ranches that today are the basis of the state's agricultural economy. Descendants of the pioneering immigrants who settled North Dakota stress the importance of their heritage and work hard to preserve customs and traditions. So, too, do the various Native-American tribes, whose colorful powwows on reservations throughout the state attract many summer visitors seeking a greater understanding of these first Americans.

North Dakota Ukrainian Festival, Dickinson, ND

Just over a million Ukrainians and persons of Ukrainian descent live in the United States, and about 500,000 in Canada, constituting the largest such population outside of the Ukraine. Many Ukrainians, taking advantage of the Homestead Act, settled in North Dakota, turning the hard prairie sod into fertile farmlands. In Dickinson, the Ukrainian Cultural Institute has made an all-out effort to preserve, display, and promote the heritage of Ukrainian descendants in that area. Every July, they stage the North Dakota Ukrainian Festival, which features music, folk dancing, art exhibits, and Ukrainian Rite religious services. A highlight of the festival is the *Stepovi Dity* Dancers, ages six to forty-six.

The festival also celebrates Ukrainian foodways and traditions, many of which were not documented until the nineteenth century. With the arrival of communism in what was then the Soviet Union, many of the old customs began to fade away. Much Ukrainian cuisine has been preserved by Ukrainian immigrants and their descendants, who found new homes in North America.

Ukrainians place great emphasis on their traditional foods. Bread making is of special importance, with a different shape, texture, and taste for every occasion. The Ukrainian Festival offers a variety of breads. On Saturday, there is a buffet based on a traditional Ukrainian menu. Many dishes are chosen for their relevance to Christmas Eve Supper, a meal of twelve meatless and milkless dishes. It is believed that departed ancestors share in the celebrations and are thus personified by a sheaf of wheat called the *didukh*. A dish that has gained much favor at the Ukrainian Festival is *holubtsi*, or meatless stuffed cabbage, often served with an onion-scented mushroom gravy.

Friday Through Sunday of the Third Weekend in July

Holubtsi (Meatless Stuffed Cabbage)

The Ukrainian Cultural Institute in Dickinson, ND, shares this heritage recipe.

4 cups water
2 cups medium grain rice (not instant)
1 teaspoon salt
3 large onions, chopped
Fresh, high-quality cooking oil
Salt and pepper to taste
1 medium cabbage
1 teaspoon salt
Additional onions, sliced, for garnish

Filling: Bring water to a boil and mix in rice and 1 teaspoon salt. Return to a boil, reduce heat, cover, and cook for 20 minutes. Meanwhile, sauté the chopped onions in oil until tender. When rice is cooked, mix in the sautéed onions and season to taste with salt and pepper.

Holubtsi: Remove core and any torn leaves from the cabbage; reserve the leaves. Fill a large pot three quarters full with water and add remaining 1 teaspoon salt. Parboil cabbage about 5 minutes. Remove from cooking water and remove leaves, placing them in a covered bowl to retain heat, which will further soften them. Let cabbage cool, then pare any thick ribs on leaves to the same thickness as the rest of the leaves.

Preheat oven to 375°. Place a cabbage leaf in one hand and place a tablespoon of the filling close to the core end. Roll firmly, tucking in the sides. Place filled cabbage rolls close together in a heavy roaster or casserole dish. When all leaves are filled, cover them with the washed, reserved leaves. Cover cabbage rolls with hot water, cover roasting pan, and bake for about 1 hour, or until ribs of cabbage are soft. Sauté additional onion in oil and pour over the holubtsi just before serving. Serves: 8–10.

United Tribes International Powwow, Bismarck, ND

Since its inception in 1969, the United Tribes International Powwow has grown from an audience of several hundred spectators surrounding a basketball court to around 20,000 visitors converging on a fifteen-acre bowery known as the "Lonestar Arena." The Powwow still holds to its original purpose of celebrating Native-American culture in song and dance, with some 2,500 dancers and thirty drums competing for top honors. So prestigious is this event that it has been proclaimed "One of the Top Ten Events in North America."

Vendors offer a wide variety of traditional and nontraditional foods, including Native-American specialties like fry bread, tripe and corn soups, Chippewa bannock bread, and beef and buffalo jerky. For many, the highlight of the festival is the free (with price of admission) Beef and Buffalo Feed. This is Sunday dinner with all the trimmings, Native-American style: roast beef or buffalo accompanied by mashed potatoes and gravy, fry bread, and corn followed by blueberry *wozapi* (a type of pudding) for dessert.

Zuni Green Chili Stew

Indian Recipes, compiled by the United Tribes Technical College, is an excellent source of Native-American heritage recipes, including this one.

3 pounds boned lamb, cut into 1½-inch cubes
Flour for dusting
2 tablespoons cooking oil
¼ teaspoon freshly ground black pepper
6 dried juniper berries, crushed
2 yellow onions, peeled and chopped
5½ cups canned hominy, including liquid
1 medium dried hot red chili pepper, crushed
1 tablespoon salt
2 cloves garlic, peeled and crushed
2 teaspoons oregano
½ cup minced fresh parsley
6 green bell peppers, washed, cored, and
    quartered (include some seeds)
1 quart water

Dust lamb cubes lightly with flour. In a large heavy skillet, brown lamb slowly on all sides in the cooking oil. As the meat browns, add the black pepper and juniper berries. Drain the meat on paper towel. In the same skillet, sauté the onions slowly until golden brown. Return the meat to skillet. Mix in remaining ingredients, cover, and simmer for 1½ hours, stirring occasionally. Serves: 12–14.

Always the First Thursday through Sunday after Labor Day

Oklahoma

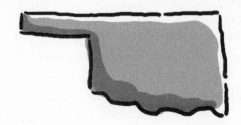

Oklahoma is truly a crossroads between the West and the South: it looks western, but the food has a definite southern touch. In fact, the official state meal is fried okra, squash, cornbread, barbecued pork, biscuits, sausage and gravy, grits, corn, strawberries, chicken-fried steak, pecan pie, and blackeyed peas.

The number one pecan-producing state may be Georgia, but that doesn't impress folks in Oklahoma, who come in fifth. Because pecans are not native to Georgia, pecan hybrids are planted. By comparison, the trees are native to Oklahoma and therefore yield "natural pecans." Blackeyed peas may not be a huge commercial crop, but local farms and markets feature them throughout most of the state. All dolled up in a spicy mixture that includes fresh celery and peppers, they make their appearance as Oklahoma Caviar. And then there's okra, widely cultivated and served in as many ways as there are cooks in Oklahoma.

Harmon County Blackeyed Pea Festival, Hollis, OK

In the late 1980s, Hollis, Oklahoma, found itself in the same situation as many small towns across America: people wanted to shop in nearby cities, and merchants needed a new way to attract business. The Harmon County Historical Museum needed a way to earn money to keep its doors open, and after some discussion, it was decided to hold an annual Blackeyed Pea Festival, an event that attracts around 2,500 people every August.

The festival features an arts and crafts show, a parade, children's games, and contests like cowpaddy bingo, pea shelling, and husband calling. At a tiny dot on the map called Jackrabbit Junction just east of Hollis, there's a Western show. A favorite entertainment is Hollis' version of *Hee Haw*, which plays to a packed house annually.

There used to be a blackeyed-pea–cooking contest. Although it has been discontinued, the *Harmon County Blackeyed Pea Festival Recipes* book is still available. In the heat of August, festivalgoers rapidly work up a thirst, and plenty of free watermelon and ice water is passed out. But the real culinary treat is the Blackeyed Peas and Ham Dinner at the grade-school cafeteria. Few miss the chance to savor the slowly simmered victuals served up with cornbread and all the trimmings of this traditional Southern meal.

Harmon County Caviar Salad

Angie Hubanks' winning recipe from the cooking contest is reprinted from *Harmon County Blackeyed Pea Festival Recipes*.

2 cups cooked fresh blackeyed peas
1 medium tomato, chopped
1 clove garlic, minced
½ red bell pepper, chopped
½ cup chopped fresh parsley
1 (8-ounce) can white hominy, drained
2 green onions, chopped
1 small green bell pepper, chopped
¼ cup chopped onion
½ cup Italian salad dressing

Second Saturday in August

Combine all ingredients except dressing; mix well. Pour salad dressing over mixture. Cover and refrigerate. Marinate for at least 2 hours. Drain well and serve with tortilla chips. Yield: About 5 cups.

Okrafest! and Fall Food Festival, Checotah, OK

For years, Checotah, Oklahoma, has been best known as the "Steer Wrestling Capital of the World," but now, it is also known for the Okrafest. More than a few people were dubious when banker Robert Jennings sold the Checotah Main Street Program on the idea of this festival. After all, okra isn't the most popular vegetable. Its texture has been described as spiny, furry, and slimy. Common in Southern cooking, okra has few fans north of the Mason-Dixon Line.

But in Checotah, okra is celebrated. According to the folks at Okrafest, this hearty vegetable was a mainstay for Native Americans and early homesteaders in the area because it could withstand drought.

Okra Surprise

The Okrafest! and Fall Food Festival supplied this recipe, which won rave reviews from both official and unofficial judges.

2 cups okra sliced ½ inch thick
2–3 large potatoes, washed and chopped, with skins on
2 onions, chopped
2 yellow squash, chopped
1 zucchini, chopped
1 jalapeño pepper, chopped
1 green bell pepper, chopped
2–3 green tomatoes, chopped
Vegetable oil

Fry the okra, potatoes, and onion in oil for 5 minutes. Add remaining ingredients and cook over medium heat until done, 30–40 minutes. Serves: 12–14.

Today, more than 7,500 people attend the Okrafest! and Fall Food Festival. And no doubt about it, this festival has a sense of humor. The day begins with karaokra at the Okrayland Stage. Having worked up an appetite, the audience and contestants head over to the Okra Pot for free okra supplied by Checotah Main Street. Next is the okra-eating contest and the okra slime balloon toss, which calls for tossing balloons filled with okra slime. Finally, there's the Okra Olympics, which lets entrants demonstrate their prowess in games like bobbing for okra pods and the okra race, in which contestants pick okra from a plate without using their hands and take it to a teammate.

Meanwhile, entrants in the Okra Cooking Contest have been hard at work. Visitors can buy tasting kits and choose the People's Choice Award winner. With the festival concentrating on the many ways to cook okra and other fall foods, there's plenty of good eating. Specialties include okra gumbo, okradogs (pickled okra deep-fried in a spicy batter and mounted on a stick), okra salad (fried okra with bacon, onions, tomatoes, and bell peppers) and, believe it or not, okra ice cream. No one goes home without plenty of new recipes featuring okra.

Pecan Festival, Okmulgee, OK

In 1984, the Okmulgee Chamber of Commerce came up with a plan to promote tourism and a local product at the same time. They founded the Pecan Festival, a spin-off of the Pecan Growers Association's annual meeting. Since then, they've gone on to set the Guinness World Record for the largest pecan pie ever produced, at forty feet in diameter. In subsequent years, these indefatigable folks have also delivered the world's largest pecan cookie, brownie, and ice cream and cookie party.

Any pecan devotee will surely enjoy the Pecan Festival. Every year, a ten-foot-diameter pecan pie is baked in a specially designed oven in downtown Okmulgee. Festivalgoers can sample a big slice of the pie or purchase Pecan Diamond Cookies, another specialty. There's lots of other food, including funnel cakes and barbecue.

It would be hard to leave the festivities without a copy of the *Pecan Festival Cookbook*, produced in celebration of the festival's tenth anniversary in 1993. It's absolutely loaded with fantastic recipes for things like Turtle Cake, Spiced Pecans, and Toasted Butter Pecan Cake.

Okmulgee's Own World's Largest, Record-Breaking Pecan Pie (Ministyle)

This is the recipe for a festival specialty from the *1993 Pecan Festival, Okmulgee, Oklahoma Cookbook*.

2⅔ cups granulated sugar
2 tablespoons butter
¼ teaspoon salt
1½ cups corn syrup
7 large eggs, well beaten
1½ teaspoons vanilla
2 unbaked (9-inch) pie shells
3 cups pecans

Preheat oven to 325°. Mix the sugar, butter, and salt until smooth. Slowly add the corn syrup until well mixed. Add the eggs, one at a time, beating until well incorporated. Be sure to scrape the mixing bowl while adding the corn syrup and eggs. Stir in the vanilla. Place the pecans in bottoms of unbaked pie shells. Add filling. Bake until the filling has set medium-firm, about 35–45 minutes. Cool and serve. Yield: 2 pies.

Third Weekend in June

South Dakota

Approximately nine-tenths of South Dakota consists of ranches and farms, many involved in the production of livestock and wheat. Since World War II, state officials have placed a priority on attracting new industry and building tourism to decrease South Dakota's dependence on agriculture. The development of the Missouri River Basin, creating the "Great Lakes of South Dakota," has helped make tourism the state's second largest industry. Visitors have always come to see Mount Rushmore and the Black Hills and Badlands areas, but today, they are finding more entertainment than ever. Many communities feature rodeos, powwows, and heritage celebrations, and others are creating unique attractions that bring in tourist dollars.

International Vinegar Festival, Roslyn, SD

When Lawrence Diggs, "The Vinegar Man," arrived in Roslyn, South Dakota, change was definitely in the wind. Diggs is a vinegar expert and a worldwide consultant on all aspects of the product. Having lived a hectic lifestyle, he wanted a home where no one knew him, and he chose Roslyn. But fate was about to intervene. A hamlet of 251 people, Roslyn is in the midst of South Dakota's grain-producing region. And grain is a basic vinegar ingredient. When flooding threatened the local economy in 1998, the townspeople turned to Diggs for inspiration; together, they have taken the first strides toward diversification of the local economy.

In 1999, after a lot of hard work, the International Vinegar Museum opened its doors. The only one of its kind in the world, it is designed to put this locale back on the map as "a beacon and a magnet for vinegar fans around the world." The museum contains displays on the history of vinegar and how it is made. Along with a research kitchen, it has a vinegar-tasting bar, and the museum shop sells some fifty different types of vinegar. Open from June 1 to October 31, the museum has become an international attraction. Serious vinegar fans can join the museum's club, Vinegar Connoisseurs International.

Not content with a museum, Diggs and the townspeople launched the International Vinegar Festival in 2000. The first year's attendance of 500 is sure to grow by leaps and bounds, outstripping all hopes and expectations and providing a huge boost for the local economy. Everyone gets involved, including area restaurants.

Always the Third Saturday in August

Festival events include a Dog Jog, which lets pets race for prizes, as well as a marathon from Roslyn to nearby Eden and back for humans. The festival features kids' games, a kiddie parade, music, crafts, and chef's demonstrations on the many uses of vinegar in cooking. Participation in the Mother of All Vinegar Contests brings in vinegar entries from all over the world to be judged by selected chefs. There is even a doll-making contest in which dolls are fashioned from vinegar bottles.

Typical carnival food is available, along with festival specialties like pickles-on-a-stick and vinegar pie. According to *The Encyclopedia of American Food and Drink*, both vinegar candy and vinegar pie were popular treats among settlers of the

Midwest, especially in winter when they craved the sweet-tart flavor of fruit.

The Vinegar Recipe Contest offers cooks an opportunity to strut their kitchen prowess. Because the annual state fair was held too early in the season to include the judging of homemade pickles, that event has been officially transferred to the Vinegar Festival, where representatives from South Dakota State University also give pickling seminars. Other uses of vinegar have been incorporated in the Vinegar Cooking Contest, with categories from vinaigrette dressings to salads or main dishes and desserts.

3-2-1 Salad Dressing

Louise Blank of Roslyn, SD, won first place at the first Vinegar Cooking Contest at the first International Vinegar Festival with this recipe—a lot of "firsts" for one cook!

3 tablespoons heavy cream or sour cream
2 tablespoons sugar
1 tablespoon vinegar
Dash of mustard
Dill or celery seed (optional)

Mix all ingredients thoroughly. Use as a dressing for lettuce or cabbage salad.

Vinegar Pie

Courtesy of Lawrence Diggs of the International Vinegar Festival.

4 eggs
1½ cups granulated sugar
¼ cup melted butter
1 teaspoon vanilla extract
1½ tablespoons cane vinegar
1 deep-dish (9-inch) piecrust, unbaked

Toppings (optional):
Whipped cream
Chopped nuts

Preheat oven to 350°. In a blender or large mixing bowl, combine the eggs, sugar, butter, vanilla extract, and vinegar. Mix well and pour into piecrust. Bake for 50 minutes, or until firm. Remove from oven and cool on a wire rack. Serve plain or topped with whipped cream and chopped nuts.

Chapter 5

The West and Southwest

Arizona | Colorado | Idaho | Montana
Nevada | New Mexico | Texas | Utah | Wyoming

Arizona

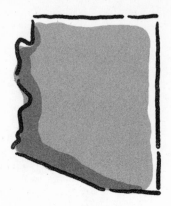

Arizona has experienced enormous population growth. With as little as two to five inches of annual precipitation in the desert portions of the state, Arizona enjoys an abundance of sunshine that also attracts millions of tourists. But with its explosive growth come concerns about energy efficiency, and Arizona is a leader in striving to meet the 1997 Million Solar Roofs Initiative, which calls for the installation of one million solar energy systems on buildings throughout the United States by the year 2010. Solar energy is viewed as a required resource in the new millennium, as it conserves resources, preserves the environment, and cuts costs on utility bills. For solar enthusiasts and activists, Arizona provides leadership and direction by example.

Tucson Solar Potluck and Exhibition, Tucson, AZ

Second Saturday in May

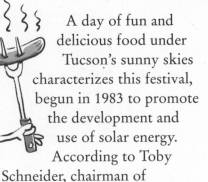

A day of fun and delicious food under Tucson's sunny skies characterizes this festival, begun in 1983 to promote the development and use of solar energy. According to Toby Schneider, chairman of Citizens for Solar, "The original organization was made up of a bunch of guys who liked to eat and who were handy with table saws required to make the ovens. For the first few years, it was a small solar Woodstock, hippie-type event. We're more respectable now!" Indeed.

Over 1,000 people annually head out to Catalina State Park, where members of the organization cook massive amounts of food using only solar power. While they spend a good deal of time explaining and demonstrating solar products in action, the solar cooks also hand out free food samples all day long.

Members compete with each other to make the biggest or the hottest ovens. Their big pizza oven can make thirty pizzas a day, six at a time. One oven cooks fifty pounds of turkey and twenty pounds of potatoes in a day, and another produces eight pans of lasagna at a time.

At 5:00 P.M., the ovens are emptied and the tables are loaded with food. Attendees line up to enjoy the free, "like the sun" buffet, which includes a staggering number of soups, stews, casseroles, breads, and vegetarian dishes. To raise funds, the Citizens for Solar sell a cookbook and how-to guide entitled *Cooking with the Sun*.

Solar Garden Soup

Toby Schneider, chairman, Citizens for Solar, shared his winning recipe, which can be cooked by solar power as well as in an electric cooking pot or on top of the stove.

2 cups dried beans such as "13 Bean Mix" or red kidney beans.
3 large carrots, peeled and chopped
2 onions, peeled and chopped
1 red bell pepper, cored and chopped
3 small unpeeled potatoes, cubed
2 cups fresh string beans, trimmed and chopped
3–4 tomatoes, cored and sliced
3 stalks celery, chopped
1 (16-ounce) can stewed tomatoes
⅓ cup ketchup
½ teaspoon cumin seeds, crushed
1 tablespoon Italian seasoning or oregano
½ teaspoon whole peppercorns
1 tablespoon olive oil
2 bay leaves
2 tablespoons dry vegetable broth or chicken bouillon
As many jalapeño peppers as you dare

Wash beans, then place in a 4-quart pot, cover with water, and let soak overnight. Drain water and discard. Combine beans with all other ingredients, add water to fill the pot, cover, and place in a solar oven by 10:00 A.M. You will have 4 quarts of soup by 5:00 P.M.

Colorado

Colorado was a sparsely settled region until prospectors discovered gold on Cherry Creek near what is now Denver. Amid cries of "Pike's Peak or Bust," nearly 100,000 prospectors converged on the area within a year's time. One of the best known of the early mining towns was Silverton, which was a supply center for area gold and silver mines in the San Juan range throughout the 1880s and 1890s. But in 1893, the U.S. economy plunged, and the government canceled its contracts to purchase large amounts of silver. After that, it was all downhill for Silverton, and even its last gold mine, the Sunnyside, shut down in 1991. Today, Silverton is a National Historic District and cashes in on Colorado's enormous tourist industry. In contrast, the mountain community of Boulder, a bit northwest of Denver, boasts a dynamic, modern economy. Referred to as "the little town nestled between the mountains and reality," it's the perfect Colorado birthplace for the National Pie Council.

Great American Pie Festival
(Location Varies Annually)

National Pie Day was established in 1979 by a group of pie lovers who banded together to form the American Pie Council. The only national organization devoted to preserving the art of making pie, which they saw as a dying art, the APC's motto is "In crust, we trust."

In 1995, the APC resolved to take further steps in their efforts to draw attention to what they claim is America's favorite dessert, and the first annual National Pie Championships were held in Laughlin, NV, Later events were held in Boulder, CO, one-time headquarters for the APC, Orlando, FL, and Celebration, FL. The championships include amateur, commercial, and professional pie-making divisions.

Once the pies are made and the judges go to work, festival attendees are invited to sample a huge array of donated pies from the World's Largest Pie Buffet, watch pie-making demonstrations, attend pie seminars, and check out a pie history lesson. There are even pie-making events for the kids. Needless to say, everyone gets a piece of the pie.

Nancy Neiss' Prize Pecan Pie

Nancy Neiss of Littleton, CO, won best of show with this pie at the 1997 National Pie Championships.

Dates Change Annually

Easy piecrust:
2 cups all-purpose flour
1 teaspoon salt
¾ cup butter flavor shortening
5–6 tablespoons ice water

Filling:
3 eggs
1 cup dark brown sugar, packed
1 cup light corn syrup
2 tablespoons butter, melted
1 teaspoon pure vanilla
1–2 tablespoons bourbon
1⅓ cups coarsely chopped pecans

In a large bowl, combine flour and salt. With a pastry blender, cut shortening into flour until mixture is crumbly and shortening is the size of small peas. Add water 1 tablespoon at a time, tossing well with a fork. Mixture should form a ball in bottom of bowl. Roll out crust and place in a 9-inch pie pan.

Preheat oven to 350°. In a medium bowl, beat eggs slightly. Add sugar, corn syrup, butter, vanilla, and bourbon. Stir until well blended. Stir in pecans (or place them in the unbaked piecrust) and pour filling into unbaked piecrust. Cover edge of pie with foil to prevent overbrowning. Bake for 25 minutes, remove shield from edge of piecrust, and continue baking for another 25–30 minutes or until a knife inserted halfway between center and edge comes out clean. Remove from oven and cool on a rack.

Note: As a time saver, use a deep-dish, frozen piecrust defrosted according to the manufacturer's instructions.

International Rhubarb Festival, Silverton, CO

High in the San Juan Mountains of southwestern Colorado lies the town of Silverton, population 500. The major occupation used to be silver mining, but now it's tourism. The most common crop is rhubarb, one of the three things that flourish here—horseradish and dandelion being the other two. In fact, town statistics cite 400 rhubarb plants for a total of 350 households. Rhubarb was thus a hands-down choice when the local Chamber of Commerce began looking for ideas for a Fourth of July celebration theme.

The main event of the Rhubarb Festival is a cooking contest that includes desserts, beverages, jams, entrees, frozen desserts, and even a category called "industrial uses." Winners are awarded much-coveted "Rhubarb Certificates," and after the contest, attendees may purchase a plate and sample anything they wish. There is also a rhubarb pie-eating contest.

In addition to plenty of baked goods, including pies, cobblers, and cakes, the specialty of the festival is delicious rhubarb ice cream. Folks who want to duplicate these goodies at home can pick up a copy of *The Silverton Public Library's International Rhubarb Cookbook and Other Little Gems*. All proceeds benefit the Silverton Public Library, built in 1906 with funds donated by Andrew Carnegie.

Rhubarb Ice Cream

Robert Zinser of Silverton, CO, whips up his famous festival specialty for visitors.

Rhubarb swirl mixture:
4 cups rhubarb, peeled, trimmed, and chopped
1 cup sugar

Ice-cream mixture:
1 gallon milk
2 quarts heavy cream
2 cups sugar
2 tablespoons pure vanilla

Always the Fourth of July

Combine ingredients for rhubarb swirl mixture and cook down over low heat until it is the consistency of jam, about 1 hour. Cool completely before making ice cream. Mix together ingredients for ice cream mixture and freeze in an ice cream maker according to manufacturer's directions. After ice cream has begun to freeze, swirl in rhubarb mixture. Yield: 1½ gallons.

Note: For a richer consistency, adjust proportions to half milk and half heavy cream.

Idaho

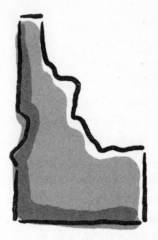

With a great deal of wilderness area still relatively inaccessible, Idaho is a land of rugged, unspoiled terrain, wide-open spaces, and great beauty. It boasts 3,100 miles of river, more than any other state. It ranks number one in the United States for production of both potatoes and trout. The Snake River, which wends its way through the southern portion of Idaho, is the focus of much of the state's economy relative to agriculture, food processing, and tourism. Along the Snake are Blackfoot, known as the "Potato Capital of the World," and Buhl, called the "Rainbow Trout Capital of the World." The people of Idaho honor the largesse of land and river in annual celebrations that draw visitors from all over America as well as many foreign countries.

Fisherman's Free Breakfast, St. Anthony, ID

Always the Friday before Opening Day of Fishing in Late May

For great trout fishing, thousands annually converge on the area surrounding the town of St. Anthony in southeastern Idaho. Most fishermen arrive on the Friday preceding opening day to participate in the fun and gustatory delights of the Fisherman's Free Breakfast sponsored by the Greater St. Anthony Chamber of Commerce and the Fisherman's Breakfast Committee.

Lucky is the visitor who runs into Eddie Clark, a local booster who can provide an enthusiastic and detailed history of this event, which goes back to 1955. The first year, travelers on U.S. Highway 91 were stopped by the townspeople and invited to partake of free doughnuts and coffee provided by local restaurants—part of a clever publicity effort to promote St. Anthony as a great place to visit and purchase supplies before heading into the fishing country of Fremont County. The success of this event culminated in an annual Fisherman's Free Breakfast held on a city-owned island surrounded by the Henry's Fork of the Snake River. From 6:00 A.M. until 2:00 P.M., visitors enjoy breakfast outdoors with Idaho's glorious Teton Peaks towering in the background.

Volunteers mix 630 pounds of pancake mix with gallons of buttermilk in a gigantic steel mixer to make the hotcakes, topped with butter and syrup, served at the breakfast along with sausage, Idaho hash brown potatoes, juice, milk, and coffee. The chokecherry jelly, made from berries gathered in the desert, provides a special, hometown touch. It's all free, with the majority of supplies donated by area merchants and the rest of the tab picked up by the Chamber of Commerce.

In 1958, the Fisherman's Free Breakfast got national attention when Jack Edwards, host of the television show *Queen for a Day*, attended with a winning contestant. Every year, invitations go out to Idaho's governor and the president of the United States. While no president has ever attended, the governor and other politicians often do, especially in election years. With an average of 5,000 people lining up for breakfast, the wait can be long but worthwhile. A few hours can pass swiftly when there is beautiful scenery accompanied by musical entertainment and lots of tall fishing tales.

Sagebrush Days, Buhl, ID

Surprisingly, there is no Idaho trout festival. But Buhl's Sagebrush Days, every July Fourth, features a not-to-be-missed Fish Fry that also includes a parade, sidewalk sale, antique car show, and an International Dutch Oven Society Cookoff.

Buhl, located in the Hagerman Valley near Twin Falls, is home to numerous federal and state fish hatcheries and boasts operations like Clear Springs Foods, the largest trout-raising farm in an area that produces nearly eighty-five percent of all commercial trout sold. Trout farming is supported by an underground aquifer that stretches from eastern Idaho almost all the way to Boise. Clear Springs Foods donates its breaded rainbow trout fillets for the annual Fish Fry, which benefits the Buhl Chamber of Commerce. Over 1,000 people line up to buy generous fish dinners that also include coleslaw, baked beans, rolls, and tartar sauce.

Pistachio-Crusted Rainbow Trout with Cilantro Citrus Hollandaise

This recipe was supplied courtesy of Clear Springs Foods, the largest trout farm in the world and developer of trout-based recipes guaranteed to win awards for any cook.

Cilantro citrus hollandaise:
4 egg yolks
2 tablespoons lime juice
2 tablespoons orange juice
2 tablespoons grapefruit juice
1½ cups clarified butter
¼ cup chopped cilantro
Salt and pepper to taste

Trout:
3 cups pistachio nuts, shelled, finely chopped, and toasted
½ cup chopped fresh cilantro
Salt and pepper to taste
12 (8-ounce) boneless, butterfly-cut rainbow trout fillets
¼ cup fresh lime juice
Flour as needed
4 eggs, lightly beaten
¾ cup clarified butter

Cilantro citrus hollandaise: Whisk together the egg yolks and citrus juices. Whisk over a *bain marie* until sauce is light and fluffy. Remove from the heat and slowly whisk in the clarified butter. Season with cilantro, salt, and pepper. Keep warm. Yield: 2 cups.

Trout: Mix together pistachio nuts and cilantro. Add salt and pepper to taste. Sprinkle each fillet with one teaspoon lime juice. Dredge fillets in flour, dip in beaten egg, and coat with pistachio mixture. Place fillets on a hot, lightly oiled griddle or in a sauté pan, flesh side down. Drizzle each fillet with 1 tablespoon clarified butter. Sauté until just done, about 2 minutes per side. Split butterfly fillet; overlap on serving plate. Ladle 1 ounce of hollandaise sauce over each fillet and serve. Serves: 12.

Idaho Spud Day, Shelley, ID

Located just south of Idaho Falls, Shelley is one of Idaho's major potato-growing areas. Since 1929, folks here have paid homage to the local crop with Idaho Spud Day in the city park. It's a country-style event with plenty going on. The day starts with a breakfast of pancakes, scrambled eggs, sausage or bacon, and, of course, Idaho hash brown potatoes. Fun runs are held for various age groups, along with a parade, a talent show, the Miss Russet Pageant, musical entertainment, and a demolition derby.

Few miss the Spud Tug, a rope-tugging contest with a definite twist, Idaho style. Prior to the festival, a two-foot-deep pit is dug. Then a cement mixer truck fills the pit with mashed potatoes! Losing teams end up wallowing in more mashed potatoes than they ever dreamed existed.

Those not participating in the Spud Tug also get their fill of Idaho potatoes. In the old days, train passengers were probably startled by local boosters who climbed aboard to pass out free baked potatoes on Spud Day. Free baked potatoes are still served annually to some 5,000 visitors who choose from a variety of toppings, including butter, sour cream, and bits of bacon. At one time, all those potatoes were prepared by commercial bakeries in Idaho Falls and then shipped the nine miles by train to Shelley. These days, they are baked in local school kitchens.

The Dutch Oven Cookoff at Spud Day encourages the creative use of potatoes in various categories like "Side Dish or Dessert" and "Yeast Rise Bread." In the "Main Dish" competition, potatoes are a mandatory ingredient. Since this competition is a sanctioned satellite cookoff of the International Dutch Oven Society, winners qualify for participation in the yearly international competition in Logan, Utah. Organizers of Shelley's Dutch Oven Cookoff have produced a cookbook featuring numerous recipes for Idaho potatoes.

Always the Third Saturday in September

MISS RUSSET

Mushroom Sherry Pot Roast and Potatoes

Clyde and Terrie Miller of Roy, UT, won the 1999 main dish division of the Spud Day Dutch Oven Cookoff with this recipe. Raised in the Shelley area, Clyde returned home to demonstrate his Dutch oven expertise.

15 baby red potatoes
1 (2–3 pound) beef roast
½ cup dry sherry for injecting
Seasoned meat tenderizer
3 tablespoons vegetable oil
¾ pound mushrooms, sliced
⅓ cup dry sherry
⅓ cup water
1 bay leaf
⅛ teaspoon salt
2 tablespoons flour

Mushroom potatoes: Push an apple corer up into the center of each potato. With a sharp knife, cut away the potato around the corer. Carefully pull out the corer and place potatoes in ice water. Approximately 1 hour before serving, cook the potatoes in salted water in an 8-inch Dutch oven until tender. Set aside 3 tablespoons of the cooking water.

Inject the roast with the ½ cup sherry and rub the outside of the roast with meat tenderizer. In a shallow, 14-inch Dutch oven, heat the oil and brown the roast on all sides to seal in juices. Slice the mushrooms and add to the pot along with ⅓ cup sherry, water, bay leaf, and salt. Cover and simmer 2½–3 hours or until meat is tender. When the roast is done, remove it from the pot, cover, and keep warm. In a cup, blend the flour and the reserved cooking water. Gradually stir this mixture into the liquid in the Dutch oven. Cook, stirring, until slightly thickened. Discard the bay leaf. To serve, pour some gravy over the roast and pass the remaining gravy. Serve with mushroom potatoes. Serves: 6.

Montana

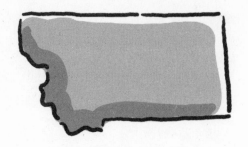

Much of Montana's history is reflected in Lewistown, located in the central part of the state. This area was originally the domain of Native Americans and buffalo. As trappers and hunters moved in, trading posts were established. In 1879, mixed-blood descendants of the French and Indians, called *Metis*, led by a French Canadian trader named Francis Janeaux, established homesteads. Cattle and sheep ranchers followed. With the discovery of gold in the Judith Mountains in 1880, hundreds of prospectors rolled into the region, and in 1883, a post office was established with the formal name of "Lewistown." These were the days of the Wild West, with vigilantes dealing out their own form of justice to the desperados who felt themselves above the law or, in its absence, common morality. Today, Lewistown serves as a ranching and business center, just as it did over a hundred years ago. Framed by the lovely Judith and Snowy Mountains, the town has been featured in several movies, commercials, and documentaries. And while sweet black cherries are Montana's major fruit crop, Lewistown celebrates the wild chokecherry, which grows in profusion across central Montana's rolling prairie.

Chokecherry Festival, Lewistown, MT

In the heart of Big Sky Country is Lewistown, Montana, "Chokecherry Capital of the World." While the hardy chokecherry, a member of the rose family, is found in many areas of the United States, it is especially common in central Montana. The "choke" in the name refers to the sour, bitter taste of the raw fruit, a quality that carries a warning of its own: uncooked, the chokecherry is poisonous because it contains cyanide. But when properly prepared, the berries produce wonderful jams, jellies, and syrups, which are available for purchase at the annual Chokecherry Festival.

The celebration opens with a breakfast of pancakes accompanied by chokecherry syrup and progresses to the Chokecherry Pit-Spitting Contest. Over in Chokecherry Lane, there's the Chokecherry Culinary Contest, which includes not only edible delights but "antichoking" creations such as cough drops and cough syrup. One year, top honors went to a woman who entered a chokecherry pie, a project that required the assistance of her entire family. With only about one-eighth inch of fruit surrounding each pit, it was a laborious effort to pit enough of the fruit to produce the required amount of pulp for the pie. A cookbook entitled *Chokecherry Recipes* was once sold by the festival but is currently out of print.

Cherry Colettes

Featured in *Chokecherry Recipes*, this dessert is the prize-winning creation of Donna Davis of Lewistown, MT.

12 ounces semisweet chocolate chips
2 tablespoons butter
3 cups baked, coarsely crumbled pound cake
⅔ cup maraschino cherries, drained and chopped
6 tablespoons chokecherry brandy
1 cup heavy cream, whipped
Cocktail cherries, stemmed, as garnish

Line the cups in an 8-cup muffin pan. Melt the butter and chocolate in the microwave. Coat the inside of the cups with chocolate and chill until firm. Remove the paper cups from the chocolate shells. Blend together the crumbled pound cake, maraschino cherries, and 4 tablespoons of chokecherry brandy. Spoon the mixture into the chocolate shells. Fold the remaining chokecherry brandy into the cream. Swirl on top of the filled shells. Garnish with stemmed cocktail cherries. Refrigerate until serving. Yield: 8 colettes.

Note: Cherry brandy may be substituted.

Always the First Saturday After Labor Day

Nevada

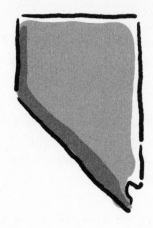

The Basques first arrived in the West to seek their fortune in the California Gold Rush. Disillusioned, they quickly turned to sheep herding, taking advantage of California's open ranges. As sheep bands proliferated, the ranges became overcrowded. By 1870, the Basques moved on, many of them into the frontier of central and northeastern Nevada. Elko became an early staging center for the itinerant herders. The Basques maintained their itinerant lifestyle until 1934, when passage of the Taylor Grazing Act largely excluded them from the open range. Many returned to Europe, while a few obtained employment with landed sheep men. Basque-Americans held their first National Basque Festival in Sparks, Nevada, in 1959. It was the prototype for the Elko event, which dates back to 1962 and has now assumed the title. It attracts participants from throughout the far-flung Basque colony of the American West, which extends into California, Idaho, and Utah.

Genoa Candy Dance, Genoa, NV

The Sierra Mountains were a formidable barrier for settlers heading to California. Research by historian Henry Chenoweth tells more of the story. On the east side of the trail leading to Placerville, a rest stop called "Ragtown" sprang up in Nevada, named for the laundry strung on bushes to dry. When the rest stop became a provisioning center, the name was changed to "Leeteville." In 1849, when Brigham Young sent a colonizing party to the area, it became known as "Mormon Station." Eventually, around 1851, an Italian settler called it "Genoa," the name stuck, and the town became Nevada's first settlement.

In 1919, the women of Genoa started what was to become a charming tradition to raise funds for the town's streetlights. They staged a dance and sold candy. There's still a dance with a huge buffet on Saturday evening, but the two-day festival now centers around a large arts and crafts show. Upward of 30,000 visitors are attracted to this town of 200. Their main purpose is to buy the famous candy made by the women of Genoa; over two tons of candy are sold during the two days of the festival.

Buyers face a dizzying array of candies: fudge, divinity, turtles, brittles, dipped chocolates, caramels, penuche, pralines, taffy, toffee, truffles, bon bons, and mints. One of the most popular is the unique almond candy made by Genoa's postmaster, Emmy Dombrowski. The *Genoa Candy Book* contains treasured recipes for the confections sold each year at the festival's candy booth.

Emmy's Almond Candy

Emmy Dombrowski, postmaster in Genoa, cleverly created this winning candy that tastes just like a famous commercial confection. Reprinted from the *Genoa Candy Book*, with permission from the Town of Genoa.

1 cup whole almonds
1 pound butter
2 cups sugar
12 ounces chocolate chips
½ to ¾ cup almonds or walnuts, finely chopped

The Last Full Weekend in September

Line a large cookie sheet or pan with heavy-duty foil. Coarsely chop the almonds. Over high heat, melt the butter and add the sugar. Bring to a boil, stirring constantly with a wooden spoon. After mixture boils, reduce heat to medium high. Cook for 5 minutes, stirring constantly. Add almonds, bring back to a boil, and boil another 5 minutes. The butter and nut oil will start to separate, so continue stirring in order to fold the nuts back in. Test by dropping a small amount of the candy mixture in cold water. Mixture should harden to a crack stage, with a medium-gold color. Pour candy into a foil-lined pan and spread thinly. Cool completely. Melt chocolate chips and coat cooled candy with chocolate. Sprinkle with finely chopped nuts and press the surface gently. When set, turn and coat the other side with finely chopped nuts. When chocolate has set completely, break candy into small pieces.

National Basque Festival, Elko, NV

Elko is in the high country of northeast Nevada. This is the heart of "Cowboy Country" and home to a significant number of Basque-Americans. The National Basque Festival, billed as "Basquing in America's Freedom," is today the largest of its kind and attracts an attendance of around 8,000, including many "old country" contestants from Spain who compete in weight-lifting and wood-chopping events, as well as dancing.

Great attention is paid to the serving of traditional foods. The chorizo booth is a major attraction. Served in hot-dog buns, the chorizo is washed down with cold beer.

Out on the range, Basque sheepherders were a self-reliant bunch, doing most of their cooking with a Dutch oven, which was essential for hearty stews and soups. The Dutch oven was also used to produce what came to be known as "Sheepherder's Bread," baked by burying the pot in hot embers. The herder would carve the sign of the cross on top of the baked loaf and then serve the first piece to his invaluable dog. A main event of the festival is the Sheepherder's Bread Baking Championship. After judging, the bread is auctioned off, with proceeds benefiting the Basque dance troupe.

The "Festival Meal" is served midday on Sunday and features barbecued lamb and steak. Some 2,000 people partake of the meal, which is rounded out with barbecued beans, a specially dressed salad, rolls, cake, coffee, and wine.

Cookbooks featuring Basque specialties include *Traditional Basque Cooking*, *From the Basque Kitchen*, *The Art of Basque Cooking*, and *Basque Recipes*. Another worthy tome on Basque cooking is *On Egin* produced by Elko Arñak Dancers.

Always the First Weekend in July

Sheepherder's Bread

Karen Larrinaga contributed this heritage recipe to the Elko Ariñak Dancers Cookbook *On Egin*.

3 cups very hot tap water
½ cup shortening
¼ cup sugar
2½ teaspoons salt
2 packages dry yeast
8½ cups flour (approximate)
Vegetable oil

In a large bowl, combine hot water, shortening, sugar, and salt. Stir to melt shortening. Let cool to lukewarm. Stir in yeast. Cover and set in a warm place until bubbly, about 15 minutes. Add 5 cups of flour and beat with a wooden spoon to form a thick batter. Stir in enough remaining flour to form a stiff dough.

Knead dough on a floured board for about 10 minutes or until smooth. Add flour as needed. Turn dough over in a greased bowl; cover and let rise in a warm place until doubled in size, about 1½ hours. Punch dough down and knead on a floured board to form a smooth ball. Cut a circle of foil to cover the bottom of the Dutch oven. Grease the inside of the Dutch oven and the inside of the lid with oil. Place the dough in the Dutch oven, cover, and let rise until the dough touches the lid.

Preheat oven to 375°. Bake for 12 minutes, then remove lid and reduce heat to 350°. Bake for 35 minutes or until golden brown. Remove from oven and take bread out of Dutch oven. Place on a wire rack to cool.

Babarrun Gorriak Azakin (Basque Beans with Cabbage)

Marcelino Ugalde of the University of Nevada, Reno, Basque Studies Program shares his family's recipe for this traditional Basque dish.

2 pounds dried red beans
2 carrots or 1 potato
1 head of cabbage, quartered and cored
4 cloves garlic
Olive oil
2 chorizo, cut into chunks
2 morcilla (blood sausages), cut into chunks

Soak beans overnight and drain. Cover beans with fresh water and boil with the carrots or potato until half done. Place cabbage in a separate pot of salted, cold water, bring to a boil, and cook until tender.

While the beans and cabbage are cooking, in a small fry pan sauté 2 cloves of the garlic in a small amount of olive oil. Add the garlic and oil, chorizo, and *morcilla* to the beans and cook on low heat for 30 minutes.

Meanwhile, sauté the remaining 2 cloves of garlic with a small amount of olive oil. When beans are ready, drain cabbage and place on a platter. Pour remaining garlic and oil over cabbage.

Typically, the beans and the cabbage are served together, with diners ladling beans over a serving of cabbage. Serves: 6.

New Mexico

When Spanish explorers arrived in New Mexico in the 1500s, they found an agrarian-based Pueblo Indian culture. Initial attempts to convert the Indians to Catholicism were met with resistance, and it was many decades before the two cultures reached the level of cultural commingling that we see in New Mexico today. The colonists did, however, adapt quickly to vital foodstuffs long used by the native population, including corn, which became a staple of their diet. Today, New Mexico is the number one producer of chiles (spelled with an "e" by order of the state legislature) and also produces such crops as pecans and onions in the lush and fertile valley of the southern Rio Grande. This river, which bisects the state from north to south, is also home to a thriving wine industry that dates back to plantings first made in 1629. New Mexicans proudly salute their culture and their economy with numerous festivals throughout the year.

Hatch Chile Festival, Hatch, NM

Chile lovers from all over the world annually convene at the Hatch Chile Festival on Labor Day Weekend. The festival is held at the Hatch Airport two miles west of town. Hatch, known as the "Chile Capital of the World," is located in the fertile Rio Grande Valley and is home to around 1,000 residents, mostly farmers and migrant workers. Hatch now annually hosts nearly 15,000 folks in search of some of the finest chiles produced in the state.

The festival offers a real feel for New Mexico's culture and people, with story telling, dancing, strolling mariachi musicians, and chile-related arts and crafts. There is plenty of chile in the form of fresh produce, chile *ristras*, and chile-based foods. At the food concessions, Southwest cuisine abounds: burritos, enchiladas, rellenos, salsas, chile, and even the all-American burger crowned with chiles.

A highlight is the Chile Cook-off, where contestants compete to produce the best tasting or hottest chile dish. There is also a *ristra* arrangement competition in which chiles are strung and dried.

A jalapeño-eating contest tests the mettle of entrants, while others vie for honors with original recipes in the cooking contest. Many of the winning formulas have been compiled into a cookbook, *Recipes from Hatch: Chile Capital of the World*. The book contains a wealth of chile recipes plus instructions on roasting chiles, preparing red chile sauce from scratch, and making *ristras*.

Chimichangas

Teresa Berridge's winning recipe appears in *Recipes from Hatch: Chile Capital of the World.*

2 tablespoons vegetable oil
2 pounds beef stew meat
1 clove garlic, minced
1 pound onions, diced
1 cup water
1 teaspoon salt
4 ounces chopped green chiles
2 cups refried beans
10 flour tortillas
Vegetable oil
Prepared red chile sauce

About 3 hours before serving, heat oil in a 3-quart saucepan and begin browning the beef. Add the garlic and onion and cook until beef is browned. Stir in the water and salt and heat until boiling. Lower heat, cover, and simmer until the meat is very tender, about 1½ hours, stirring occasionally. Shred the meat with forks, mix with the chiles, and cook until all liquid has evaporated, about 5 minutes. Meanwhile, heat the refried beans.

Spread about 2 tablespoons refried beans on each tortilla. Top beans with ¼ cup of meat mixture in lengthwise strips. Fold left and right sides of the tortilla over mixture, then fold ends up, forming a package. In a 12-inch skillet over medium heat, heat ½ inch oil to 375°. Fry tortillas with folded sides down, two at a time, for 1 minute or until golden brown. Turn and fry about 1 minute longer. Remove to paper towels to drain and keep warm while making the rest of the chimichangas. Serve with red chile sauce. Yield: 10 chimichangas.

La Fiesta de Santiago y Santa Ana, Taos, NM

La Fiesta de Santiago y Santa Ana is one of the great traditions of the town of Taos (as well as Taos Pueblo) and commemorates the patron saints of Taos: Santiago (St. James) and Santa Ana (St. Anne), whose feast days are July 25 and 26, respectively.

Fiesta was originally held in the fall and featured foot and horse races. In the 1930s or 1940s, the celebration became connected with the Catholic Church. Today, the fiesta begins on Friday evening with a Spanish-style candlelight procession around Taos Plaza and then on to the church, where mass is celebrated. A time of family gatherings and reunions, Fiesta also draws visitors who enjoy the colorful pageantry of music and dancing. Most of the events are held in the historic plaza, laid out in 1615. Parades, a puppet theater, and crafts are included. At Taos Pueblo, Fiesta is celebrated with a traditional corn dance.

Northern New Mexican delicacies abound, and many of the dishes served at Fiesta are "special occasion" food. Labor-intensive tamales are often reserved for Fiesta time. Bowls of raging hot red chile, served up with fresh flour tortillas, are as irresistible as another local specialty, prune pie. Then there are *biscochitos*, an anise-flavored cookie that is served at every northern New Mexico fiesta or holiday. As they say in Taos, "Que viva la fiesta!"

Fresh Corn Tamale Casserole

Fayne Lutz, of the *Taos News*, a renowned authority on the cooking of northern New Mexico, has spent some thirty years researching and documenting this regional cuisine. Here is Fayne's shortened version of a classic tamale, made with fresh sweet corn rather than the stiff masa harina more commonly used. The recipe originated at the now defunct restaurant, Peralta's.

12 ears fresh corn
2 teaspoons salt
3 tablespoons melted butter
1½ cups cornmeal
Sharp cheddar cheese, cut in strips
Canned whole green chiles, cut in strips

Preheat oven to 350°. Shuck corn and reserve husks. Cut kernels from corncobs. Grind the corn in a grinder or food processor to make 3 cups total. Add salt, butter, and enough cornmeal to make the mixture spreadable. Line bottom and sides of an ovenproof casserole with the green corn husks, leaving ends rising above edges of casserole. Layer corn mixture, cheese strips, and chile strips. Top with a layer of corn mixture. Fold ends of husks over the top to cover, adding more husks if necessary. Seal casserole with aluminum foil. Bake about 1 hour. Serves: 6.

Friday through Sunday on a Weekend in Late July

New Mexico Wine and Chile War Festival, Las Cruces, NM

When it comes to vineyards and wine, New Mexico doesn't immediately come to mind. That's why the state's wine growers annually participate in events that promote local vintages and educate the public on how to match various wines with the spicy foods of the region, many of which are based on chiles.

New Mexico's vineyards flourish along the shores of the Rio Grande. European settlers brought grape cuttings to the valley in the 1600s. Doña Ana County, where Las Cruces is located, lays claim to nearly thirty percent of New Mexico's chile production.

The Wine and Chile War Festival is held at the New Mexico State Fairgrounds, providing plenty of space for all the activities. A reasonable entry fee entitles visitors to taste New Mexico wines, enjoy continuous musical entertainment, and check out the juried art show.

A number of New Mexico's other agricultural products, including pecans, pistachios, and garlic, make their appearance in the exhibits. Vendors sell barbecue and regional specialties like gorditas and fajitas. There's even an entire tent devoted to the enchilada.

In 1993, the New Mexico Legislature declared war on Texas by passing a legislative mandate calling for an annual competition at the fairgrounds to determine which state has the best chile. There are four different chile competitions. Professional chefs compete to produce the best dish in five categories covering red chiles, green chiles, unique dishes, salsa, and Texas chile. Home cooks compete to produce the best chile salsas. A Chile Cook-off is held under the auspices of the Chile Appreciation Society International. Finally, home cooks from Texas and New Mexico compete for glory in the same five categories as professional chefs.

Memorial Day Weekend

The Wine and Chile War Festival was so successful that in 1997, it was decided to hold a similar fall celebration called the New Mexico Wine and Food Classic. The Western Pecan Grower's Association was a major participant and handed out brochures containing winning recipes from their annual Food Fantasy Contest. While the Wine and Food Classic turned out to be a one-time event, many of the recipes have become favorites, including the Grand Champion Turtle Cheesecake featured here.

Bill Gomez, New Mexico Cooperative Extension Service economist and Wine and Chile War coordinator, says that two of his favorite dishes are winners of the chile competitions. For Bill, a few Rio Grande Egg Rolls topped off with a piece of "killer" Chile Lover's Pecan Pie (a pecan pie laced with green chiles) make for a truly satisfying meal!

Rio Grande Egg Rolls

Kana Gershom of Las Cruces, NM, won the New Mexico Wine and Chile Festival
Chile Cook-off with this recipe.

½ pound ground beef
¼ cup onion, chopped
1 cup cooked pinto beans
1 cup grated Cheddar cheese
1 (4-ounce) can chopped green chiles
¼ cup ketchup
2 teaspoons chile powder
¼ teaspoon cumin
Wonton wrappers
Oil for frying
Salsa

Cook ground beef and onion until done; drain fat. Stir in beans, cheese, chiles, ketchup, and spices. Place 1 tablespoon of filling in center of each wonton wrapper and fold as for egg rolls. Moisten with water and seal. Fry in 375° oil for 1 minute. Drain on paper towels. Serve hot with salsa. Yield: 5 dozen.

Note: If prepared in advance, reheat the egg rolls in a 400° oven for about 10 minutes.

Turtle Cheesecake

Cheryl Welch was named grand champion of the New Mexico Wine and
Food Classic Food Fantasy with this entry.

Chocolate cookie crust:
14 chocolate sandwich cookies, crushed
3 tablespoons butter, melted
3 tablespoons chopped pecans

Filling:
3 (8-ounce) packages cream cheese, softened
⅔ cup dark brown sugar, packed
⅓ cup dark corn syrup
5 teaspoons cornstarch
3 eggs
1 egg yolk
1¼ teaspoons vanilla
5 teaspoons unsweetened cocoa powder
2½ tablespoons dark brown sugar
½ cup praline liqueur
¼ cup chopped pecans

Garnish:
Milk chocolate, melted
Caramels, melted
Chopped pecans

Crust: Stir cookies, butter, and pecans together and press crumb mixture into a buttered 10-inch springform pan.

Filling and assembly: Preheat oven to 325°. In a mixing bowl, combine cream cheese, ⅔ cup brown sugar, corn syrup, and cornstarch. Beat with a mixer until smooth. Add eggs and yolk, one at a time, beating after each addition. Add vanilla. Remove ⅔ cup of the cream cheese mixture and put into a small bowl. Stir in the cocoa powder and 2½ tablespoons brown sugar. Set aside. Stir liqueur and the pecans into remaining cream cheese mixture. Pour half of this pecan mixture over crust. Then spoon half of the cocoa mixture on top. Repeat layering with the remaining pecan mixture followed by the remaining cocoa mixture. Without disturbing the crust, swirl a knife through the cake to create a marble effect. Bake for 15 minutes, then lower to 225° and bake 1 hour more. Cool. Decorate by drizzling with melted milk chocolate and caramels. Sprinkle with pecans. Refrigerate until serving.

The Whole Enchilada Fiesta, Las Cruces, NM

Friday through Sunday during the First Weekend in October

Las Cruces, New Mexico, is the fiesta headquarters of the Southwest. It seems there's always something to celebrate, and The Whole Enchilada Fiesta may be the best excuse yet for crowds to gather in honor of New Mexico's culinary heritage. Some 70,000 converge upon the Mesilla Valley to feast and frolic at this event, which began in 1980 as a small, homegrown get-together.

The fiesta's centerpiece is what is claimed to be the world's largest enchilada, with 750 pounds of masa, 175 gallons of vegetable oil for cooking, 75 gallons of red chile sauce, 175 pounds of grated cheese, and 50 pounds of chopped onions. It takes fourteen men to carry the tortillas, lower each one into the cooking vat, and then carry the cooked tortillas to the assembly area. When completed, the enchilada rests on a ten-foot-wide serving plate and measures more than six feet in diameter. It is then served to thousands of applauding bystanders.

Those who can't wait for the largest enchilada to be served on Sunday can still have their whole enchilada at the fiesta's Enchilada Tent. New Mexico's passion for red chile sauce is evidenced by the sheer volume of red enchiladas sold. Other Southwestern specialty foods are available, including gorditas, burritos, tamales, chiles rellenos, flautas, and nachos. Those who want less spicy food enjoy turkey legs, bratwurst, and barbecue, most of which is followed by a couple of sopaipillas (deep-fried pastries) drizzled with honey. Visitors can purchase items such as fresh or dried New Mexico chiles, chile jelly, and pungent chile sauce.

In 1996, Heritage Days was incorporated into The Whole Enchilada Fiesta. Multicultural diversity is celebrated with a parade, musical entertainment, storytellers, weavers, an adobe workshop, and historical exhibits. The fiesta also encompasses a pet parade, games of skill, street dances, and a carnival. A number of cookbooks, especially those on New Mexico regional cooking, are sold at booths throughout the festival.

Chilaquiles (Enchilada Strips)

Roberto Estrada of Roberto's Restaurant in Las Cruces provides his recipe for this heritage dish which is so popular in the cuisine of New Mexico.

1 dozen corn tortillas
Vegetable oil for cooking
1 medium onion, chopped
½ cup chopped ripe olives
Salt to taste
2 cups enchilada sauce (mild, medium, or hot)
¼ pound grated cheese (cheddar or Monterey Jack) or more, to taste

Preheat oven to 350°. Cut the tortillas into strips, 1 inch long and ½ inch wide. Fry in a skillet with hot oil until light brown; drain on paper towels. In 2 tablespoons of oil, sauté the onion until translucent. Mix in the olives, salt, and enchilada sauce. In a baking dish or casserole, layer one-third each of the sauce, tortilla strips, and cheese. Repeat layering twice more. Bake for 15–25 minutes or until hot and bubbly. Serves: 6–8 as a side dish.

Texas

Texas is as diverse as the state is large. Mexico's influence has been felt since the 1500s and has been a major culinary influence. African-Americans have been in Texas for hundreds of years, first arriving with the Spanish. Germans appeared around 1830 and comprise the fourth largest group. Czechs arrived by the thousands between 1850 and 1920, and their heritage festivals are among the state's most popular. The annual Texas Folklife Festival celebrates diversity with foods from over a hundred ethnic groups.

Rice, fifth among cash crops, nets one billion dollars annually. The lower Rio Grande Valley is a leader in fruit and vegetable cultivation. In 1912, the first Girl's Tomato Clubs were formed to teach rural women canning techniques. Along with Corn Clubs for boys, they were the forerunner of 4-H programs. Texas accounts for eighty percent of U.S. cantaloupe acreage and sends over a million bushels of peaches to market every year. Poteet, in the truck farming region south of San Antonio, became the "Strawberry Capital of Texas" by the early 1990s with production of forty percent of the state's crop. Texas' fishing industry nets an annual catch valued at around $200 million, making it a leading state in shrimp production. Texans also harvest rattlesnakes and wild hogs, cooking them at seasonal festivals, but chili was adopted as the official state dish in 1977 and is a favorite food of many residents.

Fiesta en la Playa, Rockport, TX

The Rockport Navigation Festival Site comes alive every Labor Day weekend with the sounds of mariachi bands and Tejano concerts. It's time for Fiesta en la Playa, or "Celebration on the Beach," an annual scholarship fundraiser.

Folklorico dancers and arts and crafts add to the entertainment. Then there's the Macho Leg Contest and the famous Jalapeño Eating Contest, in which entrants gobble down as many hot peppers as they can in the allowed time. The Tamale Eating Contest is a big draw because it features delicious tamales made by Helen Nava of Rockport.

The fiesta offers plenty of good Mexican food. The gorditas made by vendor Sophie Cortez of San Antonio are so good that no one, it seems, can pass them up.

A former mariachi vocalist, Sophie's real passion is food, and she prepares everything as if for her own table. In 1984, 1985, and 1986, Sophie entered and won the gordita competition in San Antonio's April Fiesta in Market Square. In 1987, they wouldn't let her enter, a fact that under-scores the quality of Sophie's gorditas! She also makes tamales that are sold by mail order at Christmas. In addition to chili, pork, beef, bean, and jalapeño tamales, Sophie makes sweet tamales filled with raisins, coconut, cream cheese, and pecans. The *masa* contains cinnamon, butter, and sugar. Who could resist such delights?

Saturday and Sunday of Labor Day Weekend

Sophie Cortez' Chicken Gorditas

Sophie Cortez of San Antonio, TX, has won numerous gordita competitions with this recipe.

Filling:
1–2 cups water
1 tablespoon tomato paste
Small strips of green bell pepper or chopped
  red bell pepper
Salt
Garlic powder
Ground comino
1 chicken, boiled, skinned, boned, and shredded

Gorditas:
3 cups masa harina
1 teaspoon salt
1 tablespoon lard
1½ cups water (more if necessary)

Garnish:
Lettuce
Tomato
Avocado

Filling: Combine 1 cup water, the tomato paste, and the bell pepper. Season with salt, garlic powder, and comino. Cook sauce at full boil for about 10 minutes, then reduce heat and add shredded chicken and more water if necessary. Heat through, then allow to set off heat while making gorditas.

Gorditas: Mix the masa harina with the salt; add lard and water and knead lightly to a soft dough, adding a bit more water if necessary. When making the gorditas, it's important not to make them too thick or too thin. They should be in the form of a small cake. Dampen your hands so the mixture doesn't stick to them and pull apart. Cook gorditas on a very hot grill until brown spots appear. Then dunk the gorditas into oil heated to about 350°. The gorditas will puff up as soon as they hit the oil. Cook on both sides until a little stiff, then remove and drain on paper towels. Slit each gordita open, and using a slotted spoon to drain off any excess juice, fill them with the chicken mixture. Garnish with lettuce, tomato, and avocado and serve. Yield: About 24 gorditas.

Fort Bend County Czech Fest, Rosenberg, TX

Friday through Sunday on the First Full Weekend in May

In the mid-1800s, Bohemians and Moravians, most from what are today Slovakia and the Czech Republic, immigrated to Texas in search of inexpensive farmland. By the turn of the century, there were around 40,000 Texans of Czech descent settled in tiny communities like Rosenberg.

Czechs throughout Texas still honor the old traditions in annual festivals. The Fort Bend County Czech Fest is a triumph of Czech heritage. Authentic Czech arts, crafts, and antiques compete for attention with Czech language and cultural classes and continuous entertainment.

According to *The Czech Texans*, published by the Institute of Texan Cultures in San Antonio, a wedding in the old days was often characterized by "a virtual orgy of eating, drinking, and visiting." This might also be a description of the Czech Fest, where fabulous food predominates.

Noodles are the basis for many favorite Czech dishes. In the old days, noodles were always homemade, and a good cook was judged by how thinly she could cut and shred her noodles. In an effort to keep the old ways alive, the festival has homemade noodle demonstrations.

There is a Kolache Bake-Off with both amateur and commercial divisions covering four categories: fruit, sausage, miscellaneous, and sweet breads. Local authorities say that a good *kolache* (Czech pastry) dough should go through no less than three risings to achieve its feathery lightness. At the Czech Fest, folks generally plough their way through nearly 10,000 fruit-filled *kolaches* between 10:00 A.M. and midafternoon.

Festival visitors also dig into hundreds of plates of homemade *segedinsky gulas*, or goulash. Other foods available are barbecue, sausage, potato pancakes, and corn on the cob. Most visitors go home with a copy of a local Czech cookbook, *Narodni Domaci Kurcharka*, translated from the original 1904 version by Marie Rosická.

Nudle (Noodles)

This heritage Czech recipe is from *Narodni Domaci Kurcharka*.

2 cups flour
2 eggs, slightly beaten
1 teaspoon salt
Water

Sift flour into a bowl. Add eggs and salt to make a stiff dough. If not enough liquid, add water, 1 teaspoon at a time. Work the dough well with your hands. Roll out to 1/16 inch thick on a lightly floured board. Cover and let dry 30 minutes. Cut lengthwise into 2-inch strips. Stack strips and cut into noodles, as narrow or as wide as you want. Dry the noodles thoroughly and store in a covered jar. To cook, boil noodles in salted water for 8–10 minutes and drain. Yield: 4 cups.

Galveston Caribbean Mardi Gras Carnival, Galveston, TX

The Caribbean Carnival owes its origins to French settlers in Trinidad. In 1783, and for half a century thereafter, they embellished the carnival season with lavish balls and elegant festivities from Christmas to Ash Wednesday. After the Emancipation Bill of 1833 was passed, the freed Africans began to officially participate in these festivities. Over time, the contributions of many racial groups added their own unique elements. Carnival is a continuing example of the fruits of cultural diversity.

Carnival is freedom, abandonment, fun, and a tantalizing slice of the islands on Texas' Galveston Island. It is a visual experience coupled with the aromas of Caribbean culinary delicacies and the sounds of joyful laughter. In addition to a costumed dancing procession, there is a calypso competition, folkloric dancing, and all sorts of music.

The food is as varied as the "rainbow people" of the Caribbean, with a huge variety of tropical fruits in addition to dishes like chicken, beef, and shrimp curry, potato roti, and Caribbean corn soup. Coo-coo, a cornmeal cake, is a favorite dish throughout the Caribbean islands. On Barbados, it often includes okra.

Cornmeal Coo-Coo

Mary Philip of Galveston, TX, is proud of her Caribbean culinary heritage and provided this recipe, which never fails to win her praise and honors.

2 cups boiling water
1 medium fresh coconut, peeled and grated
½ pound fresh okra, cleaned and sliced
  ¼ inch thick
1 teaspoon salt
Pepper to taste
1 cup yellow cornmeal

Pour boiling water over grated coconut and let stand until cool. Squeeze out liquid and place liquid in a pan with okra, salt, and pepper. Bring to a boil over high heat. Reduce heat to low, cover, and cook for 10 minutes, or until okra is tender. Slowly add cornmeal, stirring constantly. Add a bit more water if necessary. Cook over medium heat, stirring constantly, for about 5 minutes or until the mixture is stiff and forms a ball, or a *panada*. Place mixture on a serving plate, slice, and serve hot. Serves: 6.

Friday through Sunday on the Second Weekend in June

Germanfest, Muenster, TX

Muenster, Texas, was founded in 1889 by people of German heritage. The town was named after the capital of Westphalia, Germany, the birthplace of many of the immigrants. With a population now numbering approximately 1,500, this little community throws one of the biggest parties in Texas.

Thousands are attracted to Germanfest by events such as a 5K and 15K Fun Run, a Metric Century Bicycle Rally, and the North Texas Championship Arm Wrestling Contest. Nonstop entertainment, characterized by dancing, music, arts, and crafts, provides adults with plenty of activity, while kids can enjoy a carnival, magicians, clowns, and storytellers.

Germanfest is also the home of the North Texas BBQ Cook-Off, which includes categories for sausage, ribs, brisket, and chili. Visitors come to Germanfest with a *guten apetit* to enjoy mouthwatering German sausage, potato salad, scrumptious apple strudel, hearty cheeses, and homemade baked goods. Of course, there's plenty of beer to quench everyone's thirst.

Apfelstrudel (Apple Strudel)

For many years, Margie Starke of Muenster, TX, has carefully preserved the formula for this winning German specialty.

Pastry:
3¼ cups sifted flour
Pinch of salt
2 tablespoons shortening
2 eggs
2 tablespoons sour cream
Lukewarm water
Butter, melted

Apple filling:
6 apples, peeled, cored, and thinly sliced
½ cup raisins
½ cup chopped pecans
½ cup sugar
½ teaspoon cinnamon
1 tablespoon flour

Glaze:
2 tablespoons sugar
1 tablespoon sour cream
1 egg yolk, beaten
Powdered sugar

Pastry: Mix flour, salt, and shortening. Combine eggs and sour cream and add to flour mixture with enough water to make a soft but firm dough. Knead for 15–20 minutes or until dough is elastic and bubbles on the surface. Cover and set in a warm place for 30 minutes.

Apple filling: Combine all ingredients and set aside.

Glaze: Combine all ingredients and set aside.

Preheat oven to 400°. Place a large, clean cloth over a large table, sprinkle with flour and place the dough in the center. Roll out the dough and then lift, pull, and stretch carefully until the dough is as thin as paper. Trim the edges and brush with butter. Spread filling over the surface to within 1½ inches of one end. Roll up into a long, thin roll, working toward the edge with no filling. Place carefully, seam-side down, on a well-greased baking sheet, twisting to fit pan. Brush with glaze. Bake for 20–25 minutes or until golden brown. Sprinkle with powdered sugar. Cut into thick slices and, if desired, serve with a scoop of ice cream.

Hopkins County Fall Festival and World Champion Hopkins County Stew Contest, Sulphur Springs, TX

According to Bill Elliott, executive vice president of the local Chamber of Commerce, the actual beginning of the Hopkins County Fall Festival is shrouded in the mists of the past. In 1969, this eight-day celebration took on a formal semblance of order and now encompasses the county fair. Tradition holds that the Texas State Fair actually evolved out of this festival.

The World Championship Hopkins County Stew Contest is almost as old as the festival and begins at dawn on the festival's last day. It's claimed that Hopkins County Stew was "invented" in the early years of this century, whereupon it was produced and sold commercially.

Today, in honor of Hopkins County's stew tradition, over 100 stew-cooking teams (which must include at least one individual from Hopkins County) compete for several thousand dollars in prize money. Each team dons authentic home-spun and denim costumes and re-creates a "heritage campsite," with huge cast-iron cooking pots set up over open wood fires. Then the heat is on to produce the best stew in either of two divisions, chicken or beef. Even an occasional squirrel stew has been known to surface. By 11:00 A.M., folks who have purchased entry tickets to the stew contest begin sampling as many stews as they like, along with crackers and cheese made from Hopkins County milk.

Hopkins County Stew, Family Size

The Chamber of Commerce in Sulphur Springs, TX, shared this prize-winning stew recipe.

2 pounds boneless, skinless chicken (or beef) pieces
4 cups water
1½ teaspoons salt
4 medium potatoes, diced
1 large onion
1 (15-ounce) can tomato sauce
1 (14½-ounce) can peeled, diced tomatoes
1 teaspoon salt
1 teaspoon pepper
1 teaspoon chili powder
1 teaspoon paprika
1 (16-ounce) can whole kernel corn
1 (16-ounce) can cream-style corn

Begins Second Saturday in September through the Third Saturday in September

Add the chicken, water, and salt to a 5-quart saucepan and cook until chicken is tender. Setting aside the broth, remove the chicken pieces to be cooled, deboned, and diced. Add the reserved broth to the potatoes and onion. If needed, add enough water to cover the vegetables and cook until the potatoes are done. Add diced chicken, tomato sauce, diced tomatoes, salt, pepper, chili powder, and paprika. Bring to a boil. Add the whole kernel and cream-style corn while stirring to prevent scorching. Reduce heat to simmer. If needed, add water to fill the pot. Cover and simmer for 15 minutes, stirring as needed. Serve with crackers or cornbread, cheese, and pickles. Serves: 6–8.

Note: This is a basic stew recipe, and other ingredients may be added to suit individual taste.

Jacksonville Annual Tomato Fest, Jacksonville, TX

At one time, Jacksonville, Texas, claimed to be the "Tomato Capital of the World." While Texas ranks tenth in tomato production in the United States, the crop is no longer a mainstay of Jacksonville's economy.

The Tomato Fest, however, continues to commemorate past tomato glory. Around 12,000 people turn out to participate in a full roster of events from a longhorn cattle display and a volleyball tournament to arts and crafts booths and an auction. For the kids, there's a tomato shoot where they test their aim with a bow and arrow. In the Couch Tomato "No Sweat" Olympics, there are events like tomato pool, tomato putting, and a tomato toss.

While visitors can purchase fresh tomatoes to take home, they must content themselves with turkey legs on a stick, nachos, and barbecued beef sandwiches. Worthy of note, however, is the fact that festival organizers are trying to encourage more tomato-based foods, and there is now a homegrown tomato contest. For those who like their salsa, the Tomato Fest is a different story indeed. The Hot Sauce Contest brings in a variety of home-canned salsas that are later auctioned off.

Hot Salsa

From the Jacksonville Annual Tomato Fest comes this recipe that won the 1996 Hot Sauce Contest.

5 pounds ripe tomatoes
3 cups chopped onions
2 cups chopped serrano peppers
2 cups chopped jalapeño peppers
3 tablespoons salt
1 cup cider vinegar (5% acidity)

Peel, core, and chop tomatoes. Combine with rest of ingredients in a large pot. Bring to a boil, stirring often, then simmer about 45 minutes. Fill hot pint jars, remove trapped air bubbles, and seal. Process in a hot water bath for extended storage.

Second Weekend in June

Kolache Festival, Caldwell, TX

Second Saturday in September

Caldwell, Texas, is in the heart of an entire county (Burleson) populated by people of Czech descent. In 1985, it occurred to residents that their heritage was gradually slipping away, and they resolved to rectify the situation. What followed was the annual Kolache Festival, which shares the history, language, and art of the residents' Czech ancestors.

Polka music, dancing, and singing bring smiles to visitors, who participate and watch. Demonstrations of crafts, such as tatting, quilting, egg decorating, weaving, caning, and woodworking, produce a sense of appreciation for such skills and help to keep them alive.

The star of the show is *kolache*, the original Czech wedding pastry and a favorite dessert amongst Czechs (and non-Czechs) throughout the world. There are demonstrations of kolache baking, and the annual kolache-eating contest attracts more than a few entrants intent on consuming as much of their favorite pastry as possible. The kolache-baking contest includes not only a Burleson County champion but a state champion as well. Following judging, the kolaches are offered for sale.

The *Czech Cookbook* is a best seller, with many of the festival's 40,000 attendees heading home with a copy.

Poppy Seed Kolaches (Czech Poppy Seed Pastries)

Claudia Matcek became the 1997 state grand champion of the kolache-baking contest when she squared off against some very formidable competition.

Dough:
2 packages dry yeast
¼ cup warm water
1 tablespoon sugar
2 cups milk
½ cup butter
½ cup sugar
5¼ cups sifted flour
2 teaspoons salt
2 egg yolks, slightly beaten
1 additional cup sifted flour
Additional melted butter

Poppy seed filling:
1½ cups milk
1¼ cups sugar
1 tablespoon flour
1 cup ground poppy seed
1 teaspoon butter
1 teaspoon vanilla

Glaze:
2 cups powdered sugar
½ teaspoon vanilla
2 tablespoons butter
¼ cup milk

Dough: Dissolve yeast in warm water. Add 1 tablespoon sugar and let stand. Heat milk in a saucepan until almost scalding. Remove from heat and stir in the butter and ½ cup sugar. Cool to lukewarm and add the yeast mixture. In a large bowl combine 5¼ cups flour and the salt. Add the yeast and milk mixture and combine. Mix in egg yolks. Mix in enough of the last cup of flour to create a dough that is workable and not too sticky (the entire cup is usually required). Knead dough on a floured board until glossy. Grease a large bowl and place the dough in it, rolling it around to grease the dough as well. Cover and let rise in a warm place until doubled in size.

Filling: Heat milk to a boil and add the sugar, flour, and poppy seeds, stirring vigorously. Cook over medium heat until mixture thickens. Remove from heat. Add the butter and vanilla. Cool filling before using to fill kolaches.

Glaze: Combine ingredients and mix until smooth.

Assembly: Preheat oven to 375°. Roll dough out to ½-inch thickness and cut into individual kolaches with a biscuit cutter. Place kolaches, not quite touching, on a greased pan. Brush with melted butter and let rise again until light to the touch. Make an indentation in each *kolache* and fill with about 1 teaspoon poppy seed filling. Bake until brown, about 25 minutes. Remove and brush with melted butter. While still warm, spoon glaze over kolaches. Yield: About 6 dozen.

La Salle County Wild Hog Cook-off and Fair, Cotulla, TX

Cotulla, an old-fashioned, family-oriented town, lies midway between San Antonio and Laredo, down in the south of Texas. The year 1980 marked the centennial of La Salle County, and folks wanted to make the celebration special, offering something over and above traditional fair activities. The practical Cotullans determined that a Wild Hog Cook-off was in order because of the abundance of wild hogs in the area.

Only five teams competed that first year, and rules were pretty lenient. The hog meat could be prepared in any fashion—not just barbecued—but all entries had to be cooked on the fairgrounds the day of the cook-off. Five years later, things were more competitive, and the cook-off got a little fancier. Two new categories were added. Teams needed to exhibit showmanship by calling themselves specific hog-related names and demonstrate artistic presentation by serving their entries on elaborate or unique trays. By 1989, even more categories were added.

These days, nearly 150 teams compete in the cook-off. They can cook the wild hog any way they see fit, but they must enter two pounds of cooked meat in one of two main categories: exotic or barbecue. With annual fair attendance up every year, and the local wild hog population now hopefully under control, it's assumed that much of the credit goes to the showmanship and just plain good eatin' delivered by the Wild Hog Cook-off.

Wild Hog Kabobs

Allen Schultz and John Howard of the Dulce Rooters team were named the 1993 and 1994 winners in the champion of champions competition at the Wild Hog Cook-off.

Marinade:
1½ cups vegetable oil
1 cup soy sauce
¼ cup honey
¼ cup vinegar
2 teaspoons garlic powder
3 teaspoons ground ginger
4 green onions, sliced

Kabobs:
3 pounds wild hog loin, cut in 1-inch chunks
30–40 mushrooms, halved
Cherry tomatoes

Bell pepper chunks
Pearl onions
Squash chunks

Combine all marinade ingredients and mix well. Marinate meat and mushrooms in mixture 6–8 hours in refrigerator. Soak wooden kabob sticks in water. Alternate the meat and vegetables on skewers. Place on grill over hot coals and cook until meat is done. Serves: 12.

Note: For a tamer version of this dish, use pork instead of wild hog.

May Days Bean Fest, Mineola, TX

Mineola, Texas, was once known for its production of beans, but today it's primarily a location for the Trinidad Benham Company, which packs beans shipped in from elsewhere. Nevertheless, the town's bean heritage has been celebrated every year since 1970 with the May Days Bean Fest.

Events cover a range of live entertainment, sports, an antique car show, a bike tour, a carnival, and an arts and crafts show. A pageant is held for the coronation of Little Mr. Bean Sprout and Little Miss Bean Blossom. If the festival falls on an election day, the local Rotary Club holds a pancake breakfast, and there's always a fish fry at noon on Saturday. Vendors provide a full array of typical festival foods plus ethnic foods. On Friday, local restaurants serve delicious specialties at the Taste of Mineola.

Those who know their beans are sure to participate in one of Saturday's cooking contests. At the Benham Bean Cook-Off, contestants are provided with pinto beans from one lot. Amateur chefs go to work, using the pintos to create the "Best Pot O' Beans." Judging is based on unique taste plus showmanship, a factor that produces some interesting cooking booth themes and costumes. The second event is a bean recipe contest in which prepared dishes are entered in categories covering appetizers, entrees, and desserts, plus a children's division. The Chamber of Commerce hopes to publish a book of winning bean recipes in the near future.

First Weekend in May

Nutty Pinto Bean Spice Cake with Seafoam Frosting

Bobbye Harrison of Fruitvale, TX, entered this cake and was named grand prize winner of the Bean Recipe Contest in 1997.

Cake:
1 cup butter
2 cups sugar
1½ cups cooked and mashed pinto beans
2 eggs
3 cups flour
1½ teaspoons baking soda
1½ teaspoons baking powder
½ teaspoon salt
2 teaspoons cinnamon
1 teaspoon nutmeg
Pinch of ground cloves
1 cup buttermilk
1 teaspoon vanilla
1 medium apple, peeled, cored, and chopped
1 cup pecans, chopped
Additional chopped pecans for garnish

Frosting:
2 egg whites
1½ cups firmly packed brown sugar
5 tablespoons water
Dash of salt
1 teaspoon vanilla

Cake: Preheat oven to 350°. Cream the butter and sugar. Add the pinto beans and eggs and beat. Sift the flour with baking soda, baking powder, salt, cinnamon, nutmeg, and cloves and add alternately with buttermilk and vanilla. Fold in the apple and pecans. Spread batter in three greased and floured 8-inch layer cake pans. Bake for 30–35 minutes. Cool.

Frosting: Combine egg whites, brown sugar, water, and salt in top of double boiler. Beat slightly to mix. Place over rapidly boiling water. Beat with electric mixer at high speed until frosting stands in peaks, about 7 minutes. Remove from heat. Add vanilla and beat 1–2 minutes or until thick enough to spread.

Assembly: Spread frosting between cooled layers, then frost cake, making decorative swirls. Sprinkle top and sides with additional chopped pecans.

Night in Old Pecos Cantaloupe Festival, Pecos, TX

Pecos, Texas, was established in 1881 as a railroad stop and rapidly gained fame as a hangout for rowdy cowboys and fast-draw lawmen. Pecos is even touted as the "Home of the World's First Rodeo."

Pecos is also the home of the "World Renowned Sweet Pecos Cantaloupe," grown in irrigated fields with a natural combination of alkali soil, dry air, and lots of sun. Cantaloupes have been grown in the area since the 1880s. Word of these luscious melons, served on the Texas and Pacific dining cars for forty-one years, spread quickly. Today, upward of 900,000 crates are shipped annually throughout the United States and Canada. According to locals, Pecos cantaloupes enjoy a status comparable to that of Maine lobsters, French wines, and Swiss cheeses.

The Cantaloupe Festival was established in 1980 to honor and promote the local crop as well as to kick off Western Week, which culminates in the West of Pecos Rodeo, a reenactment of 1883 events, on the Fourth of July.

A Fly-In Breakfast at the airport launches the festivities, also marked by exhibitions, a talent show, Western skits, and a cake walk. Festivalgoers enjoy roasted corn topped off with cantaloupe ice cream, a festival specialty. At the West of Pecos Museum, visitors can purchase an inexpensive booklet of cantaloupe recipes which includes innovative formulas for cantaloupe soup, cantaloupe butter, cantaloupe pie, cantaloupe cobbler, and cantaloupe pudding.

Cantaloupe Ice Cream

The West of Pecos Museum provided the recipe for this famous festival delicacy from its cookbook *Cantaloupe Recipes*.

8 cups milk
3 cups sugar
6 tablespoons flour
6 tablespoons lemon juice
6 cups puréed cantaloupe made from 2 large cantaloupes
3 cups finely ground pecans
4 tablespoons vanilla extract
3 cups heavy cream

Combine the milk, sugar, and flour. Cook over medium heat, stirring constantly, until the mixture thickens and coats a spoon. Remove from heat and cool. Add the remaining ingredients and chill thoroughly. Pour into a 6-quart ice-cream freezer and freeze according to manufacturer's instructions.
Yield: 6 quarts.

Oatmeal Festival, Oatmeal and Bertram, TX

There really is an Oatmeal, Texas, named after a German settler, Mr. Habermill, who stayed for "a season or two" at the watering hole, which was eventually named "Oatmeal Springs." Evidently, the name Habermill translated to "oats." Another story says that the town's name is taken from Mr. Othneil, owner of the first gristmill in the area.

As the population of Oatmeal dwindled, the town was removed from the official state of Texas map. This didn't sit too well with the locals, who resolved to do something about it. In 1978, an oatmeal festival, a spoof on the many chili and barbecue cook-offs in the region, was started . It played on the name of the local community and attracted a lot of attention—enough to ensure the continuation of the festival and get Oatmeal back on the map.

This is a fun, low-cost family affair. Games focus on an oatmeal theme and include oatmeal box stacking, an oatmeal coin search, and an oatmeal-eating contest. To qualify for the Ms. Bag of Oats Contest, ladies must admit to being fifty-five or older. The Oatmeal Air Force, which spills oatmeal on the parade route, is quite an attention getter.

In true Texas style, barbecue is served in Oatmeal on Friday, and *cabrito*, barbecued goat, is served in nearby Bertram on Saturday. In the Oatmeal Cook-Off, everyone's a winner. All entrants receive a box of oatmeal before judging begins. Winning recipes are often quite creative and are put into the *Oatmeal Festival Cookbook*.

Lighter Buffalo Wings

Crystal Young was a grand prize winner of the Oatmeal Festival Cook-Off with her version of the wings that made Buffalo famous.

1½ cups uncooked oats
2 teaspoons paprika (Hungarian sweet is preferred)
1 teaspoon garlic salt
3 egg whites
3 tablespoons Tabasco sauce (or more to taste)
3 boneless, skinless chicken breasts (1 pound), split and cut into 3 x ½-inch-thick strips
Ranch dressing

Blend the dry ingredients in a food processor for about 1 minute and place in a shallow dish. In another dish, beat together the egg whites and Tabasco sauce. Lightly coat the chicken strips with the oat mixture, shaking off any excess. Dip into the egg mixture, then again into the oat mixture. Place chicken on the rack of a broiler pan sprayed with nonstick coating. Completely spray the chicken with nonstick coating. Broil about 4 inches from heat for approximately 3 minutes. Remove chicken from oven, turn over, and spray again. Return to broiler for 2–3 minutes or until golden brown. Serve with ranch dressing as a dip. Serves: 6–8 as an appetizer.

Poteet Strawberry Festival, Poteet, TX

Since 1948, the annual Poteet Strawberry Festival has been drawing crowds to celebrate the area's number one crop. The event draws over 100,000 people to this town of 3,000 residents that holds the title "Strawberry Capital of Texas." Held on a ninety-five-acre site, it's the largest agricultural festival of its kind in the state.

Poteet is located in the heart of the artesian belt that supplies water necessary for strawberry production. By 1921, Poteet strawberry growers were inviting guests from San Antonio to enjoy their berries, capitalizing on early tourist opportunities.

The festival has continuous family entertainment with big-name country and western and Tejano stars, dancers, gunslingers, clowns, a parade, an arts and crafts show, and rodeo performances. A strawberry judging is followed by the strawberry auction, where the top crate of berries has sold for as much as $6,100.

Food booths sell all sorts of strawberry snacks, such as shortcake, cheesecake, fudge, Poteet Strawberry Wine, and Poteet Texas Strawberry Ice Cream. Filipino food is also popular.

The Taste of Texas Food Show is a cooking contest, and all entries must use a Texas-grown product as a main ingredient. The result is a vast array of creations based on strawberries, peanuts, peaches, and pecans. *Berry-Good Recipes* is a compilation of prize-winning strawberry recipes from past Taste of Texas Food Shows and contains recipes for many festival treats.

Friday through Sunday during the Second Weekend in April Unless Easter and Then Rescheduled to First Weekend in April

Strawberry Fudge

From *Berry-Good Recipes* comes the formula for this famous fudge enjoyed by visitors to the Strawberry Festival.

1 cup evaporated milk
3 cups sugar
2 tablespoons butter
3 cups strawberries, cut into small chunks
2 teaspoons lemon juice
1½ cups chopped walnuts or pecans (optional)

Combine milk, sugar, and butter. Heat slowly to boiling point, stirring constantly. Add the strawberries and cook over medium heat to 235° on a candy thermometer or to soft ball stage, stirring constantly to prevent burning—this may take a while. Cool. Add lemon juice and nuts, if desired. Beat until candy loses gloss. Turn into a buttered 8-inch-square pan. Mark in squares. Cool completely.

Prairie Dog Chili Cook Off and World Championship of Pickled Quail Egg Eating, Grand Prairie, TX

Chili is the official state dish in Texas, where it is commonly referred to as a "bowl of red." Chili is thought to have originated in San Antonio as early as 1825. A Texas-sized salute to the dish can be experienced every year at Traders Village Flea Market in Grand Prairie.

Traders Village has become a must stop on the chili-cooking circuit. Entrants vie for points that will enable them to compete in the annual national chili cook-off at Terlingua, Texas. Both events are sanctioned by the Chili Appreciation Society International (CASI). Crowds of up to 75,000 show up at Traders Village over the two-day gathering.

A parade and the jalapeño pepper cutting ceremony kick everything off on Saturday morning. Contests include the Original Anvil Toss, the Cuzin Homer Page Invitational Eat-and-Run Stewed Prune Pit Spitting Contest, and the Beech Nut Tobacco Spitting Contest.

The preliminary round of the World Championship of Pickled Quail Egg Eating takes place on Saturday followed by the final round on Sunday. The quail eggs used to come from a farm in Grapevine, Texas, but when it went out of business, locating a new source became a real problem. A supplier was located in North Carolina just in the nick of time. Today, the expensive quail eggs come from Louisiana. Quail eggs have a large proportion of yolk compared to the white, which makes them pretty dry. Contestants must thus prep the eggs with jalapeño pepper juice and Tabasco sauce that, reports Allen Hughs of Traders Village, "really boosts the authority of those eggs."

While chili cooking is the main purpose of the two-day celebration, many entrants go for showmanship honors, with zany chili and team names, costumes, and cook site themes. Some of the more printable entries have included Cow Pasture Disaster Chili, Hog's Breath Chili, and Preparation H Chili. The junior champions compete on Saturday, with Sunday reserved for the senior division. All first-place winners in chili cooking, showmanship, and quail-egg eating receive a much-coveted, appropriately inscribed commode seat. The audience gets to taste free samples of the chili.

Saturday and Sunday of the First Weekend in April

Pickled Quail Eggs

Allan Hughes of Traders Village in Grand Prairie hosts the World Championship of Pickled Quail Egg Eating and has shared his famous recipe for those eggs so eagerly consumed by contestants.

Pickling brine:
1 gallon water
½ gallon vinegar
3 cups salt

Peeled, hard-boiled quail eggs
Jalapeño peppers to taste
Tabasco sauce to taste

Combine brine ingredients and bring to a boil. Place eggs in glass jars. Pour hot brine over eggs and add jalapeño peppers and Tabasco sauce to taste, making the brine as spicy as desired. Other spices of choice may be added. Cover jars and refrigerate. Pickled quail eggs will keep indefinitely in the cold brine.

Note: Chicken eggs may be substituted.

ShrimpFest, Port Arthur, TX

During a weekend in August or September, residents of Port Arthur, Texas, annually set aside three days to celebrate the shrimping industry, one of the area's largest. ShrimpFest is characterized by every imaginable activity related to shrimp, including a peeling contest and a shrimp-calling contest. For children, there are a treasure hunt and a carnival, and nearly everyone checks out the arts and crafts sale. Musical groups provide entertainment, while festivalgoers taste a broad array of shrimp dishes offered by various vendors who try to outdo one another with original creations, as well as old favorites.

Serious shrimpers are sure to enter either the shrimp gumbo contest or the shrimp dish contest. Many visitors look for cooking demonstrations in which local seafood vendors, like Kris Adam of Buccaneer Seafood, prepare innovative shrimp creations and dispense plenty of advice on how to serve up this versatile crustacean.

A Weekend in August or September

Smothered Shrimp and Onions

You will understand why Kris Adam of Buccaneer Seafood is regionally renowned for his culinary creations after you try this recipe. It is a truly elegant version of comfort food.

⅓ cup vegetable oil
3 cups raw shrimp, peeled and deveined
2 medium onions, cut lengthwise and thinly sliced
2 cups water

Place skillet over high heat. Add the oil and shrimp and cook, stirring occasionally, until all shrimp have turned pink. Add the sliced onions and stir. Add 1 cup of water and cover. Let cook for about 15 minutes, or until all the water is gone. The shrimp and onions may be sticking to the pan and turning brown—this is good. Add the last cup of water and stir. The sauce will start to thicken, and any onions or shrimp that were stuck will come loose. About ninety percent of the onion will cook apart. Cook for 5–10 minutes longer, over low to medium heat, until the sauce is of the desired thickness, similar to gravy. Serve over rice, mashed potatoes (Kris' favorite), or even a baked potato. Serves: 3–4.

Note: If you prefer more firmly textured shrimp, sauté onions in oil over low heat until soft and translucent, about 15 minutes. Raise heat, add shrimp, and cook, stirring constantly, until they turn pink. Add the first cup of water and continue cooking over high heat, uncovered, until most of the water evaporates and the mixture thickens and begins to stick to bottom of pan. Add the second cup of water and cook over medium heat for 5 minutes longer. Serve immediately.

SPAMARAMA*, Austin, TX

Held at Auditorium Shores on Town Lake in South Austin, SPAMARAMA proves that Texans really manage to do things on a grand scale. Austin's big party—sanctioned by the Hormel Company, which employs a coordinator for these events nationwide—attracts over 10,000 people and raises more than $20,000 for the local United Cerebral Palsy Association.

SPAM*, the potted pork product, is sold in over fifty countries. Every second, nearly four cans of SPAM are sold across the United States.

Billed as the Pandemonious Party of Potted Porcine Product, SPAMARAMA has become a rite of spring in Austin. SPAM enthusiasts gather to witness and participate in numerous events celebrating SPAM. The SPAM JAM features top musical entertainment. The ever-popular SPAM Alympics includes such events as the SPAM Call, essentially a hog-calling contest, the SPAM Relay, and the SPAM Burger Eating Contest.

SPAMARAMA is essentially a SPAM cook-off in which contestants are judged in several categories, including best tasting, worst tasting, and showmanship. The showmanship factor is most likely to produce interesting props as well as the delivery of both rehearsed and impromptu skits. Entries generally exhibit an international flair with names like Spamikopita, Asti Spamanti, Moo Goo Gai SPAM, and Blackened SPAM Alfredo.

Of course, there's plenty of SPAM to go around. There are also hot dogs, hamburgers, and sausage wraps.

A Saturday in March or April, Depending on Easter Weekend

Herb-Crusted Rack of SPAM, Butternut Squash Purée, Crispy Grits, SPAMcetta Rolls with Blue Cheese, and Port Wine Reduction Sauce

Created by David L. Spooner, Austin, TX, winner of SPAMARAMA 1997.

2 cans SPAM
3 bones from French-cut lamb chops, cooked and cleaned
Dry herb mixture (basil, thyme, cilantro, and rosemary)
2 butternut squash
1 can SPAM Lite
2 tablespoons butter
2 teaspoons cinnamon
1 teaspoon nutmeg
Pinch of salt and pepper
2 cups uncooked grits
Flour
Butter for frying
¼ cup blue cheese
2 cups port wine
1 leek, blanched, with the green part of the leaf cut into a long string
Fresh herbs for garnish

Rack of SPAM: Cut a can of SPAM into 3 parts and insert a lamb bone into each piece to form the chop. Trim excess SPAM to make it into the shape of a lamb chop. Each SPAM chop should look like a French-cut lamb chop with a clean bone sticking 3 to 4 inches out the top of the SPAM. Rub each piece with the herb mixture and grill. Set aside and keep warm.

Butternut squash purée: Peel, clean and cut the squash into 1-inch cubes. Cook in boiling water until tender and drain. Cut ½ can SPAM Lite into 1-inch cubes and put into a food processor with squash, butter, cinnamon, nutmeg, salt, and pepper. Purée until smooth. If mixture is watery, cook in a sauté pan until dry and the consistency of dry mashed potatoes.

Crispy grits: Cook grits according to package instructions. Spread cooked grits ½ inch thick on a sheet pan and let cool. Cut grits with a pig-shaped cookie cutter. Dust each pig with flour and pan fry in butter until golden brown.

SPAMcetta rolls: Thinly slice remaining SPAM and heat in a pan until warm and flexible. Place 1 tablespoon of blue cheese on the end of the SPAM slices and roll up each piece, securing with a small toothpick.

Port wine reduction sauce: Reduce port wine to ¼ cup. Cool and set aside.

Assembly: Put squash mixture in center of plate and form a mound about 4 inches high. Stand the 3 SPAM chops, with the bone part of the chop toward the squash, around the mound, using the squash to hold the chops up. Cross the bones like a teepee. Tie the bones together with the leek string. Arrange several crispy grits and several SPAMcetta rolls around the chops and drizzle the port wine reduction sauce over the SPAMcetta rolls. Garnish with fresh herbs. Serves: 3.

*SPAM is a registered trademark of Hormel Foods, LLC for luncheon meat. SPAMARAMA is a trademark of Hormel Foods, LLC for an annual festival held in Austin, TX.

Stonewall Peach JAMboree and Rodeo, Stonewall, TX

Friday and Saturday of the Third Full Weekend in June

From mid-May through mid-August, peaches can be found at roadside stands in and around Stonewall, Texas. Located in the heart of Texas Hill Country, Stonewall is the peach center of the state. It's also the boyhood home and location of the Summer Whitehouse of President Lyndon B. Johnson.

Stonewall peaches have been celebrated at the Peach JAMboree every year since 1962. Growers bring their peaches to be judged on quality and uniformity, then the winning peaches are auctioned off. A single peach has been known to sell for as much as $1,000.

Visitors enjoy a parade, musical entertainment, a washer-pitching contest, historical sheep-shearing and spinning demonstrations, and a dance and rodeo each evening. With Tex-Mex foods and plenty of barbecue available, no one goes hungry.

The big bonus, of course, comes in the form of peach treats, including cobbler, pie, ice cream, and a festival favorite, peach freeze. The baking contest draws the best of peach pie and cobbler bakers, whose creations are auctioned off after judging.

Jerome's Peach Pie

Jerome Jenschke of Stonewall, TX, was the Stonewall Peach Pie Contest
winner in 1982, 1983, and 1984.

Crust:
2 cups flour
2 teaspoons baking powder
¾ teaspoon salt
⅔ cup butter-flavored shortening
½ cup hot water
1 egg yolk, unbeaten

Filling:
4 cups peaches, peeled and sliced
3 cups sugar
4 tablespoons tapioca
Cinnamon and sugar

Crust: Sift together the flour, baking powder, and salt. Combine shortening, hot water, and egg yolk and mix well. Stir into flour mixture and form dough into a ball. Chill for 30 minutes. Roll dough out to form two 8-inch piecrusts, reserving remaining dough for strips. Place dough in pans.

Filling: Preheat oven to 425°. Combine the peaches, sugar, and tapioca and divide the filling between the two pies. Place dough strips over top in lattice fashion. Sprinkle tops with cinnamon and sugar. Bake for 30–35 minutes, until strips are golden brown. Yield: 2 pies.

Peach Freeze

PJ's Peach Freeze, a vendor at the Stonewall Peach JAMboree, has generously shared

the recipe for this favorite festival drink.
2 cups semifrozen, unpeeled, sliced peaches
⅔ cup milk
2 teaspoons vanilla
½ cup sugar
Chopped ice

Place all ingredients in a blender and fill with chopped ice. Blend until mixed but still thick. Yield: 4 cups.

Texas Crawfish and Saltwater Crab Festival, Orangefield, TX

The east Texas Gulf Coast is an extension of neighboring Louisiana when it comes to festivals celebrating great food. Indeed, many of the Cajun Louisiana foodways and culture abound throughout the area, and Orangefield, near the thriving city of Beaumont, is no exception.

The Texas Crawfish and Saltwater Crab Festival was organized in 1981 by a group of locals to benefit the community and promote Cajun culture and the local seafood industry. Today, people come from miles around, and campers find easy access to Jewel Cormier Park and its RV hookups, located just three miles south of Interstate 10.

A carnival, craft vendors, and Cajun music and dance entice the fun-loving crowds. Of course, there is a crawfish race and numerous drawings and raffles.

Cajun flavor seasons the crawfish and crab dishes featured at the festival. Gumbo, crawfish boudin, crab balls, shrimp on a stick, étouffée, and boiled crawfish present an all-you-can-eat panorama of pure Cajun goodness. Crawfish cornbread is a delicious local favorite and sells like hotcakes.

Usually the Last Weekend in March

Crawfish Cornbread

Sheryl Myers of the Texas Crawfish and Saltwater Crab Festival provided the winning recipe used to make all that cornbread gobbled up by visitors.

2 (8½-ounce) packages cornbread mix
2 eggs
2 cups shredded Cheddar cheese
2 (8¾-ounce) cans cream-style corn
1 teaspoon baking soda
1 teaspoon Tony Chachere's Cajun Seasoning
1 pound raw crawfish tails, cleaned and chopped
1 cup chopped white onion
1 cup chopped green onion
1 cup chopped green bell pepper
1 (10-ounce) can diced tomatoes and green chilies, drained

Preheat oven to 350°. Combine cornbread mix, eggs, cheese, corn, baking soda, and Cajun seasoning. Stir in rest of ingredients. Pour mixture into a greased 16 x 10 x 2 inch pan and bake for 40 minutes, or until set and top is golden brown. Cut into squares and serve hot.

Note: Shrimp can be substituted for the crawfish.

Texas Folklife Festival, San Antonio, TX

Anyone longing to taste and experience the cuisines of various nations need only attend the Texas Folklife Festival, a celebration of the heritage of the many ethnic groups in Texas. Sponsored by the University of Texas Institute of Texan Cultures, the festival began in 1972 and has become such a huge attraction that it's held in San Antonio's downtown HemisFair Park.

Characterized by an atmosphere of family reunion, the Texas Folklife Festival includes forty-three different ethnic groups celebrating their heritage with food and performing groups, resulting in an extravaganza of entertainment on eleven stages from opening to closing each day. Texas pioneer heritage is celebrated with over sixty artisans demonstrating the craftsmanship of yesteryear.

At least forty vendors offer traditional ethnic and regional foods. Alsatian *Etweis* (sausage), Filipino *Pancit* (noodles), and Lebanese *Lahem mishwee* (shish kebab) are available, along with more well-known dishes like Belgian waffles, German pork ribs and sauerkraut, and Greek souvlaki.

Texan specialties are everywhere. At the Chili Booth, visitors are introduced to true Texas chili. In addition, all sorts of treats made from Texan peanuts and pecans are for sale.

From the 1500s to the 1800s, Texans shared a common history with Mexico. Much of Texas' ranching law and architecture is based on that of Mexico. Although the regional foods of Mexican-Americans in Texas vary from the traditional cooking of their homeland, ingredients remain much the same, comprising a lexicon of peppers, cumin, garlic, onions, and cilantro. Of course tortillas, made from both corn and flour, form the backbone of Tex-Mex cuisine. At the Texas Folklife Festival, the most prodigious menu is Tex-Mex cooking, covering dishes such as tacos, flautas, enchiladas, gorditas, quesadillas, and tamales.

One of the least-known ethnic groups in Texas are the Wendish. Long associated with Germans, the Wends are actually an ancient Slavic people whose ancestral homeland is the area of eastern Germany bordering on Poland. The Wends immigrated to Texas, where today, their descendants labor to preserve their church-oriented culture. Wendish cuisine is

Thursday through Sunday during the Second Weekend in June

reminiscent of that of Germany, and their delicious homemade noodles, alongside grilled and specially sauced chicken drumsticks, find a huge following at the festival.

The University of Texas Institute of Texan Cultures at San Antonio has compiled an excellent compendium of recipes entitled *The Melting Pot: Ethnic Cuisine in Texas* that has recipes for many of the festival dishes plus a well-researched synopsis of the history of the various ethnic groups represented therein. It is an invaluable contribution to the preservation of ethnic heritage in Texas as well as the United States.

Carne Guisada

Stella Bernal of San Antonio contributed this heritage recipe to *The Melting Pot: Ethnic Cuisine in Texas*, published by the Institute of Texan Cultures.

Tacos, like enchiladas, can be made with many different fillings. Tacos made with flour tortillas are frequently served with carne guisada, which can also be served on a plate with rice and beans.

2–3 pounds round steak, cubed
Vegetable oil
1 tablespoon flour
2 tablespoons chopped green bell pepper
2 tablespoons chopped onion
2 tablespoons chopped tomato
1–2 cloves garlic, finely chopped
¼–½ teaspoon ground cumin
⅛ teaspoon pepper
1 cup tomato sauce
1 (10 ounce) can RO*TEL tomatoes with peppers
Salt to taste
¼ cup water

Brown the round steak in a small amount of vegetable oil. After the meat is brown, coat it with flour and add the remaining ingredients. Cook about 30–45 minutes or until the meat is done and the sauce becomes thick. For use in tacos, the sauce should be cooked a bit longer to thicken it. Yield: 8-10 tacos.

Texas Rice Festival, Winnie, TX

The Texas Rice Festival celebrates everything to do with rice. Chartered in 1969, the event honors the rice harvest and features family entertainment with a country atmosphere. More than 100,000 people attend annually.

Rice is the oldest and most cultivated grain in the world. Ancient Chinese ceremonial records for rice date back as far as 2800 B.C., and some historians have traced it back even further. Rice cultivation in the United States can be traced to 1694, when rice first reached South Carolina. Today, Arkansas, California, Louisiana, Mississippi, Missouri, and Texas produce nearly all U.S. rice, which is one of America's most important agricultural enterprises. The United States is the world's leading exporter of rice even though its acreage totals only two percent of the world total.

The Rice Festival is a Texas-style extravaganza. Horse and livestock shows are back to back with a million-dollar farm equipment display. Activities include hay-hauling, washer-pitching, and horseshoe-pitching contests. Dancing and live music fill the streets and the community building, and there's an old-time fiddlin' contest, a rice education exhibit, and a parade. The craft show draws over fifty vendors and plenty of buyers, while others wander through the art, essay, and photography contest exhibits and quilt show.

On opening night, visitors flock to the annual BBQ and Fajita Cookoff. On Saturday morning, more serious barbecue cookoff activities begin, followed by judging. There are also an Old Timers' Breakfast and an ice-cream-eating contest for entrants up to age fourteen.

The Rice Cooking Contest is sponsored by the U.S.A. Rice Council and local mills. Categories include appetizer, vegetable or salad, main dish, miscellaneous, and dessert. Winning recipes are available from the annual program or the *Texas Rice Festival Cookbook*.

Festival foods include Texas barbecue, pork kebabs, and dishes with a distinctly Cajun flavor. Gumbo, étouffée, pistolettes, crab balls, and boudin balls are popular. Several nonprofit vendors and restaurants offer flavored rice balls, a festival favorite year after year.

A Week-Long Event Beginning the Last Weekend in September

Rice Balls

The Texas Rice Festival provided this winning recipe for a festival specialty.

3 cups short-grain rice
7 cups salted water
8 tablespoons margarine
1¼–1½ teaspoons cinnamon
1½ pounds lean ground beef
¼ cup vegetable oil
¾ cup chopped green onion
1 cup chopped celery
2 cloves minced garlic
2 tablespoons chili powder
1 (16-ounce) can tomato sauce
½ cup water
1 tablespoon chopped fresh parsley
½ cup grated Parmesan cheese
Salt and pepper to taste
3 whole eggs, beaten
5 cups seasoned bread crumbs
Oil for deep-frying

Add rice to salted water and bring to a boil. Simmer until rice is mushy. Remove from the heat and add the margarine and cinnamon. Cool.

Fry the beef in ¼ cup oil until it loses its redness. Add onion, celery, and garlic and cook slowly for 10 minutes. Add chili powder, tomato sauce, and ½ cup water. Simmer 1 hour, stirring occasionally. Remove from the heat and add the parsley, cheese, salt, and pepper to taste. Set aside to cool.

To form rice balls, grease hands with the meat grease and place ⅓ to ½ cup of rice in palm. Form a cup in the palm of the hand like a bird nest. Add 1 tablespoon of meat mixture and roll into a firm ball, enclosing the meat inside the rice. Continue making rice balls. Chill in refrigerator.

Dip chilled rice balls in the beaten egg and roll in seasoned bread crumbs. Fry in hot, deep oil until golden brown. Yield: 3 dozen.

World Championship Barbecue Goat Cook-Off, Brady, TX

Brady is located deep in the heart of Texas, where semiarid conditions are ideal for goats. Since 1974, the annual World Championship Barbecue Goat Cook-Off has celebrated the fact that this is a major U.S. goat-producing area. The event draws an average attendance of 16,000.

Festivities are kicked off with a Friday evening dance. Saturday has events like the 5K run called the Goat Gallup, a sheepdog classic, horseshoe- and washer-pitching contests, and a fiddler's contest.

The barbecuing competition begins in the wee hours of the morning, since goat requires long, slow cooking. Each entrant is given the same size half-goat. Some contestants marinate the meat, while others use barbecue sauces and rubs. All goats are cooked in open pits. An average of 140 teams vie not only for the best goat preparation but also for recognition in categories covering showmanship, campsite, and best cooking rig.

By 1996, Hazel Hodges of Brady had participated in the Goat Cook-Off every year since its inception. At first, Hazel simply loaded up a small grill and a box of cooking supplies in the back of the ranch pickup and headed into town for the cook-off. Over the years, however, the event became larger and more competitive, and eventually, Hazel ended up with a big motor home emblazoned with the name of her team, "Granny's Kitchen," on the side. On a trailer, she pulled a giant barbecue pit sporting an American flag waving overhead. "I never did win the World Championship, but it was fun, and I love this cook-off," says Hazel. In 1996, Hazel was presented with an honorary plaque for twenty-four years of participation and named "Queen of the Cook-Off."

Hazel knows all about goats and describes herself as a pioneer in cooking goat meat. When asked about her secret for preparing great barbecued goat, she is firm and opinionated. "I just hate barbecue sauce—don't like it at all. All my life, I've eaten goat meat, grew up on it and use my mother's method of cooking it. Nothing to it if you're careful. Goat is better than lamb. People around here don't eat lamb. If cooked properly, goat is very moist, and the meat will fall off the bone. It needs to be cooked until well done and ends up stringy, like pork ribs."

From 11:00 A.M. until 2:00 P.M. on Saturday, hungry visitors can enjoy a barbecued goat meal with all the trimmings: pinto beans, potato salad, pickles, onions, rolls, jalapeño peppers, and iced tea.

Always Friday and Saturday of Labor Day Weekend

Hazel Hodges' Barbecued Goat

Hazel Hodges of Brady, TX, was named "Queen of the Cook-Off" in 1997 for 24 years of participation. Here is Hazel's famous recipe.

Generously sprinkle goat with salt, pepper, and garlic salt and rub it in real good. Do NOT use barbecue sauce. I sometimes put in a little Worcestershire sauce. Put it in a covered roaster. Bake it slow the old-timey way—300°—until good and tender. If you want it brown, take the cover off, but be careful, because browning might dry the meat out. Roast the goat until it's stringy and tender.

World's Largest Rattlesnake Round-Up, Sweetwater, TX

For some forty years now, ranchers in Sweetwater, Texas, have been busy reducing the local rattlesnake population to prevent livestock losses. But this planned harvesting, if you will, takes on all the trappings of a festival in the form of the World's Largest Rattlesnake Round-Up.

This event is run by the Sweetwater Jaycees, who liven things up with such attractions as arts and crafts booths, a flea market, and dances. There is also a gun and knife show.

Rattlesnake is quite a delicacy in these parts, so there's a cook-off which includes rattlesnake in one of six different categories. Of course, fried rattlesnake meat can be enjoyed at the roundup. Anyone anxious to try rattlesnake meat in the comfort of their own home can order it from Maverick Trading Post, 2541 Valley View Lane, Farmersbranch, TX 75234; (800) 2-RATTLE.

Fried Rattlesnake

Kay Berryman of the Sweetwater, TX, Chamber of Commerce sent along this winning recipe from the festival cook-off.

1 medium sized rattlesnake (3–4 pounds), skinned and cleaned
½ cup flour
¼ cup cornmeal
¼ cup cracker crumbs
¼ teaspoon garlic powder (not garlic salt)
1 teaspoon salt
Dash of pepper
1 egg, beaten
½ cup milk
Vegetable oil for deep frying

Cut the rattlesnake into "steaks." Mix flour, cornmeal, cracker crumbs, garlic powder, salt, and pepper in a bag. Add egg to milk and dip snake steaks. Then coat the steaks by shaking them in the bag of flour mixture. Place in oil that has been heated to 400° and cook uncovered until brown or until the meat floats in the oil. Serves: 6-8.

Always the Second Weekend in March

Utah

The valleys of north central Utah were settled by several groups of Mormons in the 1840s. Led by Brigham Young, they called their new home "Deseret," a Mormon term that means "honeybee" and symbolizes industry and hard work. Valleys were irrigated, and farming was productive, but swarms of grasshoppers threatened crops until seagulls from the Great Salt Lake ate them. Now called the "Mormon Cricket," the gulls are honored as Utah's state bird.

Most of the crops in Utah are grown in the north-central area. One of the most important fruits is the peach, whose cultivation was begun in 1855 by William Brighton. He bought a hundred peach pits in Salt Lake City for $1, planted them in Brigham City, and initiated a peach production operation that was thriving by the 1890s. Today Brigham City and other towns in the Wasatch Front region produce peaches, apples, pears, cherries, and grapes. The stretch of highway along U.S. 89 between Brigham City and Willard is known as "Utah's Fruitway" and is lined with roadside stands selling fresh seasonal produce.

Peach Days, Brigham City, UT

Peach Days, begun in 1904 as a day off from the harvest, is the oldest continuously celebrated harvest festival in Utah. A 1914 edition of the *Box Elder News Peach Days Edition* proclaimed, "The Lord might have made a better fruit than the peach, but He didn't." Brigham City was once known as "Peach City." Even though peaches remain important to the economy, the town's moniker has been changed to "Tree City, U.S.A." because of its tree-lined streets.

Despite its popularity and annual crowds of around 65,000, the peach festival is still a hometown celebration marked by class reunions, a carnival, parades, softball tournaments, a library book sale, an antique car show, and many other activities.

Most food vendors sell snacks like hot dogs and hamburgers or Southwest specialties like tacos, churros, and burritos. Expert foragers, however, head for food stands offering Dutch oven specialties like barbecued ribs, cheesy potatoes, western beans, and peach cobbler. Some nonprofit groups sell delicious peach ice cream and peach cobbler, but other than that, peach treats are rare. It is hoped that the peach recipe contest, inaugurated in 1997, will rectify this omission.

A Dutch Oven Cook-Off, started in 1990, takes place on both days. Conducted under the auspices of the International Dutch Oven Society's World Championship Dutch Oven Cook-Off satellite system, the cook-off is for amateur cooks who prepare both old-fashioned and newfangled recipes. The first event is a one-pot peach specialty dish, either main dish or dessert, and peaches must be a main ingredient. The second cook-off is a traditional three-pot event. Teams are required to prepare a main dish, side dish, and dessert, one of which must be yeast or sourdough rise. In 1997, festival organizers decided to combine seven years of Dutch oven cookbooks into one volume that contains entries, as well as winning recipes from the inception of the cook-off.

Friday and Saturday of the Weekend Following Labor Day in September

Peaches 'n' Cream Pie

Mark and Debra Miles of Roy, UT, were the winners of the Peach Days Dutch Oven Cook-Off in 1995.

Piecrust:
1½ cups all-purpose flour
½ teaspoon salt
½ cup butter

Filling:
4 cups fresh or frozen, unsweetened, sliced
  peaches
1 cup sugar, dvided
2 tablespoons all-purpose flour
¼ teaspoon salt
1 cup sour cream
1 egg
½ teaspoon vanilla

Topping:
⅓ cup sugar
⅔ cup all-purpose flour
1 teaspoon cinnamon
¼ teaspoon nutmeg

¼ cup rolled oats
½ cup butter
½ cup finely chopped pecans

Piecrust: Combine the flour and salt. Cut in the butter until crumbly. Press into an ungreased 10-inch Dutch oven.

Filling: Place peaches in a bowl and sprinkle with ¼ cup sugar. Combine the flour and salt with the remaining sugar. Mix in the sour cream, egg, and vanilla and stir into peaches. Pour onto crust.

Topping and assembly: Preheat oven to 375°. Combine all dry ingredients except pecans. Cut in butter until crumbly, then stir in pecans. Sprinkle over pie, cover Dutch oven, and bake for 45 minutes. Remove from oven and cool on a wire rack.

Wyoming

Cattle drives originated around 1846 and increased after the Civil War. Soldiers moved west to work as ranch hands and cowpokes. Although westward expansion continued, initially settlers did not remain in Wyoming due to conflicts with native Americans. By the late 1860s, a treaty was signed; rich grasslands tempted settlers to establish ranching operations. With the cattle came cowboys to work the flourishing ranches. America's "cowboy" period lasted a couple of decades. With the coming of the railroads, invention of barbed wire, and taming of the West, the cattle drives and cowboys disappeared. The cowboy as an American legend remains, and Wyoming is known as the "Cowboy State." The motto of its capital, Cheyenne, is "Where the pavement ends and the West begins." Rodeos remain a favorite pastime, but in recent years cowboy poetry gatherings have attracted large crowds. Cowboy poetry has existed for over a hundred years. After a long day, cowboys would sit around the campfire and tell tall stories ("windies") or recite poems composed during long, lonely rides. According to scholars, many cowboys were of Gaelic, Anglo-Saxon, or Celtic heritage, so cowboy poetry is rooted in British oral traditions. A vast body of work has been revived and is being honored and documented. New poets of the genre are welcomed. Cowboy poetry gatherings are held throughout the West. Simple, yet complex, sometimes humorous and other times serious, cowboy poetry is the voice of grassroots America.

Chuck Wagon Cooking

Prior to 1866, food on the trail was pretty sparse, consisting mainly of what could be carried in a saddlebag: hard biscuits, beef jerky, coffee, and whiskey. Fortunately, rancher Charles Goodnight created the chuck wagon, a basic kitchen on wheels; complete with cast-iron cooking utensils and thirty days' worth of supplies, it allowed the preparation of better meals. The chuck wagon became the nucleus of the old trail drives. Everything was organized around the trail cook, since the chuck wagon had to move ahead of the herd in order to make camp and to have meals ready for hungry cowboys. Out on the range, "Cookie" was respected, and the hands were loath to cross him for fear of a bad meal as their punishment. Unfortunately, not every chuck-wagon cook was of the desired high caliber, as illustrated by the following rueful lament.

Trail Cook

Reprinted with permission from author Rod Nichols, a respected
modern-day cowboy poet who hails from Texas.

Oh fill my cup with coffee son
hot steamin' thick with cream,
some biscuits please with honey squeezed
er peppered gravy lean.

Some bacon cured in mesquite smoke
a slab er two will do,
then let 'em cook til they is crook'd
and I'll be 'bliged to you.

I'll take some eggs no matter how
a dozen from the nest,
then scramble, fry or at least try
and I'll do all the rest.

Some grits would suit me to a "T"
with red-eyed gravy son,
a big ham steak upon my plate
now that's what I call fun.

Instead we got this half-baked cook
who never heard of that,
they's jest one thing on his pea-brain
that's hard-tack, beans and fat.

That brew he touts as coffee
is shore some fitful stuff,
at least four times on one old grind
I think is long enuff.

Those rocks he claims fer biscuits
are hard enuff to eat,
I've lost a tooth and that's the truth
the second one this week.

You'd think them beans was bad enuff
before they're boiled er baked,
but cooked in lard and bullet-hard
is more than I kin take.

I don't want you should fault me son
fer speakin' ill of Slim,
but if I could I surely would
feed all this meal to him.

Cheyenne Cowboy Symposium and Celebration, Cheyenne, WY

The first annual Cheyenne Cowboy Symposium and Celebration, held in 2001, was a roaring success. Over 2,000 people attended this all-American, family-oriented event that offered something for everyone interested in the revival of cowboy poetry and paying homage to the heritage of the Old West. Mick McLean, editor of *The Wyoming Companion*, predicts huge growth for this festival.

Opening ceremonies on Thursday evening are devoted to recognizing Wyoming's pioneer families and their descendants. Also on tap is a full Cowboy Concert, with old-time cowboy music. Many of the songs are written by Barry Ward of Copeland, Kansas, who weaves tales of the land, crops, and the hardships of early settlers into his lyrics. The haunting melodies first sung on the silver screen by cowboy idols such as Gene Autry, Roy Rogers, and Rex Allen are also part of the program. The 2001 symposium included a special tribute to the late Dale Evans.

On Friday and Saturday, attendees can choose to participate in a full roster of unique educational seminars on subjects like cowboy poetry or authentic cowboy music, which includes a study of classics like "Cool Waters" and "Tumbling Tumbleweeds." Special historical presentations are a big draw. Other visitors attend workshops, such as the one on blacksmithy, or head over to the antique tractor show.

Friday and Saturday evenings are devoted to concerts, which include a large variety of cowboy singers and musicians. Cowboy poets take center stage, delivering their sometimes poignant, sometimes amusing, but always riveting verse.

Vendors are on hand selling Western products like belts, jewelry, and saddles, while artists offer original Western paintings. Chokecherry and boysenberry jellies are purchased as unique souvenirs and gifts from Wyoming.

On Sunday morning, visitors attend the nondenominational Cowboy Church. Because the cowboys made the wide-open spaces their place of worship, the service includes a special rendition of the song "Ghost Riders in the Sky." Following church services, everyone heads out to the

Always Thursday through Sunday of Labor Day Weekend

Wyoming Hereford Ranch for the remainder of the symposium. Established in 1883, it is one of the oldest and most prestigious of Western cattle operations.

The main culinary event of the Cowboy Symposium is the Milk Can Dinner, held in the old "Sale Barn" at the ranch. Few can resist the temptation of an authentic Wyoming Milk Can Dinner, featuring an entire meal composed of sausage and fresh vegetables, cooked over an open fire. Following another few hours of great entertainment, dessert in the form of an old-fashioned Ice Cream Social brings the Cowboy Symposium and Celebration to a sweet ending.

Milk Can Dinner

Pat McKelvey, chairman of the Cowboy Symposium and Celebration, is an old hand at preparing Milk Can Dinners. Here is the recipe that has won her accolades and many repeat requests over the years.

This recipe must be cooked in a 10-gallon milk can. Because vegetables require the most heat, they should be placed on the bottom.

Layer ingredients in the following order:

25 red potatoes, washed but not peeled
3 pounds carrots, washed and peeled
25 ears of corn, shucked
4 heads of cabbage, cored and quartered
6 medium onions, peeled and quartered
50 Polish sausages

Add 1½ quarts of water to the milk can. Cook 1 hour and 45 minutes on a grate placed over an open fire. Additional water may need to be added as the cooking progresses. On a hot, calm day, cooking will not require as much heat as it will on a cold, windy day. Serves: 25.

Caution: After filling the milk can, *never pound the lid down tightly*. Set the lid on gently or simply cover the top with aluminum foil. As steam builds up during cooking, it will need an escape route; otherwise the can may explode.

Chapter 6

The Pacific

Alaska | California | Hawaii | Oregon | Washington

Alaska

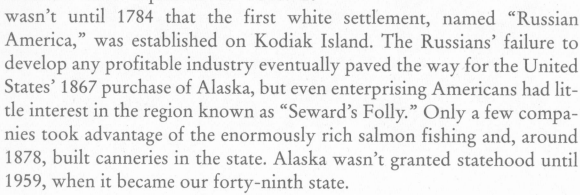

 With Alaska's most western land point only fifty-one miles from Russia, it is not surprising that the Russians were Alaska's first explorers in 1648. It wasn't until 1784 that the first white settlement, named "Russian America," was established on Kodiak Island. The Russians' failure to develop any profitable industry eventually paved the way for the United States' 1867 purchase of Alaska, but even enterprising Americans had little interest in the region known as "Seward's Folly." Only a few companies took advantage of the enormously rich salmon fishing and, around 1878, built canneries in the state. Alaska wasn't granted statehood until 1959, when it became our forty-ninth state.

 Today, Alaska's seafood industry, centered in Kodiak and Unalaska/Dutch Harbor, is valued at approximately $1.5 billion per year. The annual catch includes a broad array of fish and shellfish, but salmon and crab are most important to the U.S. market. Alaska is a primary resource for king crabs, which average about a half-pound each. The largest king crab on record was caught off Kodiak Island; it weighed twenty-five pounds and had a leg span of six feet. Tanner crabs, also called "snow crabs" because of the color of the meat, vary in weight from two to four pounds and are harvested over a six- to eight-day season in mid-February. The crab harvest varies greatly from year to year, threatened by overfishing and other issues with which Alaska continually grapples.

Kodiak Crab Festival, Kodiak, AK

While the Kodiak Crab Festival hardly sounds like an ethnic celebration, the truth is that in some years there are no crabs available, even though the festival was established in 1958 to market the crab industry. Kodiak traces its history back to the time when the Russian American Company held sway, safeguarding its interests and tremendous wealth in the territory, so festival organizers decided to capitalize on the history of the area.

The Kodiak Historical Society and the Baranov Museum, housed in a structure built by the Russians in 1808, play a significant role in the festival, and there are definite overtones of the celebration of Russian heritage. The Kodiak balalaika players perform, and there is a reception at the museum with punch and *kulich* (coffeecake). On Sunday, there is a sourdough pancake breakfast, and baked goods and jams are sold. If it's a good year, crab legs and claws are available. Newly added, the Ice Cream Social features decadent ice cream desserts.

Other events include a parade, a golf tournament, an art exhibit, and a marathon. At the annual frog-jumping contest, open to those over age twenty-one, frogs are available early-on for training, and contestants vie for trophies for the fastest frog, best-dressed jockey, and best-named frog—perhaps a sure sign that spring has finally arrived in Alaska.

Thursday Through Monday of Memorial Day Weekend

Kulick (Russian Coffeecake)

Ellen Horn Lester of the Baranov Museum in Kodiak provided this Russian heritage recipe.

Sponge:
2 packages dry yeast
4 cups warm milk
6–8 cups flour
½ cup sugar

1 cup margarine
2 cups sugar
8 eggs
2 teaspoons salt
1 teaspoon nutmeg
2 teaspoons vanilla
½ teaspoon lemon extract
1 cup peeled and slivered almonds
2 cups raisins
6–8 cups flour

Powdered sugar
Milk
Multicolored candy decorations

Early in the morning, set a sponge by first dissolving yeast in the warm milk. Add the first 6–8 cups of flour and the ½ cup sugar. Mix together well. Cover with a cloth and let rise until doubled in size, about 1 hour.

In a large mixer bowl, cream together the margarine and 2 cups sugar. Add eggs, salt, nutmeg, vanilla, and lemon extract. Add this mixture to the raised sponge and mix well with a wooden spoon. Add almonds and raisins. Add the additional 6–8 cups of flour, 1 cup at a time, until dough is stiff enough to handle. Turn dough onto a floured board. Knead until smooth and elastic. Put dough in a very large greased bowl. Let rise until doubled in size, about 4–6 hours. Punch down.

Divide dough into 8 or 16 pieces (8 for 2-pound coffee cans or 16 for 1-pound coffee cans). Shape into large buns and place in well-greased coffee cans with folded side down. Check for and remove air holes. The dough should fill the cans a third full. Let rise until double or up to the third ring of the coffee cans.

When dough is almost done rising, preheat oven to 350°. Bake for 45 minutes for the 2-pound cans and 30 minutes for the 1-pound cans. The kulich is done when you can shake it out of the can. Frost with a powdered sugar and milk glaze. The consistency of the glaze should be runny. Pour over the top of the warm bread and let it run down the sides. Immediately sprinkle with multicolored candy decorations.
Yield: 8–16 kulicks

California

When it comes to food production, California has a lot to celebrate. The Golden State has been the number one food and agricultural producer in the United States for more than fifty consecutive years and accounts for more than half, or approximately forty million tons, of our nation's fruits, nuts, and vegetables. Some 350 different crops and commodities are produced on about 80,000 farms.

California's fertile Central Valley, some 450 miles long, accounts for three-fifths of the state's farmland. Other highly productive regions include the Sacramento Valley and the San Joaquin Valley. The enormous variety of fruits and vegetables include lemons, pears, apricots, oranges, grapefruit, grapes for wine and raisins, strawberries, artichokes, carrots, eggplant, tomatoes, and lettuce. California delivers almost all of the country's supply of almonds, dates, olives, prunes, walnuts, pistachios, and kiwi fruit. Farm markets, offering fresh produce directly from growers, can be found throughout the state and do a brisk business. California exports about twenty percent of its food and agricultural products.

Not to be overlooked, the California fishing industry is valued at around $160 million annually. The tuna catch, which surpasses that of all other states, is the most valuable, followed by swordfish. Halibut, salmon, sole, crab, shrimp, and squid are but a few of the other valuable catches supplied by California waters.

Abalone Festival, Mendocino, CA

In 1914, California passed a law prohibiting the exportation of abalone, a conservation measure designed to protect what had become an endangered delicacy. Conservation laws and efforts to protect the abalone are still in force today. Mendocino's Abalone Festival, held in Van Damme State Park, is about as exclusive as it gets when it comes to food festivals. Although thousands of people from all over the United States vie for much-coveted reservations, attendance is limited to the first 450 lucky applicants. Applications are ordered seven months in advance and chosen based on the postmarked date of return. Because it's against the law to sell abalone, each guest makes a donation in order to secure an admission ticket, which includes an abalone feast.

Held under the supervision of the California Department of Fish and Game, the festival delivers plenty of entertainment, crafts, and educational displays about the abalone. Everyone's favorite event, of course, is the Abalone Cook-off in which, each year, thirty-six competitors prepare their abalone specialty. All those in attendance get to vote for their favorite dish, sending the first place winner off to a Caribbean vacation in a private villa.

When preparing abalone, it is wise to remember the advice given by cookbook author Helen Evans Brown in *Shrimp and Other Shellfish Recipes*: Overcooked or undercooked, abalone is tough and distasteful, but prepared properly, it's delicious.

Columbus Day Weekend

Abalone Garlic Noodles

Randall Dexter of Fort Bragg, CA, was a recent grand prize winner of the Abalone Festival Cook-Off.

Abalone
1 cup Garlic cloves, peeled
Extra virgin olive oil
Cracked black pepper
Chopped fresh parsley
Freshly grated Parmesan cheese
Parsley sprigs
Sourdough French bread (optional)

Abalone noodles: This technique turns abalone into noodles that can be used as you would any pasta. It eliminates the tenderizing process typically associated with making this tough mollusk edible. Access to a deli meat slicer is necessary to get very thin slices. Partially freezing the meat will give best results. Cut the abalone, foot first, into slices 1/10 inch thick. With a very sharp knife, cut slices into strips about 1/10 inch wide. Blanch the raw strips by dipping about 1 cup of strips at a time in a strainer for 10–15 seconds in a large pot of rapidly boiling water. Remove strips and immediately place in an ice water bath, then drain thoroughly. The abalone strips may be stored in the refrigerator for 2 to 3 days.

Garlic purée: Place 1 cup of peeled garlic cloves in a measuring cup and fill to 1 cup with extra virgin olive oil. Purée in a blender or food processor.

Assembly: In a frying pan, heat ¼ cup olive oil per cup of noodles. Add about 1 tablespoon of garlic purée for each cup of noodles, and sauté for 10–20 seconds. Add abalone strips and stir to coat with garlic and oil. Remember, the noodles are already cooked and only need to be warmed; the more you cook abalone, the tougher it is, so use a light hand. Add cracked pepper and chopped parsley to taste. Garnish with Parmesan cheese and parsley sprigs. Serve with sourdough French bread to soak up the garlic oil. Serves: 1.

Note: Because abalone is not generally available, this recipe was not tested.

Borrego Springs Grapefruit Festival, Borrego Springs, CA

From December through April, folks in Borrego Springs are pretty busy harvesting grapefruit. And, they will tell you, this isn't just any grapefruit—it's a local white, seedless variety called "Borrego Pink" or sometimes "Borrego Gold," which is sweeter than the popular pink grapefruit common in most grocery stores.

Borrego Springs is in the heart of the Anza-Borrego Desert State Park, about seventy miles east of San Diego. Over 2,000 acres are used for cultivation of citrus fruits, including oranges, limes, lemons, and grapefruit. The end of the annual grapefruit harvest is marked by the Grapefruit Festival, which runs from Friday through Sunday. The event is a family affair, featuring arts and crafts, a classic car show, games, entertainment, and food.

Most of the goings-on are held in the whimsically named Christmas Circle in downtown Borrego Springs. The Friday night Christmas Circle Sundowner, a cocktail party that features a delicious grapefruit drink called the "Borrego Sundowner", kicks the festivities off in a high-spirited manner. In 1997, festival volunteer Kat Gibson compiled *Citrus Delites*, a cookbook filled with tantalizing recipes collected from friends and supporters of the organization.

A Weekend in April, Depending on Easter

Borrego Sundowner

In her cookbook *Citrus Delites*, Kat Gibson notes this now-famous drink was concocted especially for the Borrego Springs Chamber of Commerce to use in their "Margaritaville" fundraiser.

4 ounces fresh grapefruit juice
1 ounce spring water
1¼ ounces gold tequila
1 teaspoon grenadine syrup

Combine grapefruit juice, water, and tequila in an 8-ounce glass. Fill with ice and stir. Drizzle grenadine on top and watch the sun go down in Borrego Springs. Serves: 1.

California Dried Plum Festival, Yuba City, CA

The California Dried Plum Festival, held at the Yuba–Sutter Fairgrounds, attracts about 30,000 visitors annually. California produces approximately seventy percent of the world's prunes, and nearly one-third of the state's plum acreage is in Yuba and Sutter counties, allowing them to claim the title "Prune Capital of the World."

The festival has a full roster of family entertainment, as well as floral displays, an arts and crafts show, a petting zoo, a 10K Prune Run, a classic tractor and motorcycle show, an artisans' village, and a photography show.

The Prune Pavilion is a good place to start. California prune packers and growers are always on hand to provide answers to questions and hand out tasty samples. Visitors interested in cooking will find the Prune Festival to be a gold medal event. The California Prune Board brings in celebrity chefs and food editors from a number of national magazines, all armed with irresistible recipes. Then there's the Farmers' Market, where shoppers can stock up on the area's freshest produce and other goodies. A wine tasting is enjoyed by many, while others head for the International Pavilion, which celebrates the cultural diversity of the Yuba-Sutter area.

Attendees can sample delights ranging from prune chili or tamales to prune ice cream and prune chocolate chip cookies and wash it all down with a prune margarita. Past festivals have featured celebrity chefs, including Martin Yan. Scott Leysath, perhaps the best-known sporting chef in America and author of *The Sporting Chef's Favorite Wild Game Recipes*, is a regular and very popular participant. Scott specializes in developing and demonstrating game recipes for preparation over campfires or in the home kitchen and owns and operates Silver Stage Caterers, an organization involved with such sports groups as Ducks Unlimited and the National Wild Turkey Federation.

Saturday and Sunday of the Second Weekend in September

Prune Festival Pheasant Breast

Scott Leysath of Sporting Chef Productions and America's most famous game chef shared this recipe, which he has demonstrated to packed audiences at the festival.

4 pheasant breast halves, skin intact
½ teaspoon garlic powder
½ teaspoon onion powder
⅛ teaspoon white pepper
⅛ teaspoon cayenne pepper
Pinch of salt
16–20 large fresh basil leaves
⅔ cup pitted prunes, thinly sliced
¾ cup grated pepper-Jack cheese
¼ cup seasoned bread crumbs
⅛ cup roasted California pistachios, chopped
2 tablespoons olive oil
½ cup game bird stock or chicken broth

Season pheasant breasts with garlic powder, onion powder, white and cayenne peppers, and salt. Place breast halves on a flat surface and cut a pocket into each with a sharp boning knife. For each breast half, lay basil leaves across bottom of pocket. Arrange prunes on top of basil leaves. Combine cheese, bread crumbs, and pistachios in a small bowl and mix well. Place cheese mixture over prunes. Fold the edges of each breast down to cover the pocket opening.

Heat olive oil in a medium skillet over medium heat; add breast halves and brown on both sides, about 4 minutes per side. Add stock or broth, and cover and cook for 3 minutes more. Remove breasts to a cutting surface and slice each into thirds before arranging on a plate. Spoon pan drippings over breasts. Serves: 4.

Note: This recipe works well with all poultry.

California Dry Bean Festival, Tracy, CA

Bean cuisine is raised to new heights at the California Dry Bean Festival. The event was founded in 1987 by Larry Texiera of Rhodes Bean Supply Warehouse as a means of promoting the dry bean industry. Today, upward of 50,000 people converge on Tracy for the festival.

Bean Boulevard and Lima Lane offer diversions in the form of arts and crafts. There is also a family bike ride, both a 5K and 10K run, and games and rides for the kids. The Bean Museum offers insight into bean lore and history, and at the Bean Pavilion, visitors can taste all kinds of strange and unusual beans.

In addition to the kick-off barbecue held on Friday evening, food vendors sell apple bean cake, barbecued oysters, Racing Bean Salad, bean burgers, and a host of typical fair foods. Delicious smells wafting from the chili cook-off draw the attention of many. Future plans include the inauguration of a Best Bean Dish Contest.

Marinated Black-Eye and Artichoke Salad

Janet Gokey, coordinator of the California Dry Bean Festival, shared this locally famous dish.

1 pound dry black-eyed peas
3 jars marinated artichoke hearts
¾ cup grated carrots
¾ cup diced celery
¼ cup diced red onion
¼ cup minced parsley
1 cup Italian salad dressing

Soak and cook the black-eyed peas just until tender (do not overcook). Drain and cool. Combine all ingredients and let stand overnight in refrigerator.
Serves: 8–12 as a side dish.

First Weekend in August

California Strawberry Festival, Oxnard, CA

Over 148,000 tons, or about twenty percent of California's strawberries, are produced in the Oxnard area. The annual Strawberry Festival pays tribute to the industry while providing affordable entertainment, great food, and support for a host of local charities.

The festival features more than 270 arts and crafts booths, three concert stages, Strawberryland for Kids, and wacky contests. For those with a big appetite and the will to beat the clock, there's the Strawberry Shortcake Eating Contest. Visitors who don't mind a few red stains on their clothes will opt for the Strawberry Tart Toss or the Strawberry Relay Race.

Food includes delectable dishes such as strawberry pizza, strawberry kabobs, sweet potato pie with strawberries, and strawberry bread, as well as such long-time favorites as strawberry shortcake and chocolate-dipped strawberries.

The annual Berry-Off recipe contest kicks off in March with recipe submissions and progresses to a finalists' challenge in April. The contest annually attracts several hundred submissions in categories covering hors d'oeuvres, soups and salads, main dishes and vegetables, breads, pancakes and crepes, pies, cakes, cookies, and desserts. Semifinalists' recipes are compiled into an annual booklet that features new and innovative ways to use strawberries.

Strawberry Truffles

One bite will tell you why Roxanne E. Chan was chosen a grand sweepstakes winner of the Berry-Off.

8 ounces cream cheese, room temperature
4 cups powdered sugar
1 teaspoon grated fresh ginger root
5 ounces white chocolate, melted and cooled
18 medium strawberries, cleaned and hulled
¼ cup finely minced crystallized ginger
½ cup toasted coconut
½ cup finely chopped pistachio nuts

Beat together the cream cheese, sugar, and ginger root until smooth. Add the white chocolate and mix well. Chill at least 1 hour or until easy to handle. If necessary, place in freezer, stirring occasionally, for 30 minutes. Using a very small melon baller, scoop out the center of each strawberry halfway down each fruit. Pat dry. Put a little crystallized ginger into each strawberry. Shape the cheese mix around each fruit. Coat 1 end in coconut and the other end in pistachio nuts. Place the truffles in candy cups. Chill until serving time. Yield: 18 truffles.

Note: An easy, but less glamorous alternative is to layer halved berries and the cream cheese mixture in a plastic wrap-lined loaf pan or paté pan with removable sides. Sprinkle top with coconut and chopped pistachios. Serve in thin slices topped with additional coconut and chopped pistachios.

Usually the Third Weekend in May

Castroville Artichoke Festival, Castroville, CA

Artichokes were first grown in the Salinas Valley in 1922, and today Castroville is billed as the "Artichoke Capital of the World." Even though more artichokes are actually grown in the Mediterranean region, folks in Monterey County and Castroville stake their claim on the basis that they have the greatest concentration of artichokes and also because the area produces about 75 percent of California's artichokes.

The Artichoke Festival offers a parade, arts and crafts, music, and artichoke exhibits. However, it's really the artichoke-based cuisine that captures the limelight.

Food booths offer artichokes fixed in every way imaginable, from battered to french fried, as a topping on pizza, and in artichoke soup. There's also plenty of ethnic food, with Indian bread tacos one of the favorites.

Usually the Third or Fourth Weekend in September

Locally renowned chefs demonstrate the artichoke's versatility and present basic cooking techniques. Sample tastings and recipes are available. For years, the cooking contest has attracted entrants from all over California who enter their prize artichoke recipes for judging.

Thistle Pie

Noel Ketsch of Prunevale, CA, won the Artichoke Festival Cooking Contest in 1991.

Filling:
4 medium artichokes
Juice of ½ lemon
Water
¼ cup olive oil
½ large onion, minced
2 carrots, cut into matchsticks
½ teaspoon salt
Fresh ground black pepper to taste
½ cup water
2 tablespoons chopped fresh parsley
¾ cup ricotta cheese
½ cup freshly grated Parmesan cheese
2 eggs, beaten

Pastry:
1½ cups flour
½ cup butter, softened
¾ cup ricotta cheese
½ teaspoon salt
Grated Parmesan cheese

Filling: Bend back the outer petals of artichokes until they snap off easily near the base. The edible portion of petals should remain on artichoke hearts. Continue to snap off and discard petals until central core of pale green petals is reached. Trim outer dark-green layer from artichoke. Slice the bottom as thin as you can lengthwise. Put artichoke slices in a bowl with enough water to cover and the juice of ½ lemon. In olive oil, sauté the onion and carrots until onions are light gold. Drain artichokes (if using fresh) and sauté with onions and carrots for 1 minute. Add salt and pepper to taste. Add ½ cup water and cook, uncovered, until tender, 7–15 minutes. Water will evaporate, leaving a thick sauce. Stir in parsley. Mix the ricotta and Parmesan cheeses with the beaten egg and add to the cooled mixture.

Pastry: Preheat oven to 375°. Mix flour, butter, ricotta, and salt in a bowl, using a fork or pastry cutter. Turn out onto a work surface and knead for 5 minutes, or until smooth. Divide dough into 2 parts, 1 twice as big as the other. Roll the larger piece out to ⅛-inch thickness on waxed paper sprinkled with grated Parmesan cheese. Place dough in a buttered and floured 8-inch springform pan, covering the bottom and letting it come up the sides almost to the top. Smooth out any thick folds with your fingers. Pour in filling and smooth with a spatula. Roll out remaining dough on parchment paper sprinkled with grated Parmesan cheese and place over the pie, completely covering the filling. Trim any excess dough, leaving ½ inch; pinch edges. Place on upper rack of oven and bake for 45–60 minutes or until brown on top. Unmold and serve lukewarm or at room temperature.

Note: Two (14-ounce) cans of artichoke hearts packed in water, drained, squeezed of liquid, and chopped may be substituted. Add to the remaining vegetables after the 15-minute cooking time.

Dixon Lambtown USA Festival, Dixon, CA

Dixon's 125 years of history in the sheep business finally resulted in the Lambtown USA Festival in 1987. What started out as a small fund-raising project to honor the local industry has bloomed into an event that attracts upward of 10,000 visitors to this rural town west of Sacramento.

California is the second largest sheep-producing state, behind Texas. In the 1940s and 1950s, Dixon earned a place on the map as a major lamb-producing area. After World War II, however, American lamb consumption decreased. Meat shortages during the war meant that many military personnel had been fed mutton, meat from older sheep that generally has an unpleasant taste and smell. Most were not anxious to try lamb again. American lamb, however, is considered meatier and more mildly flavored than imported lamb and certainly compares favorably with mutton. The mission of Dixon's Lamb Festival is to promote the fine taste of American lamb.

Musical entertainment enlivens this downtown street fair. Skilled craftspeople demonstrate spinning and weaving with wool from sheep and lambs. Arts and crafts booths sell all kinds of products related to lamb.

The smell of lamb cooking over open fires fills the air. The Lamb Cookoff draws amateur teams cooking barbecued lamb, and judging is done by media and food experts. In years past, the winning recipes have been compiled into a cookbook sold by the Dixon Chamber of Commerce.

A Saturday in July

In the food demonstration areas, chefs and local experts share tips on the preparation of lamb. Dishes like lamb fajitas and California lamb pizza have been received enthusiastically. At vendor booths in Lamb Lover's Lane, visitors line up for lamb in shish kebabs, sausage, barbecued ribs, pita bread, and burgers.

Birria de Borrego (Mexican Lamb Stew)

Henry Barraza and Frank Leal cooked up this stew and were named first place winners in the 1987 Lamb Cookoff.

Marinade:
3 ounces dried pasilla chili pods
3 ounces dried New Mexico chili pods
3 whole dried Japanese chilies (or use chili de arbol)
1 teaspoon black peppercorns
5 cloves garlic, peeled
1 (28-ounce) can whole tomatoes, undrained
1 teaspoon dried oregano
2 bay leaves
1 tablespoon sherry or white wine
1 teaspoon salt or to taste

8–10 pounds lamb with bones (shanks or ribs)
Chopped onions
Freshly squeezed lemon juice

Boil the pasilla and New Mexico chili pods, in just enough water to cover, until soft. Remove the stems and crush the chili pods, blending with left-over hot water. Purée the Japanese chilies, peppercorns, garlic, and tomatoes. Combine chili mixture in a deep bowl with the oregano, bay leaves, sherry, and salt, mixing well. Add additional chilies or spices to taste.

Preheat oven to 350°. Place the lamb in a roasting pan and top with the marinade, covering the pan tightly with heavy-duty aluminum foil. Bake for 2½–3 hours or until the meat separates easily from the bone. Serve the lamb in its own sauce, topped with onions and lemon juice. Serves: 12.

Note: This is best eaten with fresh corn tortillas, rice, and beans.

Fillmore Orange Festival, Fillmore, CA

California's Santa Clara River Valley is filled with orange, lemon, and avocado orchards. Los Angeles and the beach are only a half hour away, yet residents enjoy all the advantages of living in the country. Navel and Valencia oranges are grown here, and the oranges are sold at top dollar to the largest market, Japan.

The annual Fillmore Orange Festival honors citrus farming as the major industry in the region. In addition to parades and carnival rides, the festival features train rides through the orange groves. A variety of food is available from booths decorated in orange themes, and the festival's barbecued orange chicken remains as popular as ever.

The Fillmore Christian Academy sells a cookbook, *Taste of Fillmore,* that features local specialties such as authentic Mexican foods and a number of recipes for dishes that were served on the old Fillmore & Western Railway Dinner Trains. The book also includes a recipe for another Fillmore favorite, Grand Avenue Orange Sherbet.

Grand Avenue Orange Sherbet

In *Taste of Fillmore,* Kathy Campbell recorded the recipe for Fillmore's famous sherbet.

3 cups sugar
½ cup freshly squeezed lemon juice
4 cups freshly squeezed orange juice
7 cups milk
Finely grated rind of 1 orange
Few drops of yellow food coloring

Mix together the sugar, lemon juice, and orange juice and chill for several hours. Add the milk, orange rind, and food coloring. Freeze in an ice-cream maker in accordance with the manufacturer's directions. Yield: About ½ gallon.

First Weekend in May

Fresh Fruit Festival, Reedley, CA

Reedley, California, lies in the heart of the San Joaquin Valley, one of the richest agricultural areas in the world. Peaches, plums, nectarines, and grapes are the most common local fresh produce, but apricots, citrus, fruits, olives, nuts, avocados, melons, and many other fruits and vegetables are also grown there. No wonder that the area is known as the "Fruit Basket of the World." More fruit is grown, packed, and shipped from Reedley than anywhere else in the world.

The Fresh Fruit Festival, begun in 1996, attracts over 7,000 people each day. Offerings include a craft fair, art show, live entertainment, farm tours, and an antique farm equipment display. For the athletically inclined, the Food Olympics offers games like a grape toss, the watermelon shot put, and the Great Grape Relay Race.

An open-air Farmers' Market features the valley's freshest fruits and vegetables. Lots of folks opt for the pancake breakfast with fresh peaches and nectarines topping the hotcakes. The Fruit Bazaar is a dazzling showcase of dishes featuring fruits; crowd pleasers include chicken salad with fresh fruit and locally grown almonds, fresh fruit pies, and fresh peach ice cream. The Chamber of Commerce serves up a Caesar salad topped with fresh chilled grapes that is guaranteed to please. Area restaurants also get into the act. Jon Koobation, chef and proprietor of Jon's Bear Club in Reedly, is renowned for his cuisine using fresh fruits and can always be counted on to wow the crowds and perhaps even divulge a recipe or two.

Saturday and Sunday of the Fourth Weekend in June

Southwest Nectarine or Peach Chutney

Locals in Reedley claim there is no better chef than Jon E. Koobation, CEC, chef/proprietor of Jon's Bear Club, Inc., and when Jon shared the following recipes for which he has become noted, the reasons for his fame were clear.

1 tablespoon olive oil
½ onion, diced fine
1 clove garlic, minced
1 tablespoon ginger, minced
2 Anaheim chilies, seeded and diced
1 chipotle chili in adobo sauce, diced (canned chili)*
½ cup brown sugar
¼ cup unseasoned rice vinegar
½ teaspoon cinnamon
½ cup white wine
4 ripe nectarines or peaches, peeled, pitted and chopped**

In a stainless-steel saucepan, heat the oil and sauté the onion, garlic, ginger, and chilies over moderate heat for about 5 minutes. Add the brown sugar, rice vinegar, cinnamon, and white wine and cook until slightly thickened, stirring occasionally. Add the chopped fruit and cook an additional 15–20 minutes on medium low, stirring occasionally, until thickened. Adjust seasoning. Serve warm with chicken or pork.
Yield: About 2 cups.

*Available in the ethnic food section of the supermarket. May be omitted for a less spicy chutney.

**To make peaches easier to peel, place them in a pot of boiling water for about 20 seconds, then back into a bowl of cold water.

Chinese Chicken Salad with Plum Vinaigrette

Courtesy of Jon E. Koobation, CEC, chef/proprietor, Jon's Bear Club, Inc., Reedly, CA.

Salad:
1 head iceberg lettuce, chopped
½ cup shredded red cabbage
½ cup shredded white cabbage
¼ cup chopped cilantro
1 cup rice sticks, fried
1 cup wonton wrappers, cut in ¼-inch strips and fried
½ cup plum vinaigrette (recipe follows)
2 cooked, boneless, skinless chicken breasts, cut in thin strips

Plum vinaigrette:
½ cup rice vinegar
¼ cup sugar

1 teaspoon grated fresh ginger
½ cup soybean oil
2 teaspoons sesame oil
4 ripe plums, pitted

Salad: Toss everything except vinaigrette dressing and chicken. Toss again with the dressing and arrange on plates. Moisten chicken with a little of the dressing, arrange around the salad, and serve. Serves: 8.

Plum vinaigrettte: Place all ingredients in a food processor or blender and blend until smooth. Adjust seasoning to taste.

Gilroy Garlic Festival, Gilroy, CA

The world-renowned Gilroy Garlic Festival got its start in 1978 when Dr. Rudy Melone, then president of Gavilan College, read an article about a garlic festival in Arleaux, France. Folks there claimed the title "Garlic Capital of the World," with over 80,000 people coming to taste their garlic soup. Dr. Melone felt that Gilroy was better suited to this title, and he launched a series of events that resulted in the Gilroy Garlic Festival, which is enjoyed by more than 120,000 people every year.

This event is full of entertainment. The Children's Area has marionettes, jugglers, music, and science demonstrations. A juried arts and crafts show features one-hundred quality vendors. The Garlic Squeeze Barn Dance takes place in two barns and offers a choice of music.

Garlic is everywhere. Attendees can buy it by the bulb, in bulk, in wreathes and in braids. It's also available chopped, crushed, pickled, and roasted. Many people buy jars of salsa, pesto, mustard, mayonnaise, barbecue sauce, and stuffed olives, all containing garlic. Vendors offer a variety of garlicky foods, such as chilled garlic soup, pasta with garlic sauce, bruschetta, garlic egg rolls, corn on the cob with garlic butter, garlic bread, garlic pickles, garlic kettle corn, and even garlic ice cream. Gourmet Alley, manned by chefs and festival volunteers, is an annual tradition for fine garlic cuisine like scampi in a special wine sauce, pepper steak sandwiches, stuffed mushrooms, and calamari.

Friday through Sunday of the Last Full Weekend of July

The Great Garlic Cook-Off is a national cooking contest. Every February, the call for garlic recipes goes out. The hundred top recipes are chosen and sent to a professional food consultant, who chooses the final eight contenders. On Saturday of the festival, finalists prepare their recipes, and judges determine the winners. Past winners include dishes like Creamy Cancun Roasted Garlic Soup with Fiery Garlic Shrimp, Crispy Garlic Salmon Cakes with Roasted Corn Salsa, and Garlic and Herb-Crusted Pork Tenderloin with Creamy Garlic Gravy. Needless to say, the Garlic Festival's annual *Cook-Off Booklets* are big sellers, along with *The Greatest Hits*, a cookbook celebrating the festival's twentieth anniversary.

Creamy Potato Gratin with Gorgonzola, Pears, and Pecans

Camilla Saulsbury of Bloomington, IN, won first place in the 2000 Garlic Festival Cook-Off with this novel recipe.

10 large garlic cloves, peeled
⅓ cup Marsala wine
1¼ cups heavy cream
3 large russet potatoes (1½ pounds), peeled, thinly sliced, and partially cooked
2 large pears, peeled, cored, and thinly sliced
8 ounces Gorgonzola cheese, crumbled
Salt and freshly cracked pepper
1 cup pecans, lightly toasted and chopped
1 tablespoon fresh rosemary, chopped

In a small pan filled with water, parboil the garlic cloves until tender, about 8 minutes. Place cloves and Marsala in a blender and purée until smooth. Combine with cream and set aside.

Preheat oven to 400°. Lightly grease a 12 x 8-inch rectangular glass dish and arrange ⅓ each of the potatoes and pears. Dot potatoes with ⅓ of the Gorgonzola and sprinkle with a little salt and pepper. Top with ⅓ of the pecans and 1 teaspoon rosemary. Repeat layering 2 more times. Pour garlic-cream mixture over top.

Cover wih foil and bake for 25 minutes. Remove foil and bake 20–35 minutes longer or until almost all of the cream mixture is absorbed and the potatoes are tender. Serves: 6.

Goleta Lemon Festival, Goleta, CA

In the 1930s, Goleta, California, was the largest lemon producer in the country. While the area no longer claims that honor, many lemons are still grown in the region, and the citizens still pay homage to their lemon heritage.

The Lemon Festival was begun in 1991 and attracts around 15,000 people annually to enjoy the arts and crafts booths, musical entertainment, and, of course, the lemons, prepared every way imaginable. There's an enormous variety of fresh California produce, including lemons, at the Farmers' Market.

The Lemon Pie Eating Contest has become so popular that it's held on both days of the festival. The object is to eat as much lemon meringue pie as possible in three minutes. Contestants are not required to eat the crust but are judged on the amount of filling and meringue consumed. A few past winners have consumed an entire pie in the allotted time frame.

The food booths all have a lemon theme, selling gallon after gallon of fresh lemonade, lemon desserts, lemon chicken, lemon yogurt, and as many as 900 lemon pies. The Pie-Baking Contest consistently attracts a host of amateur cooks, and many of their recipes are featured in the official festival cookbook, *If You Love Lemon.*

Saturday and Sunday of the Third Weekend in October

Brigitte's Homemade Lemon Fettuccine with Tiger Prawns

Created by Executive Chef Felipe Barajas and Executive Sous Chef Gerardo Barajas.

Brigitte's Restaurant in Santa Barbara is famous for its dishes using local lemons. To prove it, the Greater Goleta Valley Chamber of Commerce contributed this winning recipe from Brigitte's Restaurant that also appears in the festival cookbook, *If You Love Lemon.*

Pasta:
1 pound flour (or ¾ pound flour and ¼ pound semolina)
Zest from 2–3 lemons, shredded (save lemons)
1 teaspoon salt
3 small eggs
1 cup water (approximately)
1 tablespoon virgin olive oil

Combine all ingredients to form a firm ball. Rest for 30 minutes in a cool place. Roll into fettuccine pasta following instructions on pasta machine. Boil in hot, salted water 2–3 minutes. Drain and keep warm. Toss with a little olive oil to keep the fettuccine from sticking together.

Sauce:
2 tablespoons extra virgin olive oil
1 pound peeled fresh local prawns
1 clove garlic, chopped
Juice of 1 lemon
½ cup fresh chopped tomatoes
½ cup roasted red peppers
1 tablespoon capers
½ cup white wine
¾ cup heavy cream
½ cup fresh baby spinach
½ teaspoon white pepper
Salt to taste
Parmesan cheese

Heat the olive oil in frying pan. Add the prawns and sauté for 2 minutes. Add garlic and lemon juice, then add tomatoes, peppers, and capers and cook for 2 minutes. Add white wine, cream, lemon pasta, and spinach. Cook for 1 minute or until pasta is hot. Season to taste with salt and pepper. Garnish with fresh lemon slices and/or an edible flower. Serve fresh grated Parmesan cheese on the side. Serves: 4.

Note: Large sea scallops can be used instead of prawns. Sear the sea scallops for 1–2 minutes longer than the prawns.

Holtville Carrot Festival, Holtville, CA

Located in Southern California's Imperial Valley, Holtville is still known as the "Carrot Capital of the World," even though most of the carrot farming has moved to other areas. But in 1947, around 11,000 acres were planted with carrots every year, and thus the Holtville Carrot Festival began. Today, a local seed company still supplies carrot seeds to many of the major producers in the West.

A grand parade, golf tournament, carnival, and livestock competition provide plenty to do at the festival. There is an annual deep-pit barbecue and a rib cook-off that attracts around two dozen competing teams.

The annual Carrot Banquet features a huge array of winning dishes from five decades of carrot-cooking contests. For many, the contest is a family tradition, and some competitors have entered the event for nearly forty years. The contest is held throughout the week and includes divisions from little chefs to high schoolers to seniors/snowbirds. Adults compete for recognition in categories covering salads, vegetables, main dishes, breads, desserts, microwave energy saving, and miscellaneous. Following judging, the public is invited to taste the entries. In 1948, a carrot cake made with ten eggs (seven in the cake and three in the icing) won the top award. In the calorie-conscious 1990s, more healthy concoctions, like tropical chicken salad, won the sweepstakes.

Ten Days in Late January and Early February

Tropical Chicken Salad

Emilie Dykes of Holtville entered this recipe and became a Carrot Festival Cooking Contest sweepstakes winner. Reprinted with permission from the *Holtville Tribune*.

2 cups cooked chicken
3 cups shredded carrots
1 cup chopped celery
1 cup light mayonnaise
½–1 teaspoon curry powder
1 can mandarin oranges, drained
1 (20-ounce) can chunk pineapple, drained
2 large bananas, sliced
½ cup shredded coconut
Salad greens
¾ cup salted cashews

In a bowl, combine the chicken, carrots, and celery. In another bowl, combine the mayonnaise and curry powder and add to the chicken mixture. Cover and chill for 30 minutes. Before serving, add the rest of the ingredients except the salad greens and cashews, tossing gently. Serve on a bed of salad greens and sprinkle with the cashews. Serves: 6–8.

Indio International Tamale Festival, Indio, CA

For many people, Christmas means tamales, just as Thanksgiving calls for the proverbial roast turkey. Indio's annual Tamale Festival, begun in 1992, kicks off a spicy holiday season with 120,000 visitors and dozens of tamale vendors.

With its theme based on tamales, the festival promotes Hispanic cultural pride and heritage. The event includes crafts, music, folkloric dancing, a holiday parade, a carnival, and 5K and 10K Runs.

The origin of tamales is unknown, but experts say that Aztecs ate them before the arrival of the Spanish conquistadors. Traditional Mexican tamales are made with a spiced filling of pork, chicken, beef, or vegetables, covered with a cornmeal dough called *masa,* and steamed in cornhusks.

Discriminating tamale aficionados can discern regional differences in preparation such as *estilo de Guerrero* (in the style of the Mexican state of Guerrero), where tamales contain a filling of only meat in a red chili sauce. Savory tamales may be made of pork, beef, meat, and vegetable mixtures or all vegetables. There are also sweet dessert tamales.

First Saturday and Sunday in December

Nearly 500,000 tamales are consumed annually at the festival. In 2000, the festival introduced its own signature tamale, the Desert Sweet Corn Chili and Cheese Tamale, developed by Los Angeles Chef John Rivera Sadler. Sadler, official festival spokesperson and "King of Tamales," also prepared the festival's contender for the World's Largest Tamale in the *Guinness Book of World Records.* His creation measured 40 feet long and weighed in at 1,250 pounds.

A major festival event is the Best Tamale Tasting Contest. While many traditional family recipes are used in the preparation of the festival tamales, others are clearly in the gourmet category.

Tamales with Goat Cheese, Sun-Dried Tomatoes, and Pecans

Pascal Dropsy of the Corn Maiden Company in Los Angeles is so famous for his tamales that festivalgoers immediately head for his concession. Dropsy recently opened a restaurant and retail shop in Los Angeles.

¾ pound 100% vegetable shortening
5 pounds unprepared masa
1 cup water
1 tablespoon salt
1 tablespoon plus ½ teaspoon baking powder
3¼ pounds goat cheese
1 tablespoon dried Greek oregano
½ teaspoon ground black pepper
2 ounces sun-dried tomatoes, soaked in hot
   water, drained, and chopped
¾ cup chopped pecans
Dried cornhusks, soaked in hot water until
   pliable, about 20 minutes, and drained
Salsa for serving

Masa: Place shortening in a large electric mixer bowl and beat with a paddle attachment until soft and creamy. Add the unprepared masa, water, salt, and baking powder. Beat well at medium speed for at least 5–8 minutes until light and fluffy. Transfer the mixture to another bowl, cover, and refrigerate.

Filling: In a large electric mixer bowl, place the goat cheese, oregano, and pepper. Mix well with the paddle attachment, then slowly mix in the sun-dried tomatoes and pecans.

Assembly: For each tamale, lay a husk flat with smooth-side up. Place about 3 tablespoons of masa in the center of the husk, and holding one end with your hand, spread ½ of the masa flush to one long edge. Repeat the process on the other ½ of husk, leaving a 1-inch margin on both the top and bottom of the husk. Place 2 tablespoons of filling in a band along one long edge. Fold the long edge of husk that's closest to the filling over it, then roll up snugly. Using strips from broken or extra husks, tie the tamale tightly at both ends and then make a third tie to lightly secure the center.

Cooking: Place the tamales in a rack over about 2 inches of boiling water, cover, return water to a boil, then lower heat to simmer and steam the tamales. Add more boiling water as necessary. Freshly made tamales should be steamed about 45–60 minutes or until the masa no longer sticks to the husks. Serve with salsa. Yield: About 35 tamales.

Kelseyville Pear Festival, Kelseyville, CA

Bartlett pears are the focus of the Kelseyville Pear Festival, which began in 1993. Pears were first planted in the area in the 1890s, and Lake County Bartlett pears are ranked among the finest in the world. At an altitude of 1,500 feet, the summertime climate, with warm days and cool nights, contributes to the production of sweet, juicy pears. Kelseyville is known as the "Bartlett Pear Capital of the World."

The Pear Festival was organized to celebrate the community's agricultural heritage and focuses on hometown events. An old-fashioned country feeling pervades the festival. Nearly every activity revolves around a pear theme, and visitors enjoy live music, a parade, dance demonstrations, an art show, antique tractor show, children's games, craft booths, and horse-drawn wagon rides. The festival also includes the Kelseyville Quilt Show.

Along with hamburgers and barbecued chicken, folks enjoy plenty of foods featuring pears: pies, cakes, cookies, breads, even pear milk shakes. A pear recipe contest brings out the creativity of local cooks, whose entries are judged, then auctioned off.

Marilyn's Pear Chutney

Marilyn Holdenreid, coordinator of the Kelseyville Pear Festival and owner, with husband Myron, of Maryka Orchards, shares her winning specialty.

3 pounds fresh Bartlett pears (about 7 cups), unpeeled, cored, and diced
1 pound brown sugar
2 cups cider vinegar
1 medium onion, chopped
1 cup golden raisins
¼ cup diced, preserved ginger
1 clove garlic, minced
½ teaspoon cayenne pepper
2 teaspoons salt
½ teaspoon cinnamon
½ teaspoon cloves
2 teaspoons mustard seed

Combine brown sugar and vinegar in a large saucepan and bring to a boil. Add the pears and remaining ingredients. Cook slowly, stirring from time to time, until the mixture is thick, about 1 hour. Pour into hot, sterilized jars and seal. Chutney may also be kept in the refrigerator for 3–4 weeks. Yield: 5 half-pint jars.

Note: Use as a relish with lamb or ham or as an appetizer with cream cheese and crackers.

Saturday during the Last Weekend in September

Loomis Eggplant Festival, Loomis, CA

Loomis is a rural area, characterized by ranches, fruit groves, packing sheds, and markets. In 1988, a few citizens decided that the town needed a fun event that had something to do with farming, such as fruits or vegetables. Unfortunately, everything seemed to be taken—there was already a carrot festival, a garlic festival, a strawberry festival, and even a prune festival. Eggplant seemed to be the only thing left, but there were no commercial eggplant growers in the Loomis Basin. Many folks did grow it in their own backyard gardens and they decided that was good enough. The Eggplant Festival was born, and from an initial attendance of 300, it has grown to accommodate more than 10,000 visitors each year. Local eggplant cultivation has increased as well, with veteran vegetable growers now providing several hundred pounds of eggplant in several different varieties for the event.

Eggplant serves as the inspiration for an eggplant sculpture contest and the Egganapolis 500, where eggplant drivers race down a short ramp course. There is live music and dancing, and craft people from throughout Northern California sell their wares.

Visitors taste a variety of eggplant creations which typically include things like pizza, kabobs, eggplant on a stick, and even eggplant pasties. A festival highlight is the Eggplant Cooking Contest with categories for amateurs and professionals. Winning recipes appear each year in the official *Loomis Eggplant Festival Cookbook*. Volunteers also man an Eggplant Festival booth at the California State Fair and Exposition, where they serve samples of tantalizing eggplant dip.

Third Saturday of September

State Fair Tasting Dip

The Loomis Basin Chamber of Commerce shares its famous dip.

1 medium eggplant
¼ cup lemon juice
1 cup parsley or cilantro
1 tablespoon mashed garlic
Roasted red bell peppers (optional)
Salt and pepper to taste

With a fork, poke the skin of the eggplant and place under the broiler for about 30 minutes or until soft. Cool. Remove the skin and seeds. Place the eggplant in the food processor with the rest of ingredients. The red bell peppers may be added for flavor and color. Process until smooth. Serve as a dip with crackers, tortilla chips, or vegetables. Yield: About 1 cup.

Eggplant Spinach Napoleons

Anita Miller was chosen as a recent sweepstakes winner of the Eggplant Cooking Contest when she prepared this enticing recipe.

1 medium eggplant
½ teaspoon salt
1 cup flour
½ teaspoon black pepper
¼ teaspoon cayenne pepper
Olive oil and sesame oil (or only olive oil)
1 (10-ounce) package frozen, chopped spinach, uncooked, thawed, and well drained
1 (6-ounce) package Brick cheese, sliced
1 (6-ounce) package Swiss cheese, sliced
Grated Parmesan cheese
1 small onion, grated, or onion powder to taste
Seasoned bread crumbs
Butter

Peel and slice eggplant. Salt and drain on paper towels for 10 minutes. Dredge in flour that has been mixed with salt and black and red pepper. Fry over medium heat in olive and sesame oils until brown, then drain.

Preheat oven to 350°. Butter a 9½ x 4½ x 3-inch loaf pan. Line bottom of pan with ⅓ of eggplant slices, ⅓ of spinach, and a layer of Swiss and Brick cheeses. Sprinkle with Parmesan cheese and onions or onion powder. Repeat layers twice. Top with bread crumbs and dot with butter. Bake for 30 minutes or until cheese bubbles.
Serves: 6–8.

Morro Bay Harbor Festival, Morro Bay, CA

Southern California's Morro Bay is a working waterfront and home to a significant portion of the state's fishing industry. The annual Harbor Festival represents an innovative partnership approach to community fund-raising, with more than forty-five nonprofit groups from San Luis Obispo County sharing festival proceeds. The festival always marks the beginning of National Seafood Month.

A raft of maritime-related activities draw an average of 45,000 people for ship tours, maritime heritage exhibits, and a Seas and Water Expo. The 35-ton sand sculpture is a vision to behold. There's also a Hawaiian Shirt Contest, in which entrants show off their most outrageous island garb. In the Oyster Olympics, the winner is whomever first consumes eighteen oysters, spiced however the entrant chooses.

The main festival attraction is the California Seafood Faire, featuring California-caught marine cuisine prepared by the county's top restaurateurs. The menu offers more than sixty items ranging from basic to exotic. Entrées may be paired with selections from around two dozen Central Coast wineries. Past favorites include creations based on sea bass, flounder, albacore, salmon, ahi tuna, crab, and oysters.

Morro Bay's commercial fishermen sponsor the Albacore and More Barbecue, a bit more laid back than the Seafood Faire. Attendees preferring to eat on the hoof gravitate to food stands serving up such favorites as Creamy Crab and Cheddar Cheese Soup and Vera Cruz-style fish tacos, which have drawn an enthusiastic following throughout Southern California in recent years. Many of the recipes from vendors and the Seafood Faire are in *The Official Morro Bay Harbor Festival Seafood Cookbook*.

The First Full Weekend in October

Creamy Crab and Cheddar Cheese Soup

Chef Rodney Aanerud of Rodney's Restaurant in Los Osos, CA, is justifiably famous for this soup, which he prepares at the festival. This recipe is reprinted with permission from *The Official Morro Bay Harbor Festival Seafood Cookbook.*

¾ cup butter
¾ cup flour
8¾ cups clam juice (or ½ clam juice and ½ chicken broth)
1 cup diced celery
1 bunch green onions, chopped
½ cup diced sweet white onion
1 teaspoon dried dill
½ teaspoon white pepper, or to taste
8 ounces mild Cheddar cheese, grated
1 cup sour cream
8–16 ounces snow crab meat, to taste

Roux: Melt the butter in a saucepan. Whisk in flour and cook over low heat, whisking constantly, for 2–3 minutes, until thick. Set aside.

Soup: Bring clam juice to a boil with the celery, onions, dill, and white pepper. Boil for 15 minutes. Add ¾ cup roux, a little at a time, stirring constantly to thicken. Add the cheese while stirring and reduce heat to simmer. Place the sour cream in a mixing bowl and add a little of the hot soup to temper. Add the sour cream mixture to the simmering soup. Squeeze the liquid out of the crabmeat and stir the crab into soup; up to 1 pound of crab may be added. Taste and adjust seasoning. Serve hot. Serves: 8–10.

Napa Valley Mustard Festival, Napa Valley, CA

California's Napa Valley, long known for its vineyards and premium wines, is abloom with wild mustard from January through March. The Napa Valley Mustard Festival is an annual extravaganza that attracts visitors from all over the world to explore the arts, culture, and agriculture of the area. The festival is held over a two-month period, generally February to April.

Events include art and photography competitions, as well as a golf benefit. The Blessing of the Balloons marks the launching of Napa Valley's colorful balloon fleet, now a tradition of the Mustard Festival.

Throughout the festival, casual and black-tie events are staged in various towns and locations. The Culinary Institute of America at Greystone hosts Mustard Magic, the grand opening event with delicious offerings of wine and food. Savor St. Helena and A Taste of Yountville offer wine and food tastings, with many restaurants and vendors showcasing mustard menus and specialty dishes. An awards ceremony features world-class mustards and mustard-inspired dishes, culminating in a Mustard Competition Awards Ceremony and the Napa Valley Chef of the Year Mustard Recipe Competition.

The festival's signature event is The Marketplace, where visitors can taste mustards from around the world, as well as a host of wine-country gourmet products, Napa Valley foods, wines, and craft brews. Four stages provide musical entertainment and there's an art center for children. Wine country chefs provide cooking demonstrations along with recipes for their creations. The following recipes are courtesy of Bob Hurley, executive chef of the Napa Valley Grill. Chef Hurley, a long-time supporter of and participant in the Mustard Festival, is renowned for his cuisine, which incorporates the rich, subtle flavors of mustard.

February to April

Homemade Mustard

Chef Bob Hurley, Napa Valley Grill.

There are many ways to prepare mustard, from milder champagne-based to hot sweet Chinese mustards. Most are prepared from mustard powders, which is what is left after the oil is extracted from the seeds. Many different flavors can be infused into the mustards, including green peppercorn, tarragon, dill, honey, and horseradish.

Here is a mustard that I use as a general base. I like it fairly pungent so I can use it as a flavoring, but you can tone it down with the addition of more oil and liquid.

2 teaspoons dry tarragon
6 tablespoons port wine
3 tablespoons white wine
6 tablespoons dry mustard
2 tablespoons Champagne vinegar
2 tablespoons sugar
1 tablespoon salt
5 tablespoons olive oil

Combine tarragon with port and white wine and cook to reduce to 4 tablespoons liquid. Add to the mustard, along with the other ingredients except oil. Mix to a smooth paste, then slowly add the oil until mixed. Season to taste. Yield: About ¾ cup.

Artichoke Soup with Rock Shrimp and Mustard Cream

Chef Bob Hurley, Napa Valley Grill.

Soup:
10 cups chicken stock
6 medium fresh artichokes
4 large leeks, split, washed, and trimmed of green
2 large onions, peeled and chopped
8 ounces butter
3 ounces smoked bacon, diced
8 cloves garlic, peeled
Leaves from 1 bunch fresh sage
3 medium potatoes, peeled and diced
2 cups rock shrimp

In a large pot, bring the chicken stock and artichokes to a boil and cook for 30 minutes. Remove the artichokes and separate the bottoms from the leaves. Return leaves to stock and continue cooking another 20 minutes.

While stock cooks, combine leeks, onions, butter, bacon, garlic, and sage leaves in another pot. Cook slowly on low heat until onions are translucent and bacon is limp and partially rendered. Add strained stock to this mixture along with potatoes and cook for approximately 20 minutes, until potatoes are very soft. Ladle soup in batches into a blender or food processor and purée. Put soup back into pot, bring to a boil, and add rock shrimp. Season to taste and serve with a dollop of mustard cream. Serves: 12.

Mustard cream:
1 cup heavy cream
1 tablespoon whole-grain mustard

Combine ingredients and beat until thick, but not whipped.

National Date Festival, Indio, CA

Nearly a quarter of a million people flock to Indio's National Date Festival at the 110-acre fairgrounds on Arabia Street. Queen Sheherazade rules over this festival, which features the Arabian Nights Musical Pageant every evening.

Indio is in California's Coachella Valley, and ninety-five percent of the dates in the U.S. are produced in this region. With all those date trees, Indio looks like an oasis in the middle of a desert, the perfect backdrop for the Taj Mahal that serves as an exhibit hall for local produce. The best dates are used in exhibits about date growing and the many culinary uses of dates. There are plenty of free samples and fresh dates to buy. Favorites are Deglet Noors, the most widely grown, and the large, soft Medjools, the most popular of all.

Date ice-cream cones and date shakes rank high among favorite festival foods. The date shake was first introduced at the festival in 1947, and by the following year, it was being sold at concession stands throughout the festival grounds. Today, it ranks as the festival's number one libation.

There are daily demonstrations of cooking with dates. The annual date-recipe contest hit the big time in 1996 when *Family Circle* magazine joined forces with the California Date Administration as a sponsor. The winner received a four-day trip to the Coachella Valley and attended the fiftieth anniversary of the National Date Festival. Festival cookbooks containing winning cook-off recipes are periodically produced, and ordering information may be obtained by contacting the National Date Festival office.

Date Shakes

This is a festival favorite from *Award Winning Date and Citrus Recipes.*

3 scoops vanilla ice cream
½ cup pitted dates
½ cup milk

Put ice cream in blender and whirl until liquefied. Add dates and blend until finely chopped. Add milk and blend again.
Yield: 1 shake.

Beginning in Mid-February for Ten Days

North Beach Festival, San Francisco, CA

North Beach, one of San Francisco's top tourist attractions, is the West Coast answer to New York's Little Italy, with a bit of the Beat Generation of the 1950s and 1960s thrown in. The neighborhood was settled by Italian immigrants in the first part of the twentieth century and community life here continues to retain a distinctly Italian flavor. North Beach landmarks are what most people equate with San Francisco: cable cars, Lombard Street (the world's most crooked street), Russian and Telegraph Hills, Coit Tower, and fantastic views of the city and the San Francisco Bay.

North Beach is also home to the oldest street fair in the country, dating from 1955. The festival attracts between 80,000 and 100,000 people every year to this friendly neighborhood, where Italian restaurants serve up glorious dishes from the old country. Music and dance are supplemented with small press and booksellers' booths, original arts and crafts, and an Italian marketplace. The California Olive Showcase includes an olive-oil tasting featuring only California olive oils. Worthy of note are the *Arte di Gesso*, or "chalk art" street paintings. The blessing of neighborhood pets, in honor of St. Francis of Assisi, San Francisco's patron saint, at North Beach's historic parish church lends a special poignancy to the festivities.

Many local restaurants and vendors set up alfresco booths and serve ethnic foods and beverages. Perhaps the most famous of these is The Stinking Rose Restaurant's Forty-Clove Garlic Chicken Sandwich, originally developed for the 1994 North Beach Festival and now an annual tradition. Other restaurants get into the act, too. Enrico's can be counted on for its Polenta Fries, Grant and Green goes all the way with its barbecued turkey drumsticks, and Rose Pistola's serves up grilled corn on the cob. There are also Italian sausage sandwiches, calzone, calamari fritti, mascarpone tortas, and grilled pizzette with lobster. Gelato and espresso carts provide a quick pick-me-up.

Many festival visitors check out at least a few of North Beach's shops. Charming hand-painted Majolica dinnerware and

Third Weekend in June

Della Robbia ceramics are available at Biordi Art Imports, while coffee lovers flock to Graffeo Coffee, the oldest coffee roaster in the neighborhood which produces what many consider to be the finest coffee in the country. Since 1914, Victoria Pastries has been making its famous *Saint-Honoré* cakes, confections of custard, rum, and whipped cream. The Florence Ravioli Factory and Deli delivers the best prosciutto, sausages, and pasta in town, and Iacopi's garlic sausage is a coveted treat.

The delicious smell of homemade bread lures people to Liguria Bakery for its famous focaccia.

An insider's view of North Beach is available to those who sign up for a walking tour, often conducted by *San Francisco Chronicle* food writer GraceAnn Walden. A must for cooks and gourmets, the tour includes tastings and a treasure trove of hints on where to find the best food and ingredients.

The Stinking Rose's Forty-Clove Garlic Chicken Sandwich

The Stinking Rose Restaurant in North Beach first created this famous specialty for the 1994 festival, and it has now become an annual tradition.

Olive oil
2 large, whole, boneless, skinless chicken breasts, trimmed and julienned
¼ cup sliced garlic (or more to taste)
1 medium yellow onion, sliced
1 yellow bell pepper, julienned
1 red bell pepper, julienned
1 tablespoon chopped parsley
1 tablespoon chopped basil
¼ tablespoon dried oregano
1 cup dry white wine
1 cup chicken stock
Salt and pepper to taste
1 large sourdough baguette

Heat oil in a large sauté pan. When oil is hot, add the chicken. Sauté for 1 minute, turn over, add the garlic, and sauté until the garlic starts to brown; remove from pan and keep warm. Add the onion and bell peppers and sauté for 2–3 minutes, stirring frequently. Add the parsley, basil, and oregano, stir, remove from the pan, mix with the chicken, and keep warm. Add wine to the pan to deglaze it and cook until it is almost evaporated. Add chicken stock and cook 2–3 minutes until reduced and thickened. Season sauce with salt and pepper to taste. Heat the baguette in a warm oven. Slice open, top with chicken, and pour sauce over. Slice into quarters and serve. Serves: 4 generously.

Orange Blossom Festival, Riverside, CA

The charm of a bygone era comes to life again every April when Riverside, California, holds its Orange Blossom Festival. Visitors relive the original turn-of-the-century Orange Day Celebration when citrus was king in the area. Participants wear era-appropriate costumes, and booths are decorated in theme amid the backdrop of historical downtown Riverside. It's a magical atmosphere, complete with a circus, carnival, parade, and other entertainment.

Citrus delights and orange-flavored dishes are served up in the Gourmet Grove, and professional chefs demonstrate citrus-dish preparation. Vendors sell all types of food but are required to offer at least one orange-flavored item. Orange pizza is a recent best seller.

Third Weekend in April

There's also a cooking contest that mandates that all submissions contain at least a half cup of orange juice or one orange. Every year, winning recipes, along with celeb-rity chef recipes, are gathered into an excellent cookbook entitled *The Best of the Best Orange Blossom Festival Recipes and Celebrity Chef Recipes*. The orange cheesecake recipes are outstanding.

Colors' Citrus Vegetarian Pizza

Martial Bricnet, celebrity chef at Colors' Gourmet Pizza in Carlsbad, CA, prepared this recipe for the 1997 festival.

Colors' citrus salad dressing:
1 tablespoon Dijon mustard
1 cup extra virgin olive oil
1 tablespoon orange juice
1 tablespoon lime juice
¼ cup balsamic vinegar
Ground black pepper
Sea salt to taste

Pizza:
1 teaspoon diced garlic
1 (10-inch) herb pizza crust, partially baked
12 fresh spinach leaves
¼ cup diced tomatoes
2 tablespoons pitted, sliced Kalamata olives
¼ cup sliced mushrooms
2 tablespoons diced blood oranges
2 tablespoons diced Maui onion or red onion
3 tablespoons diced red and yellow bell peppers
3 tablespoons bean sprouts
2 ounces grated mozzarella cheese
1 tablespoon chopped cilantro
1 tablespoon finely grated orange zest
2 tablespoons grated fontina cheese

Preheat oven to 400°. Combine ingredients for citrus dressing and mix well. Place garlic in center of the pizza crust and cover with ½ the citrus dressing. With a pastry brush, mix and spread the garlic and dressing evenly over the crust. Put all other ingredients in a bowl setting aside ½ the cilantro, ½ the orange zest, and the Fontina cheese. Add the remaining citrus dressing to the ingredients in the bowl and toss gently to avoid bruising the vegetables. Mix wel and distribute evenly over the crust. Spread the Fontina cheese over the pizza. Bake until golden brown, about 15 minutes. When cooked, cut into wedges. Place on a 12-inch serving platter and top with remaining cilantro and orange zest.

Paso Robles Basil Festival, Sycamore Farms, Paso Robles, CA

At Sycamore Farms in Paso Robles, California, basil is taken very seriously indeed. As a matter of fact, owner Bruce Schaumler says that he intends to do for basil what Gilroy has done for garlic. Schaumler grows 250 varieties of herbs on his four-acre farm, which he calls "a bit of heaven on earth." A lot of basil is produced for area restaurants and individuals, and when a local Italian restaurateur suggested that he start a basil festival, Schaumler took action.

Begun in 1991, the festival now attracts around 2,000 visitors a year. Basil is featured in a multitude of dishes and beverages, including pizza, salads, and bread. There's even basil-infused ice cream, beer, teas, and popcorn. Schaumler has created a basil beer and hopes to bottle it soon. In addition to live entertainment, cooks will discover basil workshops and plenty of recipes in the *Basil Festival Commemorative Booklet*.

First Saturday in August

Sycamore Farms and Buona Tavola Restaurant also sponsor a cooking contest at the Mid-State Fair the day before the Basil Festival. Three divisions cover Best o' Pesto, Best of Rosemary Focaccia, and Best of Biscotti.

Our Favorite Thai Chicken with Basil

Bruce Schaumler of Sycamore Farms in Paso Robles has become famous for his delicious recipes, which incorporate plenty of basil.

3–4 tablespoons finely chopped California green chilies, seeded
2 tablespoons soy sauce
1 teaspoon sugar
1 teaspoon vinegar
½ cup chopped fresh basil leaves
1 teaspoon chopped fresh mint leaves (or ½ teaspoon dried)
½ teaspoon cornstarch
3 tablespoons vegetable oil
2 whole chicken breasts (1 pound each), boned, skinned, cut into ¼-inch strips 2 inches long
2 cloves garlic, minced
1 large onion, halved, then sliced ¼ inch thick
Hot cooked rice

Mix together chilies, soy sauce, sugar, vinegar, basil, mint, and cornstarch; set aside. Heat 2 tablespoons of the oil in a frying pan or wok over high heat. When oil is hot, add the chicken and garlic. Cook, stirring constantly, until meat loses its pinkness, about 4 minutes. Remove chicken from pan and keep warm. Heat another tablespoon of oil in the pan, then add onion and cook, stirring, for 2 minutes. Add chili mixture and return chicken and juices to pan. Cook, stirring, until sauce thickens slightly. Transfer to a serving platter. Serve with rice. Serves: 4–6.

Patterson Apricot Fiesta, Patterson, CA

A whopping ninety-seven percent of our nation's apricots are grown in California. Patterson, a community of around 6,600, prides itself on being the "Apricot Capital of the World." In 1971, area apricot growers, businesspeople, and volunteers launched the first Apricot Fiesta, which promotes apricots and today attracts anywhere from 18,000 to 20,000 visitors.

The festival has a hometown atmosphere with events such as bingo, horseshoes, a parade, a petting zoo for kids, hot-air balloon launches, and 5K and 10K runs. A craft fair attracts scores of vendors, and tired shoppers can rest on bales of hay provided for just that purpose.

The Lion's Club offers a barbecue, and on Sunday morning, many attend Breakfast in the Park.

Along with golden fresh apricots, food vendors offer specialties like apricot smoothies and shakes, chocolate-covered apricots and apricot bars, pies, shortcakes, and tarts. An annual recipe contest, sponsored by the California Apricot Advisory Board, used to be held in conjunction with the fiesta but has been discontinued. Fortunately, festivalgoers can still purchase a cookbook entitled *Lots of 'Cots*, which includes winning recipes from the Patterson Apricot Fiesta.

The Weekend Following Observed Memorial Day Weekend

Annette's Apricot Divinity

The Patterson Apricot Fiesta provided this winning recipe from a past festival.

2 cups sugar
½ cup light corn syrup
½ cup hot water
¼ teaspoon salt
2 egg whites, stiffly beaten
1 teaspoon vanilla
½ cup finely chopped dried apricots

In a heavy 2-quart saucepan, combine the sugar, corn syrup, water, and salt. Cook and stir until the sugar dissolves and the mixture comes to a boil. Cook to hard ball stage (250°) without stirring. Occasionally wipe down the crystals from the sides of the pan. Remove from the heat and slowly pour the hot syrup over the stiffly beaten egg whites, beating constantly at high speed with an electric mixer (about 5 minutes). Add the vanilla and continue beating until mixture forms soft peaks and begins to lose its gloss. Add apricots. Pour into a lightly buttered pan or form in swirls on waxed paper.

Round Valley Blackberry Festival, Covelo, CA

Just imagine, in this day and age, a place where blackberries grow in such profusion that the briars peep from every nook and cranny and even the roadsides have to be sprayed to keep them from choking the ditches. If you yearn for unlimited quantities of luscious wild blackberries, then the place to be, come the third weekend in August, is Covelo, California, for the Round Valley Blackberry Festival. Some 190 miles north of San Francisco, Round Valley is referred to as "Nature's Hideaway" and serves as the gateway to the Mendocino National Forest.

The Blackberry Festival features loads of food-related activities, ranging from a pancake breakfast to a chili cook-off and a Mendocino County Wine Tasting. Best of all are the blackberry delicacies, including pies, jam, turnovers, and slush, which produce lovely purple smiles on the faces of all who come.

Folks who can't eat their fill at the festival can buy berries to take home. Armed with a copy of *Blackberry Bounty*, a beautifully illustrated cookbook compiled by The Friends of the Round Valley Public Library, visitors can re-create the goodies in their own kitchens.

Third Weekend in August

Blackberry Turnovers

Stella McCarty's prize recipe, featured in *Blackberry Bounty*, is used by the Covelo Girls and Boys Club to make the turnovers sold in their Blackberry Festival booth.

Pastry:
2 cups all-purpose flour
1 teaspoon salt
½ cup butter
Approximately ½ cup ice water
½ cup butter cut into small pats
1 egg mixed with 1 tablespoon water

Filling:
3 cups blackberries
6 tablespoons sugar
3 tablespoons flour

Glaze:
Powdered sugar
Water

To make the pastry, mix the flour and salt together. Then cut ½ cup of the butter into the flour as in pie dough. Add the water gradually, mixing with your hands until reaching pie-dough consistency; add more water if necessary. Using a little flour, roll dough out into a rectangle about 16 x 8 inches. Lay half the butter pats over two-thirds of the rectangle, then fold in thirds. Roll dough out again to an 16 x 8-inch rectangle and place the remaining pats of butter on two-thirds of the dough. Fold as before and roll out to 16 x 8 inches again. This time, fold the dough in half and then again in half. Refrigerate in plastic wrap until chilled, up to 3 days.

Combine the filling ingredients, mashing the berries just enough to release a bit of juice.

Preheat oven to 400°. Cut dough in half and roll each half out into 12-inch squares. Trim so edges are even. Brush with egg and water mixture. Cut in fourths, each 6 inches square. Fill with 1½ tablespoons blackberry filling, fold over, and pinch edges well. Cut slits in top and brush again with egg mixture. Freeze on cookie sheets, fit close together, about 30 minutes. Bake for 25 minutes or until golden brown. Meanwhile, to make the glaze, mix the powdered sugar and water to cinsistency of thick syrup. Remove turnovers to racks to cool, then drizzle with glaze.
Yield: 8 turnovers.

Santa Cruz Clam Chowder Cook-Off and Festival, Santa Cruz, CA

Who says chowder wars are waged only on the East Coast? Westerners have their say about the best versions of red (Manhattan) and white (New England) clam chowders every February at the Santa Cruz Beach Boardwalk. A California Historic Landmark, the boardwalk is not only California's oldest amusement park but it's also the only major oceanside amusement park on the Pacific Coast. It features a classic 1911 Looff carousel and the ever-popular Giant Dipper wooden roller coaster, built in 1924.

The Clam Chowder Cook-Off recognizes the best chowder chef in each of three divisions: restaurant, individual, and corporate/media, and annually draws around forty-five teams who compete for honors in a number of categories, including Best Individual Manhattan or Best Individual Boston, People's Choice, and Most Tasted. According to Boardwalk Promotions Manager Rich Dressler, "Most of the teams dress up with a nautical theme and don't clam up when it comes to putting on a good show." Visitors can purchase tasting kits, and the team members' silly antics, as well as the competition in trying to get the most people to try their chowder, add to the fun. For those who go a bit overboard in tasting, there's the Great Chowder Chase on Sunday, a 4½-mile race through the beach area guaranteed to burn off those excess calories.

Last Saturday in February

Best Restaurant Manhattan Clam Chowder

Chef Francisco Farias of Severino's Restaurant in Aptos, CA, created this recipe and won the Santa Cruz Boardwalk's Annual Clam Chowder Cook Off.

¾ pound raw smoked bacon, diced
2 green bell peppers, diced
2 red bell peppers, diced
2 medium yellow onions, diced
3 carrots, diced
5 large stalks celery, diced
1/2 cup diced garlic
1/2 cup diced shallots
1½ bunches leeks, diced
6 diced russet potatoes, steamed until soft
4 cups port wine
12 cups diced tomatoes in juiice
4 cups tomato paste
¾ cup lemon juice
2 bay leaves
2½ teaspoons gumbo powder
1 tablespoon Italian seasoning

2½ teaspoons garlic powder
½ bunch fresh chopped basil
¼ cup sugar
8 cups clam juice
7 cups chopped clams in juice
¾ cup dark roux
Salt and pepper to taste

Sauté bacon, then peppers, onions, carrots, celery, garlic, shallots, leeks, and potatoes. Deglaze with wine and reduce liquid. Add tomatoes and tomato paste, then add all the seasonings. Finally, add the clams and clam juice and stir in the roux. Season with salt and pepper to taste. Cook slowly for 1½ hours, stirring occasionally. Yield: About 2 gallons.

Selma Raisin Festival, Selma, CA

Selma, California, in the San Joaquin Valley, is the "Raisin Capital of the World." The fields around Selma produce ninety percent of California's raisins. It all began in 1876 when William Thompson, a Scottish immigrant in the northern Sacramento Valley, introduced the Lady de Coverly seedless grape at the Marysville District Fair. These grapes became known as the "Thompson Seedless" and were the perfect thin-skinned, sweet grape needed for full-scale raisin production. The fertile soil of the San Joaquin Valley was the ideal place for producing raisins, and the rest is history.

The Raisin Festival is a family-oriented event with a hometown feel. Families come for the carnival, as much as they do to honor "nature's candy," a term locals use for the raisin. Festivities include a photography contest, an art competition, a floriculture contest, craft vendors, and all sorts of other entertainment.

Food vendors offer a new twist on old carnival favorites, with such items as tacos with Spanish rice, barbecued pizza, carne asada tacos, barbecued corn on the cob, and tamales. The Raisin Baking Contest offers samples of items like raisin pie, raisin-oatmeal cookies, sweet tamales, carrot-raisin cake, bread pudding with raisins, and cinnamon-swirl raisin bread. The Selma Chamber of Commerce has published an updated version of the Raisin Festival cookbook, *Delightful Raisin Delicacies*, containing award-winning recipes from some of the more recent festivals.

First Weekend in May

Pineapple Carrot Raisin Cake

Stacy R. Ekberg of Selma, CA, captured the best-of-show award in the Raisin Baking Contest.

Cake:
2 cups flour
2 teaspoons baking soda
2 teaspoons cinnamon
½ teaspoon ginger
½ teaspoon salt
3 eggs
1½ cups sugar
¾ cup mayonnaise
1 cup crushed pineapple in juice
2 cups shredded carrots
1 cup chopped walnuts
1 cup raisins

Frosting:
3 ounces cream cheese, softened
⅓ cup butter
2 cups powdered sugar

Cake: Preheat oven to 350°. Combine the flour, baking soda, cinnamon, ginger, and salt in a bowl. Beat the eggs, sugar, mayonnaise, and pineapple in juice in a large mixing bowl until well blended. Gradually beat in flour mixture. Stir in carrots, nuts, and raisins. Grease and flour a 13 x 9-inch baking pan or two 9-inch round pans. Spoon batter into pans. Bake for 40–50 minutes for a 13 x 9-inch pan; 30–35 minutes for round pans. Cool in pan for 10 minutes. Invert the cake onto a wire rack to cool. Frost with cream-cheese frosting.

Cream-cheese frosting: Beat cream cheese with butter until smooth. Beat in powdered sugar until fluffy.

Taste of Solvang and Danish Days, Solvang, CA

In 1910, Danish immigrants attending the Danish Lutheran Church Convention in Michigan resolved to establish a colony on the West Coast. Central to the proposed colony would be a Danish folk school that would educate Danish Americans on the Danish way of life. The required location was found in the Santa Ynez Valley, and the new town was appropriately christened "Solvang," or "Sunny Field." The eventual result was a totally Danish town, characterized by Danish architecture, cuisine, and customs, and it is now known as the "Danish Capital of America." There's even a half-scale replica of the Little Mermaid that graces the harbor of Copenhagen.

Danish Days began in 1935 as a celebration of the twenty-fifth anniversary of Solvang's founding. By 1959, the event had attracted so many visitors that the tiny town of 2,000 was literally reeling from the effort to accommodate them. Determined "to have their party at any cost," the townsfolk moved the festival from the busier summer months to a weekend in mid-September in order to accommodate the 30,000 to 50,000 visitors.

Today, Danish Days features Danish folk dancing, traditional costumes, music, and Old World pageantry along with authentic Danish food. *Aebleskiver* breakfasts, including the famous Danish version of the doughnut made in a special pan, are one of the most popular of Danish Days events.

A Taste of Solvang, held in March, also delivers the delights of Danish cuisine. Begun in 1993, it includes a Dessert Showcase where visitors can sample scrumptious desserts. The Walking Smorgaasbord takes visitors through the village with stops at restaurants, bakeries, coffee, and gourmet shops for entertainment and samplings of more than thirty Danish specialty items. Olsen's Bakery, named by *Sunset* magazine as one of the best in the West, builds the World's Largest Danish *Kransekage*, and everyone gets a chance to munch on a piece of the pastry made by a true Danish baker.

Taste of Solvang Always the Third Weekend in March — Danish Days A Weekend in Mid-September

Aebleskiver (Danish Doughnuts)

This is the very famous and very official recipe used by Danish Days cooks.

2 eggs
2 cups buttermilk
2 cups flour
2 teaspoons baking powder
½ teaspoon salt
½ teaspoon baking soda
2 tablespoons sugar
1/4 cup melted butter
Vegetable oil or shortening

Separate the eggs and beat the whites until stiff. Mix all the other dry ingredients and the butter together and beat until smooth. Fold in the egg whites last. Put 1 teaspoon vegetable oil or shortening in the bottom of each cup in an aebleskiver pan and heat until hot. Pour about 2 tablespoons of the batter into each cup and cook over medium heat. As soon as the aebleskiver get bubbly around the edge, turn quickly (Danish cooks use a long knitting needle for turning but a fork will also work). Continue cooking, turning the ball to keep it from burning. Serve hot with syrup, jam, or powdered sugar. Yield: About 30.

The Great Monterey Squid Festival, Monterey, CA

Always Saturday and Sunday of Memorial Day Weekend

Squid is a major catch in Monterey Bay, home of a significant commercial fishing industry. In 1984, the Kiwanis Club of Monterey launched the successful Great Monterey Squid Festival, which attracts more than 30,000 people to the Monterey Peninsula on the California coast.

Squid is commonly known by its Italian name, calamari. Because of its large harvest, Monterey is billed as the "Calamari Capital of the World." Festival attendees are urged to try the "Italian Donut," so called because, precisely cut, squid results in rings that are often deep-fried and resemble tiny doughnuts.

The festival offers live entertainment on five stages, along with an arts and crafts show. Educational displays focus on the commercial fishing industry, marine life, and squid, in addition to the once lucrative sardine industry on the peninsula.

But, the festival is primarily a gastronomic event in celebration of what locals call "the incredible, edible, elegant squid, the true star of the sea." Very popular is the demonstration by local fishermen on how to clean and prepare squid for cooking. TV food personalities and chefs from local restaurants give squid-cooking demonstrations and recipes. Occasionally, there is a squid-cooking contest. At food booths, thousands of pounds of squid can be found battered, fried, grilled, and sautéed. For those squeamish about squid, there's plenty of other fresh seafood.

Marinated Calamari Salad

The Great Monterey Squid Festival shares a winning recipe from the cooking competition.

3 pounds cleaned and tenderized calamari
2 cloves garlic, minced
2 stalks celery, thinly sliced
3 tomatoes, cut into wedges
½ medium red onion, thinly sliced
1 teaspoon chopped fresh parsley
½ teaspoon oregano
¼ cup olive oil
¼ cup wine vinegar
Juice of 1 lemon
Salt and pepper to taste

Boil calamari in salted water for 5 minutes. Rinse and cool. Cut cooked calamari into ¼-inch strips. Toss with remaining ingredients. Refrigerate for 1 hour before serving. Serves: 10–12 as side dish.

Hawaii

Few people think of coffee or onions when the subject of Hawaii comes up. America's fiftieth state, a tropical paradise, plays host to seven million tourists every year, who come to enjoy beautiful scenery, sun, and beaches. Actually, Hawaii has some 4,600 farms that consume forty percent of its land, and major crops include sugarcane and pineapples. In recent years, the coffee of the Kona coast and the onions of Maui have grabbed the culinary spotlight.

The first coffee was planted in Kona around 1828 by a missionary named Samuel Ruggles. By the third quarter of the 1800s, large coffee plantations, owned by white planters, were worked by Chinese and Native Hawaiian laborers. After the crash of the coffee market in 1899, only small Japanese farms were producing coffee in the Kona area. Today, the coffee market has recovered, and many of those farms are still in the family, worked by fifth-generation family members.

Maui onions date back to the 1930s, when a variety of the Yellow Bermuda onion was introduced to the island. Grown on the fertile slopes of Haleakala Crater, a dormant volcano 10,000 feet above sea level, the Kula Maui onion is characterized by a flat shape, a pale outer skin, and its exceptionally sweet taste. The Maui onion is prized by islanders and visitors alike, and it is even said that actor Frank Sinatra spent a great deal of money in shipping hundred-pound bags of the Kula beauties to his various residences.

Kona Coffee Cultural Festival, Kailua-Kona, HI

There's plenty of activity brewing at the annual Kona Coffee Cultural Festival, begun in 1971 and now billed as "Hawaii's Oldest Food Festival." The festival honors coffee production, a major industry on the big island of Hawaii.

Coffee farms, processors, and roasters can all be found in the famed Kona coffee belt, which runs through the scenic upland slopes of Mauna Loa and Mt. Hualalai. During the festival or any time of the year, visitors can take the Kona Coffee Country Driving Tour, a self-guided exploration of farms, mills, and retail shops. Other festival events take place in Kailua-Kona and throughout the region, including a grand parade, a coffee art exhibit, an international lantern parade, and a coffee-picking contest. The Kona Coffee Farm Fair features a farmers' market, food booths, coffee basket-making, cooking demonstrations, and Kona coffee displays. Kona's Heritage Park and International Market showcases the ethnic costumes, food, arts, and crafts of the many multiethnic groups who have worked the Kona coffee fields, including those of Hawaiian, Japanese, Filipino, Chinese, English, and Portuguese descent.

Usually the First Week in November

A fabulous feast based on Big Island products awaits those who attend the Big Island Brunch and Marketplace. Both amateurs and professionals compete for honors in the Kona Coffee Recipe Contest, which always attracts innovative recipes. After talking about it for twenty-seven years, the festival produced the *Kona Coffee Festival Cookbook* in 1997, a fabulous collection of Kona coffee recipes and well worth the wait.

Kona Coffee Macnut Crust Bread Baked Shrimp with Vinaigrette

Executive Chef Vernon Wong of the Keauhou Beach Hotel created this recipe and won a recent Kona Coffee Recipe Contest.

Baked shrimp:
3 large headless shrimp (16–20 count)

Crust:
2 ounces butter
2 star anise
½ cup panko (Japanese bread crumbs)
1 tablespoon chopped macadamia nuts
½ teaspoon grated fresh ginger
½ teaspoon chopped fresh garlic
1 cup brewed Kona coffee, reduced to
  2 tablespoons
1 teaspoon chopped fresh mint leaves

Preheat oven to 375°. Slice down the back of the shrimp. Clean and lift the shrimp out of shell. Heat the butter and anise together until butter turns nutty brown. Remove the anise, add the remaining ingredients, and cook for 10 minutes over low heat to incorporate the flavor. Top each shrimp with 2 teaspoons of crust. Bake until crust is flaky and shrimp is done.

Kona coffee raspberry vinaigrette:
1 cup brewed Kona coffee
4 star anise
½ teaspoon sliced ginger
¼ cup rice vinegar
¼ cup honey
½ teaspoon vanilla
1 ounce Kahlua
¼ cup raspberry purée
¼ teaspoon sambal (red chili paste)
½ teaspoon chopped mint leaves
6 ounces vegetable oil
Fresh raspberries

Combine coffee, anise, and ginger. Reduce by half over mediium-high heat and remove anise. Add remaining ingredients and chill. Drizzle the vinaigrette over the baked shrimp. Garnish with fresh raspberries between the shrimp. Serves: 1.

Maui Onion Festival, Ka'anapali Beach, Maui, HI

Several years ago, the management of Whaler's Village, Maui's premier resort shopping destination, heard about the Gilroy Garlic Festival in California. The result was the establishment of an annual Maui onion celebration in 1990 to support Maui farmers and raise money for local nonprofit organizations like the Maui County Humane Society. Since that time, the festival has grown, and nearby hotels and restaurants get into the act with Maui onion specials on the menu and by directly participating in the event itself.

Many visitors plan vacations to coincide with the festival in order to participate in the golf tournament or the raw onion-eating contest, where one prize is a package of heavy-duty breath mints. Clowns, jugglers, and face painters entertain the kids while adults enjoy traditional Hawaiian entertainment.

Everyone lines up for Maui onion rings, fried in a huge three-foot-wide wok by members of the Maui Farm Bureau. A festival highlight is the Maui Onion Cook-Off. One year, a recipe for Maui onion ice cream took first place. For a collection of great recipes, there is none better than *The Maui Onion Cookbook* by Barbara Santos, who works hard to promote the Maui Onion Festival and to spread the word about her favorite "rotund root."

Macadamia Nut—Crusted Brie with Maui Onion and Oven-Dried Tomato Relish

This winning recipe was created by Chef Steve Armal, proprietor of The Last Stop Deli in Maui, and it is reprinted with permission from Barbara Santos', *The Maui Onion Cookbook*.

4 small wheels of brie, cold
1 cup all-purpose flour
1 cup milk
3 eggs
1 cup finely chopped macadamia nuts
Canola oil for frying
1 Maui onion, julienned
1 tablespoon Vegetable oil
⅓ cup brown sugar
½ cup chicken stock
1 cup red wine vinegar
Salt and pepper to taste
8 dried tomatoes
¼ cup capers

Brie: Toss brie wheels in the flour until well coated. Shake off the excess flour. Beat the milk and eggs together in a small bowl. Dip brie in the mixture until well coated. Dip brie in the finely chopped macadamia nuts, patting with your hands to set the nuts. Heat oil in a pan deep enough to cover the cheese. Deep-fry or bake in a preheated 475° oven until the cheese is golden brown. Serves: 4.

Relish: In a heavy pan, brown Maui onion over medium heat in vegetable oil. Stir in brown sugar. Cook until fully caramelized and glossy. Add chicken stock and vinegar. Season to taste with salt and pepper. Reduce over medium heat by ⅔, until sauce coats the back of a spoon. Remove from heat and transfer to medium-sized bowl. Add dried tomatoes and capers. Cool, stirring occasionally. Sauce will thicken as it cools. Refrigerate. Relish will keep in the refrigerator up to 2 weeks.

Oregon

Oregon's wheat and flour heritage goes back to 1828 when the first flour mill began operation at Fort Vancouver. Enough food was raised there to feed the Hudson's Bay Company employees and excess was sold to trappers. At the time, flour arriving from England was often damaged during the long voyage, and early settlers concentrated their efforts on flour production. By 1864, Standard Mills in the Willamette Valley had registered the state's first flour trademark. Today, wheat is Oregon's most valuable food crop, generating more than $220 million annually, and Portland is the nation's largest wheat-exporting gateway. Most wheat is grown in the plateau region around Pendleton. The soft white wheat grown in the Northwest is primarily used to make flour for pretzels, crackers, noodles, cookies, sponge cakes, and a variety of flatbreads.

Wild blackberries grow in profusion throughout the Illinois Valley in southwestern Oregon. The area is much like that of Covelo, California, home of the Round Valley Blackberry Festival.

Summer Loaf: A Celebration of Bread, Portland, OR

Portland's claim as the "Bread Capital of America" was staked in grand style at the first annual Summer Loaf: A Celebration of Bread in July 1997. Heidi Yorkshire, author of *Wine Savvy* and *Simply Wine* and frequent contributor to such magazines as *Bon Appetit*, was fraught with doubt, wondering if anyone would show up. She need not have worried. Thousands converged upon the Portland Farmers Market to taste breads made by participating bakeries, see flour milled, watch the city's best bakers at work, and smell fresh bread baking in a wood-fired oven. "The festival was a total smash," Heidi exuberantly reported. "We were quite overwhelmed, in a good way mostly."

The success of that first Summer Loaf has continued to rise each year, and it now attracts some 12,000 people to learn the secrets of baking good bread or sample the delicious artisan loaves baked for the event. America's first-ever bread festival promises to blossom into an enduring celebration of one of the world's most basic foods. The Portland Farmers Market, home of the festival, is on the Portland State University campus.

The Oregon Wheat Grower's League shows how wheat is grown. Representatives from Bob's Red Mill demonstrate how wheat is made into flour using an old-fashioned mill. There are also kneading and tortilla-making demonstrations. World-renowned bakers discuss their craft in special presentations. Those with questions can get help at booths manned by the Bread Baker's Guild of America and the National Baking Center. Off-site baking classes are held on days both before and after the festival.

The First Saturday in August

Participating bakeries sell their wares, ranging from fancy to homey. Selections include country French bread, baguettes, *ciabatta*, and *pugliese*, and samples are given out to all. In addition to bread, shoppers can purchase accompaniments such as olive oil, creamery butter, sea salt, and more. Also available are fine pastas, chocolates, and cheese. Delicious jams, made from the Northwest's berry crops, add a sweet dimension. The season's best produce is available from the forty-plus farmers who participate in the weekly Farmers Market.

More lasting souvenirs can be found as

well. A major book chain offers a wide selection of baking cookbooks, many of which are autographed on the spot by the authors. Wheat weavers demonstrate their craft and sell wreaths, baskets, and other items made from wheat stalks.

Amateur bakers vie for fame and prizes in the bread-baking contest. Adults compete in three categories: breads made with packaged yeast; breads made with levain, sourdough, or other starter; and quick breads leavened with baking soda and/or baking powder. In the kid's competition, breads are baked with the help of adults. Judges include professional bakers and other cooking experts.

Apricot Pumpkin Walnut Bread

Lisa Creamer was one of the very first winners in the Quick Bread Category of the Summer Loaf Bread Baking Contest in 1997. Lisa says her winning entry was based on a recipe that originally appeared in the *Atlanta Journal* in 1990.

1½ cups canned pumpkin
1 cup sugar
1 cup vegetable oil
3 eggs
2¼ cups all-purpose flour
¾ teaspoon cinnamon
¾ teaspoon nutmeg
¾ teaspoon salt
1½ teaspoons baking soda
1½ teaspoons baking powder
1 (3-ounce) package instant vanilla pudding mix
1½ cups chopped dried apricots
1½ cups chopped walnuts

Preheat oven to 350°. Lightly grease two large 9 x 5-inch loaf pans. In a large mixing bowl, whisk together the pumpkin, sugar, oil, and eggs. Sift together the flour, spices, salt, baking soda, and baking powder and whisk into pumpkin mixture. Fold in the pudding mix, apricots, and nuts, mixing until just combined.

Divide batter evenly between the two loaf pans. Bake for 1 hour or until the bread pulls slightly away from the sides of the pan and top is lightly browned. The bread keeps for several days if wrapped well.

Wild Blackberry Arts and Crafts Festival, Cave Junction, OR

The Wild Blackberry Arts and Crafts Festival was started in 1981 by Maciej "Les" Lesiecki. Les was born in 1919 and suffered from anemia. His uncle, a pediatrician, recommended he be fed plenty of spinach. Like most kids, Les hated spinach, and his mother continued to nag the doctor for a substitute. Finally, it was recommended that Les' mother make wild blackberry nectar, which contained more iron than spinach. With no further complaints, Les dutifully consumed the nectar for nearly four years. Out of gratitude to the "lifesaving blackberry," Les created the festival that today honors the area's wild blackberries and provides an outlet for the unique crafts of local residents.

The festival includes a fabulous quilt show, organized by Dorothy Wiltfong, featuring new quilts made by local women and some that have been handed down in families since the mid-1880s. Visitors enjoy an art walk, old-time fiddlers, bluegrass and jazz music, and spinning and weaving demonstrations. For fans of the wild blackberry, the food is the big draw. In addition to fresh berries, food booths and local restaurants feature blackberry specialties of every sort, including blackberry pies, jams, and jellies. The pie-eating contest and chicken barbecue draw a crowd.

Oregon Berry "Boy Bait"

Gertie Wittenberg, a venerated local cook, contributed her famous recipe to *It's the Berries Cookbook* published many years ago by the Illinois Valley Federated Women's Club, Cave Junction, OR.

2 cups flour
1½ cups sugar
2 teaspoons baking powder
1 teaspoon salt
¾ cup butter
2 egg yolks
1 cup milk
1 teaspoon almond or vanilla flavoring
2 egg whites, beaten stiff
2–3 cups blackberries, washed and drained
Fresh sweetened whipped cream (optional)

Always the Second Weekend in August

Preheat oven to 350°. Combine the dry ingredients. Cut in the butter. Remove 1 cup of the mixture and set aside.

Add remaining ingredients except the egg whites and blackberries. Mix well. Fold in the beaten egg whites. Pour the batter into a buttered and floured 13 x 9-inch pan. Sprinkle berries evenly over the batter and sprinkle with the reserved crumb mixture. Bake for 40–60 minutes, or until top is golden and a toothpick inserted in center comes out clean. This is delicious served hot, with or without whipped cream.

Washington

About one-third of Washington is farm-land, and the state grows more apples than any other, including Granny Smith, Red Delicious, and Golden Delicious varieties.

Walla Walla, Washington, is the home of the Walla Walla Sweet Onion, first cultivated by Italian immigrant gardeners from seed found on the island of Corsica around 1900. Through a process of carefully hand-selecting onions from each year's crop, growers have been able to produce today's onion, distinguished by exceptional sweetness, jumbo size, and round shape. Undoubtedly, the moderate climate and low-sulfur, high-water content of the soil in the Walla Walla region have plenty to do with the onion's quality. The Walla Walla Sweet has recently come under the protection of a Federal Marketing Order. This means that only growers within the Walla Walla Valley can grow and market the onion under the name Walla Walla Sweet.

Washington has long been famous for its seafood, which includes several varieties of salmon, in addition to oysters, crabs, shrimp, clams, tuna, flounder, and halibut. Mussels have recently become popular, and those from the waters of Penn Cove on Puget Sound are gaining in favor among connoisseurs. Mussels from this area, formally identified as *Mytilus galloprovincialis*, are originally from Spain and apparently arrived as stowaways on the ballasts of Spanish galleons in the 1700s. Known for their high meat yield, Penn Cove Mussels are in great demand today.

Penn Cove Mussel Festival, Coupeville, WA

Penn Cove mussels have consistently placed first in international shellfish competitions. They are farmed on scenic Whidbey Island in Puget Sound, just north of Seattle. Early each spring, the Captain Whidbey Inn, dating from 1907, holds its annual Penn Cove Mussel Festival to honor the local bivalve.

Mussel mania prevails throughout the three-day festival. Innkeeper John Colby Stone offers cruises of mussel farms and Penn Cove aboard the *Cutty Sark*, a classic fifty-two-foot ketch. The double-masted sailing vessel is reminiscent of the Baltimore clippers of two centuries ago.

There are mussel-farming demonstrations, as well as mussel-cooking demonstrations by recognized American chefs. Restaurants compete in the Mussel Chowder-off, cheered on by visitors who get free samplings. For die-hard mussel fans, that's just a prelude to the mussel-eating contest.

Friday through Sunday of the First Weekend in March

Two weeks prior to the festival, a mussel recipe contest is held. Awards are given for three recipes in any category. On Sunday evening, the winners are honored at a reception and dinner, which features as many of the mussel dishes as possible. Winning recipes are compiled into an annual cookbook, *Recipes from the Penn Cove Mussel Festival*.

The Best I Ever Had Mussels with Herbs and Garlic Sauce

This recipe was created by Ann Cribbs, a winner of the Penn Cove mussel recipe contest.

Garlic sauce:
2 thick slices stale French bread, crust removed
2–4 cloves garlic, peeled
¼ cup almonds, toasted, skins on
3 tablespoons white wine vinegar
¼ cup olive oil
Salt

Mussels:
1½ pounds mussels, scrubbed and debearded
½ cup best dry white wine available
¼ cup water
1 large clove garlic, peeled and crushed

Cooking sauce:
2 tablespoons butter
1 tablespoon olive oil
1 small onion, chopped
2–4 cloves garlic, minced
¼ cup chopped fresh dill
¼ cup chopped fresh fennel
¼ cup chopped fresh parsley

Jasmine rice, cooked according to package directions

Garlic sauce: Soak French bread in warm water for a few minutes and squeeze dry. In a food processor, chop the garlic and almonds.

With the machine running, add the bread and then the vinegar and oil. Process until smooth, adding a little water if a thinner consistency is desired. Salt to taste.

Mussels: Place mussels in a steamer basket above the wine, water, and garlic in a noncorrosive pan. Cover tightly and cook on high heat until steam puffs hard from under the lid, about 3–4 minutes. When mussels are well opened, move them to a baking tray to cool as quickly as possible. Strain and reserve the broth. When mussels are well cooled, shell and replace them in their broth. This may be done several hours in advance of serving, in which case, refrigerate the container of mussels and broth until ready to use. At that time, separate the mussels and broth again into 2 containers.

Cooking sauce: Heat the butter and oil in a medium-size, noncorrosive skillet and very slowly sauté onion until soft and transparent. Add garlic and heat for another minute, then add the chopped herbs. Turn heat to high, add mussels, and toss thoroughly for 1 minute. Add broth and heat well but do not boil.

Serve the mussels with their broth on a bed of jasmine rice with the garlic sauce on the side. Serves: 2.

Race to Bake the Biggest Apple Pie, Walla Walla Point Park, Wenatchee, WA

Though not an annual festival, the Race to Bake the World's Biggest Apple Pie was a worthy culinary event. It started as a scheme to raise funds for the North Central Washington Museum and promote the Wenatchee Valley and the apple industry. Washington is the top U.S. producer of apples and grows as many as the next five apple-producing states—New York, Michigan, California, Pennsylvania, and Virginia—combined.

Before the event was over, nearly 500 volunteers were pressed into service, washing, peeling, coring, and slicing 700 boxes of apples. Local football teams deserted the gridiron in favor of rolling pins, pounding and pressing pieces of dough into a makeshift pie pan. After apple slices were mixed with lemon and pineapple juices, the filling was dumped into the crust, and some seven hours of baking began. The pie, measuring 44 x 24 feet, weighed 34,438 pounds. An estimated crowd of 5,000 people purchased slices of the giant pie.

One-Time Event Held on August 16, 1997

On a more manageable scale, an apple-pie–baking contest was also held. For the volunteers and visitors who had worked up an appetite, the event featured an all-American meal of barbecued chicken, french fries, corn on the cob, and—what else?—all the apple pie and ice cream they could eat.

Wenatchee, Washington's Winning Apple Pie

Jackie Adamson, Wenatchee, WA, was the first place winner of the Wenatchee Apple Pie Contest.

Pastry:
- 2 cups all-purpose flour
- 1 teaspoon salt
- 12 tablespoons shortening (shortening prepared from meat fats and vegetable oil)
- 6 tablespoons cold water

Filling:
- 2 pounds (5 large) Golden Delicious apples, peeled, cored, and sliced
- ½ teaspoon lemon juice
- ½ teaspoon cinnamon
- ¼ cup flour
- ¼ cup granulated sugar
- ½ cup brown sugar, not pcaked
- 2 tablespoons butter

Pastry: Mix the flour and salt in a large bowl. Cut in the shortening. Sprinkle with cold water, 1 tablespoon at a time. Mix until flour is moistened. Shape the dough into a large ball; divide into two equal parts. Roll out the first ball on a floured surface to 1 inch larger than a 9-inch pie pan. Sprinkle the bottom crust with flour and ease it into the pie pan. Roll out the top crust.

Filling and assembly: Preheat oven to 425°. Place the apples in a large bowl. Add the remaining ingredients except the butter; stir to coat apples. Turn into pastry-lined pie pan and dot with butter. Cover with the top crust, then trim, seal, and flute edges and cut vents in the top. Bake 50–60 minutes or until crust is brown, apples are tender, and the juice bubbles.

Walla Walla Sweet Onion Blues Fest, Walla Walla, WA

Everyone in Washington's Walla Walla Valley takes pride in the local crop, and in July, thousands of Walla Wallans and visitors flock to the Sweet Onion Harvest Blues Fest in Fort Walla Walla Park. The event started out as a taste challenge from Georgia's Vidalia onion growers. Many participate in contests like the onion relay or onion sack races. Others come for the music, dancing, craft show, or car show. There is even an onion floral show and onion art show. In recent years, top-notch blues bands have been added. Many people come for the food, which features Walla Walla Sweets in everything from pizza and quiche to hamburgers and french-fried onion rings. A festival favorite is "onion flowers," sometimes called "blooming onions," which are whole crispy-fried onions cut to resemble flowers. Celebrity chefs demonstrate recipes calling for Walla Walla Sweets, and recipe collectors are in their glory. A highlight of the celebration is the onion recipe contest. Winning recipes are included in the official festival cookbook, *Walla Walla Sweet Onions*.

Walla Walla Sweet Onion Flower

The coveted recipe for this festival favorite was created for the Walla Walla Sweet Onion Marketing Committee by Susan Fowler Volland, food stylist and food editor.

2 Walla Walla Sweet Onions
½ cup flour
1 teaspoon salt
½ teaspoon freshly ground pepper
½ teaspoon dried oregano or 1 tablespoon fresh chopped oregano
¼ teaspoon paprika
½ teaspoon dry mustard
Nonstick vegetable cooking spray

Preheat oven to 425°. Lightly grease a large baking pan. Peel onions and cut the bottom level, leaving the core intact. To make the flower design, begin as if you are going to cut the onion in half, from top to bottom, but stop cutting ½ inch from the core. Cut the onion this way five times to form ten sections, or petals. Carefully loosen the petals slightly by rapping the onion lightly on the work surface and loosening them with your fingers. Remember that the flower will bloom more as it cooks.

Place the flour, salt, pepper, oregano, paprika, and mustard in a small paper bag. Spray the onions with cooking spray to lightly coat each petal. Put one onion in the bag and gently shake to coat. Remove the onion and pat off the excess flour. Put in the pan and repeat with the other onion. Spray the coated onions lightly again with cooking spray to aid in browning. Bake the onions for 35–40 minutes, until tender. Serve hot with your favorite sauce as a dip or with pork loin or grilled steak. Serves: 4.

Note: For a deep-fried onion flower, soak the cut onion in ice water for 30 minutes before frying. Pat dry with paper towels and lightly coat with flour mixture. Using a large fryer with plenty of oil heated to 375°, cook the coated onion for 3–4 minutes. Drain well and season again with salt and pepper. Serve hot.

DIRECTORY OF FESTIVALS BY MONTH

JANUARY
Holtville Carrot Festival, CA (Late January-early February, 10 days)

FEBRUARY
Fiesta Day, FL (2nd Saturday)

National Date Festival, CA (Mid-month for 10 days)

Red Snapper Festival, AL (Saturday before Mardi Gras)

Tee Mamou-lota Mardi Gras Folklife Festival, LA (Mardi Gras day)

Santa Cruz Clam Chowder Cook-Off and Festival, CA (Last Saturday)

Napa Valley Mustard Festival, CA (February until April)

Great American Pie Festival, various locations (A weekend in February)

MARCH
Penn Cove Mussel Festival, WA (1st weekend)

La Salle County Wild Hog Cook-off and Fair, TX (2nd weekend)

World's Largest Rattlesnake Round-Up, TX (2nd weekend)

Taste of Solvang, CA (3rd weekend)

World Championship Crawfish Etouffée Cook-off, LA (Last Sunday, moved up if on Easter)

Texas Crawfish and Saltwater Crab Festival, TX (Last week-end)

Parke County Maple Syrup Festival, IN (Last weekend in February and first weekend in March)

Wakarusa Maple Syrup Festival, IN (Weekend in March)

Chocolate Festival, OH (4th Friday before Easter)

SPAMARAMA, TX (Saturday in March or April)

APRIL
Prairie Dog Chili Cook-off, TX (1st weekend)

Allons Manger, LA (1st Sunday after Easter)

World Catfish Festival, MS (1st or 2nd Saturday, depending on Easter)

Poteet Strawberry Festival, TX (1st or 2nd weekend, depending on Easter)

Orange Blossom Festival, CA (3rd weekend)

Germanfest, TX (Last weekend)

Independence Italian Festival, LA (Last weekend)

International Ramp Cook-Off and Festival, WV (Last weekend)

Vidalia Onion Festival, GA (Last weekend)

Kenucky Derby Festival, KY (Begins end of April till 1st Saturday in May)

National Cornbread Festival, TN (Last weekend in April, or 1st in May)

Borrego Springs Grapefruit Festival, CA (Weekend in April)

World Grits Festival, SC (Weekend in April, depending on Easter)

The Feast of the Ramson, WV (Saturday in April)

Laurel Valley Village Spring Heritage, LA (Last Sunday)

MAY
Rhode Island May Breakfast, RI (All month)

Breaux Bridge Crawfish Festival, LA (1st weekend)

Dandelion May Fest, OH (1st weekend)

Fillmore Orange Festival, CA (1st weekend)

Fort Bend County Czech Fest, TX (1st weekend)

May Days Bean Fest, TX (1st weekend)

Selma Raisin Festival, CA (1st weekend)

Tucson Solar Potluck and Exhibition, AZ (2nd Saturday)

International BBQ Festival, KY (2nd weekend)

Mayhaw Festival, LA (2nd weekend in May)

Annual Rhubarb Fest, PA (3rd Saturday)

Springfield Highland Games and Celtic Festival, IL (3rd Saturday)

California Strawberry Festival, CA (3rd weekend)

Morel Mushroom Festival, MI (3rd weekend)

Orange City Tulip Festival, IA (3rd weekend)

Hellenic Festival, NY (2nd to last weekend)

Chocolate Fest, WI (Weekend after Mother's Day)

Houby Days, IA (Weekend after Mother's Day)

St. Anthony's Lebanese Food Festival, VA (Weekend after Mother's Day)

Asian Festival, OH (Memorial Day weekend)

Felsenthal Bream Festival, AR (Memorial Day weekend)

Jambalaya Festival, LA (Memorial Day weekend)

Kodiak Crab Festival, AK (Memorial Day weekend)

New Mexico Wine and Chile War Festival, NM (Memorial Day weekend)

The Great Monterey Squid Festival, CA (Memorial Day weekend)

Tivoli Fest, IA (Memorial Day weekend)

Fisherman's Free Breakfast, ID (Late May)

JUNE

Patterson Apricot Fiesta, CA (Weekend after Memorial Day)

Hungarian Festival, NJ (1st Saturday)

Le Festival de L'Heritage Francais, IA (1st Saturday)

French Market Tomato Festival, LA (1st weekend)

Great Wisconsin Cheese Festival, WI (1st weekend)

International Horseradish Festival, IL (1st weekend)

Troy Strawberry Festival, OH (1st weekend)

Beef Empire Days, KS (1st two weeks)

Asian Moon Festival, WI (Father's Day weekend)

Jacksonville Annual Tomato Fest, TX (2nd week)

Bradley County Pink Tomato Festival, AR (2nd weekend)

Galveston Caribbean Mardi Gras Carnival, TX (2nd weekend)

Louisiana Corn Festival, LA (2nd weekend)

Texas Folklife Festival, TX (2nd weekend)

Aebleskiver Days, MN (Weekend after Father's Day)

North Beach Festival, CA (3rd weekend)

Pecan Festival, OK (3rd weekend)

Polish Fest, WI (3rd weekend)

Stonewall Peach JAMboree and Rodeo, TX (3rd weekend)

Swedish Festival, NE (3rd weekend)

Clarkson Czech Festival, NE (4th weekend)

Fresh Fruit Festival, CA (4th weekend)

Night in Old Pecos Cantaloupe Festival, TX (Last Saturday)

Acadian Festival, ME (Last week)

Hampton County Watermelon Festival, SC (Last week)

Festival of American Folklife, D.C. (Last week of June and 1st of July)

Delmarva Chicken Festival, Delmarva Peninsula (Weekend in June)

Duncan Hines Festival, KY (Weekend in June)

JULY

National Basque Festival, NV (1st weekend)

International Rhubarb Festival, CO (4th of July)

Sagebrush Days, ID (4th of July)

Kutztown Pennsylvania German, PA (4th of July week)

Mandeville Seafood Festival, LA (4th of July weekend)

Bean Hole Days, MN (Tues & Wed following 4th of July)

National Cherry Festival, MI (1st Sat after 4th of July for 8 days)

Lauderdale County Tomato Festival, TN (1st weekend after 4th of July)

Italian Heritage and Food Festival, NY (2nd week)

Heritagefest, MN (2nd and 3rd weekends)

J. Millard Tawes Crab and Clam Bake, MD (3rd Wednesday)

National Baby Food Festival, MI (3rd week)

Burgerfest, NY (3rd Saturday)

Traditional Tea and Summer fun Lawn Party, NH (3rd Saturday)

North Dakota Ukrainian Festival, ND (3rd weekend)

SerbFest, NY (2nd to last weekend)

Central Maine Egg Festival, ME (4th Saturday)

Altus Area Grape Festival, AR (4th weekend)

After Harvest Czech Festival, KS (Last weekend)

Bagelfest, IL (Last week)

Gilroy Garlic Festival, CA (Last weekend)

Nordic Fest, IA (Last weekend)

Herb Festival, IA (Last Sunday)

La Fiesta de Santiago y Santa Ana, NM (Late July)

Dixon Lambtown USA Festival, CA (Saturday in July)

Hopkins Raspberry Festival, MN (10 days in July)

Walla Walla Sweet Onion Blue Fest, WA (Weekend in July)

An Evening at Hancock Shaker Village, MA (Mid-July till mid-Aug, mid-Sept till mid-Oct)

AUGUST

Braham Pie Day, MN (1st Friday)

Paso Robles Basil Festival, CA (1st Saturday)

Summer Loaf: A Celebration of Bread, OR (1st Saturday)

Bratwurst Days, WI (1st weekend)

California Dry Bean Festival, CA (1st weekend)

Country Threshing Days, KS (1st weekend)

Crab Days, MD (1st weekend)

Fox Run Vineyards Garlic Festival, NY (1st weekend)

Maine Lobster Festival, ME (1st weekend)

Maui Onion Festival, HI (1st weekend)

Phelps Sauerkraut Festival, NY (1st weekend)

Pig Gig Rib Fest, MI (1st weekend)

Stanton Corn Festival, KY (1st weekend)

Nebraska Czech Festival, NE (1st weekend)

Harmon County Black-eyed Pea Festival, OK (2nd Saturday)

Wild Blackberry Arts and Crafts Festival, OR (2nd weekend)

Bluefish Festival, CT (3rd week)

International Vinegar Festival, SD (3rd Saturday)

Machias Wild Blueberry Festival, ME (3rd weekend)

Pepper Festival, WI (3rd weekend)

Round Valley Blackberry Festival, CA (3rd weekend)

Slavic Village Harvest Festival, OH (3rd weekend)

International Quahog Festival, RI (4th weekend)

Houlton Potato Feast Day, ME (Last weekend)

Fall Mushroom Mania, MI (Late August through September)

Gueydan Duck Festival, LA (Weekend before Labor Day)

Rutabaga Festival, WI (Weekend before Labor Day)

Shrimp Fest, TX (Weekend in August or September)

SEPTEMBER

Lenexa Spinach and Trails Fest, KS (1st Saturday)

Cheyenne Cowboy Synposium & Celebration, WY (Labor Day weekend)

Fiesta en la Playa, TX (Labor Day weekend)

Hatch Chile Festival, NM (Labor Day weekend)

Japanese Festival, MO (Labor Day weekend)

Lake Vermilion Wild Rice Festival, MN (Labor Day weekend)

Ligonier Marshmallow Festival, IN (Labor Day weekend)

Louisiana Shrimp and Petroleum Festival, LA (Labor Day weekend)

Marshall County Blueberry Festival, IN (Labor Day weekend)

Oatmeal Festival, TX (Labor Day weekend)

Rayne Frog Festival, LA (Labor Day weekend)

World Championship BBQ Goat Cook-Off, TX (Labor Day weekend)

Chokecherry Festival, MT (1st Saturday after Labor Day)

Eastport Salmon Festival, ME (1st Sunday after Labor Day)

Cajun Heritage Festival, LA (1st weekend after Labor Day)

Peach Days, UT (Weekend after Labor Day)

United Tribes International Powwow, ND (1st weekend after Labor Day)

McClure Bean Soup, PA (2nd Tuesday through Saturday)

Hopkins County Fall Festival, TX (2nd week)

Morton Pumpkin Festival, IL (2nd week)

Kolache Festival, TX (2nd Saturday)

Okrafest! And Fall Food Festival, OK (2nd Saturday)

Old Settler's Day, IL (2nd Saturday)

California Dried Plum Festival, CA (2nd weekend)

Honey-Walnut Classic, IA (2nd weekend)

Jubilee Autumn Harvestfest, IL (2nd weekend)

Mushroom Festival, PA (2nd weekend)

Danish Days, CA (A weekend in mid-September)

Idaho Spud Day, ID (3rd Saturday)

Loomis Eggplant Festival, CA (3rd Saturday)

Applejack Festival, NE (3rd weekend)

North Carolina Turkey Festival, NC (3rd weekend)

Peanut Butter Festival, PA (3rd weekend)

Staunton's Annual African-American Heritage Festival, VA (3rd weekend)

Warrens Cranberry Festival, WI (3rd weekend)

Castroville Artichoke Festival, CA (3rd or 4th weekend)

Old Market Days and BBQ on the River, KY (4th weekend)

Persimmon Festival, IN (Last full week)

Isanti County Potato Festival, MN (Last Saturday)

Alligator Festival, LA (Last weekend)

Genoa Candy Dance, NV (Last weekend)

Hudson Valley Garlic Festival, NY (Last weekend)

Irmo Okra Strut, SC (Last weekend)

Kelseyville Pear Festival, CA (Last weekend)

Louisiana Sugar Cane Festival and Fair, LA (Last weekend)

Texas Rice Festival, TX (Last weekend)

Jordbruksdagarna, IL (Last weekend)

World Chicken Festival, KY (Last weekend)

Kentucky Bourbon Festival, KY (Weekend in September)

Waldo Sorghum Sopping Days, AL (Weekend in September)

Ohio Swiss Festival, OH (4th weekend after Labor Day, September/October)

OCTOBER
Roberts Cove Germanfest, LA (1st weekend)

Eagle River Cranberry Festival and Fitness Weekend, WI (1st weekend)

Long Beach Island Chowderfest, NJ (1st weekend before Columbus Day weekend)

Morro Bay Harbor Festival, CA (1st weekend)

The Whale enchilada Fiesta, NM (1st weekend)

North Carolina Seafood Festival, NC (1st weekend)

Scandinavian Food Fest, IA (1st Saturday)

National Apple Harvest Festival, PA (1st two weekends)

Fall Festival of Spoon River Scenic Drive, IL (1st two weekends)

Topsfield Fair, MA (10 days ending on Columbus Day)

National Lima Bean Festival, NJ (Saturday of Columbus Day weekend)

Abalone Festival, CA (Columbus Day weekend)

Apple Butter Festival, WV (Columbus Day weekend)

Gumbo Festival, LA (2nd weekend)

National Shrimp Festival, AL (2nd weekend)

Virginia Garlic Festival, VA (2nd weekend)

West Virginia Black Walnut Festival, WV (2nd weekend)

Laurel Valley Village Heritage Festival, LA (2nd Sunday)

Carver Sweet Potato Arts & Craft Festival, AL (3rd Saturday)

Circleville Pumpkin Show, OH (3rd Wednesday till Saturday)

Deutsch Country Days, MO (3rd weekend)

Goleta Lemon Festival, CA (3rd weekend)

St. Mary's County Oyster Festival, MD (3rd weekend)

Alabama Chitlin Jamboree, AL (Last Saturday)

Andouille Festival, LA (Last weekend)

French Food Festival, LA (Last weekend)

Louisiana Yambilee, LA (Last weekend)

Peanut Butter Festival, AL (Saturday in October)

South County Museum Annual Harvest Festival and Apple Pie Contest, RI (Sunday in October)

Feast of the Hunter's Moon, IN (Weekend in October)

Trigg County Ham Festival, KY (Weekend in October)

The Great Louisiana Beerfest, LA (Last October, early November)

NOVEMBER
Oysterfest, MD (1st Saturday)

Kona Coffee Cultural Festival, HI (1st week)

Founders Day Communal Meal, IA (2nd Saturday)

Annual Wild Game Supper, VT (Saturday before Thanksgiving)

Holiday Fold Fair International, WI (Weekend before Thanksgiving)

Holland Dutch Winterfest, MI (Day after Thanksgiving till 3rd Sunday in December)

Julmarknad, IL (Thanksgiving weekend and following weekend)

Karla's Great Cheesecakes Openhouse, VA (Day after Thanksgiving till Christmas)

DECEMBER
Christmas Pickle Festival, MI (1st weekend)

Norwegian Christmas, IA (1st weekend)

Indio International Tamale Festival, CA (1st weekend)

Plaquemines Parish Fair and Orange Festival, LA (1st weekend)

Laurel Valley Village Cajun Christmas Open House, LA (1st Sunday)

Lucia Night, IL (Weekend closest to December 13)

DIRECTORY OF FESTIVALS BY STATE

ALABAMA
Alabama Chitlin
Jamboree
P.O. Box 64
Clio, AL 36017-0064

Carver Sweet Potato
Arts & Craft Festival
National Park Service
Tuskegee Institute
National Historic Site
P.O. Drawer 10
Tuskegee Institute, AL
36087-0010
Tel: (334) 727-3200; Fax:
(334) 727-4597

National Shrimp Festival
Alabama Gulf Coast
Area Chamber of
Commerce
P.O. Drawer 3869
Gulf Shores, Alabama
36547
Tel: (334) 968-6901 or
(251) 745-6904; Fax:
(251) 968-5332

Peanut Butter Festival
Brundidge Historical
Society
128 South Main St.
Brundidge, AL 36010
Tel: (334) 735-3608

Red Snapper Festival
Orange Beach Sports
Association
P.O. Box 1253
Orange Beach, AL 36561
Tel: (334) 974-1672

Waldo Sorghum Sopping
Days
Town of Waldo
Route 3
Talladega, AL 35160

ALASKA
Kodiak Crab Festival
Kodiak Chamber of
Commerce
P.O. Box 1485
Kodiak, AK 99615
Tel: (907) 486-5557; Fax:
(907) 486-7605

ARIZONA
Tucson Solar Potluck
and Exhibition
Toby Schneider,
Chairman
Citizens for Solar
4417 N. Pomona
Tucson, AZ 85705-1311
Tel: (520) 292-9020

ARKANSAS
Altus Area Grape
Festival
Altus Chamber of
Commerce
P.O. Box 404
Altus, AR 72821
Tel: (501) 468-1414

Bradley County Pink
Tomato Festival
Bradley County
Chamber of Commerce
104 N. Myrtle Street
Warren, AR 71671
Tel: (870) 226-5225; Fax:
(870) 226-6285

Felsenthal Bream Festival
El Dorado Chamber of
Commerce
201 N. Jackson
El Dorado, AR 71731-
1271
Tel: (870) 863-6113; Fax:
(870) 863-6115

CALIFORNIA
Abalone Festival
Van Damme State Park
P.O. Box 440
Mendocino, CA 95460
Tel: (707) 937-4016

Borrego Springs
Grapefruit Festival
Borrego Springs
Chamber of Commerce
P.O. Box 420
Borrego Springs, CA
92004
Tel: (800) 559-5524 or
(760) 767-5976

California Dried Plum
Festival
P.O. Box 3006
Yuba City, CA 95992
Tel: (530) 671-3100; Fax:
(530) 671-3555

California Dry Bean
Festival
223 E. 10th Street
Tracy, CA 95376
Tel: (209) 835-2131; Fax:
(209) 833-9526

California Strawberry
Festival
1661 Pacific Avenue,

Suite # 15
Oxnard, CA 93033
Tel: (805) 385-4739

Castroville Artichoke
Festival
Castroville Festivals Inc.
P.O. Box 1041
Castroville, CA 95012
Tel: (831) 633-2465; Fax:
(831) 633-0485

Danish Days
Solvang Conference &
Visitors Bureau
P.O. Box 70
Solvang, CA 93464
Tel: (800) 468-6765 or
(805) 688-6144

Dixon Lambtown USA
Festival
Dixton District Chamber
of Commerce
110 E. Mayes
Dixon, CA 95620
Tel: (707) 678-2650 or
(707) 678-7386

Fillmore Orange Festival
Fillmore Chamber of
Commerce
354 Central Avenue
Fillmore, CA 93015
Tel: (805) 524-0351 or
(805) 524-7500

Fresh Fruit Festival
Reedley District
Chamber of Commerce
and Visitors Bureau
1158 G Street
Reedley, CA 93654

Tel: (559) 638-3548 or
(559) 638-5484; Fax:
(559) 638-8479

Gilroy Garlic Festival
P.O. Box 2311
Gilroy, CA 95021
Tel: (408) 842-1625

Goleta Lemon Festival
The Goleta Valley
Chamber of Commerce
P.O. Box 781
Goleta, CA 93116
Tel: (800) 646-5382 or
(805) 967-4618; Fax:
(805) 967-4615

Holtville Carrot Festival
Holtville Chamber of
Commerce
P.O. Box 185, 101 W. 5th
Street
Holtville, CA 92250
Tel: (760) 356-2923; Fax:
(760) 356-2925

Indio International
Tamale Festival
City of Indio
100 Civic Center Mall
Indio, CA 92201
Tel: (760) 342-6532; Fax:
(760) 342-6556

Kelseyville Pear Festival
Lake County Marketing
Program
875 Lakeport Boulevard
Lakeport, CA 95453-
5405
Tel: (800) 525-3743 or
(707) 279-9022

Loomis Eggplant Festival
Loomis Basin Chamber

of Commerce
P.O. Box 1212
Loomis, CA 95650
Tel: (916) 652-7252
Morro Bay Harbor
Festival
P.O. Box 1869
Morro Bay, CA 93443
Tel: (800) 366-6043 or
(805) 772-1155; Fax:
(805) 772-2107

Napa Valley Mustard
Festival
P.O. Box 1385
Sonoma, CA 95476
Tel: (707) 938-1133; Fax:
(707) 938-0123

National Date Festival
Riverside County Fair &
National Date Festival
Fairgrounds
Administration Office
46-350 Arabia Street
Indio, CA 92201
Tel: (800) 811-3247 or
(760) 863-8247; Fax:
(760) 863-8973

North Beach Festival
North Beach Chamber
of Commerce
556 Columbus Avenue
San Francisco, CA 94133
Tel: (415) 989-2220

Orange Blossom Festival
P.O. Box 1603
Riverside, CA 92502-
1603
Tel: (800) 382-8202; Fax:
(909) 715-3404

Paso Robles Basil
Festival

Sycamore Farms
2485 Highway 46 West
Paso Robles, CA 93446
Tel: (800) 576-5288 or
(805) 238-5288; Fax:
(805) 238-2187

Patterson Apricot Fiesta
P.O. Box 442
Patterson, CA 95363
Tel: (209) 892-3118: Fax:
(209) 892-3388

Round Valley Blackberry
Festival
Round Valley Public
Library
P.O. Box 620
Covelo, CA 95428
Tel: (707) 983-6736

Santa Cruz Clam
Chowder Cook Off and
Festival
Santa Cruz Seaside
Company
Attention: Marketing
Department
400 Beach Street
Santa Cruz, CA 95060-
5491
Tel: (831) 423-5590; Fax:
(831) 423-2438

Selma Raisin Festival
Selma District Chamber
of Commerce
1710 Tucker Street
Selma, CA 93662

Tel: (559) 896-1054; Fax:
(559) 896-1068

Taste of Solvang
Solvang Conference &
Visitors Bureau

P.O. Box 70
Solvang, CA 93464
Tel: (800) 468-6765 or
(805) 686-9386

The Great Monterey
Squid Festival
2107 Del Monte Avenue
Monterey, CA 93940
Tel: (831) 649-6544; Fax:
(831) 649-4124

COLORADO
Great American Pie
Festival
1200 Wilmette Avenue,
Suite 360
Wilmette, IL 60091
Tel: (847) 920-9905; Fax:
(847) 90-9886

International Rhubarb
Festival
Silverton Public Library
P.O. Box 68, 1111 Reese
Street
Silverton, CO 81433
Tel: (970) 387-5770; Fax:
(970) 387-0217

CONNECTICUT
Bluefish Festival
Clinton Chamber of
Commerce
50 E. Main St., P.O. Box
334
Clinton, CT 06413
Tel: (860) 669-3889

DELAWARE
Delmarva Chicken
Festival
Delmarva Peninsula, DE,
MD or VA
Delmarva Poultry
Industry, Inc.

16686 County Seat
Highway
Georgetown, DE 19947-
4881
Tel: (302) 856-9037 or
(410) 957-1919; Fax:
(302) 856-1845

FLORIDA
Fiesta Day
Ybor City Chamber of
Commerce
1600 8th Avenue East
Tampa, FL 33605
Tel: (813) 248-3712 or
(813) 241-8831; Fax:
(813) 247-1764

GEORGIA
Vidalia Onion Festival
P.O. Box 2285
Vidalia, GA 30475
Tel: (912) 538-8687

HAWAII
Kona Coffee Cultural
Festival
P.O. Box 1112
Kailua-Kona, HI 96745
Tel: (808) 326-7820: Fax:
(808) 326-5634

Maui Onion Festival
Whalers Village
Management Office
2435 Ka'anapali
Parkway, Bldg. H-6
Lahaina, Maui, HI 96761
Tel: (808) 661-4567; Fax:
(808) 661-8584

IDAHO
Fisherman's Free
Breakfast
Greater St. Anthony
Chamber of Commerce

114 N. Bridge Street
St. Anthony, ID 83445
Tel: (208) 624-4870 or
(208) 624-3711

Idaho Spud Day
Shelley Chamber of
Commerce
Box 301
Shelley, ID 83274
Tel: (208) 357-7661

Sagebrush Days
Buhl Chamber of
Commerce
716 Highway 30 East
Buhl, ID 83316
Tel: (208) 543-6682 or
(208) 543-2185

ILLINOIS
Bagelfest
Mattoon Chamber of
Commerce
1701 Wabash Ave.
Mattoon, IL 61938
Tel: (217) 235-5661; Fax:
(217) 234-6544

Fall Festival of Spoon
River Scenic Drive
Spoon River Valley
Scenic Drive
P.O. Box 525
canton, IL 61520
Tel: (309) 647-8980

International
Horseradish Festival
C/o Judy McCann
P/O. Box 766
Collinsville, IL 62234

Jordbruksdagarna
(Agricultural Days)
Bishop Hill State

Historic Site
P.O. Box 104
Bishop Hill, IL 61419
Tel: (309) 927-3345

Jubilee Autumn
Harvestfest
Jubilee College State
Historic Site
RR 2, Box 72A
Brimfield, IL 61517
Tel: (309) 243-9489

Julmarknad (Christmas
Market)
Bishop Hill State
Historic Site
P.O. Box 104
Bishop Hill, IL 61419
Tel: (309) 927-3345

Lucia Nights
Bishop Hill State
Historic Site
P.O. Box 104
Bishop Hill, IL 61419
Tel: (309) 927-3345

Morton Pumpkin
Festival
Morton Chamber of
Commerce
415 W. Jefferson Street
Morton, IL 61550
Tel: (888) 765-6588; Fax:
(309) 263-2401

Old Settler's Day
Bishop Hill State
Historic Site
P.O. Box 104
Bishop Hill, IL 61419
Tel: (309) 927-3345

Springfield Highland
Games and Celtic

Festival
St. Andrew's Society of
Central Illinois
P.O. Box 535

Springfield, IL 62705
Tel: (217) 241-3000

INDIANA
Feast of the Hunter's
Moon
Tippecanoe County
Historical Association
909 South Street
Lafayette, IN 47901
Tel: (765) 476-8411; Fax:
(765) 476-8414

Ligonier Marshmallow
Festival
Ligonier Visitors Center
& Radio Museum
800 Lincolnway South
Ligonier, IN 46767
Tel: (219) 894-9000

Marshall County
Blueberry Festival
Marshall County
Convention & Visitors
Bureau
P.O. Box 669
Plymouth, IN 46563
Tel: (800) 626-5353 or
(219) 936-9000; Fax:
(219) 936-9845

Parke County Maple
Syrup Festival
P.O. Box 165
Rockville, IN 47872
Tel: (765) 569-5226

Persimmon Festival
Greater Mitchell
Chamber of Commerce

602 W. Main Street
Mitchell, IN 47446
Tel: (812) 849-4441

Wakarusa Maple Syrup
Festival
Wakarusa Chamber of
Commerce
P.O. Box 291
Wakarusa, IN 46573
Tel: (219) 862-4344

IOWA
Founders Day
Communal Meal
Amana Arts Guild
P.O. Box 114
Amana, IA 52203
Tel: (319) 622-3678

Herb Festival
Under the Spell Herb
Shop
115 N. Main Street
Greene, IA 50636
Tel: (641) 823-5636 or
9641) 823-4562; Fax:
(641) 823-5636

Honey-Walnut Classic
Inn of the Six-Toed Cat
P.O. Box 6
Allerton, IA 50008
Tel: (641) 873-4900

Houby Days
Czech Village
Association
30 16th Avenue SW
Cedar Rapids, IA 52404-
5904
Tel: (319) 362-8500

Le Festival de L'Heritage
Francais
710 Davis Avenue

Corning, IA 50841
Tel: (641) 322-5229; Fax:
(641) 322-4387

Nordic Fest
Vesterheim Norwegian-
American Museum
P.O. Box 379
Decorah, IA 52101
Tel: (800) 382-3378 or
(563) 382-9681; Gift
Shop Tel: (800) 979-3346;
Fax: (563) 382-8828

Norwegian Christmas
Vesterheim Norwegian-
American Museum
P.O. Box 379
Decorah, IA 52101
Tel: (319) 382-9681; Gift
Shop Tel: (800) 979-3346

Orange City Tulip
Festival
Chamber of Commerce
P.O. Box 36
Orange City, IA 51041
Tel: (712) 737-4510; Fax:
(712) 737-4523

Scandinavian Food Fest
Vesterheim Norwegian-
American Museum
P.O. Box 379
Decorah, IA 52101
Tel: (800) 382-3378 or
(563) 382-9681; Gift
Shop Tel: (800) 979-3346;
Fax: (563) 382-8828

Tivoli Fest
Danish Windmill
P.O. Box 245
Elk Horn, IA 51531
Tel: (800) 451-7960 or
(712) 764-7472; Fax:

(712) 764-7475

KANSAS
After Harvest Czech
Festival
Wilson Chamber of
Commerce
P.O. Box 328
Wilson, KS 67490
Tel: (785) 658-2211; Fax:
(785) 658-3344

Beef Empire Days
405 N. 6th St., P.O. Box
1197
Garden City, KS 67846
Tel: (316) 275-6807; Fax:
(316) 275-7481

Country Threshing Days
Mennonite Heritage
Museum
P.O. Box 231, 200 N.
Poplar
Goessel, KS 67053
Tel: (620) 367-8200

Lenexa Spinach and
Trails Fest
Lenexa Chamber of
Commerce
11180 Lackman Road
Lenexa, KS 66219
Tel: (913) 888-1414; Fax:
(913) 888-3770

KENTUCKY
Duncan Hines Festival
Bowling Green-Warren
County Tourist &
Convention Commission
352 Three Springs Road
Bowling Green, KY
42104-7519
Tel: (270) 782-0800; Fax:
(270) 842-2104

International Bar-B-Q
Festival
P.O. Box 434
Owensboro, KY 42302
Tel: (270) 926-6938

Kentucky Bourbon
Festival
Bardstown Tourist &
Convention Commission
P.O. Box 867B
Bardstown, KY 40004
Tel: (800) 638-4877; Fax:
(502) 349-0804

Kentucky Derby Festival
1001 South Third Street
Louiseville, KY 40203
Tel: (502) 584-6383
or
Louisville and Jefferson
County Convention &
Visitors Bureau
400 South First St.
Louisville, KY 40202
Tel: (502) 584-2121 or
(800) 626-5646

Old Market Days and
Barbecue on the River
Paducah-McCracken
County Tourist Bureau
128 Broadway
Paducah, KY 42001
Tel: (800) PADUCAH;
Fax: (270) 443-8784

Stanton Corn Festival
Powell County Tourism
Commission
P.O. Box 1028
Stanton, KY 40380-1028
Tel: (606) 663-1161 or
(606) 663-2271; Fax:
(606) 663-6684

Trigg County Ham
Festival
Cadiz-Trigg County
Tourist Commission
P.O. Box 735
Cadiz, KY 42211
Tel: (888) 446-6402 or
(270) 522-3892; Fax:
(270) 522-6343

World Chicken Festival
London-Laurel County
Tourist Commission
140 W. Daniel Boone
Parkway
London, KY 40741
Tel: (606) 878-6900 or
(800) 348-0095

LOUISIANA
Alligator Festival
(Boutte, LA)
St. Charles Parish
P.O. Box 302
Hahnville, LA 70057
Tel: (985) 783-5000; Fax:
(985) 783-5015

Allons Manger
St. Jules Catholic Church
P.O. Box 38
Belle Rose, LA 70341
Tel: (225) 473-8569

Andouille Festival
St. John the Baptist
Parish
1801 West Airline
Highway
LaPlace, LA 70068
Tel: (985) 652-9569

Breaux Bridge Crawfish
Festival
P.O. Box 25
Breaux Bridge, LA 70517

Tel: (337) 332-6655; Fax:
(337) 332-5917

Cajun Heritage Festival
P.O. Box 582
Cut Off, LA 70345
Tel: (985) 537-5444

French Food Festival
Larose Regional Park &
Civic Center
P.O. Box 1105
Larose, LA 70373
Tel: (985) 693-7355; Fax:
(985) 693-7380

French Market Tomato
Festival (Creole Tomato
Festival)
French Market
Corporation
1008 North Peters Street
New Orleans, LA 70116
Tel: (504) 522-2621; Fax:
(502) 596-3419

Gueydan Duck Festival
P.O. Box 179, 1011 2nd
Street
Gueydan, LA 70542
Tel: (888) 536-6456 or
(337) 235-6263

Gumbo Festival
P.O. Box 9069
Bridge City, LA 70094
Tel: (504) 436-4712; Fax:
(504) 436-4070

Independence Italian
Festival
Independence Chamber
of Commerce
P.O. Box 790, 583 W.
Railroad Avenue

Independence, LA 70443
Tel: (985) 878-1902

Jambalaya Festival
Jambalaya Festival
Association
P.O. Box 1243
Gonzales, LA 70707-
1243
Tel: (225) 647-9566

Laurel Valley Village:
Spring Heritage Festival,
Fall Heritage Festival
and Cajun Christmas
Open House
P.O. Box 340
Raceland, LA 70394
Tel: (504) 537-5800; Fax:
(504) 537-5831

Louisiana Corn Festival
Bunkie Chamber of
Commerce
P.O. Drawer 70
Bunkie, LA 71322
Tel: (318) 346-2575; Fax:
(318) 346-6888

Louisiana Shrimp and
Petroleum Festival
P.O. Box 103
Morgan City, LA 70381
Tel: (504) 385-0703 or
(985) 256-2931; Fax:
(985) 384-4628

Louisiana Sugar Cane
Festival and Fair
Association
P.O. Box 9768
New Iberia, LA 70562-
9768
Tel: (337) 369-9323

Louisiana Yambilee
P.O. Box 44
Opelousas, LA 70570
Tel: (337) 948-8848; Fax:
(337) 948-4331

Mandeville Seafood
Festival Association
P.O. Box 1000
Mandeville, LA 70470-
1000
Tel: (985) 624-9762; Fax:
(985) 626-3493

Mayhaw Festival
Marion Town Hall
Marion, LA 71260
Tel: (318) 292-4716 or
(318) 292-4717

Plaquemines Parish Fair
and Orange Festival
(Buras, LA)
C/o Paula Capiello
P.O. Box 309
Port Sulphur, LA 70083
Tel: (504) 564-2951
Or
Plaquemines Parish
Economic Development
&Tourism
P.O. Box 937
Belle Chasse, LA 70037
Tel: (888) 745-0642 or
(504) 394-0018; Fax:
(504) 394-0052

Rayne Frog Festival
Rayne Chamber of
Commerce
P.O. Box 383
Rayne, LA 70578
Tel: (337) 334-2332; Fax:
(337) 334-8341

Roberts Cove
Germanfest
7166 Roberts Cove Rd.
Rayne, LA 70578
Tel: (337) 334-8354 or
(877) 783-2142; Fax:
(337) 334-5950

Tee Mamou-Iota Mardi
Gras Folklife Festival
Larry Miller
886 McMillan Avenue
Iota, LA 70543

The Great Louisiana
BeerFest
St. Tammany Humane
Society
20384 Harrison Avenue
Covington, LA 70433
Tel: (504) 892-PETS

World Championship
Crawfish Etouffée
Cook-Off
Eunice Chamber of
Commerce
P.O. Box 508
Eunice, LA 70535
Tel: (337) 457-2565; Fax:
(337) 457-0200

MAINE
Acadian Festival
Madawaska Chamber of
Commerce
378 Main Street
Madawaska, ME 004756
Tel: (207) 728-7000; Fax:
(207) 728-4696

Central Maine Egg
Festival
P.O. Box 82
Pittsfield, ME 04967
Tel: (207) 368-4698

Eastport Salmon Festival
Eastport Area Chamber
of Commerce
P.O. Box 254
Eastport, ME 04631
Tel: (207) 853-4644

Houlton Potato Feast
Days
Greater Houlton
Chamber of Commerce
109 Main Street
Houlton, ME 04730
Tel: (207) 532-4216

Machias Wild Blueberry
Festival
Centre Street
Congregational Church
P.O. Box 265
Machias, ME 04654
Tel: (207) 255-6665

Maine Lobster Festival
P.O. Box 552
Rockland, ME 04841
Tel: (800) LOB-CLAW
or (207) 596-0376

MARYLAND
Crab Days
Chesapeake Bay
Maritime Museum
P.O. Box 636
St. Michaels, MD 21663-
0636
Tel: (410) 745-2916; Fax:
(410) 745-6088

J. Millard Tawes Crab
and Clam Bake
Crisfield Area Chamber
of Commerce
P.O. Box 292
Crisfield, MD 21817
Tel: (800) 782-3913 or

(410) 968-2500; Fax:
(410) 968-0524

Oysterfest
Chesapeake Bay
Maritime Museum, Inc.
P.O. Box 636
St. Michaels, MD 21663-
0636
Tel: (410) 745-2916; Fax:
(410) 745-6088

St. Mary's County
Oyster Festival
P.O. Box 653
Lewistown, MD 20650
Tel: (301) 863-5015; Fax:
(301) 863-7789

MASSACHUSETTS
An Evening at Hancock
Shaker Village
Hancock Shaker Village
P.O. Box 927
Pittsfield, MA 01202
Tel: (413) 443-0188

Topsfield Fair
P.O. Box 134
Topsfield, MA 01983-
0234
Tel: (978) 887-5000; Fax:
(978) 887-3016

MICHIGAN
Christmas Pickle Festival
Box 316
Berrien Springs, MI
49103
Tel: (616) 471-9680

Fall Mushroom Mania
Springbrook Hills Resort
P.O. Box 219
Walloon Lake, MI 49796

Tel: (800) 530-9009 or
(231) 535-2227

Holland Dutch
Winterfest
Holland Convention and
Visitors Bureau
100 East 8th Street, Suite
120
Holland, MI 49423
Tel: (800) 506-1299 or
(616) 394-0000; Fax:
(616) 394-0122

Morel Mushroom
Festival
Boyne Area Chamber of
Commerce
28 South Lake Street
Boyne City, MI 49712
Tel: (231) 582-6222; (231)
582-6963

National Baby Food
Festival
Fremont Chamber of
Commerce
93 Main Street
Fremont, MI 49412
Tel: (231) 924-0770; Fax:
(231) 924-9248

National Cherry Festival
108 West Grandview
Parkway
Traverse City, MI 49684
Tel: (231) 947-4230; Fax:
(231) 947-7435

Pig Gig Rib Fest
P.O. Box 9
Bay City, MI 48706
Tel: (989) 684-8410 or
(989) 893-4567; Fax:
(989) 684-4173

MINNESOTA

Aebleskiver Days
Tyler Tribute
Box Q
Tyler, MN 56178
Tel: (507) 247-5502; Fax:
(507) 247-5502

Bean Hole Days
Pequot Lakes Chamber
of Commerce
P.O. Box 208
Pequot Lakes, MN
56472
Tel: (800) 950-0291 or
(218) 568-8911; Fax:
(218) 568-8910

Braham Pie Day
P.O. Box 383
Cambridge, MN 55006
Tel: (612) 689-4229; Fax:
(612) 689-4229

Heritagefest
P.O. Box 461
New Ulm, MN 56073
Tel: (507) 354-8850; Fax:
(507) 354-8853

Hopkins Raspberry
Festival Association
P.O. Box 504
Hopkins, MN 55343
Tel: (952) 931-0878

Isanti County Potato
Festival
Isanti County Historical
Society
P.O. Box 525
Cambridge, MN 55008
Tel: (763) 689-4229; Fax:
(763) 689-5134

Lake Vermilion Wild
Rice Festival
Tower-Soudan Chamber
of Commerce
P.O. Box 776
Tower, MN 55790
Tel: (218) 753-5711

MISSISSIPPI

World Catfish Festival
P.O. Box 385
Belzoni, MS 39038-0385
Tel: (800) 408-4838 or
(662) 247-4838

MISSOURI

Deutsch Country Days
Luxenhaus Farm
5437 Highway O
Marthasville, MO 63357
Tel: (636) 433-5669; Fax:
(636) 433-5275

Japanese Festival
Missouri Botanical
Garden
P.O. Box 299
St. Louis, MO 63166-
0299
(800) 642-8842

MONTANA

Chokecherry Festival
Lewistown Area
Chamber of Commerce
408 NE Main
Lewistown, MT 59457
Tel: (406) 538-5436; Fax:
(406) 538-5437

NEBRASKA

Applejack Festival
Office of Tourism &
Events
806 1st Avenue

Nebraska City, NE
68410
Tel: (800) 514-9113 or
(402) 873-3000

Clarkson Czech Festival
City of Clarkson
126 W. Second Street,
Box 18
Clarkson, NE 68629-
0018
Tel: (401) 892-3100; Fax:
(402) 892-3141

Nebraska Czech Festival
Wilber Chamber of
Commerce
P.O. Box 1164
Wilber, NE 68465
Tel: (888)-4WILBER or
(402) 821-2331; Fax:
(402) 494-5237

Swedish Festival
P.O. Box 715
Stromsburg, NE 68666
Tel: (402) 764-2226

NEVADA

Genoa Candy Dance
Town of Genoa
P.O. Box 155
Genoa, NV 89411
Tel: (775) 782-8696

National Basque Festival
Elko Basque Club
P.O. Box 1321
Elko, NV 89803

NEW HAMPSHIRE

Traditional Tea and
Summer Fun Lawn Party
Remick Country Doctor
Museum and Farm
58 Cleveland Hill Road

P.O. Box 250
Tamworth, NH 03886
Tel: (800) 686-6117; Fax:
(603) 323-8382

NEW JERSEY

Hungarian Festival
Hungarian Civic
Association
P.O. Box 1144
New Brunswick, NJ
08903
Tel: (732) 846-5777; Fax:
(732) 249-7033

Long Beach Island
Chowderfest
Southern Ocean County
Chamber of Commerce
265 West 9th Street
Ship Bottom, NJ 08008
Tel: (609) 494-7211; Fax:
(609) 494-5801

National Lima Bean
Festival
Alys Dolmetsch
19 Debbie Lane
W. Cape May, NJ 08204

NEW MEXICO

Hatch Chile Festival
Hatch Chamber of
Commerce
P.O. Box 38, 112 W. Hall
Hatch, NM 87937
Tel: (505) 267-5050

La Fiesta de Santiago y
Santa Ana
Taos County Chamber
of Commerce
Post Office Drawer 1
Taos, NM 87571
Tel: (800) 732-TAOS;
Fax: (505) 758-3873

New Mexico Wine and Chile War Festival
Box 30003, Department 3AE
Las Cruces, NM 88003
Tel: (505) 646-4543; Fax: (505) 646-3808

The Whole Enchilada Fiesta
Las Cruces Convention & Visitors Bureau
211 N. Water
Las Cruces, NM 88001
Tel: (800) FIESTAS or (505) 541-2444 or (505) 524-1968

NEW YORK
Burgerfest
Hamburg Chamber of Commerce
8 South Buffalo St.
Hamburg, NY 14075
Tel: (716) 649-7917; Fax: (716) 649-6362

Fox Run Vineyards Garlic Festival
Fox Run Vineyards
670 Route 14
Penn Yan, NY 14527
Tel: (800) 636-9786 or (315) 536-4616

Hellenic Festival
Hellenic Orthodox Church of the Annunciation
146 West Utica Street
Buffalo, NY 14222
Tel: (716) 882-9485

Hudson Valley Garlic Festival
Kiwanis Club of

Saugerties
P.O. Box 443
Saugerties, NY 12477
Tel: (914) 246-3090; Fax: (914) 246-0858

Italian Heritage Festival
Parisi O'Brien Marketing & Promotions
43 Folger Street
Buffalo, NY 14220

Tel: (716) 823-0158 or (716) 691-6864; Fax: (716) 823-0158

Phelps Sauerkraut Festival
Canandaigua Chamber of Commerce
113 S. Main Street
Canandaigua, NY 14424
Tel: (716) 394-4400 or (315) 462-2276; Fax: (716) 394-4546

SerbFest
St. Stephen Serbian Orthodox Church and Cultural Center
177 Weber Road
Lackawanna, NY 14218
(716) 823-2846

NORTH CAROLINA
North Carolina Seafood Festival
P.O. Box 1812
Morehead City, NC 28557
Tel: (252) 726-6273; Fax: (252)726-0318

North Carolina Turkey Festival
101 N. Main Street

Raeford, NC 28376
Tel: (910) 875-5929

NORTH DAKOTA
North Dakota Ukrainian Festival
Ukrainian Cultural Institute
Box 6
Dickinson, ND 58602
Tel: (701) 225-1286 or (886) 8574-6029; Fax: (701) 225-4366

United Tribes International Powwow
United Tribes Technical College
3315 University Avenue
Bismarck, ND 58504
Tel: (701) 255-3285

OHIO
Asian Festival (Columbus, OH)
Manjula Sankarappa
1367 Wingate Drive
Delaware, OH 43015-7991
Tel: (740) 464-5888; Fax: (740) 881-6516

Chocolate Festival
American Red Cross - Lorain County Chapter
2929 W. River Road North
Elyria, OH 44035
Tel: (440) 324-2929; Fax: (440) 324-5338

Circleville Pumpkin Show
Circleville-Pickaway Chamber of Commerce
159 East Franklin Street

Circleville, OH 43113
Tel: (888) 770-7425 or (740) 474-3636

Dandelion MayFest
Breitenbach Winery
5934 Old Route 39 N.W.
Dover, OH 44622
Tel: (800) THE-WINE or (330) 343-3603; Fax: (330) 343-8290

Ohio Swiss Festival
P.O. Box 158
Sugarcreek, OH 44681
Tel: (330) 852-4112

Slavic Village Harvest Festival
Slavic Village Broadway Development Corporation
5620 Broadway
Cleveland, OH 44127
Tel: (216) 429-1182 ext. 124; Fax: (216) 429-2632

Troy Strawberry Festival
Troy Strawberry Festival, Inc.
P.O. Box 56
Troy, OH 45373
Tel: (937) 339-7714; Fax: (937) 339-4944

OKLAHOMA
Harmon County Blackeyed Pea Festival
Harmon County Historical Museum
102 W. Broadway
Hollis, OK 73550
Tel: (580) 688-9545

Okrafest! and Fall Food Festival

Checocah! Chamber of
Commerce
201 N. Broadway
Checotah, OK 74426
Tel: (918) 473-4178

Pecan Festival
Okmulgee Tourism
112 N. Morton
Okmulgee, OK 74447
Tel: (918) 756-6172

OREGON

Summer Loaf: A
Celebration of Bread
Portland Farmers Market
P.O. Box 215
Portland, OR 97207
Tel: (503) 241-0032

Wild Blackberry Arts
and Crafts Festival
P.O. Box 1077
Cave Junction, OR
97523
Tel: (541) 592-3508

PENNSYLVANIA

Annual Rhubarb Fest
Kitchen Kettle Village
P.O. Box 380, Route 340
Intercourse, PA 17534
Tel: (800) 732-3538 or
(717) 768-8261; Fax:
(717) 656-2773

Kutztown Pennsylvania
German Festival
P.O. Box 306
Kutztown, PA 19530
Tel: (888) 674-6136

McClure Bean Soup
McClure Bean Soup
Committee

Box 8
McClure, PA 17841
Tel: (800) 388-7389

Mushroom Festival
P.O. Box 1000
Kennett Square, PA
19348
Tel: (888) 440-9920 or
(610) 793-3909

National Apple Harvest
Festival
Upper Adams Jaycees,
Sponsors
P.O. Box 38
Biglerville, PA 17307
Tel: (717) 677-9413

Peanut Butter Festival
Brundidge Historical
Society
128 South Main St.
Brundidge, AL 36010
Tel: (334) 735-3608

RHODE ISLAND

International Quahog
Festival
P.O. Box 1437
Wickford, RI 02852
Tel: (401) 885-4118 or
295-2444; Fax: (401) 294-
1040

Rhode Island May
Breakfasts
Rhode Island Economic
Development
Corporation
Tourism Division
1 West Exchange Street
Providence, RI 02903
Tel: (401) 277-2601; Fax:
(401) 273-8270

South County Museum
Annual Harvest Festival
and Apple Pie Contest
South County Museum
P.O. Box 709
Narragansett, RI 02882-
0709
Tel: (401) 783-5400; Fax:
(401) 783-0506

SOUTH CAROLINA

Hampton County
Watermelon Festival
P.O. Box 516
Hampton, SC 29924
Tel: (803) 943-3784 or
(803) 943-4978

Irmo Okra Strut
P.O. Box 406
Irmo, SC 29093
Tel: (803) 781-7850; Fax:
(803) 732-2376

World Grits Festival
P.O. Box 756
St. George, SC 29477
Tel: (843) 563-4366

SOUTH DAKOTA

International Vinegar
Festival
The International
Vinegar Museum
P.O. Box 41
Roslyn, SD 57261
Tel: (877) 986-0075

TENNESSEE

Lauderdale County
Tomato Festival
Lauderdale County
Chamber of Commerce
123 S. Jefferson Street
Ripley, TN 38063

Tel: (731) 635-9541; Fax:
(731) 635-9064

National Cornbread
Festival
P.O. Box 247
S. Pittsburg, TN 37380
Tel: (423) 837-0022

TEXAS

Fiesta en la Playa
P.O.D.E.R
P.O. Box 2334
Rockport, TX 78383
Tel: (361) 729-3431 or
(361) 729-4552 or (361)
729-6172

Fort Bend County
Czech Fest
Fort Bend County
Czech Alliance
P.O. Box 1788
Rosenberg, TX 77471
Tel: (832) 342-4898 or
(832) 342-5934 or (832)
595-3300

Galveston Caribbean
Mardi Gras Carnival
African-American
Chamber of Commerce
of Galveston County
P.O. Box 116
Galveston, TX 77553-
0116
Tel: (888) 275-7329 or
(409) 643-7944 or (409)
763-5700

Germanfest
Muenster Chamber of
Commerce
P.O. Box 479
Muenster, TX 76252

Tel: (800) 942-8037 or
(940) 759-2227

Hopkins County Fall
Festival and World
Champion Hopkins
County Stew Contest
Hopkins County
Chamber of Commerce
P.O. Box 347
Sulphur Springs, TX
75483
Tel: (903) 885-6515 or
(903) 885-8071; Fax:
(903) 885-6516

Jacksonville Annual
Tomato Fest
Jacksonville Chamber of
Commerce
P.O. Box 1231
Jacksonville, TX 75766
Tel: (800) 376-2217 or
(903) 586-2217; Fax:
(903) 586-6944

Kolache Festival
Burleson County
Chamber of Commerce
P.O. Drawer 87
Caldwell, TX 77836
Tel: (979) 567-3218

La Salle County Wild
Hog Cook-off and Fair
P.O. Box 547
Cotulla, Texas 78014
Tel: (800) 256-2326 or
(830) 879-2326

May Days Bean Fest
Mineola Chamber of
Commerce
P.O. Box 68, 101 E.
Broad Street
Mineola, TX 75773

Tel: (903) 569-2087; Fax:
(903) 569-5510

Night In Old Pecos
Cantaloupe Festival
Pecos Chamber of
Commerce
P.O. Box 27
Pecos, TX 79772
Tel: (915) 445-2406; Fax:
(915) 445-2407

Oatmeal Festival
Box 70
Bertram, TX 78605
Tel: (512) 355-2197 or
(512) 355-2268

Poteet Strawberry
Festival
Poteet Strawberry
Festival Association, Inc.
P.O. Box 227
Poteet, TX 78065
Tel: (830) 742-8144 or
(830) 276-3323; Fax:
(830) 742-3608

Prairie Dog Chili Cook
off and World
Championship
of Pickled Quail Egg
Eating
Traders Village
2602 Mayfield Rd.
Grand Prairie, TX 75052
Tel: (972) 647-2331; Fax:
(972) 647-8585

ShrimpFest
Greater Port Arthur
Chamber of Commerce
4749 Twin City
Highway, #300
Port Arthur, TX 77642
Tel: (800) 235-7822 or

(409) 963-1107; Fax:
(409) 963-3322

SPAMARAMA
Austin, TX
Tel: Hotline (512) 834-
1827 or (512) 416-9307;
Fax: (512) 447-9709

Stonewall Peach
JAMboree and Rodeo
Stonewall Chamber of
Commerce
P.O. Box 1
Stonewall, TX 78671
Tel: (830) 644-2735; Fax:
(830) 644-2411

Texas Crawfish and
Saltwater Crab Festival
Sheryl Myers
P.O. Box 226
Orangefield, TX 77639
Tel: (409) 735-3571 or
(409) 735-4152

Texas Folklife Festival
The University of Texas
Institute of Texas
Cultures
801 South Bowie
San Antonio, TX 78205-
3296
Tel: (210) 458-2249; Fax:
(210) 458-2218

Texas Rice Festival
P.O. Box 147
Winnie, TX 77665
Tel: (409) 296-2231; Fax:
(409) 296-9293

World Championship
Barbecue Goat Cook-
Off
Brady/McCulloch

County Chamber of
Commerce
101 E. First St.
Brady, TX 76825
Tel: (915) 597-3491; Fax:
(915) 597-2420

World's Largest
Rattlesnake Round-Up
Sweetwater Chamber of
Commerce
P.O. Box 1148
Sweetwater, TX 79556
Tel: (915) 235-5488; Fax:
(915) 235-1026

UTAH
Peach Days
Brigham City Chamber
of Commerce
P.O. Box 458
Brigham City, UT 84302
Tel: (435) 723-3931; Fax:
(435) 723-5761

VERMONT
Annual Wild Game
Supper
The Congregational
Church of the United
Church of Christ
P.O. Box 387
Bradford, VT 05033
Tel: (802) 222-4610

VIRGINIA
Karla's Great
Cheesecakes Open
House, Fredericksburg,
Virginia
Retail Outlet Shop &
Open House:
41 Cool Springs Road
Fredericksburg, VA
Tel: (540) 371-3754; Fax:
(540) 373-4821

Mailing Address Only:
Karla Seidita
4085 Summerduck Rd.,
VA 22742

St. Anthony's Lebanese
Food Festival
4611 Sadler Road
Glen Allen, VA 23060
(804) 270-7234; Fax:
(804) 273-9914

Staunton's Annual
African-American
Heritage Festival
Staunton Convention
and Visitors Bureau
P.O. Box 58
Staunton, VA 24402
Tel: (540) 332-3865 or
(800) 332-5219 or (540)
332-3865 or (540) 332-
3972; Fax: (540) 332-3807

Virginia Garlic Festival
Richard Hanson
Rebec Vineyards
2229 N. Amherst
Highway
Amherst, VA 24521
Tel: (434) 946-5168

WASHINGTON, DC
Festival of American
Folklife
Smithsonian Institution
Center for Folklife &
Cultural Studies
750 9th Street NW, Suite
4100
Washington, DC 20560-
0953
Tel: (202) 275-1150

WASHINGTON
Penn Cove Mussel
Festival
The Captain Whidbey
Inn
2072 West Captain
Whidbey Inn Rd.
Coupeville, WA 98239
Tel: (360) 678-4097; Fax:
(360) 678-4110

Walla Walla Sweet Onion
Blues Fest
Walla Walla Valley
Chamber of Commerce
P.O. Box 644
Walla Walla, WA 99362
Tel: (509) 525-0850

WEST VIRGINIA
Apple Butter Festival
Berkeley Springs-
Morgan County
Chamber of Commerce
304 Fairfax Street
Berkeley Springs, WV
25411
Tel: (800) 447-8797 or
(304) 258-3738

International Ramp
Cook-Off and Festival
Randolph County
Convention & Visitors
Bureau
200 Executive Plaza
Elkins, WV 26241
Tel: (800) 422-3304 or
(304) 636-2717: Fax:
(304) 636-8046

The Feast of the Ramson
Richwood Area
Chamber of Commerce
P.O. Box 267

Richwood, WV 26261
Tel: (304) 846-6790

West Virginia Black
Walnut Festival
P.O Box 1
Spencer, WV 25276
Tel: (304) 927-1780; Fax:
(304) 927-5953

WISCONSIN
Asian Moon Festival
(Milwaukee, WI)
Wisconsin Organization
for Asian Americans
P.O. Box 11754
Shorewood, WI 53211

Bratwurst Days
Sheboygan County
Chamber of Commerce
712 Riverfront Drive
Sheboygan, WI 53081
Tel: (800) 457-9497 or
(920) 457-9495

Chocolate Fest
P.O. Box 411
Burlington, WI 53105
Tel: (262) 763-3300

Eagle River Cranberry
Festival and Fitness
Weekend
Eagle River Area
Chamber of Commerce
P.O. Box 1917
Eagle River, WI 54521
Tel: (800) 359-6315 or
(715) 479-6400; Fax:
(715) 479-1960

Great Wisconsin Cheese
Festival
200 W. McKinley Avenue
Little Chute, WI 54140

Tel: (920) 788-7390 or
(920) 788-7380; Fax:
(920) 788-7820

Holiday Folk Fair
International
International Institute of
Wisconsin
1110 North Old World
Third Street, Suite 420
Milwaukee, WI 53203
Tel: (414) 225-6220; Fax:
(414) 225-6235

Pepper Festival, North
Hudson, WI (Usually
Friday through Sunday
the Third Weekend of
August)

Polish Fest (Milwaukee,
WI)
6941 South 68th Street
Franklin, WI 53132
Tel: (414) 529-2140

Rutabaga Festival
Cumberland Chamber of
Commerce
P.O. Box 665
Cumberland, WI 54829
Tel: (715) 822-3378

WYOMING
Cheyenne Cowboy
Symposium and
Celebration
Pat McKelvey
3321 Warren Ave.
Cheyenne, WY 82001
Tel: (307) 635-5788

INDEX

Becky Mercuri, Author

Becky started collecting recipes when she was only nine years old, so it is no wonder her cookbook collection numbers over 7,000 volumes. She also has a collection of over 3,000 cookie cutters and molds. Becky houses her ever-growing culinary collections along with three dogs and a dozen cats (and a husband squeezed in there somewhere) in a lovely lakeside home in the Enchanted Mountains, part of the Allegheny Mountain chain. All of her pets were rescued from homeless or abusive situations and Becky is donating a portion of the proceeds of this book to the cause of animal welfare.

Becky attended the State University of New York and received a BA in Cultural Studies with a double major in literature and journalism. She must have had some inkling that writing skills would come in handy in the future. Although she chose to pursue a successful career in sales and marketing in the communications industry, she never completely forsook her love of all things culinary. Becky is a contributing editor for *Cookbook Collectors Exchange,* a nationally distributed newsletter and was food editor of *The Wellsville Daily Reporter* for three years. She is a member of the Southern Foodways Alliance and remains an avid student of culinary history. She is actively engaged in completing a comprehensive bibliography of all English language cookbooks published between 1940 and 1949, along with a compilation of biographical information about the cookbook authors of this period.

Following the terrible events of 9/11, Becky has been actively involved in numerous charitable organizations. Never one to turn down a challenge or a worthy cause, Becky volunteered to make 275 pounds of fudge, thousands of cookies, and several cheesecakes while working a full time job and meeting publishing deadlines.

Becky's inspiration for this book was her discovery of the unique recipes and the heritage aspects of food festivals. With the homogenization of the American palate, the food historian in Becky wanted to capture America's rich cultural and ethnic diversity as embodied in the foods of our forebears. The results are well worth it and we believe that Becky's warmth and wit shine through the pages of her book, which are a culinary travelogue of our great country's distinctive foodways. The recipes are unique, innovative, traditional, ethnic, and delicious! The festivals are all-American, exciting, educational, fun, family-oriented and affordable. She hopes you enjoy her book whether as an on-the-road resource or a stay-at-home cookbook.

Tom Klare, Illustrator

For almost two decades Tom Klare has been creating works of whimsey. From his home studio in San Diego, California, he has cooked up quirky depictions of people and critters for publication in more countries than morels in Michigan. Klare is a frequent contributor to *Food Arts Magazine* and his work has also appeared in such places as *The Wall St. Journal, Forbes Magazine, The Dallas Morning News* and in Frommer's guidebooks. He also creates a weekly cartoon called "Glitch," which is an irreverent poke at technology and computers. His previous lives have included designer, art director, freelance photographer and bicycle mechanic. Although his cuisine preferences are quite liberal, he admits to drawing the line at pork rinds.
Find out more about Tom and his art at: *www.tomklare.com.*